MANAGING A
GLOBAL RESOURCE

MANAGING A
GLOBAL RESOURCE

Challenges of Forest Conservation
and Development

Uma Lele
editor

World Bank Series on Evaluation
and Development

Volume 5

Transaction Publishers
New Brunswick (U.S.A.) and London (U.K.)

Copyright © 2002 by Transaction Publishers, New Brunswick, New Jersey.

All rights reserved under International and Pan-American Copyright Conventions. No part of this book may be reproduced or transmitted in any form or by any means, electronic or mechanical, including photocopy, recording, or any information storage and retrieval system, without prior permission in writing from the publisher. All inquiries should be addressed to Transaction Publishers, Rutgers—The State University, 35 Berrue Circle, Piscataway, New Jersey 08854-8042.

This book is printed on acid-free paper that meets the American National Standard for Permanence of Paper for Printed Library Materials.

Library of Congress Catalog Number: 2002066842
ISBN: 0-7658-0137-X (cloth); 0-7658-0940-0 (paper)
Printed in the United States of America

Library of Congress Cataloging-in-Publication Data

Managing a global resource : challenges of forest conservation and development / Uma Lele, editor
     p. cm. — (World Bank series on evaluation and development ; v. 5)
    Includes bibliographical references and index.
    ISBN 0-7658-0137-X (alk. paper) — ISBN 0-7658-0940-0 (pbk.: alk. paper)
    1. Forest conservation. 2. Forest policy. 3. Natural resources—Management. 4. Forests and forestry. I. Lele, Uma. II. Series.

SD411 .M358 2002
333.75'16—dc21   2002066842

This book is devoted to forest-dependent poor
so their lives may improve

Contents

Foreword

In 1991, the World Bank adopted a forest strategy whose chief goals were to retard the exploitation of tropical moist forests and to encourage the planting of trees. The new strategy was prompted by reports that tropical moist forests were disappearing at a rate of between 17 million and 20 million hectares a year, and that this deep encroachment was also leading to significant losses of plant and animal species while reducing forest absorption of carbon dioxide, a significant factor in global warming. It was concern about developments like those that led the world's countries to discuss emerging threats to the earth's environment at the 1992 "Earth Summit" in Rio de Janeiro. In 1998, the Bank's board and management asked the Operations Evaluation Department (OED) to independently assess the effectiveness of the forest strategy in view of its limited implementation since 1991.

This book presents the main findings of the OED review, which concludes that the 1991 forest strategy's "ambitious goals were not matched by commensurate means to implement the strategy." The review also found that certain elements of the strategy including its ban on the use of Bank funds for commercial logging in tropical moist foresthad a chilling effect on innovation in forest management. The review concluded that the effectiveness of the Bank's 1991 forest strategy had therefore been modest.

The OED Forest Strategy review included a comprehensive analysis of 700 World Bank Group and Global Environment Facility (GEF) activities and an in-depth review of its implementation outcomes in six developing countries—three of them in countries classed as forest-rich (Brazil, Cameroon, Indonesia), two classed as forest-poor (China, India), and one country in transition from forest-poor to forest-rich (Costa Rica). The review found that the forest-poor countries, alarmed by encroachment on their own forests, have adopted policies along the lines of the Bank's 1991 approach to forest conservation. But the Bank's strategy, according to OED, has served less well in the three forest-rich countries because it paid insufficient attention to the important role of natural forests in economic development. The review also found that the poor have been less a source of deforestation and forest degradation in the forest-rich countries than was assumed in the 1991 strategy. Instead, the inefficiency and inequitable nature of forest loss in those countries are associated with governance.

The World Bank's 1991 strategy recognized the divergence in costs and benefits of forest conservation as perceived by the global community and by developing countries and hence the need for international financial transfers to underwrite forest conservation on a global scale, but it failed to generate the momentum needed to establish adequate financing and financing mechanisms. Meanwhile, there has been little borrower demand for Bank funds to finance protection of natural forests.

Demand has also declined for loan funds to enlarge forest cover by tree planting, which could help relieve the pressure to exploit natural forests, both as sources of timber and as lands to be cleared for agricultural and development purposes. The long time needed for trees to reach maturity—a period during which there is no cash flow from forested land and risks to the investment are high, in combination with tight credit, high domestic interest rates, and the continued supply of timber from natural forests, often through uncontrolled logging have weakened demand for investment in small-scale tree planting and plantation forests.

It is also clear that the amount of financial resources provided by the GEF for environmental purposes are much smaller than the need. Bank leverage on forest strategy in individual countries through strategy loan conditionality is more limited than popularly believed. But increased environmental consciousness, even in the forest-rich countries, provides more opportunities for World Bank involvement in forest production, development, and conservation activities.

The OED review identified seven elements that will make the Bank's forest strategy more relevant to current circumstances and strengthen the Bank's ability to achieve its strategic objectives:

- Mobilize international grant resources to bridge the gap between the costs and benefits of forest conservation as perceived by global and national stakeholders.
- Form partnerships with all relevant stakeholders.
- Broaden the application of the forest strategy to include all types of natural forests, including temperate and boreal forests and other highly endangered biologically rich types of forests
- Streamline and align conservation and development efforts with the overall development goals of the Bank's client countries.
- Attend to the problems of poor governance and illegal logging.
- Focus on efforts to overcome rural poverty.
- Allow for internal implementation capacity to match Bank intentions in the forest sector.

Based on these recommendations—and on extensive consultations throughout the developing and developed worlds—the Bank is adopting a new forest strategy and an operational policy. This book, with updated country studies and descriptions of new instruments for forest management, is intended to help implement that new policy. The book also examines the prospects for forest conservation in light of new financial instruments and possible financing mechanisms currently being debated in the international community.

Can other donors assist in forest conservation by providing much-needed investments in poor countries while the Bank contributes to progress in the countries' forest sectors through economic and sector work and policy dialogue? Without additional grants or concessional assistance, governments are unlikely to be interested in long-term Bank involvement in the controversial forest sector. Yet, despite growing awareness of the importance of the physical environment to sustainable economic development, international willingness to provide grant funds appears to be weaker today than it was in 1991.

Robert Picciotto
Director-General

Preface

The foundation for this book was established through the research conducted and the extensive consultations held during the Operation Evaluation Department's Review of the World Bank's 1991 Forest Strategy and Its Implementation. The Review's findings are synthesized in OED's volume, *The World Bank Forest Strategy: Striking the Right Balance,* published in November 2000, which includes an evaluation report on the Global Environmental Facility (GEF) entitled *Financing the Global Benefits of Forests* and six country studies.

The Operations Evaluation Department's comprehensive evaluation of the World Bank's 1991 forest strategy included analysis of more than 700 forest sector operations of the Bank, the International Finance Corporation (IFC), GEF, and the Multilateral Investment Guarantee Agency (MIGA). It also included non-forest operations and activities of the World Bank Group and GEF that have indirectly affected the forest sectors of developing countries. The review also included regional portfolio reviews in Latin America and the Caribbean, the Middle East and North Africa, Europe and Central Asia, Africa, South Asia and East Asia and the Pacific.

The World Bank's forest sector lending through 128 forest projects and projects with forest components in all regions of the world amounted to $3.5 billion between 1992 and 1999, although most avoided dealing with tropical moist forests, the focus of the Bank's 1991 forest strategy.

The IFC operations are typically post-harvest processing activities that use timber or its byproducts, and so are expected to have "direct" impact on forests. The IFC approved investments of $578 million in 65 forest operations in 29 countries during the 1992–98 period. This reflects a 17 percent decline in IFC commitments for forest projects over the period 1985–91. After 1991, the IFC forest sector lending increased in all regions except Latin America and East Asia, which contain a large share of the world's tropical moist forests. The IFC, through analysis conducted during OED's Forest Strategy Review, was unable to establish if the investments it turned down because of Bank policy in tropical moist forests were financed by others (possibly with less environmental scrutiny than in the IFC).

The MIGA was established in 1988 to provide political risk insurance for new foreign direct investment. It does not participate in project financing or lending. Until 1999, MIGA had no direct involvement in the forest sectors of its clients. By December 1999, its portfolio included only two guarantees in the forest sector, one for an existing pulp and paper mill in the Svetogorsk region of Russia, and another for the rehabilitation of an existing cocoa plantation in Côte d'Ivoire.

The GEF provides grants and concessional funds to countries eligible for World Bank assistance for the "incremental costs" of global environmental benefits in four areas: climate change, biological diversity, international waters, and depletion of the ozone layer (land degradation issues as they relate to these four focal areas are also addressed). Established in 1991 and restructured in 1994, the GEF is the single largest source of funding for biodiversity conservation in the world. It has invested $1.2 billion over the past nine years and has leveraged an additional $2 billion in cofinancing. It is also the financial mechanism for the UN Framework Convention on Climate Change (UNFCCC), Convention on Biological Diversity (CBD), a focal area on international water and the ozone layer and it will serve as a financial mechanism for the Stockholm Convention on Persistent Organisms. The GEF has implemented its programs in the last decade through the World Bank, the United Nations Development Programme (UNDP), and the United Nations Environment Program (UNEP). In 2001, the GEF Council approved the addition of the four regional development banks, the United Nations Industrial Development Organization (UNIDO), the United Nations Food and Agriculture Organization (FAO) and the International Fund for Agricultural Development (IFAD) as possible executing agencies of GEF funding. As of 2000, 60 percent of the $2.9 billion committed by GEF had been implemented through the Bank. Approximately 16 percent of the total GEF allocation up to June of 1999 ($2.4 billion) was for projects protecting or sustainably managing forest ecosystems or resources. While large, these resources are small in relation to estimates of the financial resources needed to save biodiversity and protect forested areas.

But it is the case studies in six countries summarized in this book that provided the most insights into the nature and extent of forest and biodiversity loss and demand for Bank involvement in the forest sectors of its borrowing countries. Together, the six countries account for 44 percent of the world's population and 27 percent of the world's forest cover. Between 1992 and 1999, they had received 31 percent of the Bank's total lending, but an overwhelming 59 percent of the Bank's forest lending and 45 percent of the Bank's lending in other operations that contained forestry components. These six countries have also been major recipients of GEF funding.

The six case studies offer a menu of approaches that developing countries have adopted to contain deforestation, often of their own accord. The interplay of each of their political circumstances, demographic factors, resource endowments, stages of resource exploitation, and development imperatives have all played a role in their policy and institutional choices. Some of their efforts have been supported by, or devised with, the assistance of external actors. The country studies provided the most useful insights into the extent and causes of forest loss and thus played a key role in OED's assessment and recommendations to the Bank's management to adopt a forest strategy more attuned to the realities in developing countries.

The assessment also benefited from extensive discussions with Bank borrowers, Bank management and staff, forest sector analysts, timber companies, and environmental non-governmental organizations (NGOs). Views of developing country stakeholders were also secured by mobilizing authors with deep knowledge of their respective country cases and through workshops in Brazil, China, India, and Indonesia, communications over the Internet, regional consultations, and a global workshop involving forest experts, environmental activists, representatives of industry, donors, and international organizations, and government policy makers.

The case studies had three purposes:

- To develop a deeper understanding of the sources and causes of deforestation across a broad spectrum of the Bank's client countries.
- To obtain the views of stakeholders within these countries about the costs and benefits of forest exploitation.
- To develop a better understanding of the Bank's approach to forest sector issues in those countries.

The main questions addressed in the six case studies were as follows:

- How have the forces of development affected the country's forest sector?
- Did the Bank's 1991 forest strategy make a difference to the Bank's ongoing forest strategy in the country? Or was the Bank's strategy largely a result of its historical relationship with the country and the policies and needs articulated by the government?
- How consistent were the country's forest operations with the Bank's 1991 forest strategy?
- Was the Bank's forest strategy in the country relevant to the country's needs in the forest sector, as identified by the country?
- Were the Bank's overall and forest sector activities effective and efficient from the viewpoint of the intentions of the 1991 strategy as well as from the country's perspective? Did they achieve policy and institutional impacts pertinent to sector management? Are these impacts likely to be sustainable?
- What are the prospects for future Bank country interaction in the forest sector and for outcomes in the sector under the 1991 Forest Strategy?

The country case studies in this volume illustrate the intricacy of the design, implementation, monitoring, and evaluation of interventions aimed at forest production and conservation and highlight the central importance of political will, information, and capacity in stimulating, fostering, and meeting the demand for environmental services. Developing countries and their external well-wishers can learn much from this experience.

Uma Lele
Editor

Acknowledgements

I appreciate the willingness and patience of all authors of this book to update the case studies since the OED review was published. It was surprising to see how much the world had changed in two years, including the environment for forests in developing countries. The publication of this book owes much to Robert Picciotto, the Director-General of the Bank's Operations Evaluation and to Gregory Ingram, the Director of the Operations Evaluation Department who provided a demanding environment but unstinting support for the intellectual enquiry leading to this book. Its content owes much to the generous input and advice of several of my colleagues in the Bank including, but not limited to Gonzalo Castro, Ken Chomtiz, Laurent Debroux, James Douglas, Luis Gamez, Jarle Harstad, John Kellenberg, Asmeen Khan, Eugenia Katsigris, Nalin Kishor, Kanta Kumari, Judith Lisansky, Ridley Nelson, Kenneth Newcombe, Saeed Rana, Susan Shen, William Magrath, Christian Peters, Robert Schneider, John Spears, Loretta Sprissler, Giusseppe Topa, Claudio Volonte, and Tom Walton. Irwin Horowitz provided useful comments on the early draft.

The foundation for this book was established through the research conducted and the extensive consultations held during the Operation Evaluation Department's Review of the World Bank's 1991 Forest Policy and Its Implementation. The Review's findings are synthesized in OED's volume, *The World Bank Forest Strategy: Striking the Right Balance*, published in November 2000, six country studies and a report on the Global Environmental Facility (GEF). *Managing a Global Resource* would not have been possible without the support and valuable contributions of a large number of individuals and organizations that were consulted during the review stages

The OED Review was guided by an Advisory Committee composed of experts: Conor Boyd, Angela Cropper, Hans Gregersen, and Emmy Hafild who provided perspectives of diverse stakeholders. Colleagues both within and outside the Bank challenged the Review's work in progress, provided alternative viewpoints and inputs, and offered constructive suggestions. They included: Chris Barr, Julian Blackwood, Juergen Blaser, Edward Bresnyan, Marjorie Anne Bromhead, Mark Cackler, Gabriel Campbell, Jeff Campbell, Kerstin Canby, Wilfred Candler, Gonzalo Castro, Kenneth Chomitz, Kevin Cleaver, Luis Constantino, Arnoldo Contreras-Hermosilla, Robert Crooks,

Peter Dewees, Chris Diewold, Jim Douglas, Navroz Dubash, Julia Falconer, Gershon Feder, Vincente Ferrer-Andreu, George Greene, Jarle Harstad, John Hayward, Peter Hazell, Ian Hill, Gesa Horskotte-Weseler, William Hyde, Peter Jipp, David Kaimowitz, Chris Keil, John Kellenberg, Irshad Khan, Robert Kirmse, Nalin Kishor, Odin Knudsen, John Lambert, Tom Lovejoy, William Magrath, Dennis Mahar, Glenn Morgan, Jessica Mott, Ken Newcombe, Jan Cornelius Post, Idah Z. Pswarayi-Riddihough, Francisco Reifschneider, Jeff Sayer, Ethel Sennhauser, Robert Schneider, Richard Scobey, Frances Seymour, Susan Shen, Mariam Sherman, Kirsten Spainhower, John Spears, Susan Stout, William Sunderlin, Guiseppe Topa, Juergen Voegle, Claudio Volonte, Steve Vosti, Tom Walton, Andy White, and Tom Wiens.

Additional feedback during the Review process was provided by: Bagher Asadi, Mark Baird, Rema Balasundaram, Tulio Barbosa, Cornelis Baron van Tuyll van Serooskerken, Chris Bennett, Carlos Eduardo Bertao, Hans Binswanger, Phillip Brylski, Bruce Cabarle, Elizabeth Campbell-Page, Anne Casson, Dennis de Tray, Mohan Dharia, Hosny El-Lakany, Osvaldo Feinstein, Douglas Forno, Robert Goodland, Korinna Horte, Ian Johnson, Norman Jones, Lisa Jordan, Ed Lim, Lennart Ljungmann, Jagmohan Maini, Michael Martin, Alex McCalla, Gobind Nankani, Ilkka Juhani Niemi, Afolabi Ojumu, V. Rajagopalan, Emil Salim, Ismail Serageldin, Narendra Sharma, Trayambkeshwar Sinha, William Stevenson, Wilfried Thalwitz, Hans Verolme, and Tom Walton.

Bank colleagues in the resident missions aided in the arrangement of integral country workshops. Acknowledgements are due to: Jin Liu, Anis Wan, Melanie Widjaja, Datin Yudha, John Garrison, Ricardo L. B. Tarifa, Elisa Romano, and Neusa Queiroz. A special thank you to EMBRAPA in Brazil, the Ministry of Environment and Forest in India, Ministry of Finance and BAPENAS in Indonesia, Ministry of Forestry, State Development Planning Commission and Ministry of Finance in China for their contributions.

Phil Sawicki, William Hurlbut, Bruce Ross Larson and his team provided editorial input. Osvaldo Feinstein and Elizabeth Campbell-Page contributed through publishing coordination. My staff assistant Maisha Hyman protected me from the daily demands of the office and my research assistant Kristina Kavaliunas updated background information. This book would not have been completed without Lauren Kelly's brilliant and tireless research assistance and management of the project. Finally, when it was most needed, my friend Miriam Freilicher provided a wonderful cottage on Lake Otsego in Cooperstown, New York, where the Native American name of the lake and the beauty of nature were a constant reminder of the loss of the world's forests and biodiversity and the people who depend on it.

World Bank cannot guarantee the accuracy of the data included in this work. The boundaries, colors, denominations, and other information shown on any map in this work do not imply on the part of the World Bank any judgment of the legal status of any territory or the endorsement or acceptance of such boundaries.

Glossary

Afforestation/Reafforestation: Establishment of a tree crop on an area from which it has been always or long absent.

Agro-forestry: Land use system in which woody perennials are used on the same land as agricultural crops or livestock in some form of spatial arrangement or temporal sequence.

Closed forest: Forest with a stand density greater than 20 percent of the area and tree crowns nearly contact one another.

Conventional logging: Conventional logging has come to be viewed as less concerned with forest regeneration through management, and often lacking in government control; often unsustainable, i.e. not focused on long term timber supplies.

Conversion forest: Forest assigned for conversion to agriculture or other non-forest use.

Deforestation: Change of forest with depletion of tree crown cover to less than 10 percent. The clearing of forests and the conversion of land to non-forest uses.

Degradation: Reductions in the productive potential of natural resources in areas that remain classified as forests. Degradation may be permanent, although some forests may recover naturally or with human assistance.

Desertification: Degradation of the land that ultimately leads to desert-like conditions.

Economic Assessment: Makes three potentially major adjustments to a financial analysis: (1) the existing financial costs and benefits to "shadow values" to reflect the true opportunity cost of the resources involved; and environmental and social costs and benefits ("externalities") are included both at the (2) national level and at the (3) global level.

- The *first* modification adjusts *financial* costs and benefits to reflect *shadow prices.* A shadow price, say the price of labor or the exchange rate, differs from a financial price in that it reflects the true *opportunity cost* of the resources in question.
- The *second* modification adds in all environmental and social consequences that affect the well being of anyone within the *nation.*
- The *third* modification constitutes a *global* analysis and would additionally include the gains and losses of people outside the country in which the forest is located.

Forest: Ecosystem with a minimum of 10 percent crown cover of trees and/or bamboo, generally associated with wild flora and fauna and natural soil conditions and not subject to agricultural practices. Forests are in two categories:

- *Natural forests:* a subset of forests composed of tree species known to be indigenous to the area.
- *Plantation forests:* established artificially by afforestation on lands that previously did not carry forest within living memory, or established artificially by reforestation on land that carried forest before, with replacement of the indigenous species by a new and essentially different species or genetic variety.

Logging: The process of harvesting timber from a forest, logging has come to be used in the context of unsustainable cutting, i.e., not focused on long-term timber supplies.

Management: Relates to the management of resources, inventorying and yield calculation and to silvicultural practice (e.g., timber cutting).

Open forest: Forest in which the tree canopy layer is discontinuous but covers at least 10 percent of the area and in which the grass layer is continuous.

Optimal forest land use: Land use in forest that is judged socially as the most beneficial overall, but in which those who lose from the land use are compensated for their losses.

Optimal use of forested land: Forested land (i.e., land that still has forest on it, rather than land that has a potential to be used for forest in one form or another) may be retained as forest or it may be converted to non-forest uses such as crop agriculture, livestock, and urban expansion, or to industrial tree crops.

Preservation forest: Forest designated for total protection of representative forest ecosystems in which all forms of extraction are prohibited.

Primary forest: Relatively intact forest essentially unmodified by human activity for the past 60 to 80 years.

Private gains/losses: Refers to the private interests of the stakeholder, i.e., what benefits him/her.

Production forest: Forest designated for sustainable production of forest products.

Protection forest: Forest designated for stabilization of mountain slopes, upland watersheds, fragile lands, reservoirs, and catchment areas. Controlled sustainable extraction of non-wood products could be allowed.

Reduced Impact Logging: Well managed logging; usually supervised

Reforestation: Establishment of a tree crop on forest land.

Secondary forest: Forest subject to a light cycle of shifting cultivation or to various intensities of logging but that still contains indigenous trees and shrubs.

Social gains/losses: Refers to the wider social perspective and the jurisdiction may be local, national, regional, or global. In theory, local, national and global perspectives on "social" gains/losses may diverge. National and global agencies should take the "social" standpoint, but it is well known that this is not always the case.

Sustainable forest management: A system of forest management that aims for sustained yields of multi-products from the forest over long periods.

Sustainable timber management: A forest management system that aims for sustained timber yields over long periods.

Tropical dry forest: Open forest with continuous grass cover; distinguished from other tropical forests by distinct seasonality and low rainfall. Includes woody savannas and shrub lands.

Tropical moist forest: Forest situated in areas receiving not less than 100 millimeters of rain in any month for two out of three years, with a mean annual temperature of 24°C or higher; mostly low lying, generally closed.

Source: *State of the World's Forests (FAO 1999), The Forest Sector: A World Bank Policy Paper, 1991, and Pearce, Putz, Vanclay. A Sustainable Forest Future? DFID, 1999.*

Acronyms and Abbreviations

AAA	Analytical Advisory Activities
AEPS	Agro-Environmental Protection System
APL	Adjustable Program Loan
CACM	Central American Common Market
CAF	Certificate of Forestry Payment
CAFMA	Certificate of Payment for Natural Forest Management
CAM	Conservation Area Management Project
CAS	Country Assistance Strategy
CBD	Convention on Biodiversity
CCICED	China's Council for International Cooperation on Environment and Development
CFA	African Financial Community Franc
CFN	National Forestry Council
CGI	Consultative Group for Indonesia
CGIAR	Consultative Group on International Agricultural Research
CIFOR	Center for International Forestry Research
CIRAD	Centre de coopération internationale en recherche agronomique pour le développement
CNP	Agricultural Marketing Company
CSD	Commission on Sustainable Development
CTO	Carbon Tradable Offset
DFID	Department for International Development
DR	Dana Reboisasi
EAP	East Asia Pacific Region
ECA	Europe and Central Asia Region
ECR	Economic Recovery Credit
EMBRAPA	Brazilian Agricultural Research Corporation
ESSD	Environmentally and Socially Sustainable Development Network
ESW	Economic and sector work
EU	European Union
FAO	Food and Agriculture Organization
FD	Forest department
FESP	Forest and Environment Sector Development Program

FICP	Forestry Institutions and Conservation Projects
FONAFIFO	National Forestry Financing Fund
FREE	Forestry Research, Education and Extension
FSC	Forest Stewardship Council
FSI	Forest Service of India
GDP	Gross domestic product
GEF	Global Environment Facility
GHG	Greenhouse gas
GNP	Gross national product
GTZ	Deutsche Gesellschaft fuer Technische Zusammenarbeit
HPH	Hak Pengusahaan Hutan
HRS	Household responsibility system
HTI	Hutan Tanaman Industri
IBAMA	Brazilian Institute of the Environment and Renewable Natural Resources
IBRD	International Bank for Reconstruction and Development
ICDP	Integrated Conservation Development Program
ICFRE	Indian Council of Forestry Research and Education
IDA	International Development Association
IDB	Inter-American Development Bank
IDCF	Interdepartmental Committee on Forestry
IFAD	International Fund for Agricultural Development
IFC	International Finance Corporation
IFF	Intergovernmental Forum on Forests
IFS	Indian Forest Service
IITA	International Institute for Tropical Agriculture
IMF	International Monetary Fund
IPCC	Intergovernmental Panel on Climate Change
IPF	Intergovernmental Panel on Forests
IPK	Izin Pemanfaatan Kayu
IRR	Internal rate of return
ISO	International Standards Organization
ITTO	International Tropical Timber Organization
IUCN	International Union for the Conservation of Nature
JFM	Joint Forest Management
JI	Joint Implementation
LEI	Indonesian Ecolabeling Institute
LULUCF	Land Use, Land-Use Change, and Forestry
MIGA	Multilateral Investment Guarantee Agency
MINAGRI	Ministry of Agriculture
MINEF	Ministry of Environment and Forests
MNA	Middle East North Africa Region
MOEF	Ministry of Environment and Forests

MOF	Ministry of Forests
MOFEC	Ministry of Forestry and Estate Crops
NAFTA	North American Free Trade Agreement
NFPP	Natural Forest Protection Program
NGO	Nongovernmental organization
NTFP	Non-timber forest product
OCIC	Office on Joint Implementation
OECF	Overseas Economic Cooperation Fund
OED	Operations Evaluation Department
OP	Operational Policy
PGBC	Programme de gestion de la biodiversite du Cameroun
PNF	National Forest Program
PPAR	Project Performance Audit Report
PPG-7	Pilot Program to Conserve the Brazilian Rain Forest
PSAs	Payment for Environmental Services
QAG	Quality Assurance Group
SAC	Structural Adjustment Credit
SAL	Structural Adjustment Loan
SBS	Brazilian Sivilculture Society
SEPA	State Environmental Protection Agency
SFM	Sustainable Forest Management
SINAC	National System of Conservation Areas
TPTI	Tebang Pilih Tanam Indonesia
UNCCD	United Nations Convention to Combat Desertification
UNCED	United Nations Conference on Environment and Development
UNDP	United Nations Development Programme
UNEP	United Nations Environment Programme
UNFCCC	United Nations Framework Convention on Climate Change
UNIDO	United Nations Industrial Development Organization
VFC	Village forest committees
WDR	World Development Report
WTO	World Trade Organization
WRI	World Resources Institute
WWF	World Wide Fund for Nature

1

Managing a Global Resource: An Overview

Uma Lele

Industrialized countries tend to attach greater weight to forest and biodiversity conservation in developing countries than do the developing countries themselves, who view their resources through the lens of their own socioeconomic development.[1] The weight developing countries give to conservation objectives depends on their forest endowments, population pressures, stages of resource exploitation and economic development. In forest-rich countries and forest-rich areas within countries, natural forests are often important sources of private profit, income, and employment as well as government revenues, raw materials, and "abundant" land for alternative uses, especially agriculture. Forests can be an engine of economic development, but their exploitation often is environmentally unsustainable and socially inequitable. Rent seeking, environmental destruction, and the failure of forest exploitation to meet the needs of the poor in developing countries, have been subjects of much debate.[2] The perceived costs and benefits of forest conservation or exploitation differ, therefore, depending on whether they are seen from a local or global perspective.

There are great differences in forest endowments between regions and within countries. The Eastern Europe and Latin America regions have the most forest per capita, while South Asia and the Middle East and North Africa region have the least (see following charts).

Besides being differently endowed, each region responds differently to when natural forests grow scarce and citizens and policymakers become more aware of the value of forests. Reform-minded leaders come forward to call for change when the stark reality of irrevocable loss sets in. Policymakers develop instruments to reconcile the dual challenge inherent in forest conservation and forest exploitation for human development. These instruments include policy and institutional reforms, changes in property rights, and incentives to

1

Regions correspond to the World Bank regional classifications

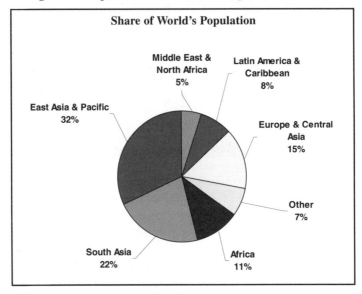

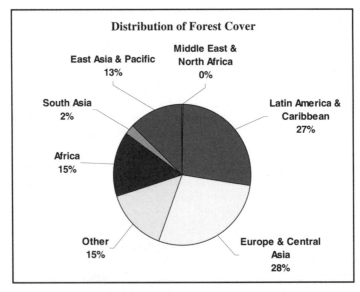

Source: FAO State of World Forests 1999 and Human Development Report 1999

support tree planting, forest regeneration, and biodiversity conservation. At that point, global environmental interests coincide with those in forest-poor regions and countries. The socioeconomic and environmental outcomes of responses to scarcity may well be positive in many respects, for example, through increased employment and income for the poor, growth of a forest industry, development of markets for environmental services including carbon sequestration and soil and water conservation. But the resulting outcome of these responses still leaves less biodiversity, although not necessarily less forest cover, than would have existed without any forest exploitation. It is fundamentally the loss of biodiversity associated with the loss of pristine natural forests, rather than tree cover *per se*, that seems to be the source of current debate in the international environment and development community.

But environmental consciousness is not just high in industrialized countries. It has been increasing rapidly in both forest-poor and forest-rich countries, and is providing new opportunities for a more constructive engagement of the global community, not simply in conservation of natural forests, but in understanding the extent of synergy, and tradeoffs, of conservation with forest production and socioeconomic development, and particularly its dynamics. The accumulating evidence is making it clearer than ever that international mechanisms and financial transfers, while not sufficient by themselves, are essential to conserve the natural forests of developing countries that the global community considers to be of global value. Grant funds, if wisely applied, can help improve substantially the synergy between environmental protection and socioeconomic development, if three additional sets of steps are taken simultaneously. First, policy, institutional and technical reforms must be put in place in developing countries to ensure "managed forests"[3] become fiscally, financially, economically and environmentally sustainable. Second, grant funds must be available on a sufficiently long-term basis to developing countries with expectations of clear performance indicators and clearly monitorable milestones of achievements in reforms so that domestic conservation policy and institutional arrangements in developing countries become effective and sustainable. Third, funds must be adequate, and enforcement and transfer payment methods effective, to compensate the agents of deforestation in developing countries for their legitimate opportunity costs of conservation until such time that conservation becomes sustainable. Without it, considerable biodiversity that the global community considers of value will likely be lost. (Although, as in developed countries and recent experience in Costa Rica, China, and elsewhere in some as yet limited parts of the developing world, forest cover may well increase over time after some initial decline, followed by stabilization, as lost natural forests are replaced by either planted forest or secondary forest regrowth).

The diverse circumstances and histories of individual developing countries show why even with these steps in place, a certain amount of deforestation is inevitable, particularly in forest-abundant countries at early stages of their natural resource exploitation—and why forests tend to be conserved and even expanded only in the later stages. Which forests are exploited, and for what purposes, depends among other things on agro-ecological circumstances, population densities, and the physical infrastructure that determines market access to forests. (This volume does not recount the story of deforestation in developed countries, but it is pertinent to mention that while tree cover is no longer declining in the industrialized world, old-growth forests are all but gone and what remains is still threatened with extinction because of demand for alternative uses of land and forest products.)

Table 1.1 provides the details of the endowments, size, and economic performance of the countries analyzed in this volume, namely, three forest-rich countries (Brazil, Indonesia, Cameroon), two forest-poor ones (China and India), and one (Costa Rica) that is now in transition from forest-poor to forest-rich due to the progressive policies it has actively pursued.

Examination of the forest policy and practices of these countries reveals the following:

- As much as 65 percent of the *benefits of forest conservation are global, but the costs are local*, borne almost completely by the local people in developing countries.[4] This means the divergence in the incidence of costs and benefits must be addressed in the design and implementation of instruments if natural forests and biodiversity are to be conserved.
- The domestic and international *factors and processes* that lead to the loss of forest cover *vary greatly among countries* and need to be understood better. In-depth country analysis and cross-country comparative analysis is necessary to understand similarities and differences between and within countries and make rapid transfers of experience, knowledge and best practices. Cheaper communication and global networking now make information dissemination possible on an unprecedented scale.

Table 1.1
Relative Developing Country Endowments

Country	Land Area (1000 km2)	Land Under Forests	Pop (M) 1998	Forest Availability (ha/capita)	Avg. Annual Pop. Growth Rate % (1998-2015)	GNP Per Capita Annual Growth % (1997-1998)
Brazil	8547	5511	165.9	3.00	1.1	-1.4
Cameroon	465	196	14.3	1.37	2.1	3.8
Indonesia	1905	1098	203.7	0.54	1.2	-18.0
Costa Rica	51	12	3.5	0.34	1.3	2.9
China	9326	1333	1238.6	0.11	0.7	6.4
India	2973	650	979.7	0.07	1.3	4.3

Source: UNDP Human Development Report 2001/World Development Report 2000

- Using the individual *country as a unit of analysis* is essential to understanding the policy and institutional reforms needed to reverse loss of forest cover. In many developing countries more than 90 percent of the gazetted forestland is listed as publicly owned, yet *de facto* property rights vary enormously between countries and over time and they tend to be poorly defined. Many of the causes of forest cover loss lie outside the country's forest sector in demographic, policy, investment, and institutional factors. Governments (federal/central, provincial/state/ regional, and local) have responsibility for formulating and enforcing (or failing to enforce) laws, fostering pluralistic institutions, including facilitating appropriate roles for civil society and the private sector and ensuring social justice. Because lack of good governance is often a problem, both *de jure* and *de facto* rules of the game vary considerably.
- *It is difficult to make global generalizations* about the causes and consequences of forest loss. The diversity and complexity has considerable implications for how the external actors generally, and the World Bank Group especially, might address the global objectives of containing forest and biodiversity loss while helping developing countries formulate forest policies, and related policies and institutions external to the forest sector, for improving forest management in the wider developmental context.

Thus, the biggest challenge is to find policies, institutions, and incentive structures that allow for the transfer of international resources to cover the global benefits that forests provide. This must be achieved without jeopardizing the ability of developing countries to manage their forests and engage in forest production and utilization for developmental purposes. It is not surprising therefore, contrary to the expectations expressed in the World Bank's 1991 forest strategy, that the Bank's impact on forest sector reform in forest-rich countries was minimal. But in forest-poor countries, which were not the focus of the 1991 strategy, the Bank made important contributions. In retrospect, these contributions too turned out to be greater than expected. They occurred both through policy analysis and advice and Bank-supported investment operations. In some cases, Bank analysis and advice improved policies, built the capacity and confidence of key stakeholders and facilitated increased participation of the poor in forest management. It also established partnerships, improved forest productivity, and encouraged forest regeneration. In each of these cases, the stimulus for forest conservation and protection has come largely from the forest-poor countries themselves, rather than being externally imposed, although in several subtle ways the Bank facilitated and accelerated the internal reform process without taking credit.

The Bank's 1991 strategy did identify a fundamental problem: national governments as well as individuals, community groups and businesses often want to realize the capital in standing trees and the land they cover, while a wider concern for the global environment presses for the conservation of forests and the protection of biodiversity. But the strategy did not address the implications of these conflicting priorities—or the implicit gap in global public and local private and community views on the management of those resources. Hence, it did not address the limitations of the World Bank's financing instruments—its IBRD loans or IDA credits—for addressing the challenge of conservation. In a marketplace where conservation faces competition for funding from other sectors offering high social returns, conservation often loses out. Instead of addressing this problem, the Bank relied almost exclusively on the emerging Global Environment Facility (GEF) to meet the demand for action on conservation.

As the only global financing mechanism for the implementation of all existing environmental conventions,[5] the GEF is clearly an important catalyst for saving the developing world's biodiversity and conserving forests for carbon sequestration. But in the case of the Convention on Biological Diversity (CBD), the memorandum of understanding states that CBD gives guidance on policies, strategies and eligibility to the GEF Council, which then operationalizes the convention. Owing to the lack of clarity in the convention, GEF has lacked a global priority agenda for its thrust on biodiversity conservation. GEF is supposed to finance the global environmental objectives within national development agendas and depends on the initiatives of the three implementing agencies—the World Bank, UNDP and UNEP—to generate country-level dialogue. Furthermore, the implementation of the GEF as a financing mechanism has raised complex conceptual issues about what constitutes biodiversity, and biodiversity of global significance, and hence, how to measure its loss or gain and whether incremental grant financing for a short duration, the approach currently followed by GEF, is sufficient for its conservation.[6] The considerable ambiguity in the convention on biological diversity in this regard has not helped.[7] Therefore, GEF's impact is difficult to determine. Moreover, GEF has limited resources in relation to the vast financial needs for conservation in developing countries. GEF grants for forest projects during 1991 to 1999 amounted to $370 million, and it does not have a mandate to compensate developing countries for the potential loss of income from forest protection, although other GEF biodiversity programs also have impacts on forests. Therefore, GEF's contribution must be addressed largely in catalytic terms, i.e., the extent to which it is contributing to knowledge on where, how and under what circumstances is biodiversity conservation achieved.

The Bank's 1991 strategy failed to recognize the sheer size of this public goods dilemma: how to persuade the global community to pay landowners and forest dwellers to conserve natural forests of global significance in developing countries while dealing with the complex developmental challenge, that is, promoting the use of forests and their biodiversity to ensure economic values and incentives are established for their conservation by the nationals of developing countries themselves (see box 1.1). To have any effect on forest conservation, global climate change, or biodiversity, the required payments in exchange for conservation of the environmental values that forests and biodiversity provide to the global community are not known with any certainty. But according to one estimate, payments of $6.5 billion to $10 billion annually would be required to ensure the conservation of 600 million hectares of forest in Latin America that could affect the climate (Lopez 1999). Some of this area constitutes natural habitats for major biodiversity, but the International Panel on Climate Change (IPCC) also estimates this amount of forested area would be lost in the next 60 years (assuming 80 percent of the needed increase in food production comes from agricultural intensification on existing cropped areas). Those estimates of annual required payments are comparable to the annual funds now being sought for the global health fund for AIDS, Tuberculosis and Malaria.

While agreeing to a similar rate of payment needed per hectare, some have questioned if the overall size of payments would need to be that large, arguing that payments for averting annual current increments of deforestation on about 13 million to 20 million hectares (about $72 million to $200 million a year) would be sufficient.[8]

Estimates of the amount needed for biodiversity conservation also cover a wide range, from $30 billion a year for a global reserve network covering each continent to a single payment of $25 billion for a "silver bullet strategy" that would compensate the owners of lands containing particularly valuable biodiversity—the so-called hotspots, a majority of which are embedded in mosaics of highly populated agricultural areas in developing countries.[9] Others, however, question the feasibility of saving biodiversity using the "cure-all" hotspot approach on a variety of socio-cultural, economic, environmental and aesthetic grounds.[10] These issues are discussed further in chapter 8.

Thus, many questions remain. How much area is under threat? Whose priorities should prevail? This particularly important question is rarely asked in the global scientific debate—a debate that has engaged few scientists from developing countries. How should concerns about conservation interact with those related to the socioeconomic development of developing countries containing these forests and the forest-dependent people within them? To be sustainable, payments for such conservation would need to be made in the context of the countries' national priorities, policies, and institutions, appropriately adapted to meet global concerns. The payments would also need to be linked to transparent agreements based on broadly understood rules that are both enforceable and enforced. What countries are doing on their own is therefore of considerable interest. For example, this realization led Costa Rica to become a world leader in Carbon Trading Offset (CTO) Certificates

Box 1.1 Global, National and Local Public Goods

Global public goods are distinguished, first, from "private" goods and, second, from "national" public goods (though it is not always easy to classify goods as global, national or local public, private or community goods). "Global" public goods are distinguished from national and local public goods by their reach. "Public goods" are distinguished from private goods by two important characteristics—non-rivalry (that is, many people can consume, use, or enjoy a public good at the same time, or, one person's consumption does not reduce the benefits that others can derive from consuming the same good at the same time), and non-excludability (that is, it is difficult to exclude from consumption those who do not pay for, or otherwise contribute to, the supply of the good). Their public characteristics, whether non-rivalry or non-excludability, spill across national boundaries. People in more than one country can consume the good at the same time. For national and local public goods, on the other hand, only those who live in a country or in a locality benefit from the provision of such public goods.

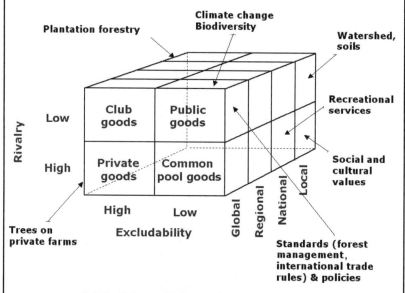

Public, Private, Club, and Common Pool Goods

Climate is often cited as a genuine global public good to which forests contribute by sequestering, conserving, or increasing the size of carbon pools. One person's enjoyment of good climate does not either exclude others nor reduce its supply. Others have considered biodiversity a global public good both because of its existence and recreational value if it is freely available, as well as its centrality to people's well-being. Natural resources, in the form of community lands, are considered "common

cont. on next page

pool" goods because often they are non-excludable but rival. What economists call "club goods" or "toll goods" are non-rival (up to the point of congestion), but excludable. Policies are considered a global or a national public good depending on their level, since all can benefit from them and no one is excluded from their application. An essential problem with public goods is that market mechanisms tend to undersupply them and oversupply "public bads," such as air pollution or biodiversity loss. Hence, public resources are often required to increase their supply, unless incentives are put in place for the markets to reduce the supply of "public bads" or increase that of public goods. These distinctions help to explain (1) why the World Bank, as a global organization, has become increasingly involved in the provision of global public goods, and (2) why the GEF was established as an international financial mechanism to provide funds to developing countries in the form of grants to conserve biodiversity of global importance.

Public, private, club and common pool goods are interchangeable and vary over time and space depending on a country's history, policy and institutional arrangements, and social preferences.

(see chapter on Costa Rica). Costa Rica has developed performance guarantees, used third-party certification, and become a leader in developing international markets for environmental services such as carbon trading. But despite its small size and forward-looking policies, Costa Rica's environmental program remains fiscally and financially fragile. International markets in environmental services have not grown as rapidly as Costa Rica had hoped, although there has been much progress in understanding the importance of developing such markets.

Growing Understanding of Forest Issues

Mounting public concern in industrial countries in the late 1980s and early 1990s about global climate change and biodiversity loss focused international attention on deforestation and resulted, among other things, in pressure from international NGOs on the World Bank to adopt a conservation-oriented forest strategy. The Bank adopted such a strategy in 1991.[11]

That was also the time of preparations for the United Nations Conference on Environment and Development, the "Earth Summit," in Rio de Janeiro in 1992. The summit produced "Agenda 21," a plan for international action on environmental and developmental matters. Agenda 21 envisaged new ways to educate people and manage natural resources in an effort to ensure a sustainable planet. The ambition of Agenda 21—a broad-ranging program of actions—was breathtaking, and its goal nothing less than to "make a safe and just world in which all life has dignity and is celebrated." Several other international agreements and initiatives followed the Earth Summit (see box 1.2), and a Rio +10 meeting is planned for Johannesburg in 2002.

Box 1.2
International Institutions and Agreements Relevant to Global Forests

Agreement on Trade-Related Aspects of Intellectual Property Rights: May affect research in forest-related biotechnology and could have a profound impact on rights to genetic material from forests, developing country competitiveness in international markets and the livelihoods of forest-dwelling people.

The Commission on Sustainable Development (CSD): Established in December 1992 to ensure effective follow-up of the Earth Summit and to monitor and report on implementation of summit agreements at the local, national, regional and international levels.

The Convention on Biological Diversity (CBD): A legally binding agreement, signed by 168 countries, on the conservation of biological diversity, the sustainable use of its components, and the fair and equitable sharing of benefits arising from the use of genetic resources.

The Convention on Combating Desertification: Relevant to forest-poor countries, principally in Africa and the Middle East.

Earth Summit + 5: A Special Session of the U.N. General Assembly in June 1997 that adopted a comprehensive document entitled "Program for the Further Implementation of Agenda 21" prepared by the Commission on Sustainable Development. It also adopted a program of work for the Commission for the period 1998–2002.

The Framework Convention on Climate Change (UNFCCC): A legally binding agreement, signed by 154 governments at the summit, whose ultimate objective is the "stabilization of greenhouse gas concentrations in the atmosphere at a level that would prevent dangerous anthropogenic (man-made) interference with the climate system."

Global Environment Facility (GEF): A global mechanism for financing implementation of environmentally related international conventions that address the loss of biodiversity, climate change, the degradation of international waters, and ozone depletion as well as land degradation issues as they relate to these four focal areas.

The Intergovernmental Forum on Forests (IFF): Established in July 1997 as an ad hoc, open-ended forum under the CSD to promote and facilitate the implementation of IPF proposals.

cont. on next page

The Intergovernmental Panel on Forests (IPF): The U.N. Commission on Sustainable Development established the IPF to continue the intergovernmental dialogue on forest policy at its third session in April 1995 to implement forest-related decisions of the Earth Summit nationally and internationally, and to promote international cooperation in financial assistance and scientific and trade issues.

The Kyoto Protocol: Adopted at the third session of the Conference of the Parties to the UNFCCC in Kyoto, Japan, in December 1997, the protocol provides three cooperative implementation mechanisms that industrialized countries—among the 84 signatories—can use to fulfill their legally binding agreements to reduce their greenhouse gas emissions. These mechanisms are:

- *Joint Implementation:* project-based financing for industrialized countries to finance and receive emission reduction units.
- *Clean Development Mechanism:* allows industrial countries to obtain "certified emission reductions" in return for carbon reduction projects in developing countries.
- *International Emissions Trading:* allows industrial country signers to use greenhouse gas emissions trading to fulfill their legally binding commitments.

The Rio Declaration: 27 universally applicable principles to help guide international action on the basis of environmental and economic responsibility.

The Statement of Forest Principles: 15 non-legally binding principles governing national and international policymaking for the protection and more sustainable management and utilization of global forest resources. These principles are extremely significant, since they constitute the first major international consensus on better use and conservation of all kinds of forests.

United Nations Forum on Forests, and Collaborative Partnership on Forests: A successor to the five-year process (1995–2000) of the ad hoc IPF and IFF with universal membership. The main purpose of the CPF is to facilitate and promote the implementation of IPF/IFF proposals to catalyze, mobilize, generate, and channel financial, technical and scientific resources to this end.

World Trade Organization (WTO): Administers the global agreement on trade liberalization that has been at the center of the Bank's structural adjustment programs (now nearly one-third of Bank lending). The removal of agricultural subsidies in industrial countries and the further liberalizing of agricultural trade by developing countries would have complex effects on forests and agriculture.

Comprehensive analysis of the implementation of the World Bank's 1991 forest strategy by OED concluded that the Bank's work, and that of other partnering multilateral and country donors, has had little effect on reducing the overall rate of tropical moist forest loss. But the efforts of the past 10 years have greatly increased our understanding of the factors causing deforestation. Some successes can be cited from among the many efforts of developing countries—mostly efforts of their own, some supported by international assistance—to reduce forest loss. There is also a far better understanding of the divergence in the costs and benefits of forest exploitation, particularly for countries, those with abundant forests and for the global community.

Forests, once seen as a source of timber for construction and other purposes, have come to be more widely appreciated for their many other benefits. For millions of poor in the rural areas of developing countries, forests supply fuelwood for household purposes and other forest products whose gathering and selling provide their livelihood. Other virtues of forests have become common knowledge. They provide habitat for millions of plant and animal species, shelter biodiversity, retain moisture, retard soil erosion, and sequester carbon dioxide. Forests influence climates, play a large role in the cultural heritage and spiritual values of indigenous societies, and serve recreational and existence values.

Is the increasing awareness of the importance of forests leading to more effective environmental protection policies? Many attempts to conserve biodiversity have failed because overly centralized, externally driven strategies have not taken local conditions and local costs and benefits into account, although much experimentation is taking place in developing countries that is leading to greater understanding of the local and global issues involved. Costa Rica has been at the forefront of experiments to reconcile such global and local values. India and China, the world's most populous countries, have independently adopted policies of no logging in natural forests (India in 1988 and China in 1998). But even the leaders of the command-and-control Chinese economy recognize the fundamental importance of incentives. They have set aside $20 billion as aid to households and enterprises affected by the logging ban over a 13-year period while also providing incentives for tree plantings and conversion of farmland to pasture and forests.[12] And the debate on forest management in Brazil, Indonesia and Cameroon has become far more active.

Knowing the Costs and Benefits

Despite our increasing knowledge, forests continue to generate controversy. Why? Because of their diffuse and long-term benefits and their concentrated and almost immediate costs. Because of the opportunity costs of the benefits forgone in alternative uses. Because of the many scales and time spans over which costs and benefits accrue. And because of the difficulty of detecting, quantifying, and measuring some of the benefits (such as microbial action on soils or cultural values). Added to these complexities are uncertain cause-and-effect relationships and the lack of congruity between different types of benefits (such as between timber production and biodiversity conservation) and between stakeholders wishing to enjoy the benefits. All of these make accurate assessment of costs and benefits difficult and contentious.[13]

The time needed to grow trees to maturity can range from 7 to 30 years, but the costs of setting aside land and financing tree planting have to be borne now. The benefits and some costs of land conversion and deforestation may be immediate—but others, particularly the environmental benefits of keeping land under forests, may be long-term. This is why the measuring of net benefits (after allowing for deforestation) is critical. Add to the costs the risks of fires, floods, and other calamities over the long life cycle of forests. Further complicating the situation is that the benefits forgone from not deforesting may be on-site, but the benefits from conservation may be off-site for people who would be displaced from lands or for consumers in urban areas. And the benefits that forests provide for the climate and biodiversity may spill over to other countries.

Not surprisingly, the many actors involved in forests—loggers, local inhabitants, small farmers, local and national forest departments, the private sector, the international community—have different interests and they perceive the costs and benefits of deforestation differently. They possess different degrees of political power and prevail differently in different situations. Understanding the processes, agents, and causes of deforestation—and the benefits and costs accruing to different actors at different levels—is crucial in determining the policies and institutions needed to manage the global commons. Among them are domestic pricing, subsidies, taxes, zoning, enforcement, the transfer payment systems, and the likelihood of sustaining such environmental outcomes as are realized.

Because the extent of the benefits is variable (see table 1.2), interrelationships are important. Exotic species, for example, offer the possibility of benefits from ecotourism and bio-prospecting but raise questions about the extent to which the benefits trickle down to the local level. As table 1.2 shows, many of the benefits potentially accrue at several levels, and there are spillovers and interactions across various levels and among the different types of benefits, their precise share depending on specific circumstances. This makes empirical, quantified estimates of benefits of utmost importance in determining financing implications.

Ninety percent of the world's biodiversity occurs outside protected areas, and the ex-situ conservation of biodiversity through such efforts as the 600,000 accessions of the publicly funded Consultative Group on International Agri-

Table 1.2
Expected Benefits from Forests

Benefits	Local	Regional	National	Global
Timber	X	X	X	X
Non-timber forest products	X	X	X	
Soil and water effects	X	X	X	
Biodiversity	X	X	X	X
Climate change	X	X	X	X
Recreational value	X	X	X	X
Cultural value	X	X	X	
Existence value			X	X

Source: Uma Lele, 2002

cultural Research (CGIAR) have provided spectacular benefits to farmers in developing countries in the form of increased productivity and to their consumers, especially poor, food-deficit households, in reduced food prices.[14] Notwithstanding the much-heralded Inbio-Merck agreement with Costa Rica, the poor in developing countries have not realized similar benefits from scientific exploitation of biodiversity in medical research because pharmaceutical research is controlled by the private sector and the high prices of the pharmaceutical products keep them out of reach for poor people. Hence, researchers have observed that the national and local benefits of bioprospecting, ecotourism, and even watershed protection within developing countries have often been exaggerated (Chomitz and Kumari 1998). Concrete, quantitative empirical information on the benefits that arise and how these benefits are distributed among the different stakeholders is often lacking.

Whereas the costs of land degradation from unsustainable timber or non-timber forest production are borne by society, the benefits are enjoyed by the agents of deforestation. The extent to which the social costs are internalized by the land owner or forest dweller depends, among other things, on tenurial rights and their security, on the enforceability and enforcement of existing laws, on market prices for sustainably managed forest products, and on the payment of taxes and fines on income earned for deforesting unsustainably. Increasing the local benefits naturally reduces the need for international transfers.

Important questions thus remain: what benefits accrue within the national boundaries of developing countries, what determines them, who derives the benefits, and who pays for them? How do they compare with the opportunity costs of alternative uses of both land and products emanating from it, for both producers and recipients of benefits? How do—and how should—

policymakers manage the divergence between the costs and benefits of conservation? Some argue that this issue will become clearer if conservation is defined as improving the allocation and use of forest resources and the associated environmental services they offer, including the various components of biodiversity and the range of ecological services and goods that the resources provide (Lutz and Caldecott 1996).

Who Pays, and How?

Given the environmental importance attached to land use and land use changes, especially in the context of the Kyoto Protocol, can carbon trading effectively transfer compensation to the national and local levels and avoid reversibility in land use? How should such global mechanisms be designed? How should GEF funding be deployed to nationals for saving biodiversity of global interest? To what extent will these mechanisms ensure sustainable conservation, and on what scale?

The complex social, cultural, legal, moral, ethical, biological, political and economic debates are by no means confined to developing countries. In a review of the U.S. Endangered Species Act after 25 years, a group of natural resource economists outlines the growing scope, the unfunded mandates, and the difficult economic choices that affect and are affected by biological needs and political realities (Shogren and Tschirhart 1999). At the global level, forests and biodiversity raise additional issues of national sovereignty, governance, corruption, and the need to develop international markets so that winners can compensate losers. The only solution to the question of compensation may be negotiated, transparent agreements involving key parties around broadly understood rules of the game that are enforceable and enforced. Yet, such solutions would depend on the availability of resources that would provide compensation to losers on a scale large enough to make a difference to global outcomes on forest cover and biodiversity.

Lopez's estimate of the huge cost of stopping deforestation in the Amazon was mentioned above. He also estimated that a tax equivalent of $1 a barrel of oil or $6 per ton of coal equivalent would generate revenues of $50 billion annually (Lopez 1999). Other suggestions to finance these global goals include the Tobin tax on international financial transactions. These international proposals, however, have not found expression in concrete financing instruments, and some argue that general taxation to achieve global goals is unlikely to receive popular support in industrial countries (Cooper 2001). So a more pragmatic case-by-case approach to resource mobilization is needed.[15] Certainly for carbon, a substantial international market may be emerging in the clean development mechanism and joint implementation discussed in chapter 8. But even if the financial resources become available on the scale needed, success will depend on the program's design, implementation, monitoring, and evaluation to ensure continuing refinement. Forests differ sub-stantially in their value, and assessing net "with project" effects, larger than without, remains a challenge.

Ways of Looking at Forests in Transition

An Evolutionary Approach

Van Thunen (1966)[16] et al. inspired by his work have taken an evolution-ary approach to characterizing forest development and deforestation and their linkages to agriculture (Hyde 1991; Sedjo 1999; Schneider 1998; Lopez 1999; Pearce 1999). In different ways, they argue that the relative levels of forest values, agricultural land values, and land protection costs will determine the levels of secure agriculture, managed forestry, open-access agriculture, and degradation and deforestation. Countries go through several phases:

- *Phase 1.* Returns to agriculture are absolutely higher than returns to forestry, leading to permanent cropping where property rights are en-forceable—that is, the marginal cost of enforcement is less than the return to agriculture. Where enforcement costs exceed the return to agriculture, forests will be degraded in favor of open-access agricul-ture (typically grazing or pasture).
- *Phase 2.* This phase is reached when permanent cropping and open-access agriculture persist. Increasing demand for forest products shifts the relative prices of agriculture and forest products, leading to pri-mary forest extraction (forest degradation, deforestation) where en-forcement costs and returns to forest products exceed returns to agriculture.
- *Phase 3.* Demand for forest products increases to levels in excess of enforcement costs, resulting in a managed forest sector, such as sec-ondary forest and plantations. Open-access forestry (some of which may be used for agriculture) continues to exist where enforcement costs exceed forest value.
- *Phase 4.* Non-market forest values (carbon sequestration, biodiversity) emerge to complement managed forest exploitation by adding en-forceable conservation to the mix. Open-access forests will persist where enforcement costs are high.

In all phases, ease of access determines which lands are exploited and the pace of exploitation. Market forces can further accelerate this exploitation. Relative prices would then reach levels that stimulate managed forestry and conservation. This line of argument suggests that a certain amount of loss is inevitable. But it is also clear that factors other than these trend variables, such as the role of interest groups, explain the socially and environmentally exploitative deforestation.

Box 1.3
What Explains Deforestation?

In an exhaustive review of the literature, Angelsen and Kaimowitz (1999) classify the explanatory variables of deforestation as follows:

- Sources of deforestation (choice variables of agents)—for instance, land use, land allocation, labor and other inputs, technological and managerial decisions.
- Immediate causes (exogenous parameters of decision making) such as prices, risks, property regimes, and environmental conditions.
- Underlying causes (policies and macro variables) such as demography, world markets, macroeconomic trends, and available technologies.

Much of the descriptive and econometric literature on Brazil, Indonesia and other developing countries, has used this approach to explain deforestation in terms of the absolute and relative prices of various agricultural commodities, prices of land and inputs, public policies toward credit, fiscal incentives, land concessions, zoning, and accessibility as determined by investment in roads and hence transportation costs. Macro variables include wages, risks, discount rates, technologies, tenure regimes, and population densities.

Empirical studies suggest that such models are not always useful in explaining deforestation, not only because the poor quality of data, but because deforestation involves a large number of variables and interactions among them (Geist and Lambin 2001). Additionally, the effects of some variables can go more than one way. Increased credit, for example, can either avert the need for deforestation by supplying working capital or increase the ability to deforest by enabling purchases of machinery. Endogeneity of some explanatory variables poses additional analytical challenges. Road access determines the relative prices of land, capital, products, and labor (say, by stimulating migration). Emerging scarcities do more than affect price signals—they help mobilize stakeholders to initiate better forest management and thus result in changes in formal or informal institutional arrangements.

Public policy can change rules, create scarcities or surpluses through logging or export bans, land use planning, the setting aside of large tracts of land for complete protection, zoning rules, construction of roads and other infrastructure, dissemination of information to interested parties, and better law enforcement. Governments can also change relative prices by using taxes, subsidies, and transfer payments as incentives to use resources differently, thus influencing decisions on afforestation, reforestation, complete protection, sustainable management of land for production, and regeneration on degraded lands (Chomitz et al. 1999).

An Income Approach

The environmental Kuznets curve provides another approach to the analysis (Panayoutou 1995). It suggests that at low income levels, economic growth will put pressure on forests and increase deforestation, but as incomes grow, deforestation will stop and forest coverage will increase because of improved government institutions and reduced dependence on agricultural and forest production. That is, higher incomes lead to increased demand for environmental and other ecological services that do not necessarily reduce forest cover. This has been the experience in several industrial economies. But critics note that the Kuznets curve does not help explain the process of institutional reforms that leads to policy changes and improved environmental outcomes (Arrow et al. 1995), does not reflect changes in international policies, and the environmental impacts on economic performance (Barbier 1994). Furthermore, median income matters more than average income and the increases in income needed for such transitions tend to be very high (Stern, Common, and Barbier 1996). Furthermore, recent evidence (including that presented in this book) suggests that the poor tend to be less responsible for deforestation than those with economic and political power. On the contrary, countries with the greatest population pressure on the land with large incidences of forest-dependent poor are making headways in arresting forest loss and restoring degraded lands using an active public policy.

An Institutional Approach

Analysis of the effects of institutional and interest group actions related to forest loss has been woefully lacking, which is not surprising. Nobel Prize-winning economist Ronald Coase has argued that economists tend to focus on the analysis of choice, and that preoccupation with choice has led to the neglect of the entities whose decisions economists analyze. This approach has often made economics lacking in substance because economic analysis of exchange takes place without any specification of the institutional setting. "Consumers are conceived without humanity. Demand is portrayed as a downward sloping curve. Firms are thought of without organizations and even exchange without markets" (Coase 1988: 3-7). Coase observed that the work of sociobiologists (and their critics) will enable economists to construct a picture of human nature in such detail that the social preference sets used by economists will be better understood.

In a similar vein, Douglas North, another Nobel Prize-winning economist, has argued that the institutional framework is a key to explaining many historical phenomena. "Institutions are the rules of the game in a society that shape human interaction...whether political, social, or economic. Institutions emerge when it is costly to transact and institutional change tends to be path dependent. Therefore, history matters. What organizations come into play and how they evolve are fundamentally influenced by the institutional framework. Organizations differ from institutions in the same way that rules differ from players. Rules define the way the game is played. Separating the analysis of the underlying rules from the strategy of the players is a necessary prerequisite to understanding institutional change. Institutions affect performance in a complex and incremental way through formal and informal means by their effect on the cost of exchange and production" (North 1990: 4-10).

According to such a broad definition of institutions, the complex interactions between policies, legal rules, and informal institutions offer new insights into understanding forest cover loss and what might be done to reverse it. Legal rules include forest laws. Informal rules include the rights of communities living adjacent to forests who have traditional rights to gather fuelwood and other non-timber products from the forest area. Forest departments constitute formal organizations, user groups informal ones.

Institutional change in the sense of changes in the relationships between these formal and informal organizations and rules occurs not as a one-time static move but as a dynamic process. Community rights to forests have been expanding, with communities owning or officially administering at least 25 percent of developing world forests (nearly 300 million hectares). Community participation in forest management shifts a share of the management responsibility from forest departments to community groups. In the process, informal community groups may become formalized. The rules of the game, crafted for forest department management of forest resources, may then become obsolete. In such situations, a formal change in the rules, including changes in laws and regulations, may be required. Similarly, logging bans and associated policies may result in substantial changes in the formal and informal rules by which communities manage forests.

A recent report on the policies needed to achieve a "sustainable Amazon" argues that if market forces continue to operate freely, land use will be based largely on predatory logging, associated with extensive ranching, leading to the risk of a boom-and-bust cycle (World Bank–Imazon 1999). The report implies that by changing the rules of the game government could help improve forest management and ensure a more stable economy (through income, employment, and taxes) than that produced by agriculture. How? By creating "national forests," restricting land use, and imposing taxes on incomes from predatory logging. But because the benefits of sustainable land use occur mostly at the national and global levels, state and local economic and regulatory instruments are not sufficient. Global transfers through such things as carbon offsets would be essential (Schneider et al. 1998). Such changes in property rights, their enforcement, and patterns of behavior through changes in incentives imply profound changes in financing and institutional arrangements both at the national and global levels.

The World Bank Group and the Global Environment Facility (GEF)

The World Bank Group and the Global Environment Facility (GEF) are the largest financiers of forest and biodiversity activities annually in developing countries (financing variously estimated at $300 to $500 million annually), and they leverage between three and six times those amounts if the contributions of national governments and other donors are considered. As compared to the World Bank's forest sector lending program between 1992 and 1999, which has financed 128 forest projects (and projects with forest components) in all regions of the world at a total cost of $3.5 billion, GEF grants for forest projects (1991–99) amounted to $370 million, *or slightly more than 10 percent of the Bank's commitments to the forest sector.* The GEF financed 44 forest projects through the World Bank between its inception in 1991 and 1999. As of 1999, 11 GEF forest projects were jointly financed, involving Bank commitments of $181 million. GEF is now expanding its reach to involving other regional banks, international and national institutions in addition to its three implementing agencies. The Bank has a presence in most economic sectors in nearly 100 developing countries. The OED review and other recent research have documented that policies and investment activities in all sectors collectively have a far larger impact on forests in the developing world than what happens in the forest sector alone. While developing countries would not want to abandon their infrastructure development plans for the sake of conservation, they might consider better placement of that infrastructure in order to minimize the adverse impacts of those investments. So, the World Bank Group's experience in the financing of forest and biodiversity conservation, as well as that of GEF, is of considerable interest.

The World Bank's 1991 Forest Strategy

The Bank's 1991 forest strategy (see box 1.4) broke new ground in several respects. It established the principle of an open participatory process in formulating Bank policies, though the consultation was confined mainly to northern-hemisphere NGOs. It brought the conservation agenda to the forefront of the Bank's activities and stressed the importance of mainstreaming environmental concerns through a multisectoral approach to forest conservation. Then-president Barber Conable established an Environment Department in the Bank to address these concerns. The strategy itself became a safeguard policy, the "do no harm" principle.[17]

The Bank's strategy also had many limitations. Its focus on the conservation of tropical moist forests led to neglect of other forest types where the rate of biodiversity loss is even greater, stock has virtually disappeared (the Atlantic forest and the cerrados in Brazil, or the coastal areas of India, for example), or where investment in tree planting is essential to meet growing national and

---

Box 1.4
The Forest Strategy

The goal of the Bank's 1991 forest sector strategy was to address the twin challenges of rapid deforestation, especially of tropical moist forests, and the inadequate planting of new trees to meet the rapidly growing demand for wood products. These challenges were viewed as being connected to five key factors:

- Externalities that prevented market forces from achieving socially desired outcomes
- Strong incentives, particularly for the poor, to harvest trees
- Weak property rights in many forests and wooded areas
- High private discount rates among those encroaching on the forests
- Inappropriate government policies, particularly land concession arrangements.

Five principles were proposed for Bank involvement in the forest sector:

- A multisectoral approach
- International cooperation
- Policy reform and institutional strengthening
- Resource expansion
- Land use controls (including zoning, demarcation, and controls associated with tenure issues) to preserve natural forests.

Bank-financed activities were expected to comply with seven conditions:

- No financing for commercial logging in primary tropical moist forests
- An institutional framework and the adoption of policies consistent with sustainability
- A participatory approach to the management of natural forests
- The adoption of comprehensive and environmentally sound conservation and development plans, with the roles and rights of key stakeholders, including local people, clearly defined
- Basing commercial use of forests on adequate social, environmental, and economic assessments of their impact
- Making adequate provision to maintain biodiversity and safeguard the interests of local people, including forest dwellers and indigenous peoples
- Establishing adequate enforcement mechanisms.

---

international demand for forest products, where the national commitment to forest conservation is greater, and hence global and national interests are more aligned. The priorities in Bank operations in the 20 moist-forest countries did not materialize because there was no demand for economic analysis or project lending by the Bank for forests in forest-rich countries. Similarly, while the logging ban had a symbolic effect, it did not address the causes of the substantial illegal logging of forests.

The ban on loans for commercial logging diverted attention from the underlying issue of providing incentives for conservation and contributed to a chilling effect on forest sector operations in forest-rich countries, which were keen to exploit their forests for production purposes and where rich and powerful interests wanted to reap profits. Indeed, the Bank Group's International Finance Corporation turned down many proposed projects for improved forest management in tropical countries for fear of violating the Bank's forest strategy. The ban thus prevented the Bank from being proactively engaged in addressing forest management along the lines later proposed by the World Bank–WWF alliance.

The Bank's major contributions to forest sector development came mostly in forest-poor countries, especially China and India, where more than 100 million people, mostly social or ethnic minorities, directly depend on forests, and hundreds of millions indirectly depend on them. China and India were the two largest recipients of investment finance, amounting to 59 percent of the Bank's lending between 1992 and 1999. The increasing scarcity of forests in India and China prompted both countries to become more environmentally conscious and to develop programs to increase or regenerate forest cover. The Bank also made an important contribution by contributing ideas to Costa Rica's forest strategy. These contributions have been central to the Bank's poverty reduction and environmental sustainability missions, but until the OED review was completed, these contributions of the Bank had remained unknown and hence unrecognized, in part because none of them involved moist tropical forests and hence were not the focus of international attention.[18]

With keen interest in conservation and biodiversity, and close connections with a number of major international conservation NGOs, Bank President James Wolfensohn launched the WWF–World Bank Global Alliance for Sustainable Forest Development and the CEO Forum. Both reinforce the principle of open dialogue with external partners. The Alliance established a concrete program of action to achieve sustainable forest management (albeit one that was inconsistent with the Bank's 1991 forest strategy).

The Alliance adopted global targets: complete protection of 50 million hectares of natural forest, another 50 million hectares of improved protection, and 200 million hectares of sustainably managed forests. The former is less than 10 percent of the forest cover needed to make a difference to the global climate (Lopez 1999). The latter goal would inevitably entail some logging, some of it commercial, and therefore would be inconsistent with the Bank's 1991 forest strategy. As this book was being completed the Bank was in the process of changing its forest strategy to address some of the limitations of the 1991 forest strategy. The revised strategy proposes to advocate three pillars: harnessing the potential of forests to reduce poverty; integrating forests in sustainable economic development; and protecting national, local and global environmental services and values. Its coverage is broadened to include all types of forests and it emphasizes partnerships and attempts to generate demand for global investment in the sustainable management of forests in developing countries.

Meanwhile, the CEO Forum is intended to facilitate consultations with the chief executive officers of timber companies, who had previously been viewed as part of the problem. The intention has been to exchange ideas on sustainable forest management with these leaders and move toward solutions.

Both groups have their critics. The Alliance has been heavily criticized by some NGOs because they shun any notion of partnership with the Bank, feel that it gives too much attention to the policies advocated by a single NGO, or object to the idea that forests in the tropics can be logged sustainably (Rice 1998). The CEO Forum was also criticized by some international NGOs when it was formed, leading to invitations to some of them to join the forum. This not only ensured the exchange of diverse viewpoints under a neutral forum, it also enabled the Bank to use its convening power to air differences on controversial issues in a transparent manner as perhaps a first step toward possible solutions to reconciling global and national objectives.

The criticism aside, both groups have opened up a dialogue on the future of forests in developing countries, but even the modest Alliance targets would require significant international finance, research and analysis in and by developing countries. They would also require policy and institutional reforms and investment in human and organizational capital, not simply support to international NGOs for research and experimentation in developing countries but also for capacity development in policy, research, and experimentation in developing countries for protection and sustainable management of forest cover.

Forest-Poor or Forest-Rich

OED research in countries reported in this volume indicated quite different policy responses among forest-rich and forest-poor countries to the loss of forest cover and biodiversity. Globally, there are three times the number of forest-poor countries relative to forest-rich countries. For example, according to FAO's *State of the World's Forests 2001* (table 2), there are only about eight apparently "forest rich" countries in West Africa, seven in Asia, three in Eastern Europe, and seven in Central and Latin America but there are about thirty "forest poor" countries in Africa, eighteen in Asia, eight in Eastern Europe, and five in central and Latin America. Hence, the analysis overtly investigated the nature of these differences and underlying causes. Given the variation in the sizes of countries and their forest cover, forest-rich countries were defined by the percentage of total land area reported under forest rather than the absolute size of their forests. It would have been more desirable to consider forest quality as well. However, data on forest areas do not provide reliable information that is internationally comparable on differences in crown cover, although such data are available for individual countries and were used. Large areas in forest-rich countries can be forest-poor, and forest-poor countries can have forest-rich areas. But the breakdown into forest-rich and forest-poor categories can shed light on the impact of differences in demography and resources on forest valuation, incentives, and perceptions within and between countries about forest conservation (see tables 1.3 and 1.4). Abundance or scarcity can trigger policy and institutional behavioral responses that lead to changes from forest-rich to forest-poor, or the reverse. Forest-poor southern Brazil has many more pro-environmental policies than the forest-rich north. Costa Rica, once forest-rich, is now in transition from forest-poor to forest-rich. It is categorized as forest-poor because its forest policies have more in common with the policies of forest-poor countries than with those of the forest-rich. China is undergoing a similar transition. Although both countries are increasing their forest cover and plantation forests serve many environmental functions, some loss of biodiversity is not recoverable.

Forest-Poor Countries: China, Costa Rica, India

Forest policies in China, Costa Rica and India were relatively consistent with the Bank's forest strategy (see Box 1.4 and Table 1.3). India's 1988 forest policy and the Bank's strategy both emphasize the environmental role of forests, particularly the role of public forests in meeting the subsistence requirements of forest-dependent populations. China's 1998 imposition of a logging ban in natural forests brought its forest policy more in line with the Bank's 1991 forest strategy. And although India and China have been the largest borrowers of IDA credits, the financing they have received has not been large enough or long-term enough to meet the resource requirements of implementing these policies.

Costa Rica has had few international concessional financial transfers to help carry out its progressive environmental policies and the country is bearing virtually all the cost. Yet the importance of this effort was recognized by the Bank in its 1993 forest sector review on Costa Rica, which estimated that nearly two-thirds of the benefits of Costa Rica's forest conservation are enjoyed globally. That review pointed out that the global community should compensate Costa Rica for conserving, managing, and planting forests. To enable the Costa Rican government to finance such environmental activities as the protection of biodiversity, the review stressed expansion of protected areas if necessary by compensating private landowners for land acquisitions to expand the network of protected areas. To finance such protection it recommended improving financial management of national parks and ensuring their sustainability, and deregulating import and export of forest products as well as harvesting in forest plantations. The small amount of economic and sector work the Bank carried out in Costa Rica has had considerable influence on the government's adoption of specific measures to make its forest sector strategies more effective, although their financial sustainability remains uncertain.

But the Bank's forest policy analysis in Costa Rica has not been without critics in Costa Rica, especially in view of the lack of international concessional financial resources to finance the purchase of private lands to establish large protected areas. Some argue that the Bank's policy advice to Costa Rica to acquire private land for conservation instead of allowing private landowners to make a living from conservation activities has had an adverse effect on incentives and led to uncertainty as to the likely government policy towards private lands for conservation. Critics also argue that the Bank's policy advice neglected the plantation sector, the development of small private forests, and post-harvest aspects of forest production, including helping Costa Rica attract more private investments. The governments of Brazil and China have also stressed the importance of Bank Group financing

Table 1.3
Forest-Poor Countries: China, Costa Rica, and India

Forest-poor countries	Principal causes of deforestation	Developments favoring conservation	Principal constraints to reform
China	Land conversion to agriculture Strong domestic demand for timber for a rapidly growing economy	Massive investments in forest plantations Participatory forest management including household rights to land and trees Natural forest protection program Substantial commitment of federal government resources to forest protection and land conversion Logging ban	A blueprint approach to forest development Location specific needs Insecure tenure rights of households to forest lands Forest state enterprises in need of reform
India	Land conversion to agriculture Rapid growth in domestic urban demand Land expansion	Productivity growth in agriculture Social forestry Joint forest management (JFM) involving the poor	Lack of an overarching forest strategy beyond community forest management A reform-resistant forest department Insufficient financial resources Limited role of the private sector
Costa Rica	Land conversion to agriculture	A multisectoral approach Private and public protected areas Third-party certification Carbon offsets Bioprospecting Ecotourism Fossil fuel tax Institutional diversity	Fragility of reforms and fiscal situation Insufficient international financial support

for tree planting and for post-harvest activities, but the Bank has discouraged subsidies for tree planting. And in a period of rising domestic interest rates and a credit crunch, the long-term nature of investments in forest plantations have reduced demand for credit for tree planting.

Forest-Rich Countries: Brazil, Indonesia, Cameroon

The experience in the three forest-rich countries discussed in this volume—Brazil, Indonesia, and Cameroon—has been quite different. While they vary greatly in population and forested areas, they have far greater per capita forest area (ranging from 0.54 to 3 hectares) than India, China, or Costa Rica. (See table 1.1.) In all three countries there is a clear divergence between the global interest in maintaining forest cover and the national imperative to use natural forests for private profit or development (see table 1.4). An overwhelming cause of deforestation in these three countries has been the use of forests for national (industrial and agricultural) development, as a source of land for agriculture, raw material (fuelwood or timber), capital (finance and savings), and private profit.

The sources of demand for forest products have varied. As much as 85 percent of the timber produced in Brazil goes to meet domestic urban/industrial demand. Industrialization through forest exports to meet international demand has been the most significant source of demand in Indonesia and Cameroon. Indeed, those two countries are the largest exporters of tropical forest products from their regions. In all three countries, some of the land converted from forests has been used for agricultural production—ranching in Brazil and tree crops in Indonesia. Each use reflects the countries' comparative advantage and international competitiveness in agriculture and agricultural exports.

Governance has been a more serious issue in forest management in forest-rich countries, although it has not been absent altogether in forest-poor countries. Forests have allowed huge scope for private profits, and the short- and medium-term interests of the state in the form of increased government revenue, income and employment, and exports have often been congruent with those of private entrepreneurs, although these practices have had adverse environmental and social consequences. In Brazil and Indonesia, the entrepreneurial class benefiting from forest exploitation has consisted of nationals, whereas in Cameroon it has been mainly foreign. Forest interests have been closely aligned with the ruling political elite at the national level in Indonesia and Cameroon. Although ranchers and loggers have been politically well connected with the local ruling elite in Brazil, there has been no such political alliance at the national level.

Reforms and dialogue with the Bank are under way in all three countries. In Cameroon and Indonesia, economic crises have increased dependence on

Table 1.4
Forest-Rich Countries: Brazil, Indonesia, and Cameroon

Forest-rich countries	Principal causes of deforestation	Developments favoring conservation	Principal constraints to reform
Brazil	Large domestic consumption of forest products Migration to the Amazon Investment in roads, logging, and agriculture (including ranching)	Increased federal government role in forest policy formulation, land use planning, forest regulation and enforcement Increased awareness and role of civil society, progressive private sector interest in third-party certification Increased domestic debate on forest policy	Divergence between global and national (including state and local) objectives Insufficient finance to compensate state and local interest groups, and insufficient planning and implementing capacity for detailed policy planning, implementation, and enforcement
Indonesia	Thriving international demand for tropical timber Large forest-related industrial capacity Overextended loans to the financial sector Tree crop expansion Migration to outer islands Divergence between global and national objectives	Abolition of the plywood processing monopoly Increased government and NGO interest in policy reforms	Established industrial capacity International market for tropical timber Breakdown of law and order, corruption Increased and more widespread distribution of benefits of deforestation in a decentralized state
Cameroon	Thriving international demand for tropical timber Powerful multinational private timber interests Low-productivity agriculture Divergence between global and national objectives	Reform of land concessions policy Third-party monitoring	Governance, resistance of multinational corporations, weak institutional capacity Corruption Limited enforcement Lack of monitoring capacity

the Bank and other donors. The Bank is trying to affect forest outcomes through a combination of adjustment-related policy conditionality and a policy dialogue based on increasingly active donor coordination and consultations with the stakeholders in the countries.

The Bank's failure to have a larger impact in the three forest-rich countries was a result of several factors. Given the Bank's "precautionary" strategy focused on conservation, and the strong rent-seeking interests in the countries in exploiting their forests, the Bank's involvement in the forest sector was not welcome. The Bank's successive reorganizations and decentralization has increased the voice of developing countries in determining areas for Bank involvement. Its ban on the financing of commercial equipment for use in the primary tropical forests led Bank staff to be risk-averse when it came to getting involved with the management of any forests unless the activity was small scale and involved indigenous people. Furthermore, even in primary natural forests, the Bank had no incentive to deal with the complex issues of illegal activity, weak enforcement capacity and a lack of political will or national consensus for policy reform. Success would require sustained long-term effort to nurture consensus among competing stakeholders through dialogue, empirical analysis and capacity building.

This would involve substantial transaction costs and entail a high risk of failure as well as a reputational risk of "guilt by association" in the event of failure. The country case studies outline the evolution of the Bank's involvement in the forest-rich countries.

An additional challenge is that the problem cannot be "fixed" quickly. Illegal logging is difficult to contain without improved information and stronger enforcement capacity. There is agreement about the importance of increasing the value of forests through increased enforcement, but no consensus on whether such instruments as improved concession policies, bans on exports of logs, or increased royalties will by themselves result in improved incentives for and outcomes in forest management. A long-term, integrated approach is needed. Markets for environmental services are needed but they require a complex web of institutions and there are no resources to fill the gap between the globally and nationally perceived optimal quantities of forest exploitation. Without appropriate policy instruments and additional resources, budget-strapped governments find it difficult to afford stronger enforcement or to make payments for environmental services.[19]

The impact of the ban on Bank financing for commercial logging in tropical moist forests has been mixed. The ban has had a strategic and symbolic value. It eliminated the likelihood of the Bank being associated with illegal, large-scale, and unsustainable logging, but it did not discourage wasteful forest exploitation practices. It made the Bank largely irrelevant in the drama of extensive illegal logging—a view shared by key borrowers and two-thirds of Bank staff working in the forest sector who responded to an OED questionnaire.[20] The Bank has since become more active in the forest policy dialogue; in encouraging donor coordination to support monitoring and sharing of information on illegal activity; and convincing the governments of the fiscal, environmental, and equity costs of their forest policies.

More important, the aversion to ecological risk associated with the 1991 strategy had unintended consequences. It discouraged the Bank from using its resources to promote new attitudes toward forest resource management, to help build internal capacity in borrowing countries and provide conservation-oriented forest constituencies a voice in their country's internal decision making.[21]

In many forest-rich countries, local rent seeking in the forest sector may have restricted Bank involvement. The 1991 strategy may also have affected the demand for Bank services, a result of successive internal reorganizations that have enabled borrowers to play a larger role in deciding priorities for Bank involvement. Without substantial support for compensating them for the fiscal and development costs of conservation, forest-rich countries have been reluctant to internationalize the forest issue. One reason is the economic benefit they see in exploiting the forests. Another is the close connection between resource exploitation and governance issues. In Brazil, as in Indonesia and Cameroon, economic crises and large-scale projects (such as Brazil's Rondonia Natural Resource Management Project) have brought these issues to the fore.

Forests and Poverty Alleviation

Nearly a quarter of the population in developing countries lives in extreme poverty, subsisting on less than a dollar a day. Nearly 90 percent of the them, about 1,080 million, live in Asia and Sub-Saharan Africa. South Asia (SA) remains the poorest region with 43.5 percent of the world's poor followed by Sub-Saharan Africa (SSA) and East Asia and the Pacific (EAP), each with slightly less than a quarter of the total poor. While poverty has declined dramatically in the EAP region, mainly due to the achievements of countries such as China and Indonesia, South Asia's progress in poverty alleviation has been slower. In Sub-Saharan Africa, the number of poor increased from 242 million in 1987 to 291 million in 1998, so that almost half the continent's residents now live in poverty (figure 1.1). Internal conflicts, civil war, adverse weather, decline in terms of trade and HIV/AIDS have added to the burden.[22]

When poverty is juxtaposed against the forest cover across regions, the pressures seem even more stark. More than half of the world's forests are in two regions, Latin America and the Caribbean (LAC) and Europe and Central Asia (ECA). But together these regions contain only 8 percent of the world's poor. South and East Asia, in contrast, contain only 15 percent of the world's forests, yet they support 54 percent of the world's population (figure 1.1). Low per capita availability of forests (only .06 hectares in South Asia and .23 hectares in EAP) and land (only 0.19 hectares in South Asia and 0.14 hectares in EAP), increases the pressure on land and forests. Sub-Saharan Africa is better placed in terms of forest and land per capita, but land quality and the low productivity of agricultural land put immense pressure on natural resources.

In the economies of forested regions, hundreds of millions of poor derive their monetary and non-monetary (subsistence) income from a variety of products and services on lands that range widely in ownership, including public lands, degraded forest margins, common property resources, and private lands. Their income-generating assets and products are also diverse and lack standardization or scale economies in handling, marketing, and processing. With huge transport costs relative to their market value, forest products require location-specific understanding and analysis to determine if there is scope for their commercialization.

Population pressure, the incidence of poverty, and the role of forests in people's livelihoods vary in the six countries studied but mirror the overall situation in their regions. For example, 109 million hectares have been set aside for 936,000 indigenous people, 117 hectares of forest land per indig-

Figure 1.1
Number of Poor Living Below $1 Per Day in Developing and Transitional
Economies, 1987 and 1998 (millions)

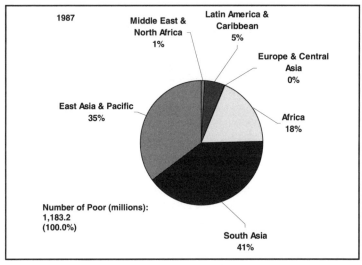

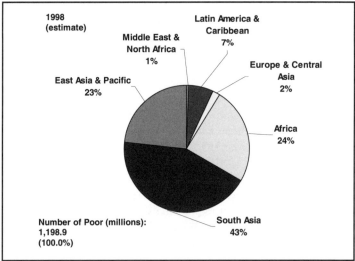

Source: WDR on Poverty and Development 2000/01

enous person, under the Amazon Cooperation Treaty in 8 Latin American
countries.[23] In contrast, in Asia well over 100 million poor make a living out
of a quarter to a third of that area. If serious progress is to be made on reducing
global poverty, then international attention on the issues of forest and liveli-

hoods must focus on the Asian and African regions, whereas environmental concerns led to center it on the Amazon and other tropical moist forests.

But information on forest dependence is very limited and estimates range widely. The estimated number of forest-dependent people in Indonesia, for example, ranges from 1.5 million to 65 million, and in India from 1 million to 50 million. Meaningful estimates are also hampered by a lack of uniformity or consistency in definitions of forest dependency.

Arnold and Bird (1999) describe dependence on forest products and services as:

- Subsistence goods (fuel, food, medicinal plants)
- Farm inputs (soil and nutrient recycling, windbreaks, shade trees, mulch)
- Income from the sale of products and labor
- Sources of income diversification and risk reduction, since they almost never offer enough income for all subsistence needs.

Forest-based subsistence activities (low input and low output) do little to help people climb out of poverty and are rapidly abandoned once incomes begin to grow and better alternatives become available. Prospects for adding value and commercialization that will help the poor depend on increasing their share of the assets (trees), the related forest products—even if they come from public forest land—and an equitable share of the value of the final product when it is sold in the market.

Turning forest activities into significant sources of income and livelihood therefore requires a focus on the rules that define property rights (not simply land rights, often the focus of analysts' attention, but also rights to the products of the land),[24] community organization, infrastructure, information, related institutions (including markets for products and services), and not the least important, human and organizational capital, including basic levels of skill. All these tend to be in short supply among the remote forest-dependent poor. The Brazil case study discusses the rapid progress in land settlement efforts underway in that country. Some forest products, such as fashion products made of Amazon rubber for urban and European markets, have been recognized as improving the lives of indigenous South Americans. More such efforts are needed, together with well-documented empirical evidence on their achievements.

Improving conditions of the rural poor as a whole and those of indigenous minorities in the forests and mountains often entails mitigating enormous social conflict. China and Indonesia (until the economic crisis of 1997) achieved rapid economic growth and substantially reduced the percentage of people below the poverty line, but transmigration schemes and forest concessions to Javanese migrants in Indonesia's forest-dependent outer islands unleashed ethnic tensions and violence of unexpected proportions among the native and migrant households. China's logging ban, while important environmentally, has caused hardship for well over a million of its forest-dependent minorities, despite large subsidies and food aid. Although China's economic strength has enabled it to commit substantial financial and food aid resources to provide alternative sources of income for these minorities, it is too early to determine if the policy will be environmentally and developmentally sustainable. To ensure sustainability will require substantial location-specific planning and implementation capacity to address location-specific issues rather than blanket approaches, and they must be linked to national policy objectives and resources. The international community can help to develop such capacity.

In India, two-thirds of the forest cover lies in tribal districts, and the incidence of poverty among tribal people is higher than average. Efforts to improve conditions have generated considerable conflict between tribal people and other poor. India has begun to shift rules of the game, sharing a significant portion of timber and, increasingly, non-timber income from public lands with forest-dependent households (in states such as Madhya Pradesh and Andhra Pradesh) with considerable success in improving forest cover and providing incentives for households to protect degraded forests, enabling them to increase their household incomes over the medium to long term. But protection of rights of some has also meant denial of rights to others, particularly the poor encroachers on the lands. Progress in giving rights to income and responsibility for forest management to village communities has varied among Indian states, as has progress in addressing long-term tenure to communities on the margins of forests.

China can be said to have been ahead of India in this regard. Under the reforms China introduced in the forest sector in the 1980s, under its "responsibility system," it decentralized control of public lands to villages, communes, and individuals through long-term leases assigning them greater responsibility for planning and implementation. But the 1998 logging ban and land conversions have reversed some rights to land and trees while reducing household incentives to invest in tree planting. These changes in policies illustrate both the dynamic nature of the rules, particularly property rights, and the need to remain vigilant in understanding their impacts on incentives and outcomes.

In Indonesia, reforms in the long-term concessional leases for timber exploitation awarded as part of policy reforms to stimulate improved management of forestlands may have violated the rights of village communities. Critics have argued that liberalizing licensing of oil palm estates as part of the IMF conditionality may have accelerated land conversion. Decentralization to the districts in the post-Suharto era also appears to have accelerated the rate of deforestation and created conditions that have made rent seeking by local elites more widespread. These problems underscore not only the importance of location-specific research to ensure that reforms are tailored to meet local realities but also that some economic reforms undertaken to foster overall growth will have adverse effects on the forest cover.

Indonesia, China and India illustrate the complex nature of issues involved in ensuring equity in benefits among different types of households. An unfortunate consequence of the controversy over the application of the World Bank safeguards for indigenous people—and the increased cost of doing business with the Bank for borrowing countries—is that even well-intentioned governments become reluctant to get the Bank involved in such issues for fear of inviting international attention and controversy. The Bank is then less able to help developing countries improve their policies in ways that reconcile complex environmental and social objectives.

Research by international organizations and international NGOs on these issues has increased in the past decade, attracting increased international attention to the rent seeking in forest activities. However, to ensure long-term sustained impacts on fine-tuning policies and institutions in response to the lessons of experience, such research would need to become institutionalized nationally, and nationals would need a voice in policy-making processes. Hence, building capacity of developing countries for sustained high-quality research and policy inputs into the reform of domestic policy is of utmost importance.

Box 1.5 offers examples of how investments in forestry have the potential to help the poor.

Major Forces Affecting Deforestation

Explosive Demand

The 1991 forest strategy did not fully envisage how much the explosive growth in demand for forest and agricultural products would exacerbate forest degradation, forest conversion, and deforestation. Globalization, international trade liberalization, and lower tariffs have made forest-product imports from forest-rich countries cheaper in forest-poor countries. Logging bans in forest-poor countries, China for example, have increased the need for imports but made domestic investment in trees less profitable. China (at $5.6 billion) and India (at $764 million) are among the world's largest importers of timber and other wood products. According to government estimates, China's 1998 decision to ban logging in natural forests will reduce China's domestic timber supply by almost 20 million cubic meters a year. Imports—slight in the 1980s—have grown commensurately, while exports have fallen. This trend is of regional and global importance. Without investments in production forests and tree plantations, China's rising demand for wood products will likely lead to defiance of the logging ban at home, with local communities continu-

---

Box 1.5
How Forest Investments Can Help the Poor

- Creating wage employment in the planting and regeneration of forest areas.[a]
- Developing human and social capital by upgrading the skills needed to operate nurseries, graft fruit trees, and manage tree crops.
- Creating assets by using trees to help meet subsistence needs for fuel, food, fiber, and other non-timber forest products.
- Ecotourism
- Bio-prospecting.
- Improving recreational activities.
- Securing land tenure through land registration.
- By introducing participatory approaches to improve the relevance and quality of projects. When villagers in China were consulted about which tree species to plant in the community, the number of species increased from 4 to 16 and the emphasis shifted from timber to fruit trees. Because there are fewer harvesting and marketing restrictions on produce from fruit trees, the outcome was greater and more reliable income for households (Rozelle et al. 2000).
- Reducing overall risks and diversifying sources of income.
- Creating social capital by increasing the collective ability of forest-dependent communities to plan, manage, grow, and equitably share common property resources.

   [a]   The Bank-financed National Afforestation Project in China significantly raised the incomes of 12 million people.

---

ing to exploit natural forests. The surge in imports has also exacerbated deforestation of natural forests in exporting countries, particularly Russia and Indonesia. In India, demand for industrial wood is expected to triple or quadruple in the next 25 years. Increased imports could also accelerate deforestation in tropical countries supplying India.

Sources of Demand Have Varied

Indonesia is now the world's largest exporter of tropical timber. By contrast, nearly 86 percent of Brazil's huge timber supply is consumed internally, placing its per capita domestic consumption ahead of Western Europe's. The development of plantations and alternative sources of energy (such as natural gas supplied through the new Brazil-Bolivia pipeline) have, however, reduced the impact of Brazil's domestic consumption on its natural forests. Cameroon's mostly foreign-owned timber companies, a powerful lobbying group promoting timber exports, have expanded their exports to Europe, making Cameroon the largest exporter of tropical forest products in Africa. These market considerations and the interest groups that organize themselves to seek favorable rules have become an integral part of discussions on the management of the global commons.

Land Conversion and Agriculture

No universal principles govern the conversion of forestland to agricultural purposes. The extent to which agricultural intensification can reduce the pressure to encroach on forests is highly location-specific, depending on the rate and nature of technical change and transportation costs. The impact of agricultural productivity growth in land-surplus countries (such as Brazil) has been to increase incentives for land conversion, a phenomenon reinforced by globalization and the liberalization of markets. But in densely populated countries, such as China and India, land productivity growth associated with agricultural intensification has helped relieve pressure on forestland to a point that forest cover appears to be stabilizing and even growing, helped along by increased tree planting by farmers and increased forest protection by communities.

The conversion of forestland to agriculture in order to expand exports has become a particularly significant issue in the three forest-rich countries— Brazil, Cameroon, and Indonesia—which experienced irregular macroeconomic performance, huge pressures on the domestic budget, and trade imbalances in the 1990s. In the Amazon, land conversion for soybean production and livestock grazing is common. Returns to agricultural conversion are sizable, partly because the forest sector is more heavily regulated than agriculture.[25]

Regulations without transparency and accountability, however, increase the potential for corruption and the cost of managing forestlands. Currency devaluations in the three forest-rich countries have increased incentives for all exports, but agricultural exports have increased more than exports of forest products.[26] The little evidence available on financial returns to managed forests suggests that the absence of enforcement (evident in extensive illegal logging) and virtually unrestricted agricultural sectors, there is little financial incentive for improved or low-impact logging.[27]

Institutional Issues

The institutional heterogeneity of the six countries ranges from the decentralized democracies of Brazil, Costa Rica, and India to the more state-controlled China. But China is more decentralized than appears on the surface, having given a strong and active role to its provincial, county, and township governments. India's community forest management programs differ greatly from those of China in terms of devolution to communities and the evolution of communities. Indonesia and Cameroon were slower to decentralize, but

Indonesia accelerated the process following the cataclysmic political changes of the late 1990s. When the Indonesian government nationalized community lands (*de facto*) in 1967, concessions were awarded to the politically well-connected to maintain their political support (Gautam et al. 2000), but its decentralization efforts post-Suharto make it one of the most decentralized countries in some respects. However, a lack of preparation for such decentralization also means lack of local enforcement capacity.

The various state governments in the six countries also differ greatly in governance capabilities and in capacity to manage the forest sector; institutional arrangements, both formal and informal, tend to be dynamic. Devolution, decentralization, the diverging interests of multiple stakeholders, and the likelihood of conflicts among them, all have implications for governance.

There are also major differences in the forest sector administrations of the six countries. Costa Rica enjoys the most organizational plurality in the public sector, along with committed NGOs and private associations, all interacting to address the many multisectoral functions and equally diffuse costs and benefits of the forest sector. Cameroon is the weakest in institutional capacity, followed by Indonesia and several of the states in the Brazilian Amazon. In Brazil, rents from forest exploitation are decentralized and broadly distributed at the local, municipal, state, and national levels and among different actors. In Indonesia, however, rents have been concentrated in the hands of a few who are close to political power, although that situation is changing. Because Brazil is far richer than Indonesia in its forest resources (nearly three times the reported area under forest and five times the actual forest cover, as shown in table 1.1) its per capita income is four times that of Indonesia. Furthermore, its economy depends less on forests and unsustainable forest management poses fewer environmental costs and huge financial benefits from Brazil's national perspective, but there are considerable environmental costs from the global perspective.

Land Tenure

The 1991 forestry policy stressed secure land tenure as a way to increase incentives to invest in trees and reduce incentives for resource mining. Support for the underlying hypothesis has varied from place to place. The extent to which tenure security affects land conversion to agriculture and deforestation is a controversial issue in Brazil (Lele et al. 2000). Some argue that securing land title increases smallholders' access to credit, information, and extension services, facilitating the clearing of land for agriculture. Others argue that farmers with no access to credit cut trees to finance their agricultural operations. Either way, the net effect in the short run tends to be deforestation. The merits of secure land rights for indigenous populations are more generally accepted. The government of Brazil has considerably accelerated the demarcation of indigenous reserves—some of it with Bank support—although the actions of many external exploiters lead to *de facto* loss of land rights and forest cover.[28]

The chief land rights issue in Cameroon and Indonesia is timber concessions. Until the mid-1980s, the Bank considered customary tenure rights in Cameroon an impediment to the development of "unused" forest resources. It recommended overhauling land tenure legislation so that land expropriation in support of state and private development of industrial plantations could become operational (Nssah and Gockowski 2000). Now, however, Bank strategy favors improving Cameroon's legal and regulatory framework, although both the forest law and the implementation decree have failed to provide an adequate legal framework for planning land use and integrating forest conservation and production activities with agriculture. The prevailing land tenure regime assigned usufruct rights to anybody who cleared and cultivated land in the state-owned forests, which make up most of Cameroon's dense forest (O'Halloran and Ferrer 1998). This has probably encouraged deforestation. In Indonesia, by contrast, the Bank recommended revenue sharing with communities, but the government was not interested in devolving rights to communities until democratization began in 1999. The short run effect in Indonesia of devolving rights to communities appears to be even more rapid deforestation.

In China, the effect of land tenure on investment in forests and the protection of forest resources is part of a debate about whether the reforms of the 1980s—giving control of forestlands to farm households—helped or hurt forest management. After successful reform to decollectivize the agricultural sector in the early 1980s, leaders in the forest sector sought to further devolve control and increase incentives to households and forest users. The reforms did not go as far as those in agriculture in the early stages of implementation, but several innovative programs have been launched in the past decade to improve forest investments. The academic and policymaking communities disagree about the success of this movement in terms of forest sector outcomes, but China's more equitable initial distribution of land and local power has ensured more socioeconomically equitable outcomes (Rozelle et al. 2000).

Decentralization

Experience in Brazil, China, and India shows that, contrary to popular belief and some positive experiences, decentralization does not always improve environmental management. It may even worsen it in the short and medium term, when local institutions are in their infancy and checks and balances are limited. Even if local capacity for environmental management increases substantially, it may not be an adequate substitute for the functions previously performed by the central government. The precarious financial condition of many states and municipalities is an increasing concern as countries decentralize. Logging and forest industries generate revenue and employment at several levels, making it profitable for local governments to lease forest concessions. Politically powerful loggers and ranchers in Brazil (typically supported by municipal and even state assemblies) compete with small agents and indigenous people for control of forestland.

National governments may be more concerned about national environmental objectives than their local counterparts and may pursue policies of conservation—such as China's introduction of a logging ban—seen as costly at the local level. But national economic and political interests may also be aligned with the state and local elite (as in Brazil, Cameroon and Indonesia). Forest sector reform should address issues of interest to key stakeholders, such as employment, income generation, and government revenues. Most responses will involve investing in increased productivity for all forest products and services—investing in research, extension, and markets, for example, areas the Bank has given less attention than conservation.

Stimulating a Sound Forest Policy

It is clear that international objectives can differ from the needs and priorities of the Bank's borrowers, as they have in Brazil, Indonesia, and Cameroon. A broadly shared, cohesive, and consistent diagnosis of the problems is required. That in turn requires a reliable information base, political will, good institutional and human capacity, and financial resources. The international community has only just begun to develop a common vision and understanding of the needs, aspirations, and constraints of developing countries. The forest sector is well suited to a holistic approach to development that emphasizes client ownership, partnership with other development actors, program design through interaction with all stakeholders, and concrete results.

Notwithstanding past and current differences between the international community and some governments—especially those in forest-rich countries—and given the ambitious goals and meager resources that the international community has been willing to bring to bear on the problems, can the World Bank harness increased environmental awareness, active domestic stakeholders, and active environmental institutions (especially NGOs) to improve forest management? The Bank's new forest strategy reflects a new international commitment to coordinate approaches, assist developing countries in the development of national forest strategies, and recognize that grant resources are needed to achieve global objectives. Some of the Bank's new instruments—the Learning and Innovation Loans and Adaptable Program Loans—could also find an important niche by helping to fill the needs of countries reluctant to take on a large debt burden (Velozo et al. 2000). The

experiences of Costa Rica, China, and India in developing successful policies and institutions for improved forest management provide examples that
need to be disseminated to other developing countries. Chapter 8 discusses
the promise and limitations of a variety of new approaches and instruments
for forest management.

Notes

1. "Biodiversity," short for "biological diversity," has acquired currency since the
    1991 Earth Summit in Rio de Janeiro. It is described in terms of a hierarchical
    organization of biological organisms based on genes, species, and ecosystems. For
    an excellent discussion of the intersection of biological and economic consider-
    ations, see David Pearce and Dominic Moran, *Economic Value of Biodiverisity*,
    IUCN, London: Earthscan, 1994.
2. See, for instance, the two publications of WWF, "IMF Intervention in Indonesia"
    by Heine Mainhardt, and "Banking on Sustainability: Structural Adjustment and
    Forestry Reforms in Post Suharto Indonesia" jointly with CIFOR by Christopher
    Barr (2001).
3. An increasingly common term used to suggest improved forest management that is
    environmentally more sensitive than traditional forest management methods, in-
    cluding those that were based on concerns of sustainability of the timber supply.
4. See "Forest Management and Competing Land Uses," Nalin Kishor and Luis
    Constantino, LATEN Dissemination Note #7, October 1993, Washington, D.C.:
    The World Bank.
5. The GEF deals with climate change, biodiversity, community-driven development,
    and persistent organic pollutants.
6. In the area of terrestrial biodiversity, GEF has largely pursued a protected area
    approach and hence its biodiversity conservation effort has been largely synony-
    mous with conservation of forests and related habitats.
7. This issue was identified in the first evaluation of the GEF and has been identified
    in a second evaluation as an important challenge for GEF. Gareth Porter, Raymond
    Clémençon, Waafas Ofosu-Amaah, Michael Phillips, *Study of GEF's Overall
    Performance,* 1997; and "Focusing on the Global Environment: The First Decade
    of the GEF"—Second Overall Performance Study (OPS2) by Leif Christoffersen
    et al. January 25, 2002.
8. Personal conversations with Robert Schneider and John Spears.
9. See Stuart Pimm et al., "Can We Defy Nature's End?" In *Science* 239 (September
    2001):2007, and Norman Myers et al., "Biodiversity hotspots for conservation
    priorities," *Nature* 403 (February 2000):853–858.
10. Paul Jepson and Susan Canney, "Biodiversity Hotspots: Hot for What?" *Global
    Ecology and Biogeography* 10(3), May 2001, p. 225.
11. Deforestation here is defined as loss of forestland to other uses. Although the
    problem of forest degradation is also considerable, it is less easily detected and less
    quantifiable.
12. An opinion survey in the 20 largest developed and developing countries in 2001
    rated environment as the greatest concern. A national opinion poll on proposed
    changes to the Forest Code, released by the Brazilian environmental organization
    Instituto Socioambiental (Socio Environmental Institute) and partner groups found
    that, of 503 people interviewed, 88 percent believed that the protection of Brazil's
    forests should increase, not decrease, and 90 percent believed that increasing de-

forestation in the Amazon for agricultural lands will probably not reduce hunger. When questioned about the restoration of fragile areas to prevent siltation, landslides, or floods, 87 percent stated they believe that property owners who deforest should be fined and forced to restore the vegetation. Similar changes in public opinion are evident in Indonesia.

13. Whereas social gains and losses refer to the wider social perspective, the jurisdiction may be local, national, regional, or global. In theory, local, national, and global perspectives on "social" gains/losses may diverge. National and global agencies should take the "social" standpoint, but it is well known that this is not always the case. Private gains and losses refer to the private interests of stakeholders; that is, what benefits him or her. (D. Pearce, Francis Putz, Jerome K. Vanclay. *A Sustainable Forest Future? 1999)*

14. P. Pardey and N. Beintema, "Slow Magic—Agricultural R&D a Century after Mendel," IFPRI, October 2001. See also OED's forthcoming meta-evaluation of the CGIAR, Bruce Gardner, "Global Public Goods form the CGIAR: Impact Assessment," Draft, December 2001.

15. Recent international public opinion polls in 20 major developed and developing countries suggest that whereas environment remains at the top of the global community's agenda, the people of developed countries have more trust in NGOs than in governments, international organizations, and multinational corporations to address the problems. This is presenting a profound challenge in situations where governments have large roles in crafting international agreements, financing instruments, and implementing them within their borders.

16. See references for author's original thesis in an *Isolated State*. This thesis has been treated extensively by William Hyde. See W. F. Hyde and D. H. Newman, "Forest Economics and Policy Analysis. An Overview," Washington: World Bank; 1991.See also F. William and Roger A. Sedjo, " Managing Tropical Forests: Reflections on the Rent Distribution Discussion ," *Land Economics* 68(3), August 1992, 343-50.

17. The Bank has since established 10 safeguard policies that are applied to every project investment.

18. Forest specialists in the Bank were concerned about the controversy surrounding the formulation of the Bank's strategy. They felt that they had not been consulted. Having attempted to express their views and been discouraged by the reception from senior managers responsible for the sector, many experienced forest sector staff left the Bank within a few years of finalization of the strategy.

19. A recent analysis of a cross section of 90 countries show a strong indirect impact of governance (i.e. defined as rule of law, control of corruption, government effectiveness, lack of regulatory burden, voices and accountability, and political stability and lack of violence) on deforestation, working largely through per capita income. However, the analysis suggests only limited evidence of a direct beneficial impact of improved governance on deforestation. See Nalin Kishor and Arati Belle's paper prepared for "Illegal Logging in the Tropics: Ecology, Economics, and Politics of Resource Misuse," organized by the Society of Tropical Forests, Yale Student Chapter and the Yale School of Forestry and Environmental Studies. March 29-30, 2002.

20. Uma Lele et al., "The World Bank Forest Strategy: Striking the Right Balance," Operations Evaluation Department, Washington D.C. 2000.

21. The OED review observed that if the ban on the purchase of logging equipment for commercial operations is extended to the natural forests of Eastern Europe *beyond its old growth forests*, it could jeopardize promising efforts under way with World Bank support to improve forest management in production forests there. It could

also have a chilling effect on the Bank Group's ability to mobilize funding from other international sources for promoting responsible forest management.

22. Although a much smaller percentage of the poor live in the ECA region the number is growing, tripling from 7 million in 1990 to 24 million in 1998 (WDR 2000). Among the new poor are people who were formerly employed in forest industries or provided social services to the company towns that were closed during a shift to the market economy.

23. Davis and Wali, 1993.

24. A major thrust of Joint Forest Management in India has been on redistributing the products of land. Some have observed that JFM is one of the most powerful ways of reducing abject poverty, but by "enclosing" common property resources to allow forest regeneration the approach has denied the poorest access to land to which they previously had open access. See the chapter on India.

25. Schneider et al. (1998) have disputed whether returns to livestock are indeed higher than sustainable forest management in parts of the Amazon, but available research did not produce alternative explanations for the growth of ranching in the Amazon after examining such alternative hypotheses as expected returns to investment in land and land mining.

26. Using a computable general equilibrium (CGE) model to determine how the magnitude and impact of deforestation in the Brazilian Amazon are affected by changes in policy regimes and technology, Cattaneo (1999) shows that devaluation shifts agricultural production in favor of exportable products. How devaluation affects agricultural incentives in different regions depends on migration flows. If migration occurs only between rural areas, a 30 percent devaluation increases deforestation rates 5 percent. If urban labor is willing to migrate to the Amazon and farm, the deforestation rate increases 35 percent. San et al. (2000) analyzed the short- and medium-term impacts of structural adjustment through devaluation on regional production, deforestation, factor markets, income distribution, and trade for the Sumatra region of Indonesia. The study found that devaluation encourages deforestation, while exports of forest products as both final products and intermediate inputs for wood processing industries increase. (See also Lele et al. 2000 and Gautam et al. 2000, OED's Brazil and Indonesia case studies, respectively). A recent piece of environmental sector work on Brazil argues that rainfall determines the potential of agricultural production and may mute some of the effects of improved incentives from globalization (see Schneider et al. 2000). Technical change, on the other hand, may expand agricultural options even in high-rainfall areas. These examples merely demonstrate the complexity and location-specificity of outcomes.

27. A recent paper prepared for ESSD (Pearce et al. 1999) includes an extensive literature review on relative returns to conventional and low-impact logging, and supports the findings of the OED studies of Brazil, Cameroon, and Indonesia. According to Lele et al. (2000c): "Protection of Brazil's Amazon forests beyond the short term requires an increase in the value of standing forest, an increase in the costs associated with unsustainable logging practices, and an increase in incentives for and profitability of sustainable (or improved) forest management. It must pay to keep trees and other forest products in the forest and improve management practices, and predatory exploitation of the timber must become unprofitable. In evaluating measures that might address these challenges, it is useful to distinguish between the processes taking place at and beyond the forest-agriculture frontier. At the frontier, agriculture, logging, and road-building create a mutually reinforcing system of forest conversion. Beyond the frontier, deeper in the forest, illegal

logging of higher value tree species threatens protected areas and the livelihoods of indigenous communities and extractivists."
28. Zoning and demarcation, among the most intensely political of issues, are particularly important challenges (Mahar et al. 1998).

References

Acheson, James. 2000. "Varieties of Institutional Failure." Keynote Address for the Meetings of the International Association for the Study of Common Property Resources. Bloomington, Indiana.

Agrawal, Arun, and Clark C. Gibson. 1999. "Enchantment and Disenchantment: The Role of Community in Natural Resource Conservation." *World Development* 27(4):629–649.

Alexandratos, Nikos. 1996. *World Food and Agriculture: Outlook to 2010.* United Nations Food and Agricultural Organization.

Angelsen, Arild, and David Kaimowitz. 1999. "Rethinking the Causes of Deforestation: Lessons from Economic Models." *The World Bank Research Observer* 14(1):73–98.

Arnold, J. E. M. and P. Bird. 1999. "Forests and the Poverty-Environment Nexus." Prepared for the UNDP/EC Expert Workshop on Poverty and the Environment, Brussels, Belgium, January 20–21.

Arrow, K.J., B. Bolin, R. Costanza,, P. Dasgupta, C. Folke, C. S. Hollings, B. O. Jansson, S. Levin, K. Maler, C. A. Perrings, D. Pimentel. 1995. "Economic Growth Carrying Capacity and the Environment." *Science* 268, 520-521.

Baland, Jean-Marie, and Jean-Phillippe Platteau. 1999. "The Ambiguous Impact of Inequality on Local Resource Management." *World Development* 27(5):773–788.

Barbier, E., J. Burgess, and C. Folke. 1994. "Paradise Lost? The Ecological Economics of Biodiversity." London: Earthscan.

Barr, Christopher M. 2001. "Bank on Sustainability: Structural Adjustment and Forestry Reform in Post-Suharto Indonesia. WWF Macroeconomics October 2001.

Bebbington, Anthony. 1999. "Capitals and Capabilities: A Framework for Analyzing Peasant Viability, Rural Livelihoods and Poverty." *World Development* 27(12):2021–2044.

Binkley, C. S. 1999. "Forest in the Next Millennium: Challenges and Opportunities for the USDA Forest Service." Resources for the Future. Discussion Paper 99-15. Washington, D.C.

Bruner, Aaron G., Raymond E. Gullison, Richard E. Rice, Gustavo A. B. da Fonseca. 2001. "Effectiveness of Parks in Protecting Tropical Biodiversity." *Science Magazine* 291:125–128.

Byron, Neil, and Michael Arnold. 1999. "What Futures for the People of the Tropical Forests?" *World Development* 27(5):789–805.

Chomitz, Kenneth M., Esteban Brenes, and Luis Constantino. 1999. "Financing Environmental Services: The Costa Rican Experience and Its Implications. *The Science for the Total Environment* 240:157–169.

Chomitz, Kenneth M., and Kanta Kumari. 1998. "The Domestic Benefits of Tropical Forests: A Critical Review." *World Bank Research Observer* 13(1):13–35.

Coase, R. H. 1988. *The Firm, the Market and the Law.* Chicago: The University of Chicago Press.

Cooper, Richard. 2001. In Christopher Gerrard, et al., *Global Public Policies and Programs: Implications for Financing and Evaluation.* Operations Evaluation Department. Washington, D.C.: The World Bank.

Dauvergne, Peter. 1997. *Shadows in the Forest: Japan and the Politics of Timber in Southeast Asia.* Cambridge, MA: The MIT Press.

Gautam, Madhur, Uma Lele, Saeed Rana, William Hyde, Hraiardi Kartodiharjo, Azis Khan, and Ir. Erwinsyah. 2000. *The Challenges of World Bank Involvement in Forests: An Evaluation of Indonesia's Forests and World Bank Assistance.* Washington, D.C.: The World Bank.

Geist, Helmut J., and Eric F. Lambin. 2001. "What Drives Tropical Deforestation: A Meta Analysis of Proximate and Underlying Causes of Deforestation Based on Sub-National Case Study Evidence." LUCC Report Series No.4, CIACO; Louvain-La-Neuve.

Hyde, W. F. and D. H. Newman. 1991. *Forest Economics and Policy Analysis. An Overview.* Washington D.C.: The World Bank.

Imazon. 1999. "Hitting the Target: Timber Consumption in the Brazilian Domestic Market and Promotion of Forest Certification."

Keipi, Kari (ed.). 1999. *Forest Resource Policy in Latin America.* Inter-American Development Bank. Washington, D.C.: The Johns Hopkins University Press.

Leach, Mellissa, Robin Mearns, and Ian Scoones. 1999. "Environmental Entitlements: Dynamics and Institutions in Community-Based Natural Resource Management. *World Development* 27(2):225–247.

Lele, Uma et al. 2000. *The World Bank Forest Strategy: Striking the Right Balance.* Operations Evaluation Department. Washington D.C.: The World Bank.

Lele, Uma, Virgilio M. Viana, Adalberto Verissimo, Stephen Vosti, Karin Perkins, and Syed Arif Husain. 2000. *Forests in the Balance: Challenges of Conservation with Development. An Evaluation of Brazil's Forest Development and World Bank Assistance.* Operations Evaluation Department. Washington, D.C.: The World Bank.

Lopez, Ramon. 1998. *The Tragedy of the Commons in Cote d'Ivoire Agriculture: Empirical Evidence and Implications for Evaluation Trade Policies.* Washington, D.C. The World Bank.

_____. 1999. "Policy and Financing Instruments for Sustainable Use of Forests." In Kari Keipi (ed.), *Forest Resource Policy in Latin America,* Inter-American Development Bank. Washington, D.C.: The Johns Hopkins University Press.

Lopez, Ramon, and Mario Niklitschek. 1991. "Dual Economic Growth in Poor Tropical Areas." *Journal of Development Economics* 36:189-211.

Lutz, Ernest, and Caldecott, Julian. 1996. *Decentralization and Biodiversity Conservation.* A World Bank Symposium Paper. Washington D.C.

North, Douglass C. 1990. *Institutions, Institutional Change and Economic Performance.* London: Cambridge University Press.

Nssah, B. E., and James Gockowski. 2000. "Forest Sector Development in a Difficult Political Economy: An Evaluation of Cameroon's Forest Development and World Bank Assistance." Operations Evaluation Department. Washington D.C.: The World Bank.

O'Faircheallaigh, Ciaran. 1998. "Resource Development and Inequality in Indigenous Societies." *World Development* 26(3):381–394.

O'Halloran, E., and V. Ferrer. 1998. "The Evolution of Cameroon's New Forestry Legal Regulatory and Taxation System." Washington, D.C.: The World Bank (draft).

Panayotou, T. 1995. "Environmental Degradation at Different Stages of Economic Development." In I. Ahmed and J.A. Doeleman (eds.). *Beyond Rio: The Environmental Crisis and Sustainable Livelihoods in the Third World.* London: Macmillan Press Ltd.

Pimm, Stuart L. et al. 2001. "Can We Defy Nature's End." *Science Magazine* 293:2207–2208.

Pearce, David, Francis Putz, and Jerome K. Vanclay. 1999. "A Sustainable Forest Future?" Natural Resources International. UK and UK Department for International Development.

Reardon, Thomas, and Stephen A. Vosti. 1995. "Links between Rural Poverty and the Environment in Developing Countries: Asset Categories and Investment Poverty." *World Development* 23(9):1495–1506.

Rice, R., C. Sugal, and I. Bowles. 1998. *Sustainable Forest Management: a Review of the Current Conventional Wisdom.* Washington D.C.: Conservation International.

Rosegrant, Mark. W., Michael S. Paisner, Siet Meijer, and Julie Witcover. 2001. *Global Food Projections To 2020: Emerging Trends and Alternative Futures.* International Food Policy Research Institute.

Rozelle, Scott, Jikun Huang, Syed Arif Husain, and Aaron Zazueta. 2000. "From Afforestation to Poverty Alleviation and Natural Forest Management: An Evaluation of China's Forest Development and World Bank Assistance." Operations Evaluation Department. Washington, D.C.: The World Bank.

Schneider, Robert. 1992. "Brazil: An Analysis of Environmental Problems in the Amazon, vol. 1—Main Report." Washington, D.C.

_____. 1992. "Brazil: An Analysis of Environmental Problems in the Amazon, vol. 2—Annexes." Washington, D.C.

Schneider, Robert, Adelberto Verissimo, and Virgilio Viana. 1998. "Logging and Tropical Forest Conservation." Submitted to *Science*.

Sedjo, Roger A. 1999. Carbon Projects in Latin America. Inter-American Development Bank Forest Policy Roundtable, June 28. Washington D.C.

Shogren, Jason, and John Tschirhart. 1999. "The Endangered Species Act at Twenty Five." *Choices*, Third Quarter.

Songorwa, Alexander N. 1999. "Community Based Wildlife Management (CWM) in Tanzania: Are the Communities Interested?" *World Development* 27(12):2061–2079.

Stern, D. I., M. S. Common, and E. B. Barbier. 1996. "Economic Growth and Environmental Degradation: The Environmental Kuznets Curve and Sustainable Development," *World Development* 24:1151–1160

Thunen, Johann Heinrich von. 1996. Hall Peter Geoffrey (ed.). *Isolated State,* an English edition of *Der isolierte Staat.* New York: Pergamon Press.

Velozo, Ronnie de Camino, Olman Segura B, Luis Guillermo Arias, and Isaac Perez. 2000. "Forest Policy and the Evolution of Land Use: An Evaluation of Costa Rica's Forest Development and World Bank Assistance." Operations Evaluation Department. Washington, D.C.: The World Bank.

2

Costa Rica: At the Cutting Edge

Ronnie de Camino V., Olman Segura B., and Lauren A. Kelly

During the 1970s and early 1980s, the small and biologically rich Central American country of Costa Rica experienced high rates of deforestation (Peuken 1993). But by 1986, when the country's forest cover had declined from over 50 percent to only 29 percent, Costa Rica realized the importance of sustainable development and the economic value of its natural resources. Today, the trend has been reversed and the country's forests cover approximately 1.5 million hectares, or 40 percent of its land area (CCT, CIEDES, and FONAFIFO 1998).

Many factors played a role in Costa Rica's decision in the mid-1980s to rein in the expansion of its agricultural sector, which had been the chief driving force in its economic development, at the expense of its forests. Those factors included a worldwide decline in agricultural prices, economic advice from the World Bank while making structural adjustment loans (SALs) to Costa Rica to reduce agricultural subsidies, and the public's gradual realization that a more diversified economy could sustainably produce greater welfare.

The seeds of new thinking on the economy and the environment fell on fertile ground in Costa Rica, which has been a well-functioning democracy for well over a century despite its location in a region where several other countries endured armed internal conflicts in the 1960s, 1970s, and 1980s. Indeed, in 1987, then president Oscar Arias Sanchez won the Nobel Prize for Peace in promoting the end of civil strife in Nicaragua and El Salvador.

Unlike many of its neighbors, Costa Rica has a large and educated middle class, and its human development indicators are among the highest in the developing world. One reason why its case is unique is that the country has no military and can instead use resources that would have gone into military spending on investments in social programs. It is not plagued by the problems

45

that arise from great inequalities in wealth and income, property rights are secure, and it has a large number of innovative educational and technical institutions.

Costa Rica has established a legal framework that gives the government a large role in protecting forests. This has been done directly through the establishment of national parks, and indirectly by giving private landowners strong financial incentives to conserve forestland.

Along with its role as a leader in remaking its own economic development and environmental policies, Costa Rica has shown strong interest in working with the international community to establish new financially rewarding ways to achieve conservation of biodiversity and its environmental services, such as carbon sequestration under the 1997 Kyoto Protocol to the United Nations Framework Convention on Climate Change (UNFCCC)—the so-called Earth Summit in Rio de Janeiro in 1992. Costa Rica has developed a system of Certified Tradable Offsets (CTOs) that appears to meet the Protocol's criteria for negotiable securities when, as is hoped, a worldwide market in environmental stocks will be established that rewards countries for actions that protect their domestic physical environment.

All this is not to say that a positive outcome for Costa Rica's forests and other natural resources is assured. The economy has been vulnerable in the past to external shocks, and the country is burdened by a large fiscal deficit and a very substantial domestic debt. Shifts in popular opinion means that presidential elections arouse strong emotions about the future direction of economic development. Although Costa Rica devotes relatively high percentages of total public expenditures to education and health programs, the quality of those services has weakened during the past decade. In addition, much of the country's infrastructure is in disrepair. As a developing economy, Costa Rica strives to position its natural capital and its environmental services as an axis of its sustainable development policy.

Costa Rica's Economic Development in the Twentieth Century

In the decades that followed Costa Rica's achievement of independence from Spain in 1821, the Costa Rican economy was dominated by agricultural and plantation production. Its warm climate, rich soil, and abundant rainfall made production of coffee, bananas, and sugarcane the traditional production options for large-scale farming, and even today those three crops are among Costa Rica's leading exports. After World War II, the agricultural sector expanded to include large-scale production of cocoa and beef.

Given high world prices for beef and other meat products, the government was prompt to respond to lobbying by ranchers' groups that sought the adoption of more favorable policies for cattle-raising, including guaranteed prices and soft loans for farmers and the elimination of restrictions on converting forests to pasture. Between 1970 and 1983, real interest rates on government loans for livestock production were negative, falling to as low as minus 10 percent (Kaimowitz 1996). Meanwhile, beef prices continued to rise. By 1982, Costa Rica's livestock sector was receiving half of all government loans for agriculture.

This interest in cattle production was easy to rationalize. Cattle production has certain natural advantages over other land uses. It requires little seed capital, ranchers can use cattle as collateral for loans, and it provides a yearly income. Meanwhile, the introduction of "green revolution technologies" such as bulldozers, chainsaws, and herbicides, speeded up the conversion of forested land into pasture.

Like a host of other developing countries, Costa Rica adopted a general economic development policy of import-substituting industrialization in the 1960s. To facilitate the success of this new policy, Costa Rica agreed in 1962 to join the Central American Common Market (CACM) that included El Salvador, Guatemala, Honduras, and Nicaragua. The common market included free trade among the five countries and common tariffs on imports from countries outside the CACM.

By the end of the 1970s, however, import-substituting industrialization began to seem less and less the answer to further economic development. Intraregional trade was declining as a proportion of total trade, the growth rate of gross domestic product (GDP) was declining in all five countries (Bulmer-Thomas 1987), and political instability had begun to roil Central America. In 1978, Costa Rica also faced a sharp decline in coffee prices and, suffered the effects of the worldwide oil crisis in 1979. External financing dried up, and the government was forced to suspend the servicing of its external debt. These events set the stage for an economic stabilization program supported by the International Monetary Fund (IMF) in 1982, and structural adjustment lending by the World Bank in the mid-1980s.

The structural adjustment loans of 1985 and 1988 were designed to introduce and then extend Bank support for certain fundamental changes in the Costa Rican economy—a reduction in the government's role in the economy and a corresponding increase in exposure to the economic disciplines of open markets, and a strengthening of the country's finances to make it more attractive to external investors. Among the important changes in economic policies that occurred in the last half of the 1980s were the elimination of subsidized government loans and the elimination of price guarantees for agricultural producers, the privatization of subsidiaries of CODESA (a state-owned corporation), reductions in tariffs, the introduction of a flexible exchange rate, and the elimination of taxes on nontraditional exports. There was also a reduction in general government spending to reduce Costa Rica's substantial budget deficit. Quota restrictions on imports of basic grains and beans were eliminated.

In 1993, the Bank approved a third structural adjustment loan for Costa Rica, but the loan was never implemented. New elections in 1994 brought a new administration into power that had reservations about some of the conditions in the newest structural adjustment program being urged by the Bank.

Costa Rica's economy experienced important transformations during the 1990s. Traditional agricultural activities were displaced by the rapid growth of new and dynamic sectors, such as information technology and tourism. Since 1993, tourism has become Costa Rica's largest source of revenues. According to the Institute for Tourism, international visitors rose from 435,000 in 1990 to 787,000 in 1997, while tourism earnings rose from $275 million to $714 million. Some 38 percent of those tourists visited national parks. Their growing popularity impelled the government to raise the admission fee to the parks from $1 to $15 per visitor. Currently, the fee is set at US$ 6 for international visitors. After 1997, high technology exports (Intel and others) abruptly became the most important foreign currency generator, with an overwhelming performance substantially over the traditional coffee and banana sectors.

The Evolution of Costa Rica's Forest Sector

Government policies in general, and economic policies in particular, have affected the use of forest resources in Costa Rica. Incentives for forest conservation and management have been redesigned and redirected several times since their introduction, but incrementally they have been successful in promoting reforestation, forest management, and forest protection. Few reforestation efforts took place before specific economic incentives were introduced in the late 1970s.

The main change in Costa Rican land use between 1950 and the mid-1980s was the transformation of forests to pastures and farmland. Between 1950 and 1984 the amount of land in pastures increased from 0.8 million to 2.2 million hectares. But the government of Costa Rica had begun to pay some attention to the country's forests as early as 1969, when it enacted a general law (Law 4465) on the environment that included sections devoted to forestry.

The new law's chief environmental components gave the government the responsibility to establish and manage national parks, national forests, and wildlife reserves. The law also created a General Directorate of Forestry within the Ministry of Agriculture to manage national forests, national parks, and wildlife reserves, and a National Forestry Council.

Among the specific tasks of the General Directorate of Forestry were the preparation of studies of timber and wood exports and imports, and analysis of reforestation methods on experimental plots of land. To pay for the operations of the National Forestry Council, the law also created a "forest tax" that was then collected at related industrial sites, such as sawmills.

Box 2.1
Fiscal Incentives for Environmental Protection

The following fiscal incentives were the predecessors of Costa Rica's current system of payments to landholders for environmental services (PSAs).

Income Tax Deduction (1979)
Through an income tax deduction introduced in 1979, the government promoted plantation forests as sources of raw timber to relieve the pressure on natural forests. Although this incentive was intended to be extensive and motivate landowners, the measure was regressive, since only large landowners pay income taxes. Most of the rural population was excluded. When the incentive was instituted, reforestation technologies were not well developed. Also, knowledge about nursery management of exotic and native species and about reforestation techniques and silvicultural management was lacking. The quality of the first areas planted as a result of this incentive was generally poor.

Soft Credits (1983)
In 1983, the National Banking System and a program known as COREMA AID-032 established soft loans for reforestation with an 8 percent interest rate and a ten-year grace period. Payment periods were as long as 30 years, depending on the species planted. Currently, four trusts are in effect.

Forest Payment Title (*Certificado de Abono Forestal*, CAFs, 1986)
The forest payment title, established in 1986, aimed at distributing resources for forest activities democratically. CAFs are tax-exempt nominative titles with which any type of tax may be paid. The titles were accessible to all landowners and can be negotiated in the marketplace. Therefore, forest owners not paying taxes could benefit from this incentive. The CAF was available to any farmer. Through the CAFs, the supplementary technical aid facilitated the knowledge of tree species, reforestation, and forest management techniques improved, and farmers were more motivated to plant trees. As a result, the quality of reforested areas improved. Yet because the amount of the CAF in local currency was maintained with only small adjustments, the amount in real terms diminished through inflation and currency devaluation. The CAF allowed reforestation of 26 percent of the area covered by plantations.

Fund for Municipalities and Organizations (1986)
Forest Law 7032 established a tax on forest activities and allocated 20 percent of the amount collected from the exploitation of timber to regional organizations and municipalities. These funds may be used to implement reforestation projects, manage watersheds, establish nurseries, promote the extension and development of forests, and build infrastructure, such as forest roads. These funds have served a very important function in developing local organizations and have provided a financial

cont. on next page

incentive to mainstream environmental activities at the local level. But critics of the government argue that the funds allocated have not been allowed to grow commensurately to meet the local demands.

Forest Advance Payment Titles (*Certificados de Abono Forestal por Adelantado,* CAFA 1998)

A major conceptual change in reforestation incentives occurred when the government began to grant CAFs under special conditions (CAFAs) to small farmers. CAFAs were created in 1988 because small landowners were unable to invest in reforestation and wait for the payment of titles (box 2.2). The amounts are paid before reforestation activities are conducted, but recipients must be organized into farming associations. The Department of Forest Development for Farmers (*Departamento de Desarrollo Forestal Campesino*) was instrumental in organizing small farmers for forest development purposes.

Fund for Forest Development (1998)

This fund (FDF) was created from Costa Rica's CAFA revenues and Dutch and Nordic revenues from debt-for-nature swaps to support forest activities among small farmers. The fund covered 35 percent of reforestation costs.

Farmers funded 15 percent of operations through valuation of their own labor contribution. CAFAs covered the remaining 50 percent. Once a reforestation project concluded, the farmer paid the loan back to a revolving fund managed by a community organization to continue supporting reforestation activities.

In another innovation, the law gave industrial companies the right to deduct all expenses incurred in reforestation investments from their corporate income taxes. In general, however, the owners of lands appropriate for reforestation did not benefit from this provision because they were smallholders who paid no corporate income tax. Law 4465 also protected the domestic forestry industry from foreign competition by imposing a customs fee on imported wood products while prohibiting the export of roundwood. However, the law made it possible for landowners to establish or harvest forests without a state permit—in other words, allowing them to replace forest on privately owned land with pastures or cropland.

In 1973, in an administrative change, the government shifted the responsibility for national parks to a National Parks Service. In 1979, another change in tax law was made to encourage landowners to establish tree plantations and thus reduce the need to cut timber in natural forests for industrial and construction purposes. This change in the tax law was also regressive, however, since there were relatively few landowners with holdings large enough to be turned into plantation forests. Then, in 1983, the state banks set up a program that gave landowners a further incentive for reforestation. Under the program, loans for that purpose became available at a rate of 8 percent (compared to approximately 25 percent for conventional loans), with a ten-year grace period, and repayment periods of as long as 30 years.

The next significant legislation regarding forestry was enacted in 1986, when a centralized Forestry Institution was established under Law 7032 to oversee the planting, managing, cutting, and transporting of forest products anywhere in the country, whether publicly or privately owned. Some landowners, who saw the new law as an encroachment on their property rights, raised objections to the law. The same law gave the private sector additional representatives on the National Forestry Council (CFN), which advises the CFN minister on reforestation. But it also established a tax on timber exploitation, with part of the proceeds going to municipal and other governmental agencies for such purposes as implementing reforestation, building infrastructure, and managing watersheds.

Under earlier law, persons who prepared forest management plans were not required to have professional qualifications. In addition to its other provisions, Law 7032 established standards for forest management by requiring forest management plans to be reviewed and signed by a registered forest professional.

In 1998, the government created a Fund for Forest Development that uses revenues from CAFA activities, along with financial aid from The Netherlands and Scandinavian countries, to make debt-for-nature swaps to support the forest activities of small farmers. The fund reimburses smallholders for 35 percent of their reforestation costs.

Box 2.2
Conservation Incentives for Small Farmers

The Forestry Loan Certificates (CAFAs)—reforestation incentives in advance for small farmers—and payment for environmental services have supported the development of such landowner associations as the Association for Forestry Development of Guanacaste (AGUADEFOR), the Foundation for the Development of the Central Volcanic Mountain Range in central Costa Rica (FUNDECOR), and the Commission for Forestry Development (CODEFORSA) in the Huetar Norte Region.

Founded in 1983, CODEFORSA has more than 1,000 members, all of whom own forests or small or medium-size farms. CODEFORSA has a team of 12 forest engineers who assist members with technical problems, management of 34,000 hectares of natural forests, and reforestation efforts. By 1997, CODEFORSA members had reforested 7,800 hectares.

Source: Alfaro 1998.

Table 2.1
Investment in Incentives for Small Farmers, 1979-95

Type of Incentive	Hectares	Investment million US$
Deduction from income	35,595	52.22
Forest payment title	38,086	26.74
Forestry loan certificates	33,818	22.51
Fund for forest development	12,789	13.01
Art. 178	2,802	3.63
Art. 87	16,071	19.87
Certificate payment for natural forest management	22,120	6.33
Forest Protection certificate	22,200	4.25
Total	167,443	148.56

Source: Castro and Arias, 1998

Table 2.2
Land Use Changes in Costa Rica, 1979-92

From	To	Area change (hectares)	Share of total area changed (percent)
Natural forests	Pastures	322,515	6.3
Secondary forest	Pastures	401,828	7.9
Secondary forests	Seasonal crops	13,324	0.3
Secondary forests	Permanent crops	43,073	0.8
Permanent crops	Pastures	30,516	0.6
Permanent crops	Secondary forests	14,158	0.3
Seasonal crops	Pastures	22,892	0.4
Pastures	Permanent crops	61,696	1.2
Pastures	Seasonal crops	33,420	0.7
Pastures	Secondary forests	105,490	2.1
Seasonal crops	Secondary forests	12,415	0.2
No change		4,041,989	79.2
Total		5,103,316	100.0

Source: IMN, MINAE, and UNEP 1996

Land Use Changes in Costa Rica, 1979-92

The greatest change in land use in Costa Rica during the 1980s and early 1990s was the conversion of secondary forests (458,225 hectares, or 9 percent of the land area) to other uses, although this was not considered deforestation because the land had already been used for pastures or crops.[1]

A 1998 study discussed the most relevant aspects of the changes in forest cover from 1987 to 1997 (CCT, CIEDES, and FONAFIFO 1998). Of the 1.6 million hectares of forest studied, 164,245 hectares had been deforested and converted to other uses, while 126,873 hectares had been transformed into secondary forests and forest plantations. These changes resulted in a deforestation rate of 16,400 hectares a year and a net loss of 3,737 hectares a year. Left out of the estimate, however, were a 63,442-hectare area of caducifolious forest and 32,500 hectares reforested from 1995 to 1997. The final balance reflects an annual deforestation rate of 16,400 hectares and an annual reforestation rate of 22,282 hectares between 1987 and 1997, with a net positive annual balance of 5,857 hectares.

Costa Rica's Protected Areas System

Costa Rica's protected areas system has been an important factor in reversing deforestation and is a practical approach to protecting biodiversity. At first, the state-owned wildlands constituted the only system of forest protection; the system evolved later into a combination of public and private reserves. The system has grown from two public protected areas of about 2,500

Figure 2.1
Ownership of Forestland in Costa Rica

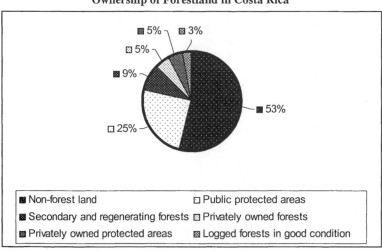

Source: Solorzano and others 1991; MIDEPLAN 1995d; MINAE and SINAC 1996a; IMN 1995; Davies 1997; Alpizar and others 1997

Figure 2.2
Evolution of Protected Areas in Costa Rica

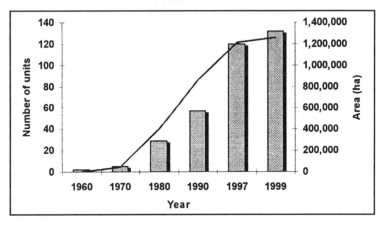

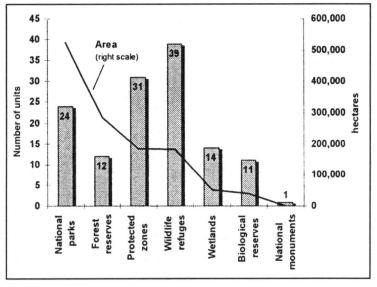

hectares in 1995 to more than 120 protected areas with more than 1.2 million hectares in 1998 and encompassing about 24.8 percent of Costa Rica's land; one-fifth are privately owned.

The government took the first steps toward developing a protected area system in the early 1900s. The 1969 forestry law provided a more solid foundation for establishing and managing protected areas. In the 1970s, the focus shifted from protecting areas of scenic, historic, and cultural value for recreation and national pride to protecting biological resources and ecosystems of scientific value. More areas were added in the 1970s and later in the 1990s. About 7.9 percent of the national territory was committed to conservation by the late 1980s; this figure grew to 16.8 percent by 1990, 23.8 percent by 1997, and 24.8 percent by 1999 (figure 2.2).

Forest and Livestock Exports

Exports of wood and wood products are beginning to outpace meat exports. Although the contribution of livestock to gross domestic product (GDP) is still higher than the contribution of the forest sector, the growth potential of forests and forest activities is much greater.

There is considerable production potential in the forest in standing timber, amounting to about 3.7 million cubic meters a year. With wood production currently at only 800,000 cubic meters a year, only 22 percent of the production potential is being used. Natural forests are overexploited, secondary forests are unexploited, and trees on forest plantations are still too young to be harvested. It will be several years, however, before the forest industry has the capacity to process annual wood growth and a market is developed for the production increase.

In order to promote a shift from cattle ranching to forestry, incentives need to be reoriented. The key land use with which any forestry incentive scheme must compete is nevertheless the grazing of livestock (Castro et al. 2000). Pastureland constitutes about one-third of the country. The opportunity cost of reforestation schemes must be weighed by cattle ranchers as they consider the local cost of renting a hectare of land compared to profits per hectare in the cattle ranching sector. Restructuring incentives for forestry ought to factor such opportunity costs into the equation.

Payments to Landowners for Environmental Services

At the end of 1995, after a decision was made to eliminate subsidies to private landholders for reforestation and forest management activities, Costa Rica shifted its approach from wood production to a more environmentally sound practice that values the life support functions of the ecosystem. This scheme is known as Payments for Environmental Services (PSAs) and is a system that compensates landowners in monetary terms for the "services" or benefits that forests provide to the national and global community. Four environmental services are acknowledged: carbon fixation, water protection, conservation of biodiversity resources, and preservation of natural scenic beauty.

PSAs were introduced in Costa Rica not simply to lighten the burden on the public budget, but also to incorporate the polluter-pays principle. Subsidies had been a necessary incentive for reforestation activities, since

Table 2.3
Land Registered in PSA Categories, 1997-2000 (in hectares)

Year	Category Protection	Reforestation	Management	Total
1997	94,621	5,035	8,533	108,189
1998	46,129	4,131	7,686	57,946
1999	55,859	3,187	5,132	64,177
2000	26,117	2,499	0	28,616
Total	222,726	14,851	21,350	258,928
Percentage	86.02 %	5.74 %	8.25%	

Source: FONAFIFO and SINAC 2000

Note: Year 2000 up to October

the revenues from traditional forest products were insufficient to make reforestation competitive with other types of land use. These subsidies reached $100 million between 1979 and 1996. Such subsidies (CAFs, CAFMAs and CPBs) not only perpetuated the image of a poor sector—a plagued branch of the economy dependent on uncertain state subsidies—but also encouraged a fixation on a single product—typically wood, valued in monetary terms—and neglected other environmental services of forests.

The PSA system is based on the reality that market failure to internalize the benefits of environmental protection results in most of the costs being borne by landowners. The landowners' inability to benefit from environmental services would consequently mean that the forests or natural habitats would be harvested or altered to benefit only local interests in the short and medium term. It is based on the right of private forest owners to direct monetary compensation for giving up a financial advantage.

Since the PSA system went into effect, the demand for forest service payments has been substantial, as can be observed in Table 2.3. The PSA system has generated an overwhelming response to reforestation, forest management, and forest protection. The demand for this last category remians high.

Sources of Funding for PSAs

The 1996 Forestry Law earmarks one-third of the revenues from a dedicated 5 percent fossil fuels tax to the PSA scheme. The tax, theoretically, has the capacity to yield up to $19.8 million annually. However, a major weakness of the current PSA system is that fossil fuel revenues go through the Ministry of Finance based on constitutional principles of "unique accounting" and "centralized tax collection" that require tax revenues to be included in the national budget. The total amount collected for PSAs has never been fully allocated for its original purpose. The amount allotted to the system varies greatly, depending on the overall government budget deficit.

The revenues collected from the fossil fuel tax are administered by the National Forest Fund (FONAFIFO), which is jointly managed by the state and the private sector. The forestry law allows funding for PSAs from a tax on fuels and other petroleum derivatives, public funds for Forest Conservation Certificates (CCBs), and revenues from sales of Carbon Tradeable Offset certificates (CTOs)[2] to international buyers.

Proponents of the environment argue that all revenues from the fossil fuel tax should be used for PSAs, and that the tax should be continued indefinitely (others want to limit the tax to five years). An annual sum per hectare per year should be paid as long as the land remains under forest cover. The Costa Rican Office on Joint Implementation should begin to recover the amounts paid to farmers for services received by the global community through the sale of carbon credits. These funds would then be invested through the National Fund for Forestry Financing.

Regardless, a major fiscal reform in 2001 targeted overlapping taxes on fossil fuels, including the major source of funding of the PSA. Only a fraction of this tax has been allowed to continue in place. This implies that full allocation of these funds has been foregone. Currently, FONAFIFO will continue to receive a fixed budget sum for the PSA system. Most rural groups are unaware of the problem and therefore have not pressured the government to change its policy.

The Carbon Fund

Costa Rica has established a Carbon Fund to serve as a depository for funds from domestic and international sources and will distribute "rights" or "credits" in exchange for such deposits. While FONAFIFO can only compensate private landowners for environmental services, the Carbon Fund is able to finance joint implementation activities related to Protected Areas Projects and to projects that do not involve land use. Landowners wishing to receive Carbon Fund money must cede their environmental services rights to the Fund. The seed money received by FONAFIFO is now being used to buy environmental services rights from farmers. The Carbon Fund markets and sells those rights internationally, producing CTOs. The Fund serves as the financing agent for the national Joint Implementation System.

The International Finance Corporation and Sales
of Wood Futures (1996)

A persistent problem in forestry for landowners is erratic cash flow. In the case of plantations, income is earned only from commercial thinning and from the final harvest. In the case of natural forests, income is produced only once in each cutting cycle, which in Costa Rica varies from 15 to 25 years. In 1996, the International Financial Corporation (IFC) of the World Bank Group established a small program for the sale of wood futures with FUNDECOR. FUNDECOR developed a system for buying wood in advance from forest management units. The system enables the owners of natural forests and plantations to earn income before harvest, thereby making money available to improve cash flow, reducing the risk of land use changes, and avoiding agreements between farmers and loggers that are unfavorable to farmers. The project, funded through the International Finance Corporation, has benefited 39 forest owners with an approximate area of 1,100 hectares and an investment of about $300,000. The project is innovative, but has a limited effect because operations are concentrated in a small area.

The Ecomarket Project

This project is designed to increase forest conservation in Costa Rica by supporting the PSA program. By providing market-based incentives to forest owners in buffer zones and interconnecting biological corridors contiguous to national parks and biological reserves for the provision of environmental services relating to carbon sequestration, biodiversity conservation, scenic beauty, and hydrological services, the project directly supports the implementation of Forestry Law No. 7575. The project contributes to environmentally sustainable development in Costa Rica by supporting the supply and demand for environmental services provided by forest ecosystems; strengthening management capacity and assuring financing of public sector forest programs administered by the Ministry of Environment and Energy (MINAE), including the FONAFIFO and the National System of Conservation Areas (SINAC); and strengthening management capacity of local non-governmental organizations

Funding consists of a $25 million loan from the World Bank, an $8 million grant from the Global Environment Facility (GEF) and $10 million from the Prototype Carbon Fund (PCF). The objective of the GEF grant is to provide an additional sum for biodiversity conservation while preserving important forest ecosystems through conservation easements on privately owned lands outside of protected areas in the Mesoamerican Biological Corridor in Costa Rica.

Key performance indicators related to the project include 150,000 hectares of land incorporated in the PSA program, a 30 percent increase in the participation of women land owners and women's organizations in the ESP program, and improvements related to democratization of the PSA through higher participation by organized groups of small farmers, women, and minorities. In 2000, the following benefited: 11 local agricultural centers, 7 cooperatives, 2 foundations, 4 forestry communities, 1 small farmer organization, and 7 indigenous groups. The percentage of PSAs registered to women is relatively high. Close to 80 percent of PSA contracts in 2000 involved areas smaller than 80 hectares (Estadio de la Nacion 2001).

Biodiversity Conservation in Costa Rica

The National Institute on Biodiversity (INBIO) has stated that the best way to conserve biodiversity is to convert it into an instrument for sustainable human development. Costa Rica has a wide variety of plant and animal species. A total of 85,891 species have been identified in Costa Rica, representing 6 percent of the world's 1.4 million known species (CONABIO 1998). Costa Rica's strategy for biodiversity conservation includes preserving representative samples of all species, learning more about biodiversity, and using plant and animal species in a sustainable way.

Biodiversity Prospecting

Costa Rica markets biodiversity through biodiversity prospecting—identifying biological aspects of plants, insects, and microorganisms that could be useful to the pharmaceutical, medicinal, agricultural, and other industries. The National Council on Biodiversity estimates that approximately 83 percent of Costa Rica's species have not been identified (CONABIO 1998). INBIO has been able to attract investments from the international business community. Such companies as Merck Pharmaceuticals, BioCatalysis, Givaudane Roure, INDENA, AnalytiCon, and the British Technology Group, Ltd. have contracts with INBIO that will allow them to benefit from biodiversity conservation and prospecting (INBIO 1998; Castro et al. 2000). The companies, in return, agree to share royalties with INBIO and the Costa Rican government if research leads to marketable products.

In another interesting approach to biodiversity prospecting, INBIO trains and works with parataxonomists. These parataxonomists, mainly are rural young men and women who live in in farm communities in the buffer zones of the protected areas. They have traditional knowledge about local biodiversity that is enhanced through special field training. Parataxonomists retain knowledge about biodiversity in their communities and their work with INBIO provides them with a livelihood alternative to traditional farming and cattle ranching.

Introducing biodiversity conservation into the economy requires organizational and institutional adaptations. Protecting biodiversity through the national park system demanded additional legislation to reduce uncertainty about land use. The Biodiversity Law is helping build trust and cooperation between the government and private landowners, promotes using indigenous knowledge about biodiversity, and established rules for conflict management in the appropriation of biodiversity. Although this law places Costa Rica far ahead of other countries in biodiversity protection, the public must be better informed if biodiversity is to be considered part of the country's natural capital, and thus part of the capital of the national economy.

The Biodiversity Resources Development Project

The project aims to demonstrate that increased knowledge about particular species enhances their value and the marketability of biodiversity services (GEF and World Bank 1998; Gámez 1999). Specific objectives include developing a framework for undertaking a biodiversity inventory in priority conservation areas, conducting collection and cataloguing activities related to the inventory, developing and testing potential applications based on the inventory, and strengthening the institutional capacity of INBIO.

The Change in Forestry Administration

The Costa Rican forest sector has evolved from a low profile sector without the involvement of private organizations, technology, or specialized education, to a proactive sector with multiple organizations and a strong lobby for reforestation, forest management and protection incentives, innovative financing mechanisms, and possibilities for trading forest services and products in the international market. Today, most agree that in addition to forest management, forest legislation must encourage stakeholder participation. Again, Costa Rica has been at the forefront.

Decentralization has meant the transfer of personnel and logistical resources to different regions, and Conservation Areas now manage their own budgets and personnel. These regional units are now responsible for all procedures regarding permits for concessions and management of protected areas, private forests, and plantations. They also rank projects for eligibility under the PSA program and allocate PSA payments.

Institutional reform has progressed more quickly in the forest and natural resource sector than in any other area of the Costa Rican government. The National System of Conservation Areas (SINAC) is a clear example of such reform. SINAC is legally defined as a system of management and institutional coordination that is decentralized and participatory. The SINAC's creation introduced sweeping changes in the organizational culture and structure of the country's forestry administration.

Democratization has been an active principle in the reshaping of SINAC, evident in the public's participation in protected areas, buffer zones, and private forests. Although public participation was present in Costa Rica's forest policy before SINAC, such participation was one of SINAC's defining principles. The Organic Environmental Law *(Ley Orgánica del Ambiente)* of 1995 further promoted public participation by creating Environmental Regional Councils. Law 7575 assigned new responsibilities for natural resources to these councils. The Biodiversity Law of 1998 established the basic objective of "promoting active participation in all social sectors concerning conservation and the ecological and sustainable use of biodiversity in order to obtain social, economic and cultural sustainability."

Culturally, the SINAC changed its focus to customer service. SINAC also has shifted from being the sole government actor with responsibility for forests to becoming a facilitator and promoter, assigning responsibilities to more specialized, non governmental organizations. The three departments in charge of natural resources management (National Park Service, Forestry General Directorate and Wildlife Service) have been merged and a decentralized forest administration was established. The focus has shifted from a functional orientation emphasizing technical assistance to a process orientation emphasizing inputs and products. These changes have allowed more efficient use of remaining forest resources, flattened the institutional structure, made that structure more democratic, and improved the quality of services provided in the Conservation Areas.

World Bank Structural Adjustment Loans to Costa Rica

The focus of Structural Adjustment Loans (SAL) I was on: import tariff reform, public sector reform, including an employment freeze, reduction in the losses of the Agricultural Marketing Agency (CNP), privatization and a streamlined public investment program, and improvements in debt management. The thrust of the action program in SAL I was maintained for SAL II: further tariff reform, improved export incentives and an increase in public savings. In addition, improvements were sought in basic grains (corn, rice, etc.) pricing policies to further reduce CNP losses, and in banking practices

The major objective of SAL III was to support the government's structural adjustment program in four main areas: public sector reform, designed to improve efficiency and strengthen fiscal policies; reform of the trade regime and of the regulatory framework; financial sector reform to improve the financial system; and social sector reform to further improve coverage and efficiency of social programs. This was an ambitious program, covering a wide spectrum of Costa Rica's reform agenda and including an inordinate number of conditions of effectiveness and tranche releases.

But the third Structural Adjustment loan (SAL III) for $100 million approved in 1993 was never declared effective and was terminated in 1995. Past experience in Costa Rica, extracted from lessons derived from the implementation of the first two SALs, suggests that including the approval of laws as loan conditions to be met after approval by the World Bank's Board, but before effectiveness of the loan, tends to lead to long delays, although such approvals create the necessary ownership of the program essential for its success. However, the full ownership of the program was lacking in the case of SAL III: the main opposition party, which assumed office following general elections a year after approval of SAL III, had concerns about some elements of SAL III.

Costa Rica's macroeconomic indicators, however, generally suggest a much improved economy as a result of structural adjustment. Under the structural adjustment loans, Costa Rica introduced important changes in economic policies by the mid-1980s including elimination of subsidies on interest rates, elimination of price guarantees, privatization of some state-owned companies, and reduction in government spending to control budget deficits. Bank credit for cattle ranching decreased, and meat exports fell to less than 8 percent, which coincided with a decrease in international meat prices to $2.1 per kilogram in 1994.

Through these indirect impacts, the structural adjustment loans helped to eliminate the "anti-forest" bias. Deforestation rates decreased to about 18,000 hectares a year in the early 1990s, a trend that continued until 1997. In that year a positive balance in forest cover was achieved, influenced by the important amount of secondary forest growth in land that had been abandoned or was previously used for agriculture.

The new model of development promoted liberalization of markets and exports of nontraditional agro-export products. New policies to encourage the new export sector eliminated quota restrictions for imports of basic grains and beans, lowered import tariffs, and created new incentives and subsidies for reforestation. At the same time, some of the export crops were produced in deforested areas (bananas in the Atlantic region, for example) and some required intensive use of chemical inputs. The final balance between structural adjustment loans and the environment is complex and generally indirect.

Assessing the impacts of SALs on the environment is complicated by the fact that SALs have changed over time. They have evolved from the early 1980s when SALS neglected social and environmental impacts, to the recognition of social impacts in the mid-1980s, to the incorporation of social concerns and recognition of environmental impacts in the late 1980s, and finally to the consideration of supplementary and compensatory policies for social and environmental concerns in the 1990s. Although the policy changes brought by SALs have been important, they still have not explicitly assessed the relationship between the environment and the national economy. This is in part due to the hybrid policy process in Costa Rica, in part due to national politics, which includes interest group lobbying that modifies the agenda and in part because the Bank did not follow the multi-sector approach towards forests that it had adopted in its 1991 Forest Strategy (Lele et al. 2000).

It appears now that the pace of the policy reforms has slowed down, although Costa Rica's characteristically slow pace of reform has not prevented good performance in projects. In the future, it will be important to conduct further research into the environmental impact of SALs. Furthermore, environmental considerations, including forests, need to be explicitly included in future Bank loans, since even the Completion Reports of SAL I and II do not contain treatment of the environmental impacts.[3] The implementation of the Ecomarkets project reflects major progress along this line.

Costa Rica's Role in Financing Environmental Services

Joint Implementation (JI) is a unified effort by industrialized and developing countries to curb global climate change effects. Through this mechanism, some industrialized countries have agreed to reduce their greenhouse gas emissions in compliance with the U.N. Framework Convention on Climate Change and to finance carbon reduction measures (such as reforestation, forest management, and forest conservation) in developing countries. Parties to the convention may count the carbon sequestered and emissions avoided toward their national emission reduction targets. The Costa Rican Office on Joint Implementation (OCIC) believes that joint implementation is the most important potential financing instrument for environmental services.

Under the JI regime, Costa Rica has been at the forefront in trying to negotiate payment for global services by trading CTOs, the only environmental services traded internationally. The National Forest Fund, responsible for financing national forest projects, disburses payments to forest owners, who then relinquish their right to market their forests' carbon sequestrations potential. The National Forest Fund also calculates the quantities of carbon bound by forest activities for OCIC, and is trying to sell CTOs to countries and firms willing to pay for sequestering to compensate for emissions.

Costa Rica has done more than any other developing country to establish a joint JI regime as a strategy to meet the objectives of the climate treaty and promote its own development goals. The Costa Rican government began to develop official JI policies and programs in 1994. A high level Consultative Committee on Climate Change was formed to shape JI policy, within the context of the national greenhouse gas emissions inventory. In September 1994, Costa Rica and the United States signed a bilateral statement of intent on cooperation for sustainable development and joint implementation (Castro et al. 2000).

Costa Rica signed a bilateral treaty with Norway in 1996 under the joint implementation mechanism for the purchase of carbon bonds for 200,000 tons of carbon at $10 a ton, yielding $2 million for reforestation. Forest owners have already received these revenues. Another transaction with the government of The Netherlands reduces the equivalent of 500 tons of methane gas through anaerobic treatment of coffee waste and energy savings through biogas use. The Dutch government also financed reforestation of 78 hectares and will receive CTOs for both investments (Castro et al. 2000). More important, the agreement amounted to official recognition by the Dutch government of the value of environmental services well before the climate change treaty began to acquire international headlines in 2000.

The Influence of the World Bank on Costa Rica's Conservation Policy in the 1990s

Before 1991, there was no World Bank activity in Costa Rica's forest sector. However, the Bank prepared a Costa Rica Forest Sector Review in 1993. Since 1991, a total of US$368 million in World Bank projects have been directed to Costa Rica. But only two projects, totaling $7.5 million, were related directly to biodiversity or forest conservation until the EcoMarkets Project for a total of $32 million was approved in 2001. The Bank's most important influence on Costa Rica's forest sector has been its role in pushing for change in agricultural policies, which led to reduced rates of deforestation and emphasis on natural forest management, forest conservation, and management of secondary forests and forest plantations. Despite its flaws, the second most important contribution was the Bank's Forest Sector Review. It provided an intellectual foundation for many of the radical changes that Costa Rican policy has brought to forestry at home and abroad.

Forest sector studies conducted by the Bank have typically concluded that undervaluation of forests, poor regulation of the private sector, unwise promotion of alternative land uses, and macroeconomic policies have had significant impacts on forest resources. The Forest Sector Review confirmed many of these ideas. The review noted the difficulty of capturing the value of forests' environmental benefits. It concluded that about 66 percent of the benefits of Costa Rica's forests are enjoyed globally and that the global community should compensate Costa Rica for conserving, managing, and planting forests. The review calculated that global benefits from Costa Rica's 1.3 million hectares of forests totaled between $119 million and $286 million and recommended transferring a minimum of $62 million to Costa Rica annually. The review also stated that the only mechanisms for identifying carbon sequestration values are grants from bilat-

eral organizations, private sector and international NGOs, Global Environmental Facility (GEF) funds, and debt-for-nature swaps (none of which are
market mechanisms).

To protect biodiversity the review suggested improving the financial management of national parks. It also proposed increasing entrance fees, especially for foreign tourists. Costa Rica adopted this recommendation, reasoning
that foreign tourists can pay higher entrance fees if nationals are already
contributing through their taxes to protect the forests. Although this measure,
generated heated debate in the tourism sector, the final agreement was congruent with the recommendation.

The review recommended deregulating harvesting in forest plantations
and trade in forest products, including logs. Both recommendations were
adopted, although logs were exempted. Thus, foreign competition may reduce Costa Rican log prices, especially for pine and other fast-growing species from the natural forests.

The Forest Sector Review also noted that:

- Too many incentives for agriculture and pastures and too few for forestry have been a principal cause of deforestation.
- Subsidies for natural forest management should be increased. Depending on the interest rate, the subsidy could range from $779 to $781 per
  hectare per crop rotation, with an annual equivalent of $117 to $156
  per hectare.
- Landowners who sign a management agreement should be protected
  against expropriation and squatters and fires and pests, and receive
  priority forest land titling and demarcation and compensation up to
  $50 a year. The forest law included most of these suggestions, although
  the amount of compensation is much lower.[4]
- Natural forest management should be compatible with conservation
  objectives. Costa Rica needs funds to administer the management system, criteria for forest protection, and allocating institutional responsibilities in the Conservation Areas.

Alongside these helpful recommendations were biased opinions and misconceptions. The Bank strongly emphasized environmental protection instead of sustainable development. Some analysts are concerned about an
exponential increase in wood exports when 150,000 hectares of trees planted
on plantations become mature, more than doubling the country's supply of
industrial wood (Watson et al. 1998). The Forest Sector Review failed to
discuss the large investments in the forest industry that would be needed to
make these exports possible.

The Bank ignored the important role of plantations in improving land use
and increasing wood production, viewing plantation subsidies as subsidies
for private commercial activities that are environmentally insensitive and

yield lower biodiversity or carbon sink benefits than natural forests. Yet plantations are not environmentally insensitive if they use land that was previously used for pastures or agricultural crops. Plantations are more efficient carbon sinks than secondary and primary forests.

It would be better for Costa Rica to invest in incentives for existing secondary forests than to change subsidies from plantations to natural forest regeneration. The government is trying to develop a balanced strategy for supporting plantations, forest management, and conservation. Both plantations and management of secondary forests need to be promoted under the objective of sustainable development. Forest plantations are highly profitable, even more profitable than cattle ranching at interest rates up to 15 percent. Indeed, since 1996 wood exports have outstripped meat exports. With incentives, plantations have higher border prices than do cattle, up to an interest rate of 20 percent.[5] Therefore, reforestation is an attractive alternative to cattle farming in forest soils (Kishor and Constantino 1993). The review's recommendations for protecting biodiversity reserves leave great doubt about sustainability, efficiency, and institutional development in the forest sector. Instead of creating opportunities for the local and international economy by recommending initiatives favoring biodiversity protection, tourism, research, and other forms of community participation, the Bank recommended environmental protection measures only. Because this alternative is economically inefficient and socially inequitable, the evidence unfolding in the 1990s has demonstrated beyond doubt that in absence of creating livelihoods, income, and revenue this approach will be difficult to sustain.

The Bank has so far avoided natural forest management because the Bank's 1991 forest strategy mandated that the Bank Group would not provide financing for commercial logging in primary tropical moist forests. The joint Forest for Life Initiative of the World Bank/World Wildlife Fund targets good forest management and certification of 100 million hectares globally. It provides an opportunity to promote sound forest management in natural primary forests using certification as a monitoring tool. In the end, neither objective was achieved. The Conservation Area Management Project (CAM) was proposed to protect Costa Rica's biodiversity, balance the country's resource needs with global demands for biodiversity preservation, and help curb deforestation. CAM was never approved, but was expected to begin with a $70 million investment. The last version considered an investment of only $23.2 million, including a $15 million loan from the Bank.

The natural resources management, institutions, and policies of the proposed project included the following elements:

- Identification and establishment of the boundaries of key protected areas;

- Description of physical and economic characteristics of the country's natural resources through cartography and geographic information systems;
- Improvement of forestry technology in forest plantations;
- Analysis of sectoral policies and institutions to improve MINAE's decision making ability.

The early proposal became the prototype for more elaborated and better designed projects, such as the Biodiversity Resources Development Project in 1998 and the EcoMarkets Project. These two captured the essence of the CAM, but their goals went further in terms of sustainability content and the actual adoption of the recommendations of the Forest Sector Review and testing the creation of markets for the environmental benefits of the Protected Areas System, while addressing rural community welfare through opportunities in conservation. The former materialized as a joint INBIO-WB/GEF project of $12 million. INBIO participates with a matching fund in the amount of $4 million. The latter project, EcoMarkets, materialized in early 2001 and involves a $ 25 million Bank loan plus a GEF $8 million grant and a PCF $10 million contribution. FONAFIFO and OCIC are the counterparts and contribute approximately $20 million.

Costa Rica's Influence on World Bank Forest Policy

It is premature to try to determine whether developments in forestry and natural resource management in Costa Rica have influenced the Bank in the same way that the Bank influenced Costa Rica's bold policies. However, the following changes in Costa Rican forest policies have been innovative and may have already served to widen the Bank's perspective and may benefit its other borrowers:

- The country's forest law has evolved substantially since the 1960s into a comprehensive environmental code that includes the Environmental Law, the Biodiversity Law, and the Forest Law. This is an area where many developing countries are currently behind and one which calls for greater attention in international assistance than before (see the discussion of this issue in the chapters on Indonesia and India, for instance).
- The Conservation Areas System (SINAC) has guaranteed the protection of a large proportion of the country's natural forests. While the other five developing countries in this volume show the same trend, Costa Rica has gone further in developing financial and other mechanisms to ensure that they are well funded and managed—an important contrast with Indonesia, for example.
- A wide-ranging system of incentives for forest activities has evolved, beginning with reforestation. Such incentives are being developed in

China, India, and Brazil as well, but again Costa Rica has been ahead of them in integrating forest policy with policies in other sectors, such as the use of the fossil fuel tax.

- SINAC changed from a strongly centralized, command-and-control administration that put its responsibilities for forests, protected areas, and wildlife into separate categories to a decentralized and democratic organization that delegates decision making and budget authority to the regions, with participation from citizens and communities. Virtually all five countries discussed in this volume are experimenting with decentralization, but the initial impact of decentralization has been accelerated deforestation in part because the interacting conditions have not yet been created through incentives in those other countries. In other areas, too, the five countries discussed in this volume are behind Costa Rica.
- Farming organizations have been strengthened through incentives for small farmers that transferred technology from the government to the private sector.
- The "polluter-pays" system was introduced through establishment of a fossil fuels tax to pay for the environmental services of forests.
- FONAFIFO specializes in the financial issues of forests and natural resources, disbursing PSAs, providing credits, etc.
- OCIC trades CTOs in the international markets and solicits funding for the conservation, management, and reforestation of more than 2.5 million Hectares.
- INBIO assigns a value to biodiversity.
- The National Certification System provides national criteria for the management of forest plantations, secondary forests, and natural forests. Proper implementation of the system could help decentralize administrative control of forest activities.
- Responsibility for forest management has been transferred to private owners by the *Regentes*, foresters responsible to the government for application of government ordinances.
- The invention of CTOs could serve as a model for trading other environmental services.
- Ecotourism has benefited from many of these policies and is contributing revenues for forest protection.

The Future Role of the World Bank in Costa Rican Forestry

The World Bank Group including the International Financial Corporation [IFC] and MIGA could play a much more active role in the sustainable development of the forest sector in Costa Rica by supporting the construction of timber mills and futures purchases of wood. As of 1998, more than 147,000 hectares of trees had been planted in Costa Rica, most of them between 1988 and 1995. This means that between 2000 and 2005 Costa Rica must increase its processing capacity more than five times. This will require $60 million of increased investments in the timber milling and drying industry. This investment does not include secondary wood processing, which would make the figure much larger.

- An important limitation to reforestation in Costa Rica has been the lack of steady, predictable cash flow for small and medium-size farmers who reforest. After the fifth year, when forest incentives have been fully disbursed, these farmers have no more income from the forests till thinning or harvest. To solve this problem, some owners of small and medium-size farms are cutting high-quality trees that are easier to sell in the market, leaving the worst trees for the future harvest and thereby decreasing the long-run profitability of the plantation. The IFC-FUNDECOR sales of wood futures have successfully addressed this problem. A new project of this kind under The National Forest Fund will extend the experience nationally.
- The EcoMarkets Project provides the support Costa Rica needs to fortify its financial strategy. The Prototype Carbon Fund should include not only mitigation through renewable energy production but also through forest activities envisaged in the Kyoto Protocol. Alternative options for managing biodiversity and other forest services are also needed. Property rights generally are not well defined in forested areas. This lack of clarity causes problems, since the structure of property rights affects both the allocation of resources and the distribution of wealth in the economy. Having a good definition of property rights for natural resources (including forest services) is important for sustainable development, but it is not the total solution. Another socially acceptable practice would be to introduce biodiversity management on private lands or let landowners share the profits of management and the potential profits of future discoveries. Other common property alternatives also may be feasible.

Flexible and innovative lending instruments and incentives are urgently needed for forest management. These could include longer-term financial alternatives and cooperative alternatives among NGOs, the private sector (large landowners as well as small), and financial institutions like FONAFIFO. Encouraging the use of standing forests as collateral for loans and selling futures in timber may be good options for developing forest plantations and forest management. Costa Rica could be a showcase for other countries in the world on how to develop forest goods and services.

Notes

1. If the conversion of secondary forests is included, total deforestation from 1979 to 1992 was 780,740 hectares, or 15.29 percent of the total area undergoing land use change, for a deforestation rate of 1.18 percent a year.

2. Certifiable Tradeable Offsets (CTOs)—a financial instrument designed by Costa Rica that can be used to transfer greenhouse gas offsets in the international marketplace. A CTO represents a specific number of units of greenhouse gas emissions expressed in carbon equivalent units reduced or sequestered.
3. Similarly, Bank loans for the agricultural sector have not explicitly considered forest or environmental areas. If a loan indirectly addressed these it linked them to macroeconomic or broad sector policy reforms. The Export Financing Fund and other export funds have not promoted forest sector activities and lending systems. In other cases, loans that could have indirectly benefited the forest sector, such as the 1992 Agricultural Sector Investment and Institutional Development Loan, were terminated because of critical delays in legislative procedures and the country's failure to comply with effectiveness conditions. The loan included such elements as soil erosion programs and demarcation of national parks and reserves, but it was conditioned on quota, tariffs, and price reforms for basic grains and beans.
4. For 2001, the officially approved level of payment of PSAs per hectare are $570 for reforestation, $348 for natural forest management, $222 for forest conservation, $222 for natural regeneration, and $222 for plantation management. These values are calculated with an exchange rate of 330 colones per dollar because the amounts are fixed in colones. Payments are in different percentages over five years until the total amount is reached. For example, for a plantation with one forest management activity and a rotation cycle of 20 years, the amount of the PSA is $39.6 per hectare per year. For forest management and a cutting cycle of 20 years, the amount is $17.4 hectare a year. Both figures are lower than the amounts suggested by the World Bank.
5. From 1979 to 1986 Costa Rican incentives were targeted to wealthier people, companies, and farmers through tax deductions (affecting 24 percent of the planted area of large landowners until 1998). In 1986 and 1987 such incentives as CAFAs were established for small landowners as well (affecting 49 percent of the planted area of all owners regardless of size). Plantation incentives are now accessible to all farmers.

References

Alfaro, M. 1998. La Conservación de los Bosques Privados a través de la Red Costarricense de Reservas Naturales. San José, C.R.

Alpizar, W. 1997. "Joint Implementation in the Forestry Sector Makes Viable Sustainable Development an Option in Developing Countries: Costa Rica—A True Life Case." Proceedings of the Eleventh World Forestry Congress. Ankara, Turkey. September.

Boyce, J. K, A. Fernández, E. Fürst, and O. Segura. 1994. "Café y Desarrollo Sostenible: del Cultivo Agroquímico a la Producción Orgánica en Costa Rica." Universidad Nacional, San José, Costa Rica.

Brockett, C. 1988. Land, Power and Poverty: Agrarian Transformation and Political Conflict in Central America. Boulder, CO: Westview Press.

Bulmer-Thomas, Victor. 1987. The Political Economy of Central America Since 1920. Cambridge: Cambridge University Press.

Castro, Rene., L. Gámez, N. Olson, and F. Tattenbach. 2000. "The Costa Rican Experience with Market Instruments to Mitigate Climate Change and Conserve Biodiversity." Journal of Environmental Monitoring and Assessment 61: 75-92. Kluwer Academic Publishers. March.

Castro, Rene, and G. Arias. 1998. Costa Rica: Towards the Sustainability of its Forest Resources. MINAE-FONAFIFO.

CCT (Tropical Science Center), CIEDES (Center for Research on Sustainable Development) CI (Conservation Internationa), and FONAFIFO (National Forestry Financing Fund). 1998. Survey of Forest Cover in Costa Rica Using LANDSAT Images 1986/87-1996/97. San José, Costa Rica.

CONABIO. 1998. Comisión Nacional Para El Conocimiento Y Uso De La Biodiversidad: Registro De Bases De Datos De Proyectos (database).

Constantino, L., and N. Kishor. 1993. Forest Management and Competing Land Uses: An Economic Analysis for Costa Rica. World Bank LATEN Dissemination Note 7. Latin America Technical Department, Environment Division. Washington, D.C.: World Bank.

De Camino, Ronnie, and M. Alfaro. 1997. "La Certificación Forestal en Centroamérica." Paper presented at the Third Central American Forestry Congress. San José, Costa Rica. September 15-17.

Edelman, Marc. 1992. *The Logic of the Latifundio: The Large Estates of Northwestern Costa Rica Since the Late Nineteenth Century*. Stanford, CA: Stanford University Press.

Estadio de la Nacion. 26, June 2001. "Intervención del Secretario General del Psoe, Jose Luis Rodriguez Zapatero.

Fondo Nacional de Financiamiento Forestal (FONAFIFO). 1999. Informe anual. Costa Rica.

FUNDECOR-Energía Global S.A. 1997. Acuerdo Contractual para el pago de servicios ambientales entre FUNDECOR—Compañía Energía Global S.A.: Proyecto Hidroeléctrico Río Volcán y Don Pedro. San José.

Gámez, R. 1999. "Biodiversidad y la Agenda de Costa Rica." Lecture to the participants of the First International Workshop on Analysis and Design of Forestry and Natural Resources Policies, University for Peace, San José, Costa Rica.

GEF (Global Environment Facility) and World Bank. 1998. "Costa Rica: Biodiversity Resources Development Project." GEF/World Bank Semester Bulletins. Washington, D.C.

Gorbitz, Adalberto. 1998. Personal communication. Manager, Costa Rican Office for Joint Implementation (OCIC) IMN (National Meteorological Institute), MINAE (Ministry of Environment and Energy), UNEP (United Nations Environment Programme), MAG (Ministry of Agriculture and Livestock), IGN (National Geographical Institute), and DGF (General Forestry Directorate). 1996. Evaluación del Cambio de Cobertura de la Tierra en Costa Rica 1979–1992. San José, Costa Rica.

INBio (National Biodiversity Institute).1998. Annual Report. Santo Domingo, Costa Rica.

Kaimowitz, D. 1996. "Livestock and Deforestation.Central America in the 1980s and 1990s: A Policy Perspective. Center for International Forestry Research (CIFOR), Deutsche Gesellschaft für Technische Zusammenarbeit (GTZ), Instituto Interamericano de Cooperaciónpara la Agricultura (ICA), International Food Policy Research Institute (IFPRI). CIFOR Special Publication. Jakarta, Indonesia.

Kishor, Nalin M., and Luis F. Constantino. 1993. "Forest Management and Competing Land Uses: An Economic Analysis of Costa Rica." Latin American and the Caribbean Regional Office. Technical Department, Env. Division, Washington, D.C., The World Bank.

Lele, U., N. Kumar, Syed A. Husain, Aaron Zazeuta, and Lauren Kelly. 2000. "The World Bank Forest Strategy: Striking the Right Balance." The World Bank.

Leonard, J. 1986. Recursos Naturales en América Central: un Perfil Ambiental Regional. CATIE. San Jose, Costa Rica.

Masís, German, and C. Rodríguez. 1994. "La Agricultora Campesina en Costa Rica: Alternativas y Desafios en la Transformación Productiva del Agro." IDEAS. San José Costa Rica.

Mena, Y., and G. Artavia. 1998. Parques Nacionales y Otras Areas Silvestres Protegidas de Costa Rica. National System of Conservation Areas (SINAC) and Ministry of Environment and Energy (MINAE), San José, Costa Rica.

MINAE (Costa Rica, Ministry of Environment and Energy) and SINAC (National System of Conservation Areas). 1996. Información Relevante sobre el Sector Forestal-1972-1995. Mimeo. SINAC, Area de Fomento. San José, Costa Rica.

Peuker, Axel. 1992. "Public Policies and Deforestation: A Case Study of Costa Rica." Regional Studies Program Report 14. Latin America and the Caribbean Regional Office, Technical Department, World Bank, Washington, D.C.

Proyecto Estado de la Nación. 2000. Estado de la Nación en el Desarrollo Humano Sostenible: sétimo informe. San José, Costa Rica

RUTA (Regional Unit for technical Assistance). 1998. "Progress Report: RUTA III and RUTA III Extended."San José, Costa Rica.

Segura, Olman. 1999. "Competitiveness and Sustainability of the Forest Sector in Central America." Ph. D. thesis. SUDESCA Research Paper No.24. Aalborg University, Denmark.

Sistema Nacional de Áreas de Conservación (SINAC). 1999. Evolución y perspectiva. Ministerio de Ambiente y Energía. San José, Costa Rica.

Solórzano, R., R. de Camino, R. Woodward, J. Tosi, V. Watson, A. Vásquez, C. Villalobos, J. Jiménez, R. Repetto, and W. Cruz. 1991. *Accounts Overdue: Natural Resources Depreciation in Costa Rica.* San José, Costa Rica: Tropical Science Center (CCT) and World Resources Institute.

Stewart, R., and G. Gibson. 1994. "El Efecto de las Políticas Agrícolas y Forestales sobre el Ambiente y el Desarrollo Económico de América Latina." In H. Cortés, *Libro de Lecturas del Taller sobre Reforma de Políticas de Gobierno Relacionadas con la Conservación y el Desarrollo Forestal de América Latina.* Washington, D.C.: Center for International Forestry Research, United States Agency for International Development, Inter-American Institute for Cooperation in Agriculture, Environmental and Natural Resources Policy and Training, Inter-American Development Bank, and World Bank.

Trejos, R. 1992. "El Comercio Agropecuario Extraregional." In C. Pomareda (ed.), *La Agricultura en el Desarrollo Económico de Centroamérica en los 90.* Inter-American Institute for Cooperation in Agriculture (IICA). San José, Costa Rica.

Vieto, R., and J. Valverde. 1995. Efectos de las compras de tierras con fines de conservación. RNT. Recursos Naturales Tropicales por encargo de la Friedrich Ebert Stiftung. San José, Costa Rica.

Watson, V., S. Cervantes, C. Castro, L. Mora, M. Solís, I. Porras, and B. Cornejo. 1998. Costa Rica: Políticas Exitosas para el Bosque y la Gente. Tropical Science Center, International Institute for Environment and Development, JUNAFORCA (National Board of Forestry Farmers). San José, Costa Rica.

World Bank. 1998. Biodiversity in World Bank Projects: A Portfolio Update. Washington, D.C.

World Bank. 1994. "Review of the Implementation of the Forest Sector Policy." Agricultural and Natural Resources Department Report 13850. Environment Department, Washington, D.C.

3

China: The World's Largest Experiment in Conservation and Development

Scott Rozelle, Jikun Huang, and Uma Lele

China, the world's most populous country, has had the world's highest rate of economic growth in the last two decades and has had the world's deepest decline in poverty. China's real gross domestic product (GDP) increased an average of 9.7 percent between 1989 and 2000, with the percentage of people earning more than $1 a day rising from 20 percent in 1978 to 80 percent in 1998. Such explosive change has placed great pressure on both China's forest resources and, as the world's second-largest importer of forest products, on forests of timber-exporting countries. China ranks fifth in the world in forest area and is among the 12 countries in the world with the greatest biodiversity.

In the late 1980s, anticipating imminent timber shortages, the government began taking steps to expand supply and manage demand. Choosing to increase domestic supply rather than increase imports, the country embarked on an ambitious program to massively enlarge its forest cover, mainly through plantations. Although deforestation in natural forests has continued unabated (estimated to be about 500,000 hectares a year until 1998), the rise in the area covered by tree plantations, shelterbelts, and orchards is driving the growth in total forest cover, which increased by about 43 million hectares between 1981 and 1998 (Table 3.1).

These plantations will help China meet more of its annual demand for timber and other wood products from domestic sources, although they will not make up for the loss of biodiversity that occurs when natural forests are harvested. But plantation forestry has substantially increased total forest productivity while at the same time generating rural employment and incomes for over two million people, many of them indigenous and forest-dependent. China has also managed to meet part of its large and growing demand for raw timber by requiring, through government regulation, the substitution of non-timber products for wood products in industry and construction.

Thus, China's approach to forest sector development has evolved over the past 20 years from relatively simple forest plantation projects to a complex strategy involving all aspects of the environment and its relation to economic development. Beginning in the mid-1980s, the country focused on aggressive reforestation and forestation, albeit at the expense of the country's natural forests. It has transformed the structure of at least 30 percent of its forest area, reversing the worst excesses of deforestation in the 1950s and 1960s with protection forests planted across wide areas of fragile lands.

Following successful decollectivization in the agricultural sector in the early 1980s, forest leaders sought to further devolve control and increase incentives to households and forest users. In the decade or so since then, China has launched innovative programs to improve its investment in forests. Although the Chinese governance system has been largely state-based and state-driven, the country has been skillfully combining its traditional command-and-control approach with a web of innovative incentives in property rights. This has encouraged households to take responsibility for land and trees, fiscal decentralization to the provinces, and a household, county, and enterprise responsibility system has emerged.

Catastrophic flooding along the Yangtze River in 1998 heightened public awareness of the severity of the degradation of China's natural vegetation over the years and the potential environmental and economic consequences. In response to the flooding, the government implemented a Natural Forest Protection Program (NFPP) that includes a logging ban in natural forests on the upper reaches of the Yangtze and Yellow rivers (along with logging reductions in natural forests in other regions), a 1999 program that calls for the conversion of cropland and wasteland on slopes of more than 25 degrees to forest or grasslands, and a Great West Development Program to compensate farmers, loggers and other groups harmed by the logging ban and land conversion policies. For the year 2000, the goals of the land conversion program included planting trees and other vegetation on 340,000 hectares of steep cultivated (i.e., agricultural) land and on 430,000 hectares of seriously degraded wasteland. The cumulative target for the land conversion program is 220 million mu by 2010. The government has also established a Forest and Grasslands Taskforce to provide independent advice to policymakers on the impact of these new policies.

The most important factor in China's accomplishments has been the high priority assigned to the forest sector by the government—the State Forestry Administration as its implementing arm—and hence the high level of the strategy's ownership. This extends from the ministry level to the provinces, prefects, counties, and towns, each of which contributes counterpart funds through a "household responsibility system" dating from the late 1970s.

That system has profoundly influenced the incentives to make projects work. Even beneficiary households are expected to contribute their share to this system.

The role of nongovernmental institutions in China has been limited until recently, but legitimate, independent nongovernmental organizations are rapidly emerging. The voice of the academic community is greater and more independent, and the use of incentive principles in the management of public entities and resources has increased in just a few years. China is exploring other market-based approaches for financing environmental services. This diversified view is helping in evaluating China's forest policies, projects, and future scenarios in addressing the socioeconomic and environmental challenges wrought by the logging ban and other new forest policies.

But much remains to be done. Precious little is known about the distribution of the benefits of forest projects between households and production and marketing units. The implications of the logging ban require careful analysis from the viewpoint of linking expected environmental benefits to the design, implementation, monitoring, and evaluation of benefits. China needs a more nuanced, location-specific approach to its forests that will require substantial human capital and additional institutional capacity for planning, implementation, monitoring, and evaluation in various sectors at all levels to ensure that the logging ban is financially sustainable and yields the expected environmental benefits. Future trends in supply, demand, marketing, and trade for timber and some key non-timber forest products need to be better understood.

The extent to which China will be self-sufficient or draw on global forest resources will depend on the future productivity of its forestry sector, an area where the World Bank's contribution has been particularly evident. Indeed, the Bank's involvement offers a window on China's forest sector performance. The Bank's impact has been largely through lending operations. China is both the Bank's biggest overall borrower and the largest borrower for forest sector projects. As judged by the effectiveness and impact of Bank lending operations, China has been by far the best performer.

The Bank's forest sector portfolio in China has evolved to a remarkable degree over the past 20 years. The projects of the 1980s focused on relatively simple, highly practical, production and plantation management oriented forestry activities that mainly involved the managers of China's state-owned and -operated tree plantations. In the mid-1990s, the scope of the Bank's projects broadened to include forests operated by farmer-managed collectives and trees raised by rural residents on their own homesteads. Today, the newest Bank projects are engaging the central government on the extension of innovative forest and nature reserve management systems, are deeply involving local villagers (especially the poor) in forest management matters, and are beginning to deal with a broad spectrum of development, transition, and environmental issues.

Because of its successes, the Bank's forest lending in China is in jeopardy. Because of its rapid growth and higher per capita income, China has graduated from being eligible for concessional credit (at an 0.75 percent annual interest rate and 40-year maturity) from the International Development Association (IDA) to near commercial interest rates from the International Bank for Reconstruction and Development (IBRD). Unlike most other developing countries, China passes loan funds to its provinces and holds them responsible for repayment. The provinces in turn lend IDA and Bank resources to households that similarly are responsible for repayment. The lending program in the forest sector is coming under pressure because of a drop in the demand for credit among poor households as the provincial government's on-lending rates have increased to keep up with the near-commercial IBRD interest rates, although repayment periods for IBRD loans are longer than those required by commercial banks.

Overall Growth in Forest Cover and Volume
Belies Changes in Forest Structure

Although China's forest resource base is the world's fifth largest in per capita terms, it is relatively small and isolated. Forest cover amounts to only 0.11 hectare per capita, a seventh of the world average of 0.77 hectares. Most of the country's natural forests are in remote and poor areas in the northeast, northwest, and southwest, where China's more isolated and marginal minority populations live. Increasing the productivity of forests and forest-related industries is crucial to reducing poverty and improving life for indigenous people. Domestic forests provide 40 percent of China's rural energy, almost all of the lumber and plywood panels for its construction sector, and raw material for its pulp and paper industry (World Bank 1998). Supplying about 3 percent of the nation's jobs and 4 percent of its gross national product (GNP), the sector is a vital source of employment and income.

Table 3.1
Forest Cover in China, 1973-1998

Survey	Period	Forest Area (million hectares)	Forest Stock (million hectares)	Forest Cover (percent)
First	1973-76	122	87	12.7
Second	1977-81	115	90	12.0
Third	1984-88	125	91	12.98
Fourth	1989-93	134	101	13.92
Fifth	1994-98	159	113	16.55

Source: China State Forestry Administration

National statistics document an increase in the amount of land under forest cover from 12.0 percent in the 1977-81 survey period to 16.5 percent in the 1994-98 survey period, an increase of 18 million hectares between 1980 and 1993, and another 25 million hectares between 1993 and 1998. Forest volume has recovered sharply in the past decade after a long, steady decline. Much of the newly forested area was originally bare wasteland that was highly susceptible to erosion. Because the rise in forest cover has come from an increase in tree plantations, shelterbelts (barriers of trees and shrubs that protect the land from wind and storm and lessen erosion), and commercial orchards, the rise in forest diversity and its associated environmental services has been minimal.

Although tree plantations have increased, natural and old-growth forest areas have declined. This transformation limits the other environmental contributions provided by forests, since limited-species plantations do not provide the diverse flora and habitat for large groups of wildlife that are found in natural forests; on the other hand, to the extent that tree plantations indirectly reduce pressure to harvest natural forests, there is a reduced loss of diversity.

From 1980 to 1993, the latest survey period for which disaggregated data could be assembled, state forest farms and collectives increased the area put into new forestation projects, on average, by about 1.5 million hectares per year. Such large annual increases imply a total rise of 20 million hectares of new forest land from these afforestation efforts, a rise that exceeds the entire *net* increase in forest area (see figure 3.1).

Figure 3.1
**Cumulative Area of New Forestation and Reforestation on
Engineered Plantations, 1980–93**

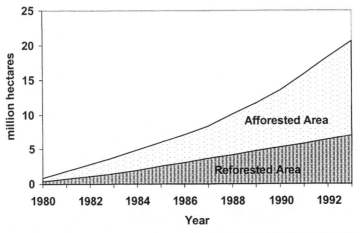

Source: ZGLYNJ 1949–86 (one volume), 1987–93. [ZGLYNJ in refs is for 1986-92, 1980-93, and 1995-97]

The dramatic jump in the reported afforested areas means that vast areas of original natural forest were clear-cut and not replanted. According to interviews with foresters in almost every major forested region in China, most plantations are being established on land that is either barren or, at most, home to scrub-covered hills. If so, and if most of the engineered forestation projects involve timber-producing species, the fact that total timber area has remained relatively constant would imply that managers of state-run and collective forests were logging and not replanting large parts of China's mature plantations and natural or old growth forests. This has major consequences for the diversity of China's forests. China's concerted effort to establish plantations has more than kept up with harvesting of older timber stands, but the species composition in the harvested forests is more diverse than in those being planted.

Newly engineered forestland can be divided into fast-growing forests and traditional forests. Fast-growing forests—species of trees that increase their volume by at least 15 cubic meters a year—have risen by almost 0.5 million hectares annually since 1986. According to Yin (1994) and species data in the national forest census, most of these fast-growing forests, which feed China's growing paper and light industrial manufacturing sectors, have been established in the collectively managed forests in the south and north-central provinces. In spite of the higher profile of fast-growing forests (which receive much attention from China's forestry community), plantations with traditional timber-producing trees are expanding faster and actually account for more of the engineered forestation.

The Effects of Reforestation

The rise in engineered reforested area has also apparently reinforced the sharp structural changes that are occurring in many important forest areas.

Table 3.2
Cost of China's Timber Imports, 1982 to 1999 (Estimated)

Year	Amount (billions of $)	Year	Amount (billions of $)	Year	Amount (billions of $)
1982	1,000	1988	2,000	1994	3,000
1983	1,400	1989	1,400	1995	2,900
1984	1,600	1990	1,400	1996	3,500
1985	1,800	1991	1,800	1997	4,800
1986	1,000	1992	2,600	1998	5,100
1987	1,900	1993	2,700	1999	6,200

Source: Chinese customs statistics, 1993-1998

During the reform era, the average annual area established as high-quality, engineered timber forests on land that had recently been logged rose from about 400,000 hectares in the early 1980s to more than 550,000 hectares in the early 1990s. Recently released forest census data are expected to show a similar analysis for the latest period. To the extent that reforestation occurs on mature plantations, its chief contribution is that it helps to maintain current forest cover. If foresters harvest in old-growth or natural forests and then replant with single (or several) species, the diversity and associated environmental services of China's forests would decline. But because plantations help meet domestic demand, afforested and reforested plantations can take pressure off of remaining national natural forests, thereby curbing the need for imports and thus taking pressure off forest resources internationally.

Trends in Forest Structure

The trends in China's forest area, drawn from census and supplementary statistics, show the accomplishments and potential environmental implications of China's forest sector (table 3.3). The primary problem is not destruction of tree cover per se—the amount of forested area in China rose by more than four percentage points between 1981 and 1998.

But disaggregated analysis shows that the forest structure changed sharply in the reform era. Engineered timber forestation efforts, shelterbelts, and commercial plantations grew by 40 percent or more during the reform period.[1] Analysis also shows that decreasing diversity and loss of old growth forests unconnected to the reforestation programs may be a serious environmental issue. Because China's traditional timber sector has in part exploited natural, old growth forests, it is plausible to think that there has been a sizable decline in natural forests of 23 million hectares (16 million hectares of clear-cut, non-replanted forest and the 7 million hectares of engineered reforested land, which also often constitutes a switch from mixed forests to single-species forests).

Continuing Environmental Threats

In many ways, China's environment is continuing to deteriorate. Pastures in northwest China and on the Xizang-Qinghai plateau continue to be over-grazed and converted to farmland, although some of the cultivated land subsequently reverts to grassland. Coastal wetlands are being drained for agriculture (primarily rice) or converted to aquaculture. Desertification seems to be increasing, although statistics are scarce. Much of the reforested area is monocultured, and the drop in natural and old-growth forest will produce a decline in biodiversity, wildlife habitats, and other environmental services from natural forests.

Table 3.3
Forest Cover and Volume, by Region

	Forest cover (%/% change)			Forest volume (billion meters³/% change)		
	1980	1988	1993	1980	1988	1993
Northeast state-run region	19.5	19.8 (1.5)	20.3 (2.5)	2.94	2.89 (−1.7)	3.00 (3.8)
Southern collective region	29.4	30.2 (2.7)	35.2 (16.6)	1.12	0.96 (−14.3)	1.09 (13.5)
Southwest mixed-managed region	16.9	21.3 (26.0)	22.1 (3.8)	2.15	2.37 (10.2)	2.41 (1.7)
North-central fast growth region	7.9	10.4 (31.6)	10.8 (3.8)	0.10	0.13 (35.8)	0.13 (3.9)
All China	12.0	13.0 (8.3)	13.9 (6.9)	7.98	8.09 (1.4)	9.09 (12.4)
Total covered area (millions of hectares)	115.3	124.7	133.7			

Note: Forest cover is measured by total forest area divided by total land area. The dates in the table are proxy dates for the three census periods. The 1980 forest census was carried out from 1978 to 1981, the 1988 census from 1986 to 1989, and the 1993 census from 1992 to 1994.

Source: QGSLZYTJ 1983, 1989, 1994

Soil Erosion and Desertification

A report by the Research Center for Environment and Development found that of all of China's natural resource problems, erosion and desertification have had the greatest negative impact on GDP. Some 1.53 million square kilometers of land out of a total of 9.6 million square kilometers are classified as more than slightly eroded. The most severely affected areas are the Loess Plateau, the red soils area south of the Yangtze River, the black soils of the Northeast Plain, and the grasslands of the northwest. It is estimated that China loses five billion tons of soil from agricultural and nonagricultural land each year.

Although the primary direct effect of erosion is a decline in soil productivity and crop yields, crop area also shrinks as erosion worsens, but this has not been captured in the statistics. Most erosion is the direct result of pasture overgrazing, inappropriate conversion of grassland to cultivated cropland,

and removal of vegetative cover through deforestation and clearing of marginal lands. Erosion was most serious in the 1950s and 1960s, when large-scale conversion of forestland and pasture to agriculture took place to meet grain production targets. Pastureland conversion has diminished in recent years, and forest conversion has reversed, but crop cultivation itself has severely degraded large areas. The government has implemented erosion control measures on almost 700,000 square kilometers of land by 1996. Land areas totaling 1.53 million square kilometers in China are classified as desert. Increasing rates of desertification have been reported but not confirmed.

Loss of Biodiversity

About 10 percent of the world's plants, mammals, birds, reptiles, and amphibians are found in China. Despite the substantial decline in the rate of population growth in China, population pressures and development activities have damaged the country's biodiversity resources. The large population and limited land have meant loss of habitat to logging, fuelwood collection, livestock grazing, and agricultural and aquacultural production. The Chinese Academy of Sciences reports that 200 plant species have become extinct in China, and 5,000 more have become endangered in recent years because of human activity (CCICED June 2001).

As in many other countries, biodiversity protection in China has focused on establishing nature reserves. New environmental protection and wildlife conservation laws put into effect in 1989 facilitated development of a comprehensive system of nature reserves and rationalized categories of protection for endangered wildlife. The amount of protected areas has dramatically expanded over the past 10 years, and China's 926 nature reserves now cover some 77 million hectares—7.6 percent of the country's land area. But staffing, management budgets, training and performance standards have not kept pace with the expansion of reserves. Few areas are protected or managed effectively, and if present trends continue, biological diversity in many critical nature reserves will diminish.

An international working group on biodiversity recently concluded that the "effectiveness of China's protected area network for the protection of biodiversity and ecosystem functioning is highly deficient due to the lack of adequate implementation. The conflict between conservation and development is more evident in the highlands, where there has been substantial improvement in the living conditions through investment in roads and other improvements. Therefore, often it is not clear who will benefit from conservation" (CCICED June 2001).The report makes a variety of recommendations, including the need for multisectoral coordinating mechanisms to increase efficiency and to reconcile conflicting goals between high productivity agriculture and biodiversity conservation through such steps as more use of native vegetative and other species, and the establishment of guidelines and criteria for ensuring biodiversity conservation. The report also points out that the ambiguity in the use of the term "ecological reconstruction" has created a sense of uncertainty among those who manage and work the land. Hence, there is need to review the implementation of government regulations for protected areas to increase the emphasis on effectiveness rather than quantity.

Staffing resources are modest, and local bureaus often have only part-time and inadequately trained staff to implement and enforce antidegradation policies. With the constrained fiscal atmosphere, local leaders frequently agree to assign resource rights to the agencies responsible for protecting state resources. Leaders then encourage the agencies to use those rights to generate income for staff salaries and other expenses, often leading agency officials to exploit the resources they are charged with protecting. The system lacks independent monitoring or oversight to resolve conflicts between growth and the environment.

Estimates of the losses incurred by environmental degradation range from 0 to 15 percent of GDP, but the higher estimates are based on anecdotes and assumptions rather than on systematic scientific data and analysis. The Research Center on Environment and Development of the Chinese Academy of Social Science (1992) estimated that environmental pollution and ecological degradation reduce GDP by 7 percent and concluded that agriculture accounted for about half of that loss. Another analysis found large but declining losses in GDP from ecological destruction between 1985 and 1993. A similar study concluded that pollution and degradation costs in 1992 were 4 percent of GDP.

China's Environmental Laws

China's environmental strategy in rural areas is based on three main policy tools:

1. Direct regulation
2. Targeting and planning cleanup and rectification campaigns
3. Reliance on state-mandated technological improvements to reduce the adverse consequences of certain production practices (Sinkule and Ortolano 1995).

In practice, little use is made of economic incentives to combat environmental deterioration (Sinkule and Ortolano 1995). Yet tough regulations and incentive-compatible institutions are essential to implement these largely administrative-based policies (World Bank 1992).

The Environmental Protection Law of 1979 is at the apex of a hierarchy of laws covering a broad range of issues, and it defines the nation's general principles and goals for protecting the environment, but it has few specific regulations (Smil 1984 contains a translation of the law). Laws to protect specific parts of China's natural resource base were supposed to be created in subsequent years, and in fact, such laws have proliferated.

Some of the strictest laws and regulations issued by the Central State Council pertain to the protection of China's forests. Rules put in place in the late 1990s state that timber-cutting quotas are to be established exclusively under the national plan. In theory, this means that central authorities determine all logging activity in China's forest areas.

China passed its current forestry law in 1984 and modified it most recently in April 1998. From a comparative international perspective, the following two features are of interest. First, the law acknowledges a high degree of decentralization in forest sector management yet asserts a high degree of central control over forestland issues and the disposal of forest products, including the requirements of permits for cutting and transporting wood approved by the Central State Council. Second, the law says little about the need for plans to ensure sustainable forest management. The exception—step-by-step felling of trees to be adopted according to different conditions—is mentioned, perhaps because the state manages all forests and has imposed strict bans on logging of most natural forests.

China has, however, begun to address issues of sustainable forest management with the support of some Global Environment Facility (GEF) projects under the World Bank–WWF alliance.

China's Environmental Agencies

The State Environmental Protection Commission is the main unit situated at the central level for managing the environment and overseeing policy implementation. The executive arm is SEPA. Below SEPA are environmental protection bureaus in all provincial administrative regions. Each provincial organization runs its own network of prefectural and county environmental protection bureaus.

This national environmental protection system is responsible for all environmental affairs in China. At the central level the main task is to work out general principles for each sector's policies and set national standards for environmental quality (Wu 1987). Local agencies are left to implement and enforce these policies (Qu and Li 1984).

China's SEPA, one of the most active in the developing world in environmental management, has been aggressively seeking international finance to support its domestic efforts in the areas of new emission-efficient technologies for industry and biodiversity conservation. The State Forest Administration is largely responsible for promoting land use changes and management of national parks. This creates rivalry and creative tensions between the two organizations, particularly in mobilizing international resources.

SEPA has chosen not to claim jurisdiction over many of China's environmental and natural resource problems (World Bank 1992), although that stance is changing. Interviews with SEPA officials reveal that leaders have prioritized the nation's problems and use their limited budget to address only a subset of them. SEPA, after being raised to the ministerial level in 1998, would like to assert itself in many areas, but has to struggle with the various ministries/departments that have traditionally handled such areas.

SEPA leaders admit that they have had to leave implementation of many sector-specific environmental policies to sectoral ministries. In particular, SEPA has elected not to become directly involved in most rural natural resource and environmental management problems, though it has begun to take an interest in reclaiming jurisdiction over the management of some natural resources, such as those in natural reserves.

Each ministry has established its own environmental management hierarchy. The implementation path for all protection measures typically passes down through the lower levels of the administrative hierarchies (provinces, counties, townships), creating a three-tier Agro-Environmental Protection System (AEPS).

At the top of the system is the provincial station, an office set up under the Bureau of Agriculture in the provincial capital. At the county level there are either established AEPS offices or the counties have built up strong, committed networks to address rural environmental problems. At the lowest level, the township, there typically is an agro-environmental specialist in charge of executing environmental rules and regulations.

Decentralized Management

China has four main forest regions managed by one of two regimes. Since the 1950s, two distinct management forms—the state and the collective—have shared control of China's forests (Ross 1988).

Collective management began in the 1950s, with 96 percent of the land in rural areas placed under the jurisdiction of village (brigade) leaders (Richardson 1990). In the 1960s and 1970s, however, the emphasis on national grain policy and party ideology discouraged local villages from investing in forests, and state forest farms frequently encroached on the forests of local collectives. By the 1980s, the state managed only 20 percent of China's forests, but it controlled the vast majority of its high-quality timber reserves. Today, 4,000 state forest farms employing more than 500,000 people (ZGLYNJ 1987; Yin 1994) carry out almost all forestry production within their jurisdictions and report to local bureaus of the State Forestry Administration (Richardson 1990).

Most of the major forest areas in the south and north-central parts of China are managed by collectives. The north-central region has less natural forest than the southern region and has only begun to encourage its collectives to engage in forestry activities on a large scale. State management is mostly found in the forests of China's northeast provinces. Forests in southwestern China in Yunnan and Sichuan provinces have nearly equal division of forest area between the different regimes.

Problems in Implementation

The array of new regulations is designed to provide policy implementation guidance to leaders in specific sectors. The expanded set of laws also is supposed to give more substance to the environmental protection law. While China's environmental legal framework is impressive in scope, many observers have criticized it. The laws are said to be vague (He 1991; Smil 1984 1990) and to lack enforcement mechanisms (World Bank 1992; Ma 1997). Many are also said to lack coordination (Qu and Li 1984). Another criticism is that final ordinances do not contain specific standards, finite schedules, or other provisions to facilitate monitoring and enforcement (Sinkule and Ortolano 1995; Ma 1997). and Qu and Li (1984) concluded that since most of China's environmental laws lack substance; effective environmental control relies on the efforts of those charged with implementation.

Sinkule and Ortolano (1995) and Ma (1997) find that poor training of environmental officials impedes implementation of environmental regulations in well-funded and more experienced urban and industrial networks. The level of training of their rural counterparts is even lower. In most townships and counties, personnel at the agricultural technical station have at most a background in agronomy or agricultural management—and most have only high school technical training. Poorly trained staff have difficulty organizing and carrying out systematic monitoring and enforcement.

Another problem has been the weak commitment of local leaders to environmental concerns, but this may be changing. The logging ban has created awareness of the drastic steps that the government at the national level is adopting to deal with the problems of environmental degradation. Yet, there is no independent watchdog agency currently. In the past, production-oriented bureaus and agencies have had obvious conflicts of interests. Sectoral leaders have had an incentive to implement protection efforts less strictly. Friction between production and protection became more visible at the local level, where growth in output and income came into more direct conflict with environmental concerns. Not even better laws and a more committed and better-funded and trained central environmental protection agency could overcome the weaknesses of a system that breaks down at the lowest level of implementation.

Local officials have faced demanding production targets, receiving monetary bonuses and promotions when targets were met and facing penalties when they were not (Rozelle 1994). However, there have been almost no rewards or punishments explicitly tied to success or failure in executing environmental laws. Local leaders have had no incentive to increase the weight of protection in their decision-making calculus. If there was a tradeoff between production and the environment, the rational official would be expected to sacrifice environment goals or even make decisions that led to greater environmental degradation to meet production goals. This has been evident at many state forest enterprises where production received primacy over the long- term sustainability of the timber supply.

While charging local officials with the responsibility of protecting the environment and meeting production standards, China's system has achieved only the production-oriented goal. But the situation has changed considerably since the introduction of the logging ban and the land conversion policy.

After carrying out case studies in nine western provinces, the Forest and Grasslands Taskforce found that an absence of detailed guidelines and performance indicators has resulted in mixed implementation of the 1998 logging ban and cropland conversion policy. Without location-specific guidelines, different provinces have interpreted the policy in diverse ways and have pursued their own implementation strategies, often adding their own objectives to national policy objectives. This variation reflects both the diversity of conditions in the provinces and hence the particular needs of their populations, but also their own interpretation (and at times confusion in interpretation) of policy.

In some cases the implementation of the policy has been overzealous, as found in Xinjiang Province, which introduced a total logging ban of its own, rather than implementing the more flexible national logging ban. At the same time, the province has allowed free grazing of cattle in forested areas, with less than expected policy results of the soil erosion goals (CCICED 2001).

The Reform of Forest Policy

The policies of the reform period that began in the early 1980s represented a sharp break from the preceding socialist era and were pursued as a more effective way to use the forest sector's natural resources. Before the reform era, China's forest management system relied on command and control to implement the central government's forest sector plan (Ross 1988) rather than on prices to create incentives for producers to allocate resources efficiently. Timber producers received low prices, retained little of their profits, and were promoted if they met production targets. With few positive incentives and tight financial constraints, forest managers undertook few non-harvesting activities (such as replanting). Strict control and poor incentives extended to the collectively managed forests, where local needs and the state's procurement plan determined production plans. No extra-plan or over-quota markets existed.

Recognizing the shortcomings of this system, national policymakers began to identify reforms to promote more efficient resource use—shifting the emphasis from cutting natural forests to forestation and replanting, diversifying the output of the forest sector, and reducing the economy's dependence on the output of state-run forest farms (ZGLYNJ 1992). There were also efforts to liberalize economic activity in the forest sector by eliminating rules that stifled innovation. Forest leaders pursued these goals by making a clear division of responsibilities for forests between the collective and state sector, and launched a series of measures in each sector to encourage more efficient resource use.

Reforming the State-run Sector

Despite reform rhetoric, the basic features of the centrally planned forestry industry—production plans, controlled prices, and fixed wage payments to forest managers and workers (instead of profit-sharing schemes)—remained throughout most of the early reform period (ZGLYNJ 1987). Because top-level forest farm managers almost never expected to stay long at any given site, their planning horizons were often quite short.

Reform officials promoted a farm manager responsibility system—the Household Responsibility System—to encourage farm officials to use forests more efficiently. Forest farms were given marginal latitude for investing excess profits, although forest managers-cum-bureaucrats still focused their efforts primarily on meeting annual production goals. A new accounting system effectively removed one of the main constraints on reforestation (Ross 1988)—forest farms had not been allowed to receive reimbursement for expenses incurred in reforestation efforts—while a revised price structure more accurately reflected the opportunity cost of timber (Li et al. 1987; Rozelle and Jiang 1993).

The state forest farm system evolved more slowly, and recent problems and changes in the way state enterprises are managed have gradually removed fiscal and financial support from many of the unprofitable forest farms. This has led to unemployment and reports that entire communities, frequently in remote corners of the nation, have been impoverished. Some communities have reported uneconomic and unsustainable mining of remaining old-growth forests and younger plantations.

Reforming the Collective Sector

Forest officials carried out more radical measures in the collective sector, implementing a "three-fixed" reform policy that gave individuals and village leaders more control over forest resources and more responsibility for their management (ZGLYNJ 1987). The three-pronged approach established the following:

- The first part of the policy clearly delineated the boundaries of forest land under collective control. This helped prevent state forest farm managers from claiming the forest resources of collectives, a practice that had reduced the collective's incentive to invest in forest resources (DDZGDLY 1985).
- The second part fixed the rights of individuals to the output produced on household forest plots assigned by the village (Richardson 1990; Yin 1994). These rights, which policy architects believed would induce more efficient harvesting and planting efforts, were monitored by officials in the forest ministry's local branches.
- The third part gave local forest stations the ultimate responsibility for forest use by allowing officials to limit the quantity of timber products that could be harvested and marketed by collective managers and individuals. The policy also required forestation efforts on state and collective land by all rural residents.

But the lack of a systematic method for imposing these regulations, the weakness of the enforcement mechanisms, the differing interpretations of policy directives, and the history of policy uncertainty in the rural sector created an unpredictable situation for collective forest managers. Many sources report that collective forest managers responded by quickly harvesting trees legally and quasi-legally, exploiting a resource perceived to be only temporarily under village control (Li et al. 1987; Smil 1984).

Exacerbating the atmosphere of uncertainty was a series of rapid land tenure policy changes aimed at preventing indiscriminate felling and promoting more efficient forest use (DDZGDLY 1985). Still, uncertainty of land tenure continues to be a problem. In some areas the government took private mountain lands from individuals (Menzies and Peluso 1991). In other areas it reassigned tenure several times in the 1980s (Zuo 1994a). Some regional authorities invoked rules prohibiting or circumscribing the use of the forest (Rozelle et al. 1993). Policies governing timber markets were equally unpredictable.[2]

The Recent Taskforce Analysis of China's Forest Sector

In July 2000, China established a multidisciplinary, multinational Taskforce on Forests and Grasslands in the Development of the West under the China Council for International Cooperation on Environment and Development (CCICED 2001).[3] The taskforce's objective is to support the Chinese Government in addressing knowledge, policy, planning, and implementation gaps, integrating and building upon recent and ongoing quality work, and providing independent advice to policymakers. Part of its work is to examine the impacts of the logging ban and cropland conversion policy and explore their implications for achieving sustainable environmental and developmental goals.

The taskforce completed, in phase 1 of its two-year work plan, a report on land conversion that included 10 case studies in nine provinces in which it conducted surveys of more than 1,400 households to assess the impacts of the new policies. The taskforce found that the willingness of local governments and farmers to participate has been extremely high. This can be attributed to the facts that the land being converted from agriculture to grasslands and forestland was mostly low-productivity land, and that three successive droughts had affected large parts of the upper reaches of the Yellow River in the northwest.

But the taskforce also determined that strict, top-down implementation of policy in many areas has resulted in inadequate delivery of assistance, confusion and disagreement regarding targets, a low survival rate of trees planted, a technical bias that favors tree planting over planting of other types of vegetation, and heavy reliance on activities limited to the forest sector. Location-specific solutions, substantial structural adjustment, and appropriate performance indicators are much needed.

The researchers were also worried as to whether the planting of economically profitable trees, as demanded by many households, would achieve the intended ecological objectives. To control land conversion and water and soil erosion, the taskforce suggests that a more integrated, multisectoral approach could yield better results. Tree selection needs to be improved as well. There is also a strong argument against the current policy on wasteland forestation.

In studying the impacts of the land conversion program, the task force found that land conversion has improved the economic situation of farmers in the short term, but has also resulted in reduction of on-farm household employment, and has increased uncertainty about household ownership rights to land and trees. The conversion of open access land to some form of managed land has increased the risk of local conflicts. Subsidies have benefited those households which owned more land, resulting in a wider gap between them and poorer households. The financial effects of the new policies at the provincial and local levels were found to have generally been positive, whereas achievement of national objectives was less than ideal.

The taskforce cautioned that the real challenge of the land conversion policy, after the assistance is ended, would be sustainability. Specifically, the taskforce recommends that land conversion should be integrated into watershed management, that the scale of wasteland plantings should be reduced in order to reduce costs and increase ecological benefits, that the rationality of continued compensation should be explored, and that property rights to converted land should be reinforced. For institutional and financing arrangements, a more integrated approach to policy implementation is recommended.

Taskforce Findings on the NFPP

In contrast to widespread enthusiasm about the land conversion policy among rural inhabitants, there have been mixed feelings toward implementation of the 1998 NFPP. The policy will improve the finances of state-owned forest enterprises but cause a loss of income for well-off enterprises and local communities dependent on the timber economy.

Initial implementation of the logging ban was much more problematic than that of the conversion policy. In the absence of detailed guidelines for implementation, different provinces interpreted the policy differently and pursued their own implementation strategies, often adding their own objectives to the national policy objectives at the provincial and county levels.

The policy volatility of provincially imposed bans on logging has hurt investment in forestry. The taskforce recommends compensation for private investments made prior to the logging ban. The taskforce findings show that local agencies don't have the means to respond to the emergency financial problems of households, causing further distrust of government policy.

Impacts of the NFPP

The taskforce concluded that income reduction for households affiliated with forest enterprises has resulted in local economic recession, increases in school dropout rates, etc. On the positive side, laborers have been released from the arduous work of logging. In terms of national objectives, the policy appears to have helped accelerate the process of natural forest protection. However, ecological goals have not been fully met, and there is evidence that the ban may be resulting in the exportation of deforestation to other regions and other countries.

The task force recommends lifting the logging ban in collective forests while providing compensation for the losses suffered by private investors and forest farmers.

The taskforce also recommends that a cost-benefit evaluation of the policy should be conducted because its socioeconomic costs have proven to be much higher than anticipated, that various objectives should be consolidated, that technologies that reduce costs and increase benefits should be adopted, and that monitoring and evaluation should be greatly enhanced (CCICED 2001).

The World Bank–China Relationship: Responsive to Changing Needs

The Bank has invested more than $1 billion in loans and credits in China's forests. That volume is large even for China, which is the Bank's largest overall borrower, and demonstrates the emphasis that the Bank and China have placed on the forest sector.

The Bank's program has been driven mostly by China's demand for specific projects, which have evolved from relatively simple efforts—developing forest plantations on state and collective farms—to more complex projects with objectives ranging from rural poverty alleviation to farmer participation in the production of trees, to management of protected areas and biodiversity conservation. The broader orientation in project design has been particularly noticeable since the mid-1990s.

The Bank's assistance has helped increase China's forest cover by nearly 3.2 million hectares, along with an additional 600,000 hectares of tree orchards included in agricultural projects. The program has conserved soil and water and created employment and incomes for nearly two million poor.

Forest expansion has provided for the sequestering of approximately 20 percent of China's annual carbon emissions while meeting consumption needs and reducing pressure on China's natural forests and remaining biodiversity. But the Bank's contribution, while large in absolute terms, is still small in the overall picture of forest management in China.

The Bank's project management has been responsive to new needs and changes in the government's policy priorities. The emphasis on forest projects in poorer, more environmentally fragile areas reflects the rising government priorities of poverty alleviation and natural resource management. When China first began borrowing for forest sector development, there was neither a permanent national legislation to protect the forests, nor was there an integrated national poverty alleviation policy. Now it has both.

Keys to Program Success

The reasons for the success and increasing sophistication of China's forest sector projects are difficult to determine and may not be replicable in other countries. But a review of the project documentation and interviews with people familiar with the Bank's operations suggest several underlying factors.

First, the Chinese government—not the Bank—drives policy dialogue in China. Thus, the Bank's 1991 forest strategy has had less influence on the Bank's work in China than have the needs and priorities as determined by the government. Whereas the 1991 strategy focused rather exclusively on the conservation of tropical moist forests and banned Bank financing of logging equipment for forest production activities in tropical moist forests, the Bank's program in China first focused on ways to increase alternative supplies of forest products to meet domestic needs, while reducing pressure on natural forests. It was only after the logging ban in 1998 that China could afford to bear the costs of imposing more direct measures to protect natural forests, and become actively committed to addressing the environmental concerns related to forests.

Second, China boasts macroeconomic stability and an expanding economy that have enabled it to undertake its current major investment in land conversion from agriculture to forests and grasslands.

Third, Bank staff and China's project managers have been among the more qualified and staff turnover has been low. The same staff members have managed, appraised, developed, and implemented all but two of the projects. While these people deserve much of the credit for the successes, their involvement in such a large part of the portfolio makes it hard to separate the project implementation effect from their impact, although it would be appropriate to stress that the primary responsibility for achieving results on the ground rests with the Bank's borrower and hence the credit goes largely to the Chinese.

The continued success of the Chinese forest sector can also be traced to several systemic factors. The forest sector's relatively low profile in China has made the Bank's participation important, and the support of the State Forestry Administration at all jurisdictional levels has contributed to successful project design and implementation. The progression from relatively simple and one-dimensional projects to increasingly complex ones has allowed for relatively low-cost learning. New projects incorporate lessons from old ones.

Shortcomings and New Challenges

In spite of this success, the Bank's work on China's forests has had some shortcomings and faces new challenges. Bank attempts to engage policymakers and the academic community in systematic dialogue about forest sector policy were limited until recently and, when pursued, ineffective. This may be a result of the Bank's limited sphere of contact with the section of the State Forest Administration responsible for multilateral aid. But Bank managers responsible for China at the time of the OED Review of implementation of the Bank's forest policy in China argued that the larger reason was the reluctance of Chinese officials to discuss policy at a pace and pattern other than that determined by the government. Relatively few people, even in China's central government, were aware of the Bank's large and important forest work. This had probably limited its impact. NGOs in China were also uninformed about the Bank's activities and believed that their opinions had not been heeded.

But this state of affairs has changed greatly since the controversy surrounding the Western Poverty Reduction Project and the subsequent withdrawal by the government of China of that project.

Almost no analytical work is available to assess whether the Bank is working in the right areas of the forest sector. Interviews with current and past project managers and past division leaders reveal low demand for systematic information about sector performance and project impact. Although the Bank has invested more than $1 billion in China's forest sector, it has never undertaken a sector review.

Until recently, most of the Bank's work has been in the state-run forest sector, although research shows that the most dynamic forest activities involve rural households despite the regulatory, credit, tenure, and other constraints they face. The focus on the state-run sector and work with collective forest farms may also have limited the impact of the projects on poverty. More projects are targeting the poor areas, but not necessarily the poorest in those areas (Lele et al. 2000).

Nonetheless, changes in the forest sector's portfolio during the 1990s have been surprisingly consistent with several of the non-controversial aspects of the 1991 Bank strategy. Recent projects have been more focused on poverty reduction (Loess Plateau and Forest Development in Poor Areas), institutional reforms (Sustainable Forest Development Project and Nature Reserves Management Project), and better integration of forests with agriculture and watershed management (Forest Resource and Development Protection and Loess Plateau). These shifts probably resulted from China's policy priority changes and the assimilation into forest strategy of other Bank trends (and developing countries in general), such as the greater emphasis on poverty alleviation and concern for biodiversity.

The Need for an Integrated Approach

Whatever its relative strengths and weaknesses, future Bank work on Chinese forest management faces challenges. China has graduated from low-interest to commercial-rate loans, so China's leaders may not want to continue borrowing for forest sector work—especially for loans that address poverty and environmental concerns at a time when the terms of Bank lending are hardening. As for the Bank continuing and expanding its work into the household sector, activities in the lending package should be closely monitored to determine what works and what does not. It is not known which poor counties in China benefit from forest sector projects. A more integrated approach, including projects that increase the productivity of local agricultural resources and offer off-farm job opportunities, could enhance forest work.

For forest projects to succeed, Bank staff must find cheaper forestry systems with quicker payback for which households will be willing to borrow at commercial rates. Issues of land tenure and the security of participants' investments in an environment where contractual terms are difficult to enforce must be addressed. Land tenure systems in China are complex and often play multiple roles (including social welfare and social security), and changes will be difficult to enforce unless they are designed to meet community needs.

Managing the exchange rate risk on long-term, dollar-denominated loans is also a concern. Until China can address the chronic shortcomings of its fiscal system—which systematically underfunds policy-mandated expenditures, leading to over-taxation, investment diversion, and exploitation of local resource bases (including forests), there is little hope that poverty alleviation or environmental management projects can be sustainably implemented.

Although Bank projects have had important environmental and economic benefits, the biggest impact on forests may have come through overall changes in the Chinese economy—that is, progress in poverty alleviation, economic growth, and agricultural intensification. There is evidence that China's forest policy and regulations may have negatively affected forests. Because of the investment concentration on state farms and China's early suspicion of households, China's forest policies probably have had less of a direct impact on poverty than they could have had.

The impact of government controls (harvesting quotas, transportation permits) on producer incentives has received less attention than investments related to production. This, together with production and market intelligence, will become important as emphasis on participation and private sector investments increases.

Officials in China claim that the Bank needs to be involved in policy reforms in the forest sector, particularly on issues of post-harvest processing, reform of forest enterprises, and the role of the private sector. But Bank staff argue that the government has not been willing to take steps to reform state enterprises, promote private investment, or improve incentives. Besides, the Bank has lacked the necessary expertise on policy and management issues related to the state forest enterprises. China's policy of lending to households for tree planting rather than providing outright subsidies requires close examination. The government has said that because it proposes to spend massive public funds to improve the environment, mostly in the form of transfers, the Bank must do the same or there will be severely limited demand for IBRD resources. The government has expressed doubt about farmers' interest in forest loans at higher interest rates and has also expressed concern that new projects will not be able to reach the poorest farmers. Bank task managers are mobilizing concessional or grant funds from other donors, but the task is difficult. Donor interest in China's forests is less than that for the pristine rainforests of Latin America.

China will need to increase its supply of timber and reforest large tracts of land. The Bank has helped make China's forestation programs more efficient and has improved soil and water conservation and carbon sequestration. Thus, there are good reasons to continue World Bank investment in plantations in China, which will not only help to save China's natural forests but also avert increased pressure on domestic and global forest resources. The Sustainable Forestry Development Project under preparation seeks to further expand afforested area and is a good start toward meeting the future wood needs of the people of China.

The Bank has begun to diversify the participants in its dialogue with China by reaching out to the wider academic community, a broader range of institutions, and non-governmental organizations working in the forest sector. This diversification needs to be deepened, particularly to address the socioeconomic and environmental challenges that the new logging ban poses and to consult these resources in evaluating current projects and developing future ones.

Without investment in plantations, China will have to import more, thereby increasing the pressures on regional forest resources. Chinese officials have said that they need more investment in plantations as a way of making the logging ban stick, but they are not certain that expansion of the plantations can be implemented without subsidies. Their case for concessional lending for forest sector management from the Bank is based on the fact that even a poor country like China is committing such large amounts—mostly in the form of government transfers—that the global community also needs to help with grant or near-grant funds to ensure that China protects its biodiversity, natural reserves, and poor people, while minimizing pressures on global forests.

Notes

1. If the overall timber area grew only marginally, one way that these figures can be reconciled is if there were 21 million hectares of newly afforested area that loggers clear cut, replacing only 5 million hectares of old growth or natural timber forests. Eleven of the 18 million hectares of the net increase would then be accounted for by shelterbelts and commercial plantations. Approximately 2 million hectares have been added by fuel wood forests, natural reserves, and other special forests.
2. After eliminating procurement quotas in the mid-1980s, the government temporarily closed timber markets, increased monitoring, and imposed fines (Li et al. 1987). A year later, the government partially reversed policies and liberalized markets for substandard timber products, causing some households to harvest forest products prematurely. In a subsequent period, access to all markets was again limited.
3. CCICED, an organization composed of senior Chinese policymakers and representatives from Chinese and international think tanks, is chaired by Chinese Vice

Premier Wen Jiabaoco. It is co-chaired by Professor Shen Guo Fang, Vice President of the Chinese Academy of Engineering, and Uma Lele, Senior Advisor in the World Bank's Operations Evaluation Department since June 2000. The taskforce is made up of six Chinese and six international experts and involves collaboration with several Chinese institutions in the 12 Western provinces falling within its jurisdiction. The China Council on International Cooperation for Environment and Development (CCICED) is an important innovation. It brings to bear domestic and international expertise, involves heads of line ministries and think tanks on the Council, reports to the Dy. Premier of China, and through collaborative work between international and domestic experts using a multisectoral, nonpartisan approach working outside their existing institutional structures, it provides an opportunity to offer independent advice to line ministries in a non-threatening way.

References

CCICED. 2001. Working Group on Trade and Environment Report. China: Timber Trade and Protection of Forestry Resources. August.

CFFA *(China Facts and Figures Annual)*. Gulf Breeze, FL: Academic International Press, various years.

DDZGDLY (Editorial Committee). 1985. *Dangdai Zhongguo di Linye* [Current Situation of China's Forests]. Beijing: China Social Science Press.

Ghimire, Krishna. 1994. "Conservation and Social Development: A Study Based on the Assessment of Wolong and Other Panda Reserves in China." United Nation Research Working Paper. Institute for Social Development.

Harkness, Jim. (forthcoming). "Forest and Conservation of Biodiversity in China: Threats and Prospects," *China Quarterly* 1998.

He, B. 1991. *China on the Edge: The Crisis of Ecology and Development.* San Francisco: China Books & Periodicals, Inc.

Heij, Bertlan, Zhou Fengqi, Toni Schneider. 2001. *Policy Options for Carbon Dioxide Emission Mitigation in China.* The Netherlands: Bilthoven.

Huang, J., and S. Rozelle. 1995. "Environmental Stress and Grain Yields in China." *American Journal of Agricultural Economics* 77(4):246–256 (November).

Huang, Jikun, Scott Rozelle, and Fangbin Qiao. 1998. "Private Holdings, Conservation, and the Success of China's Forest Policy in the Reform Era." Working Paper, Center for Chinese Agricultural Policy, Chinese Academy of Agricultural Sciences, Beijing, China.

Hyde, William F., Gregory S. Amacher, and William Magrath. 1996. "Deforestation and Forest Land Use: Theory, Evidence, and Policy Implications." *The World Bank Research Observer* 11(2):223–248.

Lardy, Nicholas. 1983. *Agriculture in China's Modern Economic Development.* Cambridge: Cambridge University Press.

Lele et al. 1999. "QAG Review of East Asia Rural Poverty Reduction Projects," January 12 memorandum.

Li, Jinchang, Fanwen Kong, Naihui He, and Lester Ross. 1987. "Price and Policy: The keys to Revamping China's Forest Reserves." In R. Repetto and M. Gillis (eds.), *Public Policies and the Misuse of Forest Resources.* Cambridge: Cambridge University Press.

Liu Can, Ma Tianle, and Xu Qin, Qizhen. 2000. "The Institutional Arrangements and Case Study for Community Forestry and Poverty Alleviation." Beijing: China Agriculture Publishing House.

Liu, Z., C. Findlay, and A. Watson. 1992. "Collective Resource Management in China: The Raw Wool Industry." In C. Findlay (ed.), *Challenges of Economic Reform and Industrial Growth: China's Wool War*. Sydney: Allen Unwin.

Ma, X. 1997. "Compliance, Enforcement, and Urban Waste Water Control in China." Unpublished Ph.D. Dissertation, Department of Civil Engineering, Stanford University, Stanford, CA.

Menzies, Nicholas, and Nancy Peluso. 1991. "Rights of Access to Upland Forest Resources in Southwest China." *Journal of World Forest Resource Management* 6:1–20.

Ministry of Agriculture (MOA). 1991. *Sustainable Agriculture and Rural Development in China: Policy and Plan*. Beijing: Document of Ministry of Agriculture.

Ministry of Forestry. 1998. "Report on 1993 to 1997 Wood Product Imports."

MOA [Ministry of Agriculture]. 1997. *White Paper on Agricultural Policy in 1996*. Beijing: China Agricultural Press.

National Environmental Protection Agency (NEPA) and State Planning Commission (SPC), People's Republic of China, Environmental Action Plan of China, 1991-2000. n.d.

NEPA. 1992. *Environmental Protection of Township Industries in China*. Beijing: China Environmental Science Press.

Qiao, Fangbin. 1997. "Property Rights and Forest Land Use in Southern China." Unpublished Masters Thesis, Chinese Academy of Agricultural Sciences Graduate School, Beijing, China.

Otsuka, Keijiro. 1997. "Property Rights and Forests in Africa." Working Paper, International Policy Research Institute, Washington, DC.

Qu, Geping, and Li, J. (eds.). 1984. *Managing the Environment in China*. Dublin, Ireland: Tycooly International Publishing Ltd.

QGSLZYTJ. 1991. *Quanguo Linye Tongji Ziliao* [National Forestry Resource Statistics]. Beijing: Ministry of Forestry.

_____. 1994. *Quanguo Senlin Ziyuan Tongji* [National Forest Resource Statistics]. Beijing: Ministry of Forestry, 1983–89.

Richardson, S. D. 1990. *Forests and Forestry in China*. Washington, DC: Island Press.

Ross, Lester. 1988. *Environmental Policy in China*. Bloomington: Indiana University Press.

Rozelle, Scott, Li Guo, Minggao Shen, Amelia Hughart, and John Giles. 1998. "Poverty, Networks, Institutions, or Education: Testing among Competing Hypothesis on the Determinants of Migration in China." Working Paper, Department of Agricultural Economics, University of California, Davis.

Rozelle, Scott, Susan Lund, Zuo Ting, and Jikun Huang. 1993. "Rural Policy and Forest Degradation in China." Working Paper, Food Research Institute, Stanford University.

Rozelle, S. 1994. "Decision Making in China's Rural Economy: The Linkages Between Village Leaders and Farm Households." *China Quarterly*, 137:99–124 (March).

Rozelle, S., H. Albers, and G. Li. 1998. "China's Forests Under Economic Reform: Timber Supplies, Environmental Protection, and Rural Resource Access." *Contemporary Economic Policy* 16,1:22-33.

Rozelle, S., and R. Boisvert. 1994. "Quantifying Chinese Village Leaders' Multiple Objectives." *Journal of Comparative Economics* 18:25–45 (February).

Rozelle, S. ,and L. Jiang. 1993. "Sustainable Agricultural and Rural Development Policy in China." Report to the Food and Agricultural Organization, ESPP Division, March.

Sinkule, B., and L. Ortolano. 1995. *Implementing Environmental Policy in China*. Westport, CT: Praeger Press.

Smil, Vaclav. 1984. *The Bad Earth: Environmental Degradation in China*. New York: M.E. Sharpe.
Sun, Changjin. 1992. "Community Forestry in Southern China." *Journal of Forestry* 90: 35–39 (June).
World Bank. 1992. *China Environmental Strategy Paper*. Washington, DC: World Bank.
_____. 1993. *World Development Report—Environment*. Washington D.C.: World Bank.
Wu, Zijin. 1987. "The Origins of Environmental management in China." In B. Glaeser (ed.), *Learning From China? Development and Environment in the Third World Countries*. London: Allen and Unwin.
Yin, Runsheng. 1994. "An Empirical Analysis of Rural Forestry Reform in China, 1978–90." Unpublished Ph.D. Dissertation, Warnell School of Forest Resources, The University of Georgia.
ZGLYNJ. 1986–1992. *Zhongguo Linye Nianjian* [Chinese Forestry Yearbook]. Beijing: Forestry Publishing House.
ZGNYNJ. 1995 to 1997. *Zhongguo Nongye Nianjian* [China Agricultural Yearbook]. China Agricultural Press: Beijing, China.
ZGTJNJ. 1980–1993. *Zhongguo Tongji Nianjian* [China Statistical Yearbook]. Beijing: State Statistical Bureau Press.
Zuo, Ting. 1995. "Non-timber Forest Use in China," Working Paper, Rural Development Institute, Yunnan Provincial Academy of Social Sciences, Kunming, China.
_____. 1994a. "Forest Structure Change in Yunnan, China since the 1950s—Investigations in Two Villages." Working Paper, Institute of Rural Economics, Yunnan Academy of Social Sciences.

4

India's Forests: Potential for Poverty Alleviation

Nalini Kumar and Naresh Chandra Saxena

India has the largest number of poor in the world, many of whom depend directly or indirectly on forests for a living. It is estimated that 200 million people in India are partially or wholly dependent on forest resources for their livelihoods. This estimate includes more than 68 million tribal people, a large percentage of whom live close to the forest areas and constitute the most disadvantaged section of society. Poverty, large and expanding human and livestock populations, the shrinking common property resource base, and unclear tenurial rights contribute to unrelenting pressure on the forests, resulting in severe degradation of the country's forest resources.

Degradation, not deforestation, is currently the major problem in India's forest sector. Deforestation was more important in the past. India's agricultural intensification has had a major positive impact by relieving pressure on the marginal lands on which most of the forests remain. But urbanization, industrialization, and income growth continue to place tremendous demand pressure on forests for products and services. The government owns 90 percent of the forests in India. Its past industrial policies have also adversely affected the country's forests in many ways. Subsidies on government-supplied raw materials reduced the profitability of investment in forests and encouraged wasteful use of resources. Per capita forest area in India is only 0.08 hectares, as against the world's per capita forest area of 0.64 hectares and the average of 0.5 hectares for all developing countries.

India has a well-articulated forest policy that has evolved over time. Forest policy in India since independence has passed through three distinct phases: industrial forestry, social forestry, and priority for environment and support for Joint Forest Management (JFM). But forest laws and the institutional capacity and incentives to enforce them have lagged in translating the national policy into an effectively implemented forest strategy. In addition, policy interpretation and implementation has seen India "graduating" from one phase to the next, instead of each new phase building on the preceding one with additional components to create a more comprehensive forest strategy. Graduating from one phase to another does not imply that the three phases are mutually exclusive. Although elements of the three phases overlap, the major shift in emphasis has resulted in weak support for, and implementation of the elements of an earlier phase. An ideal forest strategy for India would provide a balance among the three phases, namely industrial forestry, social forestry, and protection/regeneration, aspects that India has pursued successively in its policy phases since independence.

In the 1980s, the aim of the social forestry phase was to reduce pressure on natural forests by meeting the fuelwood and other wood product requirements of the local population from outside the forest areas, whose main use remained production of commercial timber. While social forestry was successful in increasing the supply of wood production, little community participation was achieved. The country's 1988 Forest Policy emphasized the environmental role of forests and the need to fulfill the subsistence requirements of the local population dependent on forests. This paved the way for the implementation of JFM. Since the early 1990s, the government has put increased emphasis on people's participation in forest resource protection and management. The JFM program was further promoted by a Government of India circular to all states and union territories providing guidelines for the involvement of village communities in the regeneration of degraded forests. JFM, introduced in many states in the early 1990s, involves villagers cooperating with state Forest Departments (FDs) in forest protection in exchange for a share in the usufruct and final harvest.

The JFM program in its present form can be traced to the Arabari experiment initiated by foresters in the state of West Bengal. This experiment provided a strong feedback for incorporation of the program in India's forest strategy. In many locations, voluntary groups were engaged in the protection of forests without any encouragement from the government. Subsequently, based on this initial experience, the process of institutionalizing people's participation in forest protection and regeneration began. This type of collective endeavor in protection and management of forests through people's involvement was later termed JFM.

JFM has led successfully to regeneration of forest cover in several states. However, there are several limitations of the JFM strategy. There are issues like returns from non-timber forest products (NTFPs), the relationship between JFM committees and the panchayats, intersectoral linkages, issues of gender and equity, conflict resolution, sustainability of the JFM program and benefit sharing arrangements which require urgent attention.

Multilateral and bilateral donors, have assisted the Government of India in its effort to slow losses of the country's forests and increase tree cover through a series of programs. The largest lenders for the forest sector have been the World Bank and Japan's Overseas Economic Cooperation Fund (OECF). Several donors supported the social forestry program in the 1970s, and some are currently financing JFM programs in Indian states.

Since 1991, the Global Environment Facility (GEF) has funded biodiversity conservation and climate change projects. As of January 1998, $142.38 million had been programmed for India under the GEF. A GEF grant administered by the United Nations Development Programme (UNDP) is helping India prepare its first national report to the Convention on Biological Diversity. UNDP and the Food and Agriculture Organization supported MOEF's National Forestry Action Program, completed in June 1999.

The Ford Foundation, whose activities in India began in the 1950s, has pursued several programs in the forestry sector and was instrumental in winning government support for JFM. The Foundation has also supported pioneering work on poverty measurement and alleviation policies. India is perhaps the only country in the world where the Bank has been continuously involved in the forest sector for over two decades. Since the Bank's approach has been to support the Government of India program, the Bank's forest strategy suffered from the same limitations as the government's.

The Bank's involvement in JFM is the largest experiment in participatory forest management ever funded by the Bank anywhere in the developing world. A two-pronged approach is followed to involve communities: increasing the stake of the neighboring communities in the management and utilization of the forests, and creating alternative sources of employment to reduce the pressure on forests. These include work on plantation and regeneration activities as well as building of sources of drinking water supply, approach roads, schools, check dams, and other facilities as a way of creating alternative incomes or incentives for villagers to cooperate with the FD in forest protection.

The Bank's lending to India has been relevant in the past. Through its support for India's forest strategy, the Bank has contributed positively to preserving natural forests, but it has not yet contributed to developing financially sustainable approaches to such outcomes, as was done in Costa Rica. By following a systemic approach toward building the capacity for production and management of good quality planting material, the Bank is helping build in-country capacity for production technology generation and transfer. It has helped India implement its forest strategy by bridging the financial resource gap and bringing critical but politically unpopular policy and institutional issues to the table. The Bank also has been instrumental in helping to change the attitude of the FDs toward working with the poor in tree/forest protection and regeneration to foster consensus on a new strategy of forest protection and management.

The Bank can contribute significantly to forest development and poverty alleviation in India in the future. India's legal, and institutional environments for the forestry sector are not yet right. By playing a catalytic role in bringing several policy and institutional issues to the table, the Bank can help focus attention on areas in need of reform. It could do more to focus attention on poor governance and excessive regulation, which manifests itself in poor service delivery, corruption, and wasteful public expenditure. Today, even with a well-defined forest policy, India lacks an effective strategy to meet the many diverse demands for forest products and services from the forest sector. Lack of an effective production strategy for wood products, keeps India dependent on imports, and may limit India's achievements in the long run.

The Current Status of India's Forests

About 64 million hectares, or 20 percent, of India's land are under forest cover. Those figures include both natural forests and plantations. The distribution of forest cover in India is very uneven: five states (Madhya Pradesh, Arunachal Pradesh, Andhra Pradesh, Orissa, and Maharashtra) account for more than 50 percent of the forested areas. A large part of these forests are located in the poorest regions of India which have heavy tribal concentration. Some 90 percent of the country's forests are owned by the government. In addition to the usual environmental functions (watershed protection, groundwater recharge, prevention of soil and water run-off, wildlife refuge), forests in India serve important subsistence functions for millions of forest dwellers, including tribals.

Data on the extent of India's forest cover are inconsistent. Estimates by the Forest Survey of India (FSI) and the FAO, for example, differ not only in raw numbers but also in trends. FSI data include plantations on farms and degraded lands, while FAO calculates the rate of deforestation only on natural forests and reports plantations separately (based on government data). The plantation area is based on the number of trees planted or delivered from nurseries and assumes a survival rate of 70 percent, which many consider overly optimistic. Forest degradation, generally unobservable by satellite imagery, is more difficult to monitor than deforestation.

According to the FAO, the area under natural forests declined from 55.12 million hectares in 1980 to 51.73 million hectares in 1990. Meanwhile, the area under plantations increased from 3.18 million hectares in 1980 to 13.23 million hectares in 1990. By these estimates, total tree cover in India increased from about 58.3 million hectares in 1980 to about 65.0 million hectares in 1990. FSI data, on the other hand, report that forest cover declined marginally, from 64.08 to 63.73 million hectares between 1987 and 1999 (FSI 1999), thus reversing the trend between 1970 and 1985. While the data needs improvement, most observers believe that enough is known to support actions on various fronts. The data discrepancy notwithstanding, there is evidence that the rate of decline in tree cover in India has slowed significantly since the mid-1980s.

Several factors have contributed to the improved scenario. General economic prosperity,[1] the substitution of petroleum products for fuelwood in urban areas, and the process of agricultural intensification[2] have reduced the pressure on India's forests. Meanwhile, the financial contribution of forests to the revenues of the states in India has fallen dramatically since Independence because of the expansion of the industrial and services sectors. This change enabled many states to forego incomes from logging and to clamp a general ban on green felling in the late 1980s. Other factors, such as fewer barriers to wood imports (which were about $1.8 billion in the 1999-2000 period), the natural spread of Prosopis juliflora shrubs (an excellent coppicer with high calorific value), and the success of tree crop forestry have also contributed to reducing the pressure on forests. Finally, the success of participatory policies, and joint forest management (JFM), which was introduced in many states during the 1990s, has also led to improvement in forest cover. After about a century of using a custodial approach, India today is returning to the idea of community management even though the state retains ownership of the forestlands.

India also has a network of preservation and protected areas for conserving flora and fauna and for studies of the dynamics of natural populations in undisturbed conditions. The protected area program grew from 10 national parks and 127 sanctuaries on 2.5 million hectares in 1970 to 83 national parks and 447 sanctuaries on more than 15 million hectares (about 4 percent of India's land) in 1997.

Supply and Demand for Forest Products

Data on supply and demand for timber, NTFPs, and fuelwood are also unreliable because a large amount of forest extraction is unreported. Estimates of demand for industrial wood (demand for timber, pulpwood, and poles minus demand of rural consumers for wood for house construction and agricultural implements) vary widely, as do estimates of supply. Although government forests and community and private lands are the usual sources of timber, only timber from government forests is reported in national timber production statistics.

A Center for International Forestry Research (CIFOR) paper (Mafa 2001), quoting FAO sources, concluded that per capita consumption of all main wood products in South Asia (i.e., including India) in 1995 was very low in relation to estimates for the entire Asia-Pacific region (see table 4.1). The South Asia average is particularly low (some 3 percent of the Asia average) for panel products but also for fiber and for paper and paperboard (11 percent). The low rate of consumption is only partly explained by low incomes in South Asia. The sheer numbers of the South Asian population would be expected to lead to higher levels of consumption.

Reported timber production in India accounts for less than half the demand of industrial wood. The excess demand reflects subsidies on the supply of wood to industry. The subsidies have created high profits and excess capacity in the sawmill and pulpwood industries, but without the incentives to increase domestic production, since private producers cannot compete with subsidized government supplies. The gap between demand and supply of industrial wood so far has been met through imports. If the rising demand is to be met from domestic sources, however, the area under tree cover and its productivity will need to be substantially increased. This would require India to have a clearer and stronger strategy to increase tree production.

Table 4.1
Per Capita Consumption of Timber for Wood Products

Country group	Consumption per '000 capita				
	Industrial roundwood (m3)	Sawnwood (m3)	Wood panels (m3)	Fiber for pulp (mt)	Paper and board (mt)
Industrialized Asia (Japan, Australia, New Zealand)	636	292	100	224	234
South Asia (including India)	23	16	0.4	3	3
Southeast Asia	162	32	9	14	17
Newly industrialized*	220	104	112	125	160
North Asia (excluding Japan)	81	22	9	28	24
Oceania	295	54	22	0	5
Asia-Pacific Islands	99	35	12	27	27

*Korea; Singapore; Hong Kong (SAR of China); Taiwan, Province of China

Source: FAO, 1998a, 1998b

The gathering of NTFPs (*sal* and *tendu* leaves, grasses, medicinal herbs, honey, gums and resins, oil seeds, tanning agents, dyes, etc.) is an important source of livelihood for many rural communities, whose residents remove several thousand tons of NTFPs from India's forests each year (Lele, Mitra, and Kaul 1994). Estimates of the earnings from these activities run from $208 million (Chaturevedi 1994) to $645 million annually (Shiva 1994). It is estimated that about 60 percent of the non-timber products that are removed from the forests go unrecorded and are consumed or bartered by some 15 million families living in and around forests (Shiva 1994). Large revenues flowing to the state exchequer from NTFPs have given the state a vested interest in marketing the products, with huge costs to the poor who rely on gathering them for their income and to the users of NTFPs.

Fuelwood is collected mostly for subsistence. Only about 15 percent of fuelwood is purchased; 62 percent is collected from forest and public lands, 23 percent from private lands (Leach 1987). But where fuelwood is easily accessible and the opportunity cost is low, fuelwood is also substituted for other fuels. Estimates of the demand for fuelwood vary by as much as 100 percent because it is difficult to assess the effects of such variables as local prices, the prices of substitutes, the size and location of user households, and price and income elasticity of demand. Wood, dung, and agricultural residues together meet an estimated 95 percent of the fuel needs of rural areas. Dung and agricultural waste are commonly used as fuel in such prosperous regions as the Punjab and Haryana, while wood continues to be the main domestic fuel in less endowed households and poorer regions (NCAER 1985). "Gobar" gas made from cow dung is a growing source of fuel for many better-off rural households. Consumption of wood (timber and fuelwood) in the country is substantially higher than what can be removed from forests sustainably (MOEF 1999).

Deforestation and Forest Degradation

The causes of deforestation and forest degradation in India are numerous and vary regionally. Large-scale commercial deforestation to meet the raw material needs of the expanding wood processing industry at subsidized prices continued in the postcolonial era, and rapid expansion of agricultural production caused conversion of large areas of forestland to agricultural uses. About 2.6 million hectares of forests were converted to agriculture before the Green Revolution in the 1960s slowed the process. Reduced fallow periods in shifting cultivation systems because of population pressures have also led to deforestation, especially in the tribal belts in northeastern and central India. Forest fires also degrade substantial amounts of forests in India, with about 3.5 million hectares being burned every year (MOEF 1999). Although several states have schemes to prevent forest fires, poor funding hampers their implementation.

Although the percentage of poor people in India has declined since independence, slow economic growth and rapid population growth left more than 300 million earning less than $1 a day in 2001. A large percentage of these people live in and around forests, exerting high degradation pressure. FSI data show that two-thirds of India's forest cover in 1997 was in tribal districts, where the incidence of poverty is more than 50 percent (Natrajan 1996). Approximately 1.5 million hectares of forestland are illegally occupied for agriculture and other uses (MOEF 1999).

India's large and growing livestock population also exert high degradation pressure on forests. Of the estimated 450 million head of livestock (Mukerji 1994), about 270 million graze in the forests (MOEF 1999). Fodder production has not kept pace with the increase in livestock; the fodder requirement for 2000 was projected at 844 million tons, compared with an actual supply of 504 million tons. Although India's national forest policies address grazing on state FD lands, they pay scant attention to grazing on wastelands and pastures managed by revenue departments and communities. These areas have deteriorated rapidly because of the absence of clear policy on use of the commons, thus increasing the grazing pressure on forests. Tenurial rights for these lands are also unclear. *Panchayats*[3] are expected to manage the lands, but their control is not absolute. All this suggests that there needs to be a stronger link between agricultural and forest policies than currently exists.

The Evolution of Forestry Policy and Administration in India

The relationship between the national government and the many state governments in India is a complex one, and nowhere is this more true than in matters of forest policy and administration. Forestry was the responsibility of the national government until 1935, when it was transferred to the states. It remained a state subject after India achieved independence in 1947, but steady inroads into India's natural forests for agricultural purposes and other development projects led to passage of a constitutional amendment in 1976 that added forestry to the concurrent list and made natural forests the joint responsibility of the national and state governments. In the same year, a report by the National Commission on Agriculture stressed the importance of achieving national self-sufficiency in the production of raw timber from tree plantations. Although the national government has the authority to enact laws on forestry issues, it must take the views of the states into account in doing so because the states are responsible for actual management of the forests. Moreover, the relationship between the Government of India and the state government depends on several factors, such as its contribution to the state budget and its political strength relative to the states at a given time.

The question of authority on forestry matters is also complicated by bureaucratic realities. The Indian Forest Service (IFS) is a nationwide service whose officials hold senior positions in both the national and state governments. The IFS is controlled by the Government of India. At the same time, however, the state governments control the rest of the subordinate state-level staff responsible for implementing forestry policies and budgets. The IFS has traditionally looked to the GOI for guidance, and its officers have traditionally seen state politicians as not very keen on conservation and wanting to give away forest lands for agriculture and development projects. On the other hand, they perceive the GOI to be guided by the long-term interest of the country in preserving forests.

Funding for the administration of forest policy comes from two sources: (i) the state funds routed through the principal chief conservator of forests in each state; (ii) funds received by state FDs as part of centrally sponsored schemes. GOI funding, however, accounts for less than 20 percent of forestry funding in the states, with the result that the national government's influence on state forestry administration is relatively weak.

In the mid-1970s, India adopted an overall policy on the use of forests that is customarily referred to as "social forestry." To assure that natural forests would be protected while continuing to serve as a domestic source of timber for wood processing purposes, the government decided that it would meet the needs of forest dwellers for fuelwood, fodder, and construction timber from outside the forest areas. In addition, forest development corporations were established in most of the states as autonomous public agencies whose purpose was to convert miscellaneous degraded forests into high-value plantations.

The Indian Forest Act of 1927, adopted soon after independence, continues to be the legislative foundation of the forest sector in India. Since independence, several states have enacted their own legislation, while others amended the act to suit local needs. The Forest Conservation Act of 1980 was the first legislative attempt to slow deforestation by controlling the actions of state governments. It limited the power of state governments to use forestlands for non-forest purposes without the permission of the central government. A state government wanting to do so must pay a fee and must identify an area of non-forest land of at least equal size for afforestation.

In 1984, the national government established MOEF to monitor state compliance with the law, but the ministry has proved to be a weak enforcer, and the states' record of compensatory afforestation has been poor. In the late 1980s, both the national and some state governments adopted new and more stringent policies on the use of natural forests. In 1986, an Environmental Protection Act was enacted that requires the assessment of any potentially adverse impact of public investment projects.

The awareness created by the energy crisis of the 1970s and 1980s about the importance of preserving renewable energy resources had important consequences for forests. The Report of the Advisory Board on Energy in the 1980s urged restrictions on the industrial use of wood where alternatives were available. In addition, several states imposed a ban on the felling of timber in the late 1980s.[4]

The Environmental Impact Assessment Notification Law of 1994 made environmental impact assessments mandatory for 29 categories of development activities (such as river valley projects, highways, and industrial and mining enterprises) when they involve investments of $10 million or more. With MOEF responsible for giving environmental clearance for those activities, the central government is able to identify projects with serious environmental implications and to insist on design modifications to mitigate harmful impacts. The environmental management plan provides for mandatory replacement of government forestland areas used, for example, for constructing canals. Degraded areas are to be planted with suitable tree species and protected with effective structural and nonstructural soil conservation measures.

The National Forest Policy of 1988

Even more significant was the national government's 1988 policy change. Under this policy, natural forests are to be treated first as an ecological necessity, second as a source of goods for local people (with emphasis on non-timber products), and third as a source of wood and other products for industry. The major role of Forest Development Corporations was changed to rehabilitation of wastelands. The policy set the target to increase forest cover to 33 percent of India's land area. It advocated that this area be further increased to two-thirds in the hills to prevent erosion and land degradation. Moreover, it called for an end to the practice of supplying timber to industry at concessional prices. It also advised industry to provide financial credit, technical advice, and transport services to local farmers interested in setting up tree plantations. Although the 1988 policy redefined the objectives of forest management, it did not envisage any direct role for forest dwellers in forest management.

Then, in 1990, the national government established guidelines that were sent to the state governments for the "involvement of village communities and voluntary agencies in the regeneration of degraded forests" (Saxena 1997). That was the beginning of JFM in India. For the first time, a government document specified the rights of local communities to forest lands, giving them usufruct for grasses and other non-timber forest products as well as a portion of the proceeds (ranging from 20 to 100 percent) from the sale of trees. The government also urged state FDs to take advantage of the expertise of nongovernmental organizations (NGOs) to build up community participation in the protection and development of degraded forestlands. Several state governments passed enabling resolutions to carry out the intent of the guidelines and started JFM programs. JFM is reported to be quite extensive (covering 14 million hectares out of a total of 26 million hectares of degraded forests) although the quality and sustainability of protection are variable across states.

While JFM has protected degraded forestland, it was not extended to include forestland under rich forest cover until the guidelines for JFM were revised in 2000. The Bank-supported West Bengal Forestry Project attempted to put the luxuriant forest areas in northern Bengal under JFM, but this effort was not effective. The major issue in luxuriant forest is what returns can be guaranteed to local communities to generate sustained interest in protection. Logging is banned in these areas, so communities cannot expect a share of the final harvest. If the forests are in good condition, nearby communities probably have already been getting the benefits from the non-timber forest products. This raises the question of whether there is any value in extending JFM to protect these areas.

Four factors have limited the implementation of the 1990 guidelines and the 2000 revision (see Box 4.1). Since they are non-statutory and advisory statements issued by the national government, they lack the force of law. Second, state governments control the implementation of forest policies and may have different views than the national government on what needs to be done. Third, what is implemented in the field is generally what is provided for in the budget, and many policy prescriptions are not implemented because they lack financial support. Fourth, India's powerful bureaucracy has its own predilections and may filter what is demanded of it by governments. Radical changes in policies may therefore take longer than expected if government officials are unconvinced of the need for change.

State Monopoly on Trade in Non-Timber Forest Products (NTFPs)

NTFPs were nationalized in various states in India in the 1960s and 1970s, apparently with the intention of helping the poor. Nationalization meant that state FDs control trade in forest products by issuing licenses to engage in it to a limited number of contractual buyers and sellers of such commodities. State FDs and the licensed traders get large amounts of revenue from the trade, and there is also a certain amount of rent-seeking from trade in certain NTFPs, such as *tendu* leaves, which are used in the production of a type of cigarette called "bidi." Government officials argue that the private sector would exploit the poor who gather these items if unlicensed middlemen were allowed to buy and sell in the market. Nationalization, however, has reduced the number of legal buyers, and has choked the free flow of goods, and delayed the payment to the gatherers because FDs find it difficult to make prompt

---

Box 4.1
Summary of Current MOEF Guidelines for Strengthening JFM

Legal identity: All JFM groups in the country should be registered as "Societies" under the Societies Act in order to have a proper legal identity.

Involvement of women: Half of the general body and one-third of the executive committee members should be women.

JFM in good forests: JFM should be extended to good forest areas (except protected areas), though the maximum area per JFM group should be limited to 100 hectares and maximum revenue from the final harvest to 20 percent.

Microplans: In all new working plans, a JFM Working Circle should be introduced. In the case of existing working plans, special orders may be issued by the state FD to facilitate implementation of JFM microplans.

Conflict resolution: Multi-stakeholder working groups should be constituted at the state and division levels to resolve any conflicts arising during the course of implementation of JFM.

Self-initiated forest protection groups: The existing self-initiated forest protection groups need to be identified, recognized, and registered.

Monitoring and evaluation: Systematic monitoring of the JFM program should be undertaken every three years at the Forest Division level and every five years at the state level.

Source: Saxena 1996a; MOEF 1999

payment to licensed traders. This forces the traders to operate with higher margins in order to cover the late payments as well as to bribe the police and other authorities to ignore their illegal activities. The reality is that the current system reduces the income that forest dwellers would get from the gathering of NTFPs, and thus discourages gathering itself. It has been observed that nationalization also distorts administrative priorities. Analysts note that there is a need to end the government monopoly by denationalizing trade in NTFPs gradually. Encouraging the setting up of processing units within tribal areas is also recommended.

State Obstacles to Trade in Charcoal and Fuelwood

It is reported that some of the states in India have erected unnecessary obstacles to trade in charcoal and fuelwood. The authorities in the state of

Gujarat, for instance, require people who want to convert *prosopis* into charcoal (a very simple process) to engage in the time-consuming task of obtaining permits for the harvesting, conversion, and transportation of the product. Charcoal producers in Tamil Nadu also face several problems. Forest Officers there must issue a certificate of origin for the transport of charcoal to other states after verifying its stated origin. Charcoal producers, however, have encountered difficulties in satisfying the authorities about this matter (Saxena 1996b).

Comprehensive changes are necessary. *Prosopis* occurs in abundance in some parts of India, and the transformation of it into charcoal is a way of producing wealth out of wastelands, promoting employment opportunities, and improving land use. Another ill-conceived policy in some states (such as Karnataka) is to subsidize the cost of fuelwood for urban consumers, presumably to discourage headloaders[5] from cutting trees on public lands. Subsidizing the cost of a scarce commodity makes no economic sense. Moreover, the subsidy is unlikely to check the incentive to collect and market firewood. In West Bengal, many JFM committees believe that they could receive two to three times what they earn now if they themselves marketed the poles instead of the state Forestry Department. They also think that their returns would be even higher if the West Bengal government lifted its restrictions on interstate movement of poles.

The Effect of Low Tariffs on Forest Products on India's Forestry Sector

Low tariffs on imported pulp and other intermediate products, along with India's longstanding industrial policies, have adversely affected India's forestry programs. However, cheap imports of timber mean that a large part of domestic demand is satisfied from external sources, thus slowing deforestation in India. Yet, industry access to external sources of cheaper timber has been a disincentive to invest in tree plantations in India. The paper and pulp industry could be a major market for farm forestry. Subsidies on government-supplied raw material have further reduced the profitability of investment in tree plantations and encouraged wasteful use of resources (Gadgil 1991). Meanwhile, protectionist policies in other parts of the economy have slowed overall industrial growth and employment, which makes the rural population more dependent on rural employment, with consequently greater pressure on forests. Slow industrial growth has also lowered urban demand for wood products. Because imports could meet this demand, there was little pressure to increase domestic wood production.

The lack of an effective strategy for timber plantations and the absence of top-quality research and extension programs for forests in India have been major problems. (Norman Jones, personal communication June 1999). With strong internal demand (newsprint consumption, for example, is increasing

20 percent a year) and high timber imports, India clearly needs a better strategy for growing trees on plantations, farms, and wastelands. If India continues to use imports to meet its rising internal demand, it runs the risk of creating an adverse balance of payments as well as adverse impacts on natural forests elsewhere.

Proponents of JFM argue that India's forests can meet the country's social and environmental goals, and that the tree plantation sector should meet the rapidly growing commercial needs for forest products. But the government does not have a national production strategy. Much of the focus in recent years has been on JFM and forest regeneration. The enhancement of tree production on plantations will require new laws, secure tenurial arrangements, better access to credit, and predictable pricing and marketing policies.

Tree plantations can be good investments for the rural poor if their rights to land ownership are not disputed and not impeded by other laws or bureaucratic regulations. Even though the National Commission on Agriculture supported farm forestry in 1976, the law requires the written permission of state governments to harvest certain kinds of trees on private lands. These permitting procedures are cumbersome and discourage farm forestry. Since the national government's capacity to enforce the law is weak, the law has led to both corruption and harassment. In recent years the state governments have modified the laws, but the process remains slow and lacks political support. Recent Bank projects have also pressed for changes in law—with limited success.

The Complex Question of Rights to Forest Land

The legal framework for JFM is weak and does not promote secure tenure. In addition it is often difficult to clearly identify all the users of a forest

---

Box 4.2
Permit Procedure in West Bengal for Selling Trees Grown on Private Land

Application———> village council and the chief———> standing committee consisting of the Block Development Officer, Range Officer, and some elected members———> Range Officer———> local Land Reforms Officer to verify ownership of land ———> Range Officer to estimate the value of the plantation (this decides who issues permit)———> the buyer to make an affidavit and obtain a court order———> now the buyer can cut trees and apply to Range Officer for a transit permit———> Range Officer (or his superior, depending upon the value of the trees) to inspect and hammer the trees and issue transit permit.

Source: N.C. Saxena 2001

resource. The rights and privileges of forest dwellers in now-degraded forests (rights usually established in the colonial period) continue to be in force, and those rights often include permission to cut expensive timber. Often, more than one village has rights in the same forest, making it more difficult to promote village protection committees. Another problem is that new settlers without hereditary rights to the forest are deprived of its legal benefits and sometimes engage in illegal cutting. Still another problem is that people who live at a distance from the forest and who therefore are uninterested in forest management may hold rights to the forest that allow them to forage in it for fuelwood and other forest products. Migratory tribes from other states sometimes use forests for grazing their cattle, and their rights have been upheld by the Supreme Court (Vira 1993).

Conflicts like these make it difficult to protect forested lands, and rights to forest use in JFM areas should be put in harmony with the "care and share" philosophy that is the basis of JFM. Even in unclassified forests, where no previous settlement has been done, the task is not simple due to use by a large number of stakeholders. Elsewhere, old rights may have to be modified to make forested areas amenable to the formation of village forest committees (VFC). This is easier said than done, since changes in traditional or legal rights may face political hurdles.

The Role of the Panchayat in JFM

The lack of clarity on the institutional authority of the local *Panchayat* in relation to the authority of VFCs has caused confusion. VFCs have no legal or statutory basis, and their authority is recognized only by state FDs. Since no other government agencies grant them recognition, it may be difficult for them to manage resources on a long-term basis. Another concern is that if VFCs were absorbed by village *panchayats*, vested interests might exert control over decision-making. Because small user communities may consist of less powerful groups, they may lose authority to the local elite if forest management becomes an adjunct responsibility of the *panchayat.*

The overwhelming evidence on management of natural resources by user committees is that the benefits derived from the establishment of such committees are not sustainable in the long term. After funds dry up, plantations disappear, committees are disbanded, and the livelihood of the poor remains only marginally improved, if at all. The members of *panchayats*, on the other hand, are democratically elected, have better connections with existing bureaucracies, and have the support of other forums and have a much wider say in shaping local governing policies.

Some successful VFCs charge fees from forest dwellers who gather non-timber forest products. This practice is technically in violation of the Forest Act, although the illegality can be removed administratively if the allotment of forestland to the VFCs or to the village council is done under section 28 of the Forest Act.

A Review of World Bank Projects in India

India is the Bank's second largest borrower for projects in the forest sector (China is first). Total International Development Association (IDA) commitments over the last 20 years of $830 million have funded 16 projects—12 completed and 4 ongoing. Additional forestry projects in some states are in various stages of preparation. In addition to project lending, Bank interaction with India relevant to forestry includes the country assistance strategy, economic and sector work, and policy dialogue.

In addition to two major pieces of sector work, the Bank has done a report on gender in forestry and another on JFM. In a study in 1978, the Bank stressed two major tasks for India's forest sector: improving forest productivity to meet the growing needs of the domestic wood processing industry, and developing tree plantations to meet the fuelwood, fodder, and timber requirements of rural areas. The emphasis in this sector work was on replacement of natural forests with plantations, establishment of additional wood processing facilities and research on fast growing plantations. The public sector was to concentrate on increasing the domestic supply of wood, while the private sector concentrated on developing processing facilities. The 1993 Bank study, on the other hand, emphasized sustainable management, developing partnerships with NGOs and villagers in forest management, stimulating private sector involvement in forest development, improving technology and the incentive and institutional structure, and effectively implementing forest policies.

In a 1991 report on women in forestry, the Bank noted that women play a much greater role in the forest sector than was previously documented and recommended strengthening their involvement even more. The 1998 JFM document focused two case studies on the mixed teak forest system in Gujarat and *sal coppice* forest system in West Bengal to better understand the economic and financial incentives that would encourage forest-dwelling communities to participate in JFM.

Bank sector work has neglected four important points:

- The significant contribution that tree plantations outside the forest areas have made to stabilizing the total land under tree cover.
- The special role that India's import policies have played in meeting industrial demand for wood products (thus preserving India's forests) but hurting the market for domestic forestry products.
- The close relationship between forests and poverty.
- The limitation of the 1988 Policy as a production oriented strategy.

In addition, the Bank's sector work has not defined concrete steps for addressing the key challenges that face India's forest sector, such as the crunch in financial resources and the need for reform of state FDs.

The Bank's Pre-1991 Lending

Before the Bank adopted its 1991 forest strategy, it provided $345 million for social forestry[6] in India in the form of six state projects and one national project. The objective of the social forestry program was to reduce pressure on natural forests by meeting the fuelwood and other wood product requirements of the local population from outside natural forest areas, whose main use remained production of commercial timber.

The seven projects were similar in design. Each had a farm forestry component for growing trees on farmers' lands and a community forestry component for planting trees on wastelands and on village land held by the *panchayat*. Other project components included research, training, and fuelwood conservation measures. Local participation, with government support and motivation, was central to the program design, but was not achieved. Since such an ambitious forestry program had never been undertaken in India, the government initiated several institutional and organizational reforms to make the program more effective and mobilized external funding support. Some states established separate social forestry wings within their FDs to handle the increased responsibilities. The projects provided for recruitment of a large number of forest extension workers and motivators at the field level.

The farm forestry component was more successful than the community forestry component, especially in tree production. But success occurred only in the "Green Revolution belt" in India. Little attention was given to promotion of tree plantations or research in agroforestry in rainfed areas. Overproduction of poor-quality trees and liberal imports of pulpwood created glut conditions, leading to a fall in the pole price. Farmers' enthusiasm for planting eucalyptus—the most favored tree—declined after 1986 despite considerable incentives because the tree failed to generate the kind of returns farmers were expecting. Much of the output from the projects was used to meet the needs of the pulp and paper industry, so the free and subsidized seedlings provided under the projects inadvertently subsidized well-off farmers (those who had the land to plant trees) and industry.

Individual profit and secure tenure made farm forestry attractive. Lack of it was the primary reason for the failure of community forestry. Some analysts argue that foresters and the Bank consultants who designed the projects did not fully grasp the complexity of the rural power structure and assumed that village *panchayats* represented the interests of all in the village. In reality, the *panchayats* saw the woodlots as significant sources of communal income rather than as sources of forest products to meet local needs. Hence, there was a preference for auctioning the output rather than selling it at preferential rates or distributing it. Others claim that the way these plantations were managed was responsible for the lack of community interest. Most of the lands were planted as government plantations, with little involvement of local people other than in the form of wage labor. Even *panchayat* participation was limited to signing a letter regarding land transfer and all the management decisions were taken by the FD. The research and extension component of the social forestry projects was not successful. Had the Bank paid greater attention to research and extension, including improving the quality of the planting material and farm management (in the same way as it does in JFM projects), farmers might not have ended up trying to market poor, spindly trees.

But there were a few exceptions. West Bengal's group farm forestry and Gujarat's experiment with tree tenure schemes enabled poor farmers and the landless to lease public lands at nominal fees and to benefit from the trees grown. The Tree *Patta* (lease) scheme in Andhra Pradesh granted beneficiaries ownership of trees on land leased for 20 years. Besides usufruct rights, the beneficiaries reaped the benefit when the trees were harvested.

Prior to the social forestry period, the work of the state FDs had been confined to protecting natural forestlands. With social forestry, village wastelands and common lands also came under their jurisdiction. The Bank projects helped in horizontal expansion of the FDs to meet this extended role with more staff, vehicles, and civil works. The operational guidelines that followed from the Bank's 1978 policy paper noted that the key to achieving forestry objectives was strengthening forestry institutions. For the social forestry projects, this meant increasing the size and the authority of FDs rather than improving their ability to work with local villagers. Although the social forestry projects convinced FD staff that local people were not enemies, they could not transform the departments from "guardians" of forest resources to participatory sustainable managers.

In fact, local communities rarely participated in these projects. As a result of the emphasis on achieving targets, the FDs did most of the planting on community lands, seldom consulting the public about what species to plant. The farm forestry component achieved a kind of "paternalistic participation," with FDs doling out advice and telling the people to plant trees.

Sustainability was not one of the strengths of the social forestry program. Issues of tenure were neglected. There was also a failure to define, establish, and publicize the rights to maturing trees and the procedures for marketing and allocating benefits. The focus should have been on building social capital and communities' capacity to manage common property resources. Degradation often set in once the trees were harvested. When it came time to close a project, the state had to find ways to pay the salaries of staff hired during the project. With few internal resources, the states then vied for additional Bank-supported forest projects.

Still, the Bank's social forestry projects made important contributions to the sector. They increased awareness of the importance of creating tree plantations outside natural forests. They convinced aloof FDs to accept that local people's cooperation could be enlisted in increasing tree cover. They demonstrated a way for the country to stabilize its tree cover, even under extreme population and livestock pressure. And project implementation revealed imperfections in wood markets—in the legal and procedural frameworks that make it difficult to cut and sell privately owned trees. With greater investment in research and extension and in the quality of tree planting material, the social forestry projects could have been more successful. Reports from several areas reveal that social forestry plantations have nevertheless improved water conservation, provided microclimatic stabilization and restored soil fertility.

World Bank (post-1991) Projects

The Bank's post-1991 projects were designed to support the forest sector development strategies of the state FDs. Recognizing that a much more flexible approach is required, the projects (in Madhya Pradesh, Uttar Pradesh, and Kerala) were the first of two phases in a long-term support plan. Project components included sector reform, JFM, training and research, regeneration and afforestation, technology improvement, wildlife and biodiversity conservation, fodder development, and social forestry. Policy and institutional reforms focused on state-level fiscal and market distortions that impede sustainable resource management.

The design of the later projects reflected the experience of earlier ones in Maharashtra and West Bengal. For example, although the West Bengal Forestry Project provided for supporting works in villages, the concept was not articulated into a village resource development strategy as it is in the later projects. The Madhya Pradesh Forestry Project, on the other hand, draws a distinction between JFM and the Village Resource Development Program. The strategy of the latter combines JFM with activities and investments designed to create alternative incomes or resources in villages adjacent to forests.

The design of the state projects is complex as they are attempting to deal with sector-wide concerns. However, little baseline data is available to do a before and after comparison. Monitoring and evaluation indicators in projects are also ill-suited to measure achievement in project objectives. In current projects, while project objectives stress the achievement of results, indicators are designed to measure quantitative progress.[7] Improving public sector management is a development objective in the Uttar Pradesh Forestry Project. But the monitoring indicators measure progress by the number of training courses held, number of policy studies commissioned, number of staff trained, and similar measures. Holding training courses is a means of achieving improvement in sector management but is not in itself an indicator of improved sector management. Hence, there is a disconnect between what the project states is the objective and what the indicators measure. Since the indicators do not measure progress toward results, what a project does achieve does not do justice to what it originally set out to do. At the field level, achievement of objectives then is translated into the need to fulfill quantitative targets rather than qualitative improvements. In JFM, this dilutes the participatory nature of the strategy of working with the communities in protecting forest areas. New kinds of indicators that will measure progress in achievement of qualitative progress are required.[8]

Though the projects' basic strategies remained the same, their emphases varied according to state requirements. JFM was only a pilot in the Kerala Forestry Project, since the state had no experience with participatory forest management. In West Bengal, on the other hand, JFM was already established before the project began and thus got a larger share of project funds. The Madhya Pradesh Forestry Project distinguished between JFM and the village resource development program.

Due to excessive focus on JFM, it is often stated that the state FDs have paid scant attention to tree plantations outside the forests. Given the large stretches of wastelands in the country, it has been noted that neglect of tree plantations on non-forest land was a major shortcoming of the Bank's current projects. Bank staff comment that the major reason for decline in financial resource allocation to social forestry was: (i) the belief that subsidies should be phased out (according to them these comprised the major element of SF project costs); (ii) forestry on *panchayat* and other common lands had not been successful and the FD did not have new alternative approaches. Bank staff also note that they have continued to explore ways to continue supporting farm forestry objectives (the successful component of SF) and cite the innovative features in the Uttar Pradesh Forestry Project as an example. However, the declining resource allocation by the Bank and other donors to the SF component conveys the message to the state FDs that the SF phase is no longer important.

Neglect of tree plantations on non-forest land is a mistake. First, village lands are closest to homes, and protection by the village could be organized easily, as opposed to forestlands that are far removed from the village. Second, use of these lands is generally restricted to residents of one village and intervillage conflicts can easily be avoided. Third, because common lands[9] are quite degraded, closure does not harm any group. On the contrary, degraded forests provide low-grade fuel and grasses to the poor, and therefore closing such lands for regeneration will adversely affect the poorest. Fourth, as these lands were never under the control of the Forest Department, transferring benefits, management, and ownership to the *panchayats* does not invite hostility from foresters.

The success of JFM will depend on efforts to increase productivity on land other than degraded forests: private lands, non-forest village commons, and forests remote from villages. Such programs could meet the employment and income needs of the villagers when they are required to reduce their consumption from specific forests. The village micro-plan should include all parcels of land within a village, including cropland and uncultivated village lands.

Implementation experience revealed drastic variations in performance among the forest projects, depending on the commitment of the implementing agency. In Andhra Pradesh, the rehabilitation of degraded forest land through village participation has been high on the chief minister's agenda. The state's chief secretary frequently reviewed the implementation of JFM with the district collectors. In short, there was both political and administrative leadership, and not just within the state Forest Department. In Maharastra, discontinuity in staff made it difficult to build commitment.

The Impact on the Poor

The JFM strategy implies increase in the collective ability of the communities adjacent to forests to manage, grow, and equitably share common property resources. Since a large number of the poor live near forests, the Bank's forest sector projects have a tremendous potential for meeting the needs of the poorest.

The two-pronged strategy of village development and forest protection assumes that if resources outside natural forests become more productive, people will give up gathering fuelwood, fodder, and other resources from forests. Experience so far shows that, in the absence of capable village institutions, this assumption may not be valid. Differences in perceptions of and expectations from JFM also create problems. While the state Forest Department sees JFM as a convenient means of regenerating forests, the local communities view it as a wage employment program and as a means of meeting their daily needs.

Currently, a large part of the benefit to the poor has been through wages. Alhough the regenerating forest areas have increased the physical output of NTFPs, since adequate attention to marketing issues is lacking, the benefit from increased production has not as yet trickled down sufficiently to the poor. JFM has also failed to give sufficient attention to the poorest in forest-dependent communities, such as artisans, headloaders, and *podu* (shifting) cultivators. Although the Forest Department in Andhra Pradesh does not evict

---

Box 4.3
Empowering the Tribals

Many villages in Madhya Pradesh that depend on a variety of forest products for their subsistence needs are denied access to natural forests by a variety of laws that give the state government proprietary rights to the forests. The net effect of these laws is to engender corruption in forest officials, who demand bribes for allowing the villagers into the forests. This practice, widespread in the state, has produced a web of social tensions.

The state's Forest Department contends that the major cause of forest degradation is the clandestine use of resources by the tribals, who must therefore be controlled with a heavy hand. Even though it is an open secret that it is the contractor-politician-forest official nexus that has been denuding the forests, blaming tribals comes easily since they are mostly unorganized and marginalized. The social situation in the state remained "normal" until the system of corruption was challenged by the tribals.

Some senior Forestry officers are aware of the systemic exploitation of tribals. Tracing the history of the conflict, the conservator of forests told how the political parties had accepted actions that exacerbated the problem of forest encroachment by the tribals—a situation that demanded the provision of livelihoods and programs for social and economic development. He advised that the standing crops of tribals on encroached land should not be destroyed because it would lead to an escalation of the conflict.

The Principal Secretary of Forests admitted that the joint forest committees did not have local support and needed to be reconstituted so that they are not dominated by the rural elite and representatives of the contractor lobby. He spoke against any use of force by the authorities.

Source: N.C. Saxena 2001

podu cultivators, it includes *podu* lands within the scope of management, which increases the fears of the tribes that their food supply will be jeopardized after wage-earning programs end (Oxfam 1998). In Madhya Pradesh (see Box 4.3), the Forest Department relies to a large extent on the village elite, who dominate the JFM committees. The elite do not depend on forest resources, but they benefit the most from forest protection. The long-term benefit of groundwater recharge helps wealthy farmers more than it does the landless, and elite leadership gives them control of committee finances.

It is important to distinguish between a strategy that provides resources to people and encourages them to protect trees, and a strategy that encourages building grassroots social capital for conservation and protection. Even the best projects have failed to develop a sense of ownership about government forests among the villagers (Box 4.4).

Box 4.4
Whose Forests Are These?

To what extent have the poor developed a sense of ownership about the natural resources they are supposed to be protecting? The chief minister in Andhra Pradesh was taken to a JFM village. When he asked a tribal the reasons for his participation in the program, the answer was because he got Rs 65 ($1.40) as daily wages, whereas elsewhere he would get only about two-thirds of that amount. When the chief minister asked him who owned the trees, the answer was "the Forest Department." The tribal did not know what long-term benefits he would derive from forest protection.

Thus, the immediate gain to village people through wage employment tends to be confused with true participation in management. A feeling of ownership about forests has yet to develop among the people. They see JFM as a contract: "what will *we* get if we protect *your* forests?"

In Madhya Pradesh, funds are managed by the secretary, who is also the Forest Guard, whereas higher officers in the Forest Department control technology. Participation is sought only for grazing control. Meetings of the Committee are held when senior officers visit. In almost all VFCs, the participation of men was restricted to providing them with information, while women did not even know that they were members and were not aware of the existence of a village development fund.

Source: Saxena 1999; PRIA 1998

Gender

Gender issues have continued to receive limited attention in current Bank-financed projects. The intention of increasing women's participation is present in the Bank-financed projects but they do little to address the crucial constraints that women face. The result is limited women's participation. When JFM involves the protection of a nearby degraded area, women's daily drudgery is increased because they must travel greater distances to collect fuelwood and fodder (Sarin 1998). In some places, women have had to switch to collecting inferior fuels, such as leaves, husks, weeds, and bushes. Merely shifting the protection role from the FD to the communities does not provide any immediate relief to women. Neither does it guarantee their increased participation.

The Bank-financed projects have attempted to provide for women's membership in committees, but membership in committees is not synonymous with a share in rights or of benefits. Both need to be ensured, not one or the other. Forced inclusion of women through legislation has not led to their genuine participation. In Madhya Pradesh, while men's participation in micro-planning in VFCs was restricted to providing information, women did not even do that. Their role was negligible. Women were not even aware of the existence of a village development fund (PRIA & Samarthan 1998). Often meetings are scheduled in the evenings to suit men, at the time when women tend to be cooking. When attending meetings, women rarely participate. It is considered against Indian culture for women to talk in the presence of men, much less to question their ideas. As a result, there is a bias in favor of those forest products of interest primarily to men.

NGO Participation

The post-1992 projects provide for greater NGO collaboration, especially to assist the FDs in participatory management activities in the field of training, extension, villager mobilization, formation of village protection committees and training of women's groups, and technology dissemination. There is more concern now for building social capital with NGO participation. But the NGOs, while large in number, tend to be of variable quality. Many of them started as effective bridges between communities and government (and donors), but by now they have become bureaucratic establishments focusing on their own survival. Critics argue that mobilization of donor money takes higher priority among many NGOs than community mobilization.

But there are exceptions. Some NGOs are aware of and worried about the current trends, but have no way to control them. The rejuvenation and reorientation of NGOs to serve as think tanks and forums for interaction is an unrealized goal. The development of genuine civil society organizations for increased accountability needs to be an important part of the Bank's support for forestry in India.

Institutional Development

Three levels of institutional development merit consideration: the implementing agency (the Forest Department), partnership development with other stakeholders, and grassroots capacity building for undertaking plantations and preserving forests.

Forest Department

The forest sector projects have had two kinds of effects on the state FDs. First, the projects, especially the SF projects, have helped increase the number of staff in the department. This has not necessarily been a positive development. In most states, financing the additional staff has been a huge drain on state resources when the Bank funding stopped. However, the post-1992 projects are not heavy on new staffing. Instead, they are attempting to restruc-

---

Box 4.5
NGO Evaluation of JFM in Andhra Pradesh

Samata, a grassroots organization in Andhra Pradesh, recently studied the operations of several JFM committees. It concluded that local indigenous communities have become involved in resource management programs for the first time. No other government department has built up this kind of institutional structure where there is a people's committee and joint management of committee funds. Committee members are involved in meetings where the use and disbursement of funds are discussed. However, the study also found several shortcomings.

There has been no sharing in profits, and there are a number of problems arising out of bamboo harvesting. The PCCF does not have the power to grant a 50 percent share of the proceeds from bamboo harvesting to any village forest committee. Approval must come from the national government's MOEF. All applications for a right to share in income are pending because of this.

Within most of the joint management committees, the power of decision-making lies with the upper castes and landed families, while the activities are done by the poor and the landless. Only chairpersons or a few committee members are aware of the amount of funds coming to them from the state Forest Department. Transparency has thus become a much-debated issue in the program, and corruption has trickled down to the village level.

People want to grow quick-yielding varieties like cashew, banana, coffee, and pepper, but the department has rejected these proposals while telling villagers to plant eucalyptus. Where such interests are conflicting, two things have happened—either people went ahead and planted other species and their JFM was cancelled, or people went ahead with a tacit understanding with the forest staff that villagers would be allowed to harvest species like bamboo, coffee, and cashew.

The laws on marketing are also a serious hindrance to the economic progress of JFM committees. A few benevolent field officers have given informal permission to the committees to transport and sell non-timber forest products outside their area.

The evaluation concluded that for sustainability and long-term benefits to the people, the emphasis in the program should shift from incentives (wage labor, share in produce) to building social capital and community capability.

Based on Samata 2001

ture the FD to tailor it to its new role. However, the handling of the restructuring process was poor in the West Bengal Forestry Project. In the later projects, modifications have been made to better handle the reorganization exercise. However, at this stage, it is difficult to say what the overall institutional impact of the reorganization exercise will be.

The other aspect of institutional development in the FD is the positive change in attitude toward working with the people. This began under the SF projects, when the FD became aware of the possibility of working with people, yet it continued the traditional policing approach toward protection of the forest areas. The change, however, created an atmosphere that permitted the FD to accept the idea of a cooperative strategy for management of forest resources in the post-1992 projects. The later projects then attempted to build people's participation in protection and management of forest lands. Based on the experience of West Bengal and review of the implementation experience of ongoing projects, it is possible to say that the attitudinal change in FD is a visible impact. The department staff is convinced of the advantage of including people in forest protection. Field conversations with the FD staff found that before JFM, they felt the department was fighting a losing battle. One forest guard could not effectively patrol the large number of hectares that were under his control, especially with hostility from the people. JFM has made the task of forest protection easier for the department, hence the staff conviction in pursuing it. However, this attitudinal change does not yet amount to genuine participation.

Developing Partnerships with Other Stakeholders

Although the Bank recognizes the importance of building partnerships with the private sector in forest protection, so far private sector involvement has been limited. The state FDs are generally reluctant to lease degraded forest land to industry. One major fear is that it may lead to diversion of forest land to other uses and states lack the political will and the monitoring capacity to ensure that the private sector keeps its promises. This results in a low-level equilibrium of unattended degraded lands from which the society cannot benefit. The Bank needs to take the lead in undertaking studies to explore more effective models of public private partnerships and result monitoring.

Building Grassroots Capacity

The post-1992 projects have been successful in creating thousands of FPCs in several states for forest protection and regeneration. The projects have not so far succeeded in imparting a complete sense of ownership of the JFM program and the forests among the FPC members. Except for promoting a commercial interest in planting trees, the SF projects were not able to build grassroots capacity in villages for tree plantations.

The larger political economy of development in India often does not support community empowerment (despite the rhetoric)—it favors individual advancement and dependence on the bureaucratic and political elite. Although rural development programs require a strong community, socioeconomic developments in India in the last four decades have stressed the household as opposed to the communal approach. People in the villages tend to see themselves as households and to seek vertical alliances with those with power, rather than trying to build horizontal ties within the village.

One of the major problems in India is "silent participation." The people place their trust in one or a few leaders and allow themselves to be led by them. "Established power structures, socio-political and economic inequities and rigidities, play their visible and invisible roles in obstructing institutional change. These factors dictate the pace and patterns of change processes. They determine the mix of failures and successes. Non-recognition of these aspects greatly contributes toward the persistent gaps in JFM policies and program, failures and disillusionments as well as frequent criticism of the program by reviewers and researchers" (Jodha 2000).

To increase the organizational capacity of the village so that program management is both equitable and effective is therefore not an easy task. It takes time to mobilize a village community into a coherent and empowered group. Greater transparency within village groups between local leadership and the wider group membership is essential to ensure that marginalized groups benefit from participatory forest management (World Bank Strategy Note, April 2000). The confidence gained in planning, communication, and program administration in a transparent communal manner result in plans and capabilities that extend beyond the scope of conventional forest conservation programs. Empowered communities may focus on accessing credit, creating community assets, or investing in non-farm economic activities. These economic benefits are often long-lasting and sustained, even when the JFM committee has lost its previous vigor.

Institutional Factors within the Bank

One institutional aspect in the Bank affects forest sector projects. Important changes made under the Strategic Compact and Renewal Program to increase the Bank capacity and effectiveness in project implementation, allow for more effective portfolio management and enable the Bank to respond quickly to the client's needs and responsibilities:

- presence in the field of the Bank's Country Director, as well as International Finance Corporation's Director to facilitate continuous and intensive dialogue with clients reduces project preparation and supervision costs.
- decentralization of staff work to the field. This does not involve significant relocation of headquarter staff but incremental staff resources and responsibilities will be met by national staff.

- Support for new products, particularly Adaptable Program Lending (APL).

What impact have these changes had on the forest sector lending program? It is not clear why, but overall lending to the forest sector is currently in jeopardy because lending to other sectors is considered a higher priority by both the finance ministry and the country department. Even with the decentralization, the positive role that the forest sector can play in poverty alleviation has not yet been clearly grasped by either. Individually, however, forest sector projects have benefited from the decentralization of staff work to the field, especially the presence of the procurement unit in the resident mission.

Inefficiency and Corruption

Successful implementation of forestry programs requires adequate funds, an appropriate policy framework, and effective delivery. Past experience suggests that availability of funds is no panacea for tackling the problems of environmental degradation; it may be necessary but is not a sufficient condition. The determining factor seems to be a delivery system for optimally utilizing funds. Over the decades, India's forest bureaucracy has steadily amassed functions and powers, often in the name of the poor. Donor assistance has further increased their patronage authority. Although the exercise of these powers is not untrammeled—the democratic system imposes a number of checks and balances—the labyrinthine and obscure decision-making processes, the over-regulation inherent in forest laws, the weakness of democratic institutions, and the sheer monopoly which vests with the forest service creates the ground for arbitrary exercise of power. This has led to inefficiency and corruption. The problem of inefficiency is compounded by some of the characteristics of the Indian Forestry Service: rigid hierarchical structure, one-way communication, declining cohesiveness, absence of long-term planning, lack of public contact, and short tenure (Saxena 1996a). Politicization has made matters worse, as it de-links rewards from hard work, weakens internal discipline, and promotes factionalism based on caste and similar extraneous factors. Ultimately, it saps the morale of honest officers, who sooner or later "fall into line."

Corruption is systemic and affects the forestry sector as it does all other sectors. However, in the forestry sector, corruption is primarily at the individual level; it mainly involves payments to circumvent regulations, facilitate issuance of permits, avoid prosecution, and obtain contracts or jobs. Due to the general level of forest degradation, India does not experience the large-scale corruption associated with the sale of logging concessions in many forest-rich countries. Greater decentralization and participatory transparent sharing of forest management responsibilities with local communities are effective and significant mechanisms for minimizing corruption.

It must be emphasized that the problems caused by poor administration are common to all development programs. Therefore, to attempt institutional development only in one sector through tinkering with instruments that are internal to the department, such as training, MIS, changes in formats, computerization, etc. may not lead to the desired changes unless one also looks at the policy and structural issues that affect the working of all government departments in the state. Reforms in one sector may not bring sustained results unless larger issues of governance are corrected.

The Prime Minister of India had this to say at a National Development Council meeting in 1999:

> People often perceive the bureaucracy as an agent of exploitation rather than a provider of service. Corruption has become a low risk and high reward activity. Frequent and arbitrary transfers combined with limited tenures are harming the work ethic and lowering the morale of honest officers. While expecting discipline and diligence from the administration, the political executive should self-critically review its own performance. Unless we do this, we cannot regain credibility in the eyes of the people who have elected us to serve them. (Planning Commission 2001)

Thus, an attack on weak governance and excessive regulation, manifesting itself in poor service delivery, corruption, and wasteful public expenditure should be on the top of the agenda for political reform in India. Development is an outcome of efficient institutions rather than the other way around. Focus therefore must be shifted from maximizing the quantity of development funding to maximizing development outcomes and the effectiveness of public service delivery.

Insufficient Research in Forestry

Although the Bank has made significant contributions to forest research in India, the program lags behind those of such developing countries as China and Brazil. The Bank has sought to improve the quality of planting stock and to develop sound policies (including privatization of tree nurseries). Plant propagation, silvicultural management, fire protection, and improvement in seed quality sources, and handling are central to the research agenda.

A Forestry Research, Education, and Extension (FREE) project funded by the Bank was approved for India in 1994, but the project has produced mixed results. The project has not complied with critical legal covenants and has suffered from poor disbursement, procurement delays, and staffing constraints. In spite of these problems the FREE project has improved many facets of forest technology, including production and management of improved planting stock. There are other problems in research operations in India's forestry

---

Box 4.6
Fundamental Issues in Research

- Research and technology development currently is not integrated into the strategy for forestry development. Indian Council of Forestry Research and Education (ICFRE) has done valuable research in some states, but it is spotty and variable, and the institution has so far been unable to provide national leadership in research. The states have endeavored to do their own research, also with some good results, but those efforts could have been made more effective and productive had ICFRE been able to facilitate better linkages with other state, national, and international organizations. This is partly a problem of location. Were ICFRE located in Delhi instead of Dehradun, with its director responsible to the MOEF, it might have been able to take a stronger leadership position.
- The private sector is ahead of the public sector in forestry research, but mechanisms to ensure that the benefits of that research are used in state-funded programs are currently insufficient.
- Research is not currently driven by problems encountered in the field.
- Research is currently organized according to contiguous states when ideally, it should be by agroecological zones.
- The incentive framework is not geared toward high-quality research. This could be a major reason why forestry research has lagged behind agricultural research in India. The very existence of a Forest Service like the IFS has hindered research development. Administrators do not run agricultural research. In forestry, important positions in research institutes are occupied by officers of the IFS who are frequently transferred and, hence, are not able to keep up with recent scientific advances. The presence of the IFS officers in higher research positions means that technical staff engaged in forestry research have fewer opportunities for promotion.
- Current projects give inadequate attention to research in NTFPs, production, and processing, which should be high on the state research agenda, though given the large number of NTFPs, this is a challenging task.
- Dissemination of research through field-level functionaries does not receive adequate attention.
- Development of new technologies for rain-fed areas is a priority for the country but not given adequate attention in the research agenda.
a. Bank staff, in their comments, note that several points raised in this box are being addressed through the National Forestry Research Plan that is being developed through a participatory prioritization process under the FREE project.
b. That ICFRE now also incorporates a forestry university means that staff who should be devoted to full-time research have to spend substantial time teaching. This has worked against the promotion of a research agenda (Uma Lele Personal communication with Norman Jones, June 1999).
c. Bank staff note that some good work is being done by forest corporations like the Andhra Pradesh Forest Development Corporation (clonal plantation program) and several state forest research institutes.

cont. on next page

d. Mitra, in a later communication, has clarified that the institutes are assigned (by ICFRE) responsibilities of adjoining states only. In addition, each one of them is given a set of subject areas (based on the most important issues in the region). As a result, some regional issues remain outside the scope of research of the nearby institute or any other ICFRE institute. This also sometimes leads to duplication of research among institutes working on issues in two distantly located but similar agroecological zones.

sector (see Box 4.6), but it is expected that some of these will be addressed in a National Forestry Research Plan that is being developed by the FREE project.

National Parks and Biodiversity Conservation

The six state projects and the nationwide FREE project are developing a strategy for biodiversity conservation both inside and outside protected areas. Project funding includes support for research studies, habitat, and infrastructure improvement (a long-distance telephone network, electrified fences, camp sheds, and watchtowers). GEF and IDA are financing mutually dependent activities in the Eco-Development Project, a program of targeted interventions to conserve biodiversity in seven globally significant protected areas in India by improving protected area management and involving local people in it. If this strategy is effective, the government will expand it to other protected areas.

The economic development component (EDP) in current Bank projects and the earlier social forestry program share a common assumption: if resources outside forests become more productive, villagers will give up gathering fuelwood and other items from forests. This assumption may prove to be naive. Empirical evidence linking improvements in income with reduction in gathering is not very conclusive. By itself, poverty alleviation does not reduce dependence on open resources unless accompanied by a sense of ownership about the resources, which is even more difficult to achieve in national parks than in other forests.

In the Eco-Development Project, the Bank is dealing with new and controversial issues. Analysts are concerned about the practicality of managing and implementing the Eco-Development activities and note that such issues as staffing and infrastructure have not been given sufficient attention. Do the present staff and infrastructure have the ability to implement a scheme that in some cases has doubled annual budgets and so, presumably, workloads? How much implementation will the Forest Department subcontract to other agencies and departments? The challenge is to reconcile natural forest and biodiversity conservation with economic development and poverty alleviation. The Eco-Development project supports experimental participatory processes to plan and implement voluntary resettlement, on the assumption that enough land for resettlement is available in the immediate vicinity of protected areas. In reality, however, India's scarcest resource is land. Project implementation has been slow for many reasons: lack of smooth flow of funds from the center to states to project sites, delays in hiring specialists, lack of continuity in task managers, amongst others.

How has the Bank Performed?

The Bank's forest sector strategy in India, even though largely manifested through project lending and a project-by-project approach, has been relevant for several reasons: (i) It has helped the country bridge the financial resource gap that it faced in implementing its forest strategy. (ii) It has contributed to reducing the rate of decline in tree cover through support for SF and JFM. (iii) It is helping change the attitude of the state FDs toward working with communities in tree plantation, forest protection, and management. (iv) It is contributing to improvement in the quality of planting stock. (v) It has helped to bring critical but politically unpopular policy and institutional issues to the table. (vi) It has the potential for positive impacts on the poorest—i.e., people living in and around forest areas. The Bank lending has had two major limitations: First, in supporting India's strategy for its forest sector, it has supported the idea of India graduating from one policy phase to the other, instead of treating each new phase as a part of an expanding forest sector strategy. As a result, even though the current state level sector wide projects focus attention on regeneration, social forestry, improved planting stock, and other production-related aspects, they have not sufficiently helped the country meet the diverse demands on the sector. Second, partly because it did not realize it, the Bank failed to bring this to the attention of Indian policymakers as a shortcoming.

The Bank's focus on tree regeneration and other forestry production matters has not helped India resolve the many other issues found in the sector:

- Poverty alleviation, tribal welfare, and issues of women empowerment. Benefits to the poor, other than better wages, have been limited.
- The short-term boost in local enthusiasm caused by new projects has often been interpreted as support for JFM. Often, however, the poor shift their gathering activities to other areas not under JFM.
- Forestry's links with pastures and watershed development are poorly understood and have not been given sufficient attention.
- There have been no attempts to initiate land use planning; common lands adjacent to forests have gotten a low priority in post-1991 projects. The focus on farm forestry has been diluted since 1991 despite its enor-

mous potential, especially in agriculturally backward areas. There are better social returns to be obtained by promoting agroforestry in the rainfed and semi-arid regions that contain most of India's marginal lands.

- The prospects for local value-added activities, such as the processing of non-timber forest products by villagers, have not been investigated.
- Little consideration has been given to shifting attention from timber to forest floor management and greater production of gatherable biomass. Old-style plantations still continue to be funded despite the 1988 change in policy.
- Coordination within the Bank continues to be weak. The Rural Development Department, for instance, provided free seedlings that undermined the sale of seedlings by the farm forestry sub-component of the project in Andhra Pradesh. Increasing the capacity of the departments for strategic policy/planning and coordination, including administrative and structural reforms, is not part of project strategy.

The Bank's forestry sector projects in India have also not been efficient. Sector lending should be seen in terms of the financial cost to the borrower and the country's major objective. If the objective was to prevent deforestation and degradation and to stabilize tree cover, the question is whether the $830 million spent on forest sector projects has been spent effectively. If the objective was to reduce poverty, the question is whether lending to sectors other than forests is a more efficient way of reaching the poor. Though monitoring and evaluation have improved, it is not certain that sufficient outcome information will be available by the end of the projects to permit assessment of impact.

Core activities in JFM have received relatively small amounts of investment. In most cases, a larger portion of loan funds has been spent on the support structure, including travel, meetings, training, salaries, etc., of forest departments, NGOs, and others, as well as the establishing and servicing of networks related to JFM. This tendency gets accentuated under donor-aided projects, where activities tend to be undertaken in "project mode" with a strong (spending) target orientation but with little attention to institutional transformation, which is the key goal of JFM.

Cost per village or per unit of area regenerated has been a missing factor in the design of Bank forest sector projects. The Maharashtra Forestry Project, for example, covers 150 villages. Its project costs are almost twice those in the Madhya Pradesh project, which has covered 1,150 villages in fewer years. Analysis by cost per hectare yields the same picture. Assuming the objective is to prevent forest deforestation and degradation and to stabilize tree cover, all project components (sector reform, research, NGO participation, JFM) will help achieve that goal. Analysis shows that even the planned cost per hectare varies significantly among projects, ranging from $56.23 per hectare in West Bengal to an astounding $714 per hectare in Kerala. High costs have implications for the financial sustainability of the projects, because the borrower may be unable to continue the funding of activities that were begun under the Bank project.

There are other areas where attention is needed:

- State governments continue to supply industry with raw timber, which acts as a disincentive to industry to pay a remunerative price to farmers.
- State projects should not duplicate each other. Both the Andhra Pradesh and Uttar Pradesh projects are funding eucalyptus plantations inside government forests. Since demand for eucalyptus is limited, duplicating the same species cuts into the profits of farmers and thus undermines the entire program.
- The government should review its decision to allow cheap and duty-free imports of pulp. While the lowering of import barriers on this product reduces pressure on forests, it hurts Indian farmers who grow tree varieties used for pulp, such as eucalyptus and bamboo.
- Failure on the part of government to look at personnel and organizational issues relating to quick transfers, declining morale, and inadequate financial and functional delegation. Issues of governance determine the ultimate success or failure of projects, but these are not being addressed.

The transferring of project resources to state governments may have implications for efficiency. In India, after a donor project with a state is approved, the state makes provision for that amount in their budget and claims reimbursement from the Ministry of Finance. The national government bears the foreign exchange risk and pays interest to the donor. In China, on the other hand, the central government on-lends funds to the provinces and counties, which typically bear the interest and repayment burden and sometimes the foreign exchange risk. As a result, the provinces and counties in China become more conscious about how to best use the resources to meet the needs of the sector. Indian states lack this incentive.

Donor coordination in the forest sector is generally poor. OECF shuns involvement in policy and institutional reforms and prefers to work locally. The Bank and the Ford Foundation interact regularly, but mainly on poverty programs. Cooperation between the Bank and DFID was more active. India's government does not have a strategy for setting priorities in the sector and then coordinating among donors. MOEF has only ensured that funds from the two largest donors do not go to the same state.

The Future of Bank Projects in India

A major weakness of Bank-supported projects in India has been lack of attention to their financial sustainability. For example, when the West Bengal social forestry project closed, the social forestry wing came to a complete standstill for lack of funds. In India, no department can be financially solvent independent of government as a whole. Many state governments are facing fiscal crises (Planning Commission 2001), and programs that bring primarily long-term benefits are likely to suffer budget cuts.

Though Bank-supported projects promote JFM, they lack a clear strategy to ensure that regenerated forests remain under forest cover. The strategy now is to reduce pressure on forests by creating alternative employment opportunities in the villages and involving local people in forest protection. The regenerated forest area can be kept under tree cover only if local people are compensated for the income forgone from abandoning gathering activities. This means that JFM and economic development have to be part of a single strategy. Developing grassroots social capital is the most effective way to ensure sustainability. NGOs can help by threading the projects into the fabric of the local social and economic structure. The Bank needs to give greater attention to building NGO, forest department, and grassroots capacity.

The Bank has two options: it can lend for the forestry sector when the policy and institutional environment is perfect, or it can use economic and sector analysis and project lending to push for policy and institutional reform. As in other countries, economic and sector work on forestry issues has been minimal. But the incremental approach taken by the Bank has had only limited success.

Nonetheless, Bank lending to India has been of some help and can contribute even more to forest sector development and poverty alleviation. The Bank needs to stay involved in the sector, and the government needs to view this involvement in the larger and longer-term context of poverty alleviation—not simply as a source of finance for a resource-starved sector. The Bank, too, needs to make forestry sector lending part of its long-term poverty alleviation strategy in India.

The Bank, however, has many questions to answer before it chooses a course of action. In which areas does it have the expertise to get into certain issues? What is its comparative advantage? Bank involvement in controversial issues will surely open these issues to debate. Can the Bank prevail where entrenched opposition to policy and institutional reforms and the legal framework hinder implementation?

Similarly, the Bank has to weigh all the pros and cons when it makes recommendations about reorganizing state FDs. The structure of the departments has endured for 100 years. Poorly planned reforms can do more harm than good and become an excuse for postponing future reforms.

Policies are not implemented in a vacuum. Their successful implementation should draw strength from documentation and knowledge about grassroots experience. Experience so far shows that unless the process through which participation is to be secured is described in detail and monitored, it is likely to be ignored—both because of lack of commitment and lack of knowledge about the road map to the destination.

The Bank may be better equipped to advise on policy issues (domestic trade, marketing, interaction between the public and private sectors) than on institutional issues (reform of the IFS, fiscal solvency of the state governments, building cohesive and caring communities). The institutional issues are complex and involve intricate working relationships between the central and state governments—issues in which the Bank lacks sufficient expertise and may best be left to Indian experts. But India's readiness for reform is also important. The readiness is greater in some areas (e.g., in giving incentives) than in institution building. An honest appreciation of the differing capacities and organizational abilities of different stakeholders is required. Political commitment has been strong in Andhra Pradesh, and to a lesser extent Madhya Pradesh, but political leadership alone is not sufficient. There is also need to build the capacities of village institutions and undertake governance reforms.

Notes

1. Per capita income has increased by 3.8 percent annually in the last two decades, as opposed to 1.3 percent during the 1951-79 period.
2. Foodgrain production has doubled in India in the last three decades, without any increase in net cultivated area. Had this not happened, India would have needed another 100 million hectares of land to feed its population, which would have wiped out the entire remaining forest area.
3. *Panchayats* are village political organizations based on the electoral system.
4. Before the 1988 policy was adopted, India focused on replacing natural forests with plantations. During the 1960–80 period, natural forests in several states were clear-cut and high-value trees were planted as replacements.
5. Fuelwood collection by the poor from public lands and carrying it on their heads to the nearest market. In Orissa for instance, a headloader would earn Rs 25 to 30 a day for a shoulder load and Rs 50 to 60 for a cycle load in 1992. This was against agricultural wage rate of Rs 25 per day fixed by government, and actual payment of about Rs 16-17 a day (Jonsonn and Rai 1994). Moreover, agricultural work is only available in mono-cropped areas for four months a year.
6. In India, social forestry refers to tree plantings outside the forest areas.
7. Some participants at the country workshop noted that management objectives for JFM continue to be based on physical targets of forest cover, timber production etc. and that there are no social objectives (Aga Khan Rural Support Programme India).
8. The Regional staff argue that poor M&E is due to insufficient client capability. They note that the client's capability is the only way to ensure that effective monitoring is carried out. Even if the best indicators were developed it would be difficult to measure them as the FDs are not in a position to survey, collect, and process the data in a timely manner.
9. The assertion in the PIP for Uttar Pradesh (Annex 1, p. 23) that there are few areas of unused community lands in the state is factually not correct. The Bank has a very successful land reclamation project in the plains of Uttar Pradesh.

References

Chaturvedi, A. N. 1994. "Managing Public Forests." Draft.

Food and Agriculture Organisation of the United Nations (FAO) (1998b): Report of the Asia-Pacific Forestry Sector Outlook Study. *FAO Job No D/W9615E/1/9.98/1000.* FAO, Rome/Bangkok, November 1998.

Food and Agriculture Organisation of the United Nations (FAO) (1998a): Executive summary—the Asia-Pacific Forestry Sector Outlook Study. *ISBN 974-86532-3-4.* FAO, Rome/Bangkok, November 1998.

FSI 1988 State of India's Forests. 1987. Dehradun: Forest Survey of India.

FSI 2000 State of Forest Report. 1999. Dehradun: Forest Survey of India.

Gadgil, M. 1991. "Restoring India's Forest Wealth." *Nature and Resources* 27 (2).

Gadgil, M., and R. Guha. 1992. "This Fissured Land: An Ecological History of India." OUP.

India: Forestry Prospects Report No 1745, 1978; India: Policies and Issues in Forest Sector Development. Report No. 10965, 1993.

Jodha, N.S. 2000. Joint Management of Small Gains. *Economic and Political Weekly* 35 (50), December 9.

Jonsson, Stefan, and Ajai Rai. 1994. Forests, People and Protection: Case Studies of Voluntary Forest Protection by Communities in Orissa. ISO/Swedforest New Delhi.

Leach Gerald. 1987. *Household Energy in South Asia.* London: International Institute for Environment and Development.

Lele, Uma, Kinsuk Mitra, and O. N. Kaul. 1994. "Environment, Development and Poverty: A Report of the International Workshop on India's Forest Management and Ecological Revival." Occasional Paper 3. CIFOR (Center for International Forestry Research), Jakarta, Indonesia.

Mafa E. Chipeta. 2001. *Indian Forestry on the International Stage—India's Quest for Its Own Future.* Bogor: CIFOR.

MOEF (Ministry of Environment and Forest). 1999-2000. Annual Report New Delhi, India.

Mukerji, A. K. 1994. "India's Forests: A Status Report: Concepts, Definitions, Trends and Controversies." Draft.

Natarajan, I. 1996, *Trends in Firewood Consumption in Rural India.* New Delhi: NCAER.

NCAER. 1985. *Domestic Fuel Survey with Special Reference to Kerosene*, vols. 1 and 2. New Delhi.

OXFAM. 1998. Joint Forest Management in Andhra Pradesh. OXFAM India: Trust Hyderabad.

Parthasarthy, G. et al. 1998. *Procurement and Marketing of Minor Forest Produce in the GCC Area of AP and Orissa.* Vishakhapatnam: Institute of Development and Planning Studies.

Planning Commission. 2000. Mid-term Review of the 9th Plan. Planning Commission, New Delhi.

Planning Commission. 2001. Approach to the 10th Plan. Planning Commission, New Delhi.

PRIA (Society for Participatory Research in Asia) New Dakhi and Samarthan Center for Development Support Bhopal. 1998. *Village Resource Development Programme and Ecodevelopment Programmes in Madhra Pradesh.* Mid-Tem Evaluation.

PRIA. 1998. Studies of Participation in MP Forestry Project, Participatory Research in Asia. New Delhi.

Raina, Vinod. 2001. "Tribals Must Not Organize." *Economic and Political Weekly* vol. 36.

Ram Prasad. 1998. Impact of Monopolistic Trade Practices on the Sustainability of JFM. Bhopal: IIFM.

Samata. 2001. Evaluation of JFM in Andhra Pradesh. Anand: Foundation for Ecological Security.

Sarin, Madhu. 1998. "Grassroots Initiatives vs. Official Responses: The Dilemmas Facing Community Forest Management in India." In Michael Victor, Chris Lang, and Jeffrey Bornemeier (eds.), *Community Forestry at a Crossroads: Reflections and Future Directions in the Development of Community Forestry.* RECOFTC, Bangkok.

Saxena, N. C., and Sarin, Madhu. 1998. "Western Ghats Forestry and Environmental Project in Karnataka—A Preliminary Assessment." In Roger Jeffery and Nandini Sundar (eds.), *A New Moral Economy for Indian Forests?* New Delhi: Sage.

Saxena, N. C., Tushaar Shah, Madhu Sarin, and RV Singh. 1997b. *Independent Review of Western Ghat Forestry Project.* New Delhi: DFID.

Saxena, N. C. 1997. "The Saga of Participatory Forest Management in India." Center for International Forestry Research Special Publication, Jakarta, Indonesia.

_____. 1995. "Forests, People and Profit." Dehradun, India: Natraj Publishers.

_____. 1999. "World Bank and Forestry in India." Background paper for India country study. Draft. Operations Evaluation Department, World Bank, Washington, D.C.

_____. 1996a. "Policies, Realities and the Ability to Change: The Indian Forest Service—A Case Study." In *Sharing Challenges: The Indo Swedish Development Program.* Stockholm: Ministry for Foreign Affairs.

_____. 1996b. *The Woodfuel Scenario and Policy Issues in India.* Bangkok: FAO, RWDEP.

Shiva, M. P. 1994. "Determinants of the Key Elements of the Demand and Supply of Non-Timber Forest Products." Draft.

Singh, Neera M. 1996. Communities and Forest Management in Orissa (ed.), Orissa Forest Department.

Vira, Shiraz. 1993. *JFM and Nomadic Groups—The Potential for Conflict: A Baseline Study from the Himalayan Region of Uttar Pradesh and Himachal Pradesh.* New Delhi: SPWD.

World Bank. 2001. Project Concept Document: MP Community Forestry Project, SARD (15/5/2001).

_____. 1998. *Incentives for JFM in India Analytical Methods and Case Studies.* Technical Paper 394. Washington, D.C.

_____. 1991. "Women in Forestry in India." Policy Research Working Paper. Washington, D.C.

5

A New Deal for Cameroon's Forests?

B. Essama-Nssah, James Gockowski, and Lauren A. Kelly

The highly diverse forests of Cameroon in West Africa are representative of the biological diversity of forests in the Congo Basin, which is home to about 80 percent of Africa's moist forests and 20 percent of the world's tropical moist forests.[1] Only the Amazon accounts for more. The rainforest area in Cameroon has been estimated at approximately 22 million hectares, or 43 percent of the national territory. Until a reform process took hold in 1999, however, this resource was under siege, and success in preserving it still hangs in the balance. Apart from the Democratic Republic of the Congo, Cameroon has had the second highest annual rate of deforestation in the basin in recent years, losing an estimated 200,000 hectares of natural forest annually. Yet deforestation is not the worst threat against Cameroon's rainforest. The more serious threats are forest fragmentation, forest degradation, and loss of biodiversity, which are difficult to assess.

The history of Cameroon's forest sector is linked to events in its agriculture and political economy. Between 1950 and the late 1970s, the government—with the World Bank's blessing—encouraged the conversion of its moist tropical forests to smallholder coffee and cocoa agroforests, a tactic that produced fairly equitable economic growth, averaging about 5 percent a year. Largely because of the discovery of commercial oil fields in Cameroon, real GDP per capita then increased by 7 percent a year between 1978 and 1985. But a protracted decline in the terms of trade for its main agricultural exports and overvaluation of the currency then caused a harsh depression from 1986 through 1993.[2] Per capita incomes and consumption fell by nearly half, and Cameroon's large external debt became unserviceable. Economic recovery since then has been sluggish, with real gross domestic product (GDP) per capita averaging 1.6 percent annually during the 1998-2000 period. Poverty remains widespread, and the prevalence rate of HIV/AIDS is estimated at

7 to 10 percent. Significantly, however, the leadership of Cameroon appears determined to combat the corruption that has severely damaged the economy for several decades.

Poverty in Cameroon is overwhelmingly concentrated in rural areas—86 percent of the country's poor are rural. The entire rural population relies on forest products for food, medicine, fuel wood, and construction materials. To get cash, rural residents depend on trading in medicinal plants, rattan, bushmeat, and other non-timber forest products. The collapse of commodity prices in the 1980s and devaluation of the local currency (the CFA franc) in 1994 triggered greater reliance on those activities.

The Bank has been assisting Cameroon with loans and policy advice since 1967, but the pattern of Bank assistance has been uneven. Cameroon's deteriorating economic conditions in the late 1980s and early 1990s prompted the Bank to abandon its traditional project lending in Cameroon in favor of adjustment lending. But adjustment lending, which included recommendations for forest sector reforms, had only limited success through most of the 1990s because of poor sequencing of reforms, lack of political will, weak institutional capacity, and foot-dragging by both domestic and international stakeholders.

The dialogue between the Bank and the Government of Cameroon took a distinctly positive turn in 1999. Forest sector issues have now taken center stage in the debate over Cameroon's future and have been integrated into the broader perspective of governance and poverty alleviation. The Bank has learned how to apply more relevant and effective instruments to achieve greater results both in and across sectors. Meanwhile, the revived dialogue has also raised awareness in the world at large of the importance of Cameroon's forests to the global environment.

The process of reform in Cameroon remains fragile, however. Studies on the underlying causes of deforestation in Cameroon have revealed the devastating impact of corruption. An endemic system of patronage and political rewards involving both internal and external actors fostered destructive exploitation of the country's forest resources and contributed to widespread rent-seeking. The low pay and poor working conditions of civil servants, which have worsened since 1994, have made them susceptible to bribery, but corruption over the years has hardly been limited to bureaucrats. The creation of a law enforcement system to implement the Forest and Fauna Law of 1994, the Environmental Law of 1996, and the Emergency Action Plan of 1999 remains a formidable long-term task.

The Current Status of Cameroon's Forests

Cameroon's forests range from wet evergreen forest in the shadow of Mount Cameroon in the southwest to the semi-arid Guinea Savanna Woodlands of northern Cameroon. While exhibiting most of the variations in vegetation types found in Africa, Cameroon is also one of the few places in the world where tropical mountain systems are found. These are particularly important centers of plant and faunal endemism. More than 45 endemic plant species have been found on Mount Cameroon alone (IUCN 1994).

A Global Environment Facility (GEF) grant, combined with a Dutch (DGIS) grant, for a total of $12.4 million that began in 1995 is helping the government of Cameroon protect the country's biological diversity. The grant has helped to support a network of national parks, reserves, and ungazetted sites, and was also designed to strengthen national institutions involved in research, planning, and coordination of biodiversity activities. A total of seven donors are supporting the government in the implementation of this PGBC (Programme de gestion de la biodiversite du Cameroun). Two early reviews of progress under the project found unsatisfactory outcomes because of poor design, the absence of a biodiversity conservation strategy, and inadequate enforcement of environmental rules in protected areas, but performance has improved significantly since the PGBC was restructured in 1998. The government gazetted three new national parks, and biodiversity conservation is ensured through the implementation of a landscape approach that takes into account the development needs in production areas near the parks. Land use planning is clearly mapped and negotiated with all actors, and forestry companies, agro-businesses, and local communities are all involved in protected areas management. The project has been rated satisfactory since 1999, and Cameroon's forestry agency (MINEF) intends to replicate PGBC experience in the new sector program currently under preparation.

Attempts to deal with environmental problems in Cameroon, however, are complicated by lack of reliable statistics on the country's forest cover and changes in it over time. This problem can only be resolved through accurate measuring, monitoring, and valuation of forest functions. Estimates of the extent of closed-canopy moist tropical forest in Cameroon range anywhere from 155,000 square kilometers (33 percent of national territory) to 206,000 square kilometers (44 percent of national territory). Estimates of deforestation in the 1980s and 1990s ranged from 800 to 1,500 square kilometers a year, translating into rates that range from 0.4 percent to 1.0 percent. Deforestation occurs mainly in the dry forests in the northern part of the country, which is the country's most fragile and threatened ecosystem.

In the absence of reliable data, discussions among stakeholders about the magnitude of deforestation have often centered on which data are more accurate. Technological advances, however, may resolve some of the data problems. Gaston et al. (1998), for example, combined data on carbon pool estimates for forest types with FAO maps of forest cover and data on population densities to estimate a 1.7 percent annual decline in total carbon pools in Cameroon because of deforestation and degradation.[3]

As a signatory to the United Nations Framework Convention on Climate Change (UNFCCC), Cameroon is responsible for an inventory of the country's sources of greenhouse gases, including carbon dioxide, along with its sinks for those gases, and how both sources and sinks are affected by changes in land use. For most tropical countries, however, the global convention is rather meaningless because of the limited amount of data for making carbon flux estimates. There is a clear need for a concerted international effort to improve this critical global monitoring. Efforts to improve the global environmental monitoring done by satellite, however, will not resolve all data questions regarding forests in Cameroon because forest degradation (as opposed to forest cover) is generally not revealed by satellite imagery. These degradation issues involve the long-run sustainability of logging operations and the secondary impacts of logging, agriculture, and population growth on biodiversity resources. Successfully addressing such issues will require a continuing commitment to sustainable forest management by the Government of Cameroon and by the foreign companies that have dominated exploitation of the country's forests for the past five decades.

Agents of Deforestation in Cameroon

Agricultural land clearing by smallholders is believed to be responsible for between 85 and 95 percent of the degradation and deforestation that has occurred in Cameroon. Today, however, logging is swiftly opening up the remaining tracts of primary forest. Approximately 76 percent of Cameroon's forests have either been logged or are allocated as logging concessions. Less than a fifth of the country's unprotected forests, mostly in central and eastern Cameroon, remain free from logging. Logging can take place in forest concessions (where it is meant to be sustainable), in rural lands (where it is part of the change from forest to agriculture), and in protected areas (where it is illegal). Logging in forest concessions in Cameroon means about one tree removed per hectare, with about 5 to 10 percent of the ground area disturbed, because of the scarcity of commercial species. All non-protected areas will be awarded as logging concessions in the next three years. All concessions are submitted to forest management rules which were recently clarified and simplified, and which should be adequate to ensure the long-term stability of the forest ecosystem. MINEF's capacity to enforce these new rules is still weak, but MINEF is making progress in strengthening and improving transparency of its field controls capacity, with support from the international community. The most intact forests in the country are in southeastern Cameroon, but that region also has the highest logging rates and the most extensive concessions of land for exploitative purposes. In an effort to ensure wide-scale biodiversity conservation, the government recently set aside nine concessions totaling

900,000 hectares of never-logged forest in the southeast that may be turned into conservation areas.

There are three major underlying causes of deforestation. Population growth has caused expansion of the amount of land cultivated for food production, while deteriorating job opportunities in rural areas have increased encroachment on forested land. Meanwhile, the construction of roads and bridges has increased access to the forest frontier. Much collateral degradation of the forest is associated with illegal trade in bushmeat (see Box 5.1).

The Effect of Population Growth on Natural Resources

Cameroon has seen its population grow at an average of 3 percent a year since independence in 1960. Data from the population censuses of 1976 and 1987 indicate rapid growth in the urban sector and significant rural-urban migration. In 1987 the urban population exceeded the rural population and was growing almost five times as fast. Among the forest provinces, only the Southwest province exceeded the national rural growth rate, reflecting the high influx of migrants from the adjacent and densely populated West and Northwest provinces attracted by the availability of fertile land.

Rural population densities in the forest provinces are quite low (41 percent lower than the national average) because of economic factors, a higher incidence of disease (including trypanosomiasis), and inadequate infrastructure. Before 1987 there was no rural population growth in the Center or South provinces, and rural population in some of the administrative divisions of the South and Center provinces actually declined from 1976 to 1987. Population pressures then increased in the Center and the South provinces because of

---

Box 5.1
The Bushmeat Trade in Cameroon

The most important non-timber forest product activities in the moist forest zone of Cameroon is the poaching of bushmeat. Operating in a symbiotic relationship with logging concessions, hunters place snares along newly created logging tracks to supply urban markets and logging camps with smoked and fresh game. Among the animals taken in this trade are such charismatic fauna as elephants, leopards, chimpanzees, and gorillas, although the bulk of the trade is in *duiker*, a small forest antelope. Loss of such species is irreversible.

A household consumption survey conducted in Yaounde found that estimated annual trade in bushmeat in Cameroon exceeded $4 million. No differences in expenditures across income classes were noted, though the poor consumed mainly the cheaper smoked product. For the poor, bushmeat purchases were the second most frequent meat purchase after beef.

lower rural-urban migration and return migration caused by an economic crisis in 1986, which hit urban areas harder than rural ones.

Among the economic factors that influence rural-urban migration are the expectation of employment and higher wages in the urban sector and the declining agricultural terms of trade. The agricultural terms of trade for the humid forest zone in Cameroon declined progressively from the onset of oil production in the Bight of Biafra in the late 1970s. This decline, combined with the burgeoning of the civil service (funded by oil royalties) and rising demand for non-traded goods in the urban sector, led to an exodus of rural people to urban centers. The decline in the terms of trade continued with the economic crisis and did not reverse until the devaluation of the CFA franc in 1994. The agricultural terms of trade improved with higher world prices for coffee and cocoa in 1997 and 1998. Because of the reduced probabilities of urban employment and lower urban wages, rural-urban migration has slowed (Gockowski et al. 1999; Sunderlin and Pokam 1998).

In general, the demographic shift in rural-urban migration is a result of the changing incentive structure facing farmers in the humid forest zone under the newly liberalized market context of structural adjustment. The long-run impact on forest resources will depend on the types of production systems that are expanded and the intensification process that is used. But in the short run, additional numbers of households will rely on the same basic production systems and technology that once served a smaller populace.

The Decline of Rural Income

Income opportunities in settled agricultural regions have deteriorated, thereby increasing the amount of migration and encroachment on forested land. This is most evident in the forested areas of the Southwest and Littoral provinces, where rural-rural migration from the densely populated highlands of the West and Northwest provinces has contributed to an increase in the population pressures of smallholder agriculture. Studies have found the highest incidence of rural poverty here and in the Far North province.[4]

Improved Access to Forests

New roads and bridges have steadily increased access to the forest frontier over the past 20 years. Road improvements between the major port of Douala and the timber-rich East province have been instrumental in making the province a leader in timber harvesting. But greater exploitation of the frontier forests of the East province threatens the lives of large primates and forest elephants and the livelihood of the indigenous Baka forest dwellers. The shift by the Baka from its nomadic lifestyle to a sedentary one was initiated long ago by missionaries supported by the government, and it reflects the Baka's interest in becoming more modern. Nonetheless, the European Union's financing of road improvements has been heavily criticized by international environmental nongovernmental organizations (NGOs) for its impact on biodiversity, and the EU is revising its policies. Most Cameroonians, however, applaud the new infrastructure because it has increased market access for agricultural goods while contributing to greater deforestation for agricultural purposes along the trunk roads.

The Chad-Cameroon Pipeline

The Chad-Cameroon Petroleum Development and Pipeline Project is similarly controversial because construction will displace households and remove vegetative and shade canopy along the pipeline (Thenkabail 1999).

Mechanisms of Deforestation

Deforestation and land degradation in Cameroon are caused by such dynamic mechanisms as shorter fallow cycles, direct conversion of forest to other uses, fuelwood demand, and logging.

Shorter Fallow Cycles

Shortened fallow cycles on smallholder lands are the most common source of deforestation in Cameroon. As population pressures increase and fallow periods shorten, fallow composition changes from secondary forest pioneer species, such as terminalia and musanga, to shrubs and grasses. Ultimately, the natural forest may be endangered as increased annual food cropping threatens the integrity and viability of the forest ecosystem and, with enough population pressure, transforms the landscape into the farm and forest mosaic now found in most of the former forested areas of nearby Côte d'Ivoire and Ghana.

Direct Conversion

While smallholder agriculture has gradually transformed the landscape in Cameroon, large-scale plantations have been created quickly through conversion of forest lands to other purposes, using mechanical or manual techniques to remove existing forest vegetation. Between 1967 and 1985, the Bank financed nine industrial tree crop projects in Cameroon. All of these were state enterprises that are now being privatized or have already been sold. These conversions (on more than 100,000 hectares) occurred in the Atlantic coastal forests around Mount Cameroon and south of Douala, regions recognized as the home of some of the world's most biologically diverse tropical rainforests.

Box 5.2
The Chad-Cameroon Pipeline

The Chad-Cameroon Petroleum Development and Pipeline Project, which will transport oil from Chad to the Atlantic Ocean, is expected to generate substantial revenues for both Cameroon and Chad. The pipeline will stretch through a variety of ecological landscapes and displace between 60 and 150 farming households that will be resettled around the oil field in the Doba basin. The project's construction will also involve removal of vegetative cover and shade canopy, thus increasing soil surface temperatures, decreasing soil moisture content, killing soil organisms, and increasing the potential for soil erosion. It may also increase the peak flows and sediment loads of small tributaries and reduce water quality. The project proposes to mitigate any environmental damage by:

- Controlling unauthorized use of the pipeline route during construction to minimize disturbances to forest and riverine vegetation.
- Draining surface runoff to more than one tributary to correct increased peak flows and sediment loads.
- Phasing in the digging of new water supply wells to reduce disturbances to existing wells.
- Treating sanitary wastewater discharges according to World Bank effluent guidelines.

As the largest single private investment now under way in Sub-Saharan Africa, the pipeline project is also the most controversial. Most of the nongovernmental organization community (led by the Rainforest Action Network) argues that oil projects in poor countries governed by corrupt regimes do not reduce poverty. In addition, they contend, such governments lack the capacity and the political will to implement regulatory measures to control environmental and social destruction. The Bank recognizes the risk of weak capacity and weak public and private commitment to protect the environment, but it believes that it will be possible to strengthen governmental institutions during the five years that will pass before the pipeline begins carrying oil.

The pipeline also allowed for greater political leverage and progress on sensitive matters related to biodiversity: Prime Minister's involvement in gazetting new national park, stop logging within a national park, environmental assessment prior to industrial planning around protected area, road mapping; military settlement. The Pipeline played a significant role in the improvement of PGBC.

Fuelwood Demand

Demand for fuelwood increased significantly in Cameroon when the prices of traded fuels doubled after the 1994 devaluation. Neither the Bank nor the government tried to diminish this incentive to deforest. In a survey of fuelwood consumption conducted by the International Institute of Tropical Agriculture (IITA) and the Center for International Forestry Research (CIFOR), 48 percent of urban households in the Center province of Cameroon and 71 percent of households in the South province cited fuelwood as their principal cooking fuel, up from 30 percent and 55 percent, respectively, in 1987. This problem is being addressed in the donor-supported PSFE-sector investment program.

Notwithstanding those increases, the impact of fuelwood demand on forest resources is limited. Studies by CIFOR show that most fuelwood and charcoal are byproducts of clearing for agriculture. Estimated annual per capita consumption for Cameroon is about one cubic meter, with national consumption estimated at 13 million cubic meters (WRI 1994; Millington et al. 1994). The estimated value of fuelwood consumed in Cameroon is between $45 million and $65 million, though the Ministry of Environment and Forests (1995) cited a value of $83 million. These markets are informal and not subject to government taxation or regulation.

Logging

Low agricultural productivity, combined with increased food demand, has made expansion of the cultivated area a leading cause of deforestation. But while smallholder slash-and-burn agriculture and fuelwood demand are widely believed to be responsible for 85 to 95 percent of deforestation, those are often simply the secondary effects of timber harvesting.

Historically, logging in Cameroon has been an enclave sector with high capital requirements and limited forward and backward links to the rest of the economy. Foreign owners have traditionally dominated the sector, and nearly all capital inputs, from chainsaws to heavy equipment, are imported. Between 1959 and 2001, at least 81 percent of Cameroon's unprotected forest had been allocated to logging. Abandoned, current, and future concessions cover 76 percent of the total forest area (WRI 2000).

Today, Cameroon ranks among the world's top five exporters of logs from tropical forests and is the leading African exporter, with more than $270 million in annual sales. In recent years, timber exploitation has overtaken coffee and cocoa production as the most important economic activity in its moist forests.

Timber generates more than a quarter of Cameroon's non-petroleum export revenues, along with some $60 million in tax revenues (Biki 2000).[5] Timber production has increased by 35 percent since 1980. As the country's oil reserves dry up, timber exports are projected to constitute an increasing share of foreign exchange revenue in coming years. But Cameroon's timber industry depends mostly on five species of trees. With Asia rapidly surpassing Europe as the primary market for Cameroon's timber, the trend may be toward more extensive harvesting because Asian buyers may be interested in a wider range of species than their European counterparts.

MINEF estimates Cameroon's stock of commercial timber at 310 million cubic meters, which at current FOB prices represents a standing value of about $70 billion. The average productivity of the typical Cameroonian production forest is about 260 cubic meters per hectare of standing timber—32 cubic meters of that from the 75 commercially exploited species (CIRAD-Foret 1997). Logging seldom exceeds between 5 and 15 cubic meters per hectare because of the quality of the trees and market practices. Under Cameroon's national zoning plan, more than 6 million hectares are slated to become production forests; an annual average of 415,000 hectares of concessions were leased for logging from 1994 to 1996 (Coté 1993; Eba'a Atyi 1998). This period was a transition phase between the old and the new systems: in coming years, about 500,000 hectares on concessions will be logged annually, along with an unpredictable amount of timber from the national estate (*ventes de coupe* and community forests). But the estimated average felling rate is less than one tree per hectare of production forest—a rate comparable to other African countries and very low compared with those of other countries producing tropical timber in Asia and Latin America.

On June 30, 1999, the logging ban in the 1994 law was imposed on some of Cameroon's rare hardwood trees, including *iroko*, *moabi*, and *bubinga*. The ban was a compromise between the Ministry of Forests and the Ministry of Finances, and between the government and the private sector. Initially, the government intended to impose a total ban, but the industry opposed it. Some consider a total export ban the strongest possible incentive for domestic processing. A total ban is simpler to implement and easier to monitor, but it is also inflexible. It cannot be easily adjusted as conditions change or as the local industry matures—it can only be removed or reinstated (Grut et al. 1991).[6] The Bank supports the recommendation made by the 1999 fiscal audit to award exportation rights for all species through a competitive process. This will give private sector companies the flexibility to export very high-value logs while providing the government with control over export volume. It should also maximize revenues. Management plans must be devised in collaboration with local people to decide which tree species and which areas will be safe from logging.

Aside from the ban on exports of certain tree varieties, log export policy in Cameroon includes an export tax and a domestic processing requirement. In theory, a log export tax diverts logs to the domestic market, thereby lowering domestic log prices. High export taxes on logs, combined with low or zero export taxes on processed products, are supposed to provide a strong incentive for domestic processing because they tend to lower log prices below world market prices and provide domestic processors with cheap inputs (Grut et al. 1991). Cheap prices for domestic logs will induce inefficiency in forest use and in processing plant operations. That may mean that some species will be left in the forest.[7]

A key objective of the Bank's proposed reform of Cameroon's forestry was to use economic instruments, including taxation, to guide industry behavior toward a more conservative and sustainable use of resources. Moving upstream (to the forest) part of the taxes that were previously levied at the export level was part of this strategy. Another important measure was to introduce a competitive allocation process that would significantly increase the fees paid by private companies for each concession.

In July 1995 (in the context of the Financial Law that was adopted following adoption of the Forest Law), the government tried to make the local wood processing industry pay a value-added export tax of 25 percent. The private sector lobbied intensively against that rate of taxation and eventually threatened to shut down processing operations if the tax was not reduced. At that point, the government capitulated (Carret 1998). But in 1996 the government again tried to levy the tax. This time, the processing firms responded by laying off their employees. Two days later the government agreed to set the tax at a low 3 to 4 percent (Carret 1998). In general, the Bank is in favor of promoting local industry, but the Bank did not support Cameroon's approach, which protected both international and domestic timber companies from competition through the export ban and preferential tax treatment, among other things. An equitable industrialization policy that would ensure the international competitiveness of the industry will require the training of Cameroonian technicians and managers in sustainable development techniques. The Bank has been ready to underwrite such an approach for the last ten years, but the government has shown little interest in this idea until recently.

Sustainable Forest Reform and Development

The Bank's 1996 country assistance strategy for Cameroon projected a near doubling in forest export revenues from 1996 to 2004. Ensuring that some of the revenues from that expansion are used to assure sustainable development of Cameroon's forests will not be easy. Whereas wealth from smallholder agriculture contributes directly to the livelihoods of more than 2 million people, wealth from the harvesting of timber is concentrated in fewer hands. The industry's ownership patterns, investments, employment practices, and links to the rest of the economy will determine whether sustained and equitable development is the result (see tables 5.1 and 5.2). Government revenues from the forest sector increased more than fivefold from 1986 to 1995, but in 1996, the last year for which data are available, tax revenues from the forest sector were only 3.3 percent of total revenues. That was much lower than the sector's contribution to GDP, which was estimated at 8.9 percent.

Table 5.1
Evolution of Ownership in Cameroon's Forestry Sector

Year	Domestic ownership		Foreign ownership		Joint venture ownership	
	# active enterprises	% concessions exploited	# active enterprises	% concessions exploited	# active enterprises	% concessions exploited
1988	49	18	67	77	3	6
1996	154	53	58	46	8	1

Source: Adapted from Eba'a Atyi (1998) and Afrique Agriculture (1990)

Table 5.2
Cameroon's Wood Exports and Export Value Added through Processing, 1996

Product	Vol. exported	Vol. roundwood equivalents processed (meters^3)	Total export revenues (millions of CFA francs)	Avg. export value per meter^3 of raw log processed (CFA franc per meters^3)	Total export value added (millions of CFA francs)
Raw logs	1,254,407	1,254,407	89,308	71,195	0
Sawnwood	236,340	675,257	60,369	89,401	12,294
Veneer and plywood	35,000	61,403	10,850	176,701	6,478
Total	1,525,747	1,991,067	160,527	337,297	18,772

Source: Adapted from Eba'a Atyi (1998)

The non-market values of Cameroon's forests (existence and option value, carbon sequestration, biodiversity) have yet to be transferred into local incentives and therefore have little influence over forest sector policy (Karsenty et al. 1999). But to preserve its forests, Cameroon needs a system of sustainable management that can guarantee a continued stream of economic benefits. Sustainable pathways for rural development in Cameroon's humid forests can minimize damage and in some cases even improve the environmental benefits of the forest ecosystem. Bank efforts to intensify smallholder agriculture in the humid forest zone and its periphery—though diminished since the 1970s and 1980s—have involved support for zoning, integrated rural development, and silviculture.

Zoning Plans

The Bank has called for zoning in southern Cameroon to designate protected, production, and multiple-use areas, and Cameroon's prime minister approved a national zoning plan in 1995. This kind of biodiversity management calls for respecting minimum areas for species conservation and genetic biodiversity, and allowing the possibility of transborder protected areas. In principle, 20 percent of the national territory would be included in the permanent forest estate in a zoning plan. Of particular importance to the forest sector, and the largest component of the permanent forest estate, are production forest zones, which are the designated locations for active logging concessions. The Ministry of Environment and Forests approved a zoning strategy in June 1999.

Integrated Rural Development Projects

Techniques for sustainable forest management have been investigated in several projects in Cameroon. Among these is the French-led Dimako Pilot Integrated Improvement Project in the East province, which closed in June 2001. It aimed to rationally and sustainably exploit tropical forests, conserve the forest ecosystem, and renew forest resources. As one of several such projects initiated in central Africa by the French Ministry of Cooperation and Development since 1990, the project takes into account the needs of local people and reinforces technical field services (N'djantsana et al. 1998; MINEF 1996).

Technical silviculture

Among areas needing reform, the technical silvicultural aspects of sustainable forest management have made the most progress in Cameroon. Recommended management practice consists of three interdependent parts. The first is to develop knowledge of the resource base by taking detailed forest inventories on 1 percent of concession lands to establish tree diameter distributions, taking aerial photographs and studying vegetation to draw maps of tree populations, and studying biodiversity (flora and fauna) to determine fragile or particularly rich areas that need protection. The second is developing and transferring knowledge of sustainable management to government ministries, local people, and logging companies. The third is determining the parameters of rational forest exploitation. This means calculating the optimal rotation period based on tree diameter distributions and growth rates, determining the boundaries of the *assietes de coupes* (land to be cleared), and determining the minimum exploitable diameters of different tree species. These rules have been clarified and standardized, and now apply to private companies, whose adherence will be monitored and enforced by MINEF.

The Bank's Role in Forest Sector Reform

From its first mission to Cameroon in 1967 until the late 1980s, the Bank took the position that forest resources in Cameroon were unused or, at best, underused, and that the country's long-term economic outlook depended on making use of its vast natural resources. Policy recommendations focused on removing the constraints to expansion and intensification of these resources, including transportation and port infrastructure, market arrangements, credit, and land tenure. The Bank proposed that Cameroon intensify agricultural production and increase the amount of land dedicated to it. This would bring idle resources into production and facilitate economic growth. But attempts by the government of Cameroon and the Bank to intensify agricultural production have been largely unsuccessful because of poor policies and lack of institutional capacity at the central and grassroots levels.

Cameroon's forest sector has historically been harmed by weak institutions, lack of transparency, and corruption. Legislation introduced by the Ministry of Agriculture (MINAGRI, replaced by MINEF in 1993) such as the 1981 Forest Law and the subsequent 1983 Implementation Decree did not provide an adequate legal framework for planning land use and integrating forest conservation and production activities with agriculture. It failed to address the existing concession system that encouraged rent-seeking and inefficiency, and the distorted tax system, which was designed to protect an inefficient industry. Under the traditional land tenure regime, anyone who cleared and cultivated land in the state-owned forests had usufruct rights (O'Halloran and Ferrer 1997). This was believed to encourage deforestation.

Throughout the 1980s the government paid no attention to community forest management or to fostering any sense of ownership as a mechanism to promote protection of its forest resources or to ensure that the local elite did not capture the benefits intended for the local communities. MINAGRI lacked the administrative capacity to ensure that the receipts from taxes were shared with local communities. Forest sector policy was subservient to the development of the country's agricultural sector.

But the Bank's 1989 agricultural sector review proposed a forest development strategy to help Cameroon increase its share of the world market and increase the forest subsector's contribution to employment and national income while rationalizing forest exploitation for industry, fuelwood, and agriculture. It recommended:

- Developing a forest use plan to guide forest authorities in designing and implementing a forest exploitation strategy.
- Reforming the existing concession system to encourage the private sector to regenerate the forest, install modern sawmill equipment, and reduce uncoordinated agricultural encroachment.
- Extending the five-year limit on concession leases to at least 20 years.
- Training Cameroonian technicians and managers, who then would take an active role in the development of the sector.
- Updating the status of parks and reserves, identifying areas to be included in protected zones, and creating buffer zones around the protected areas.

- Rationalizing the use of fuelwood through an overall household energy strategy.
- Reducing the number of institutions in charge of forests and clarifying their responsibilities.
- Reforming the legislative and fiscal framework, particularly as it applied to the concession system, wood processing, and the rights and responsibilities of local communities in managing forest resources.

Most of these objectives have been achieved, and those that have not are present priorities.

The 1994 Country Assistance Strategy

In 1994, the Bank prepared a country assistance strategy (CAS) for Cameroon and provided an economic recovery credit of $75 million on standard International Development Association (IDA) terms with a maturity of 40 years. The Bank intended the credit to support major economic reforms and provide general balance-of-payments support. The strategy document identified three major development challenges: halting the increase in poverty, reining in the overextended and inefficient public sector, and halting the deterioration of the human and physical capital base.

The strategy document listed three objectives:

- Improve the performance of the public sector by downsizing and reorganizing the civil service, reforming the public procurement system, and rationally using and managing natural resources.
- Improve productive capacity by reforming the legal and regulatory framework, improving macroeconomic management, developing and maintaining basic infrastructure and human resources, and strengthening the financial sector.
- Improve the delivery of social services to low-income groups.

The strategy sought to ensure more efficient and transparent management of Cameroon's forest resources by helping the government formulate and implement a new law that would change the way in which forest concessions were allocated, taxed, and managed. Implementation of the new law was a condition for the IDA credit, backed by the country assistance strategy.

The Government of Cameroon, the Bank, logging companies, and local and foreign politicians all influenced the writing of Cameroon's 1994 Forest Law, at a time when civil unrest and financial distress plagued Cameroon's executive branch. The Bank's views—on concessions, community forestry, sustainable management, and reserves and parks—prevailed at the drafting stage. But the National Assembly, which did not feel the same degree of stress as the executive branch, set out to undo some aspects of the law. New players emerged during the debate in the assembly and the Bank lost its leverage (Ekoko 1998). That debate centered on two issues: the efficiency and equity of public auctions of standing timber, and the effects of the ban on log exports.

The foreign forestry firms that dominated the private sector kept a low profile during policy formulation but joined the fight in earnest at the beginning of the implementation phase. The firms opposed every aspect of the reform, which they perceived as eroding the advantages they had enjoyed for at least 50 years, and on numerous occasions threatened to shut down their operations.

Meanwhile, the government institutions in charge of implementing the new forest policy disagreed among themselves about the right approach. The Ministry of Environment and Forests, for example, wanted to use the proceeds from forest fees and taxes to finance sustainable management activities, but the Ministry of Finance (backed by the IMF) opposed the idea. The fund was eventually established in 1996 but was not funded until 1998.

What did local forest communities have to say? Not much. An information campaign reached only some localities, with no amplification at the national level. Thus, the communication strategy adopted for the reform process ensured that actors with knowledge would benefit at the expense of those who remained uninformed. The result: an inequitable law.

Clearly, the Bank made strategic mistakes. It forgot that policymaking at all stages is a political process (Dixit 1996), and it did not take into account the government's weakened political and financial situation. The Bank should have anticipated difficulties and taken steps to ensure that the legislative phase would produce the desired results.

Although one of the Bank's stated objectives was to promote the interests of local communities, it did almost nothing to gather their views or ensure that those views were taken into consideration. No attention was paid to the interface between forestry and rural poverty, or to the fact that forest taxation was under-performing, or that forestry companies had been given no incentive to improve resource management, conservation, or renewal.

Nor did the Bank apply a forward-looking approach to policy and project design. It did not recognize that the institutional environment would constrain implementation and therefore take this information into account in policy design. The Bank recognized institutional weaknesses in Cameroon, but preferred to rely on technical assistance to deal with them. The failure to develop local institutions undermined the sustainability of any achievement.

The Bank's 1996 country assistance strategy was an extension of the 1994 CAS, with a focus on consensus building and proper sequencing of reforms. It aimed to link actual performance more closely to the availability of funding and to broaden the consensus on the reform agenda while stimulating debate within the government and between the government, the private sector, and NGOs.

The three main objectives of the 1996 strategy were to consolidate the benefits of the 1994 devaluation, alleviate poverty, and create a climate favorable for private sector development. Thanks to a reform-minded government, substantial progress was made toward the first and the third objectives, but not on the second. The Bank program placed too little emphasis on the social sectors.

Reforming Timber Concessions

Prior to 1994, the system for distributing logging concessions was not transparent and gave the industry many incentives to "mine" the forest. Companies receiving concessions were not required to practice sustainable forest exploitation. Concessions were awarded for five years and were based on unpublicized agreements between the timber industry and high government officials. Though the contracts were renewable, their short duration may have encouraged companies to use old and cheaper machinery, leading to inefficiency, with wastage rates as high as 75 percent (O'Halloran and Ferrer 1997) and overlogging of concessions. Logging companies concentrated on a few very valuable species (O'Halloran and Ferrer 1997). Although the government taxed the logging industry, it did so in a way that protected industry inefficiency. The taxes were as follows:

- A surface area tax of 98 CFA francs per hectare per year, which was raised in 1996 to 300 CFA francs, and in 1998 to a more sensible minimum, given the value of products from each hectare, of 1,500 francs.
- A stumpage fee of 5 percent of the value of a cubic meter of wood. In general, stumpage value represents the maximum price a buyer would be willing to pay for the standing timber and thus is an approximation of the price in a competitive market (Grut et al. 1991).[8] Estimation of stumpage fees requires an accurate inventory of the cutting area before logging. If there are no additional fees for additional trees cut, stumpage fees encourage the concession holder to harvest all merchantable timber because it has already paid for the trees. But in Cameroon, the stumpage fee was assessed on the basis of trees felled, not on standing volume. So, except for the area tax, standing trees were not taxed. In 1996 the stumpage fee was reduced from 7 percent to 2.5 percent.
- An export tax of 20 percent of the administratively estimated value of a log (rather than the FOB price). The export tax accounted for about 75 percent of the total taxes collected from the forest sector. The products of sawmills were exempted from the tax, which reinforced that subsector's inefficiency.
- A forest export tax of 10 percent that was designed to discourage log exporting.

Under the new regime, concessions are allocated for 3-15 years. But this new regime was not implemented immediately. There was an overlapping period from 1994 until 2000. During this period, some old licenses were extended because new procedures for making allocations were not ready. Under the new law, logging by each company is limited to 2,500 hectares a year while the holders of land concessions prepared management plans. Approval of the plan by the government resulted in a 15-year renewable contract. The first concessions were awarded in 1998, but as of 2000, few management plans had been completed and none had been approved (World Bank 2001). The government decided to extend provisionary agreement for one year to give time to private companies to finalize their management plans.

The Bank had attempted to reform the concession allocation process by insisting in the 1994 CAS that the practice of handing out concessions on a *gré a gré* basis should cease. But without the leverage that Structural Adjustment Credit (SAC) conditionality would eventually lend to encourage this change, the Bank not only failed to achieve reform but was blamed for what turned out to be a mismanaged and ineffective bidding process in late 1997 and early 1998.

The Bank had recommended a standard approach when granting concessions. First, applicants would be screened for technical expertise. Those who passed the first phase would then compete in a sealed bid first-price auction, with the highest bidder winning the concession. This was inserted in the law by the Assembly in 1994. It is separate from Bank and MINEF policy, and everyone knows how to bypass it.

Table 5.3
Forest Taxes in Cameroon

	Fiscal law 1994–95	Fiscal law 1995–96	Fiscal law 1996–97	Fiscal law 1997–98	Fiscal law 1998–99
Area tax (CFA franc per hectare per year)	98	300	300	1,500–2,500	1,500–2,500
Stumpage (percentage mercuriale)	5	7	2.5	2.5	2.5
Export tax on logs (percent)	25	25	25	17.5	17.5
Export tax on processed wood (percent)	15	15	15	12.5	3–4

Source: World Bank 1999

The Bank had hoped that this mechanism would increase government revenue and reduce corruption in the allocation of rights, but members of parliament who opposed a system of public auctions argued that national companies could not succeed in a sector that was already heavily dominated by foreign firms (Ekoko 1998). Sawmill companies also opposed auctions on grounds that they would make logs more expensive, thereby violating the implicit understanding that the government would assure cheap prices for their inputs. Local logging companies, fearful that new Asian competitors would take over the forest sector in Cameroon, also opposed public auctions.

In hopes of finding a solution that captured the economic efficiency of auctions while limiting foreign competition, the Bank allowed the government to conduct discriminatory auctions. Bidding documents issued in 1996–97 for the first 24 concessions explicitly stated that bidding would be restricted to enterprises already operating in Cameroon. There was evidence, however, that two of the legal bidders were awarded concessions even though they were not the high bidders. That prompted the Bank to send a stern letter of reproof to Cameroon's president.

The proposed auction system did not take enforcement difficulties into account and ignored some of the factors that would affect how logging companies, particularly international firms, would view the incentives. It was also based on weak information about transaction costs. Cameroon's concession contract considered species composition, tree quality, and tree density (variables that cannot be manipulated), but it ignored whether the harvesting was done with "care and diligence" (Leffler and Rucker 1991).

In August 1997, the government launched an open bidding process for 26 concessions covering 1.8 million hectares; 190 companies submitted bids, but 16 of the 26 concessions were not awarded to the highest bidder. The Bank was blamed for the result, and some industry representatives said it would have been preferable to have continued the *gré a gré* system.

In 1998, the Bank approved a third structural adjustment credit (SAC III) for Cameroon. Following lengthy internal discussions about the advisability of doing so, the Bank decided to include a forestry component in SAC III that would be aimed at creating the necessary conditions for implementation of the 1994 CAS.

Meanwhile, the Bank team involved in advising on Cameroon's forestry activities was strengthened. The combination of structural adjustment conditionality and a strengthened team eventually produced significant forest sector reforms.

Yet at the same time, there was increasing tension between the Bank and Cameroon on two aspects of forestry policy. Illegal cutting in the Campo Ma' an reserve, which was to be designated as an offset for the Chad-Cameroon Pipeline Project, was beginning to worry the Bank and other donors, and threatened the renewal of the ongoing Biodiversity Project supported by GEF, IDA, and seven other donors and NGOs. Investigation showed increasing evidence of compliance with, and even active participation of, senior MINEF functionaries in corrupt activities. In addition, Cameroon was refusing to accept the principle of a publicly reporting independent observer of the procedures for awarding concessions, and MINEF had yet to publish a strategy and action plan aimed at punishing illegal timber cutting.

Following several weeks of intense dialogue and the intervention of the president and the Prime Minister's Office, major staff changes at MINEF were announced in June 1999. All directors, subdirectors, and provincial delegates of the Ministry were replaced, and new structures for managing reserves and national parks were put in place. An important result of these changes was the reestablishment of a logical chain of command in which senior MINEF officials report directly to the prime minister.

In subsequent months, many other positive changes took place in Cameroon. The Bank and MINEF staff worked together during 1999 to review the procedures and introduce the independent observer. This new regulation was adopted in June 1999 prior to release of the SAC III tranche; it was test-implemented on *ventes de coupe* in November 1999, reviewed until April 2000 and successfully implemented in June 2000.

In November 1999, under new criteria and methods for awarding forest concessions, 110 bids out of 375 submitted were rejected because of incomplete or improper files and background information. In December 1999, MINEF conducted a field inspection of all concessions awarded in 1997 to monitor compliance with individual agreements, and the results were released to the donor community. In late 1999 and early 2000, the government carried out a detailed economic and fiscal audit of the forest sector. In June 2000, independent international observers watched the allocation of concessions by Cameroon's Interministerial Committee. In September 2000, the government halted the practice of limiting bidding on certain concessions to Cameroon nationals. Meanwhile, the conditions for release of the second fixed tranche of SAC III had been fulfilled. A new regulation is being finalized to provide local communities with priority rights to all logging in rural areas, with the option of creating community forests.

The Bank, in conjunction with a Japanese assistance agency has prepared a Forest and Environment Sector Development Program (FESP) for Cameroon. The policy distortions have been resolved, political will has been demonstrated, and international confidence has been restored. The government is now preparing a sector investment program to strengthen institutional capacity to implement and enforce recent reforms, with support from the Bank, European Commission, France, DFID, Canada, Japan, GEF, GTZ, FAO, for a long-term programmatic approach. The objectives of FESP include the following:

- Improve Cameroon's institutional capacity to implement new policies and regulations for sustainable forest and savanna management.
- Increase local community involvement in and benefits from sustainable management of rainforests and savanna lands.
- Improve management of biodiversity while increasing its contribution to local livelihoods and economic development.
- Supply environmental services of global relevance and promote mechanisms that can generate revenues from activities other than logging.

Finally, in May 2001, with the agreement of the government of Cameroon, the United Kingdom Department for International Development (DFID), and the World Bank, the nongovernmental organization Global Witness agreed to monitor corrupt practices and illegal logging in Cameroon for three years, beginning in 2002. Global Witness was asked to do so because of its earlier success as an independent monitor of Cambodia's forest sector. The NGO's aims include:

- Building a network of local communities, local and national NGOs, private sector organizations, and government officials to pool information on forestry infractions
- Providing a confidential apparatus for making such information public
- Documenting such infractions
- Providing public information on government awards of land concessions.

During the six-month transition period that began in mid-2001 prior to full implementation of its monitoring contract, Global Witness conducted six field investigations and claimed "significant results and impact on some of the companies targeted for their logging out of limits."

A New Approach to Rural Resources in Cameroon

Although reform in Cameroon has introduced new governance standards and has increased both tax revenues and the forest sector's share of GDP, the structural underpinnings of the rural sector still need to be reformed. Since smallholder agriculture is a major source of land degradation, any forward-looking multisectoral approach must start with agricultural and rural development.

An active policy-led effort to intensify perennial crop and food crop systems to deflect further encroachment on the forest margin is needed. Agroforests could provide some portion of the environmental services of tropical forests. And since food crop systems managed by women will remain an integral component of Cameroon's agriculture, better price incentives and stronger institutions are a necessity.

A viable and dynamic agricultural research and extension system is also important. Since agricultural labor is the scarcest resource in rural areas, technology systems should ensure that the return from labor is increased. The different roles of men and women also affect labor productivity and must be considered. A single innovation can sometimes increase land and labor productivity simultaneously. Labor productivity can also be increased through Pigouvian subsidies and taxes to correct for production externalities.

Fertilizer subsidies in the Congo Basin should be reevaluated; when a smallholder burns a fallow field, between 100 and 135 tons of carbon dioxide are released over the course of a year. Attempts are being made to use market mechanisms—such as ECO–OK labeling and the fair trade movement—to overcome such problems, but they are small-scale and are often without the support of such large donors as the Bank.[9] In areas already significantly degraded, institutional mechanisms for transferring carbon credits to smallholders could provide new planting incentives for reforestation through agroforests. Supportive rural institutions—such as credit markets and input markets—must also be strengthened.

Intensifying production in the forest zone is not a new idea in Cameroon. As early as the 1930s, the French were searching for ways to intensify cocoa production. Today, however, there is a better economic environment for intensification. Although the policy sequencing of reforms within the agricultural sector has been less than ideal, producers are showing renewed interest in perennial crop systems since the removal of implicit taxation on producers. The infusion of new competition into export crop marketing has also reduced marketing margins and increased producer incentives. These incentives need to be augmented even further. This will require capacity building in the public sector and the exploration of new institutional arrangements for the provision of services and inputs by the private sector, NGOs, and farmer organizations.

A promising development is the greatly increased contact between farmers and extension agents as a result of an extension project sponsored by the Bank. In many ways, the project is quite innovative—it focuses on women farmers and on recruiting women to be extension agents. Explicit support for the burgeoning farmer movement in Cameroon was provided by the liberalization of export markets in the early 1990s, which established an improved legal framework for organization. The approach is also much more participatory than previous extension efforts.

Cameroon's capacity for implementing and enforcing policy in the agricultural and forest sectors continues to be weak. The public sector was hurt by the fiscal compression required by structural adjustment, and the government chose to reduce salaries instead of staff numbers, thereby reducing efficiency. The size of the civil service has dwindled amid hiring freezes and early retirements, and low wages and inefficiency remain major obstacles to strengthening the institutions required for the sustainable development of forest and agricultural resources. Without additional support for institutional development, the significant gains in environmental and forest policies will not be realized.

As the structural adjustment program showed, it is useless to design a strategy if it cannot be implemented over the long term. Feasibility and sustainability require political and nonpolitical resources. When success hinges on the interactions among different interest groups, challenges arise in donor coordination, borrower ownership and capacity, and the appropriateness of the adjustment instrument for forest policy reform.

The conditions imposed on donor funding could not induce the Government of Cameroon to implement reforms, but the government had few incentives to do so. Add to this a lack of donor coordination, waivers, and conditions based on promises not always kept. True commitment requires costly actions that are hard to reverse. This suggests a shift in the design of funding conditions—instead of basing tranching on policy content, it should be based on an acceptable policy process, one that involves partnerships outside the central government.

Such partnerships can be built through participatory economic and sector work (involving local communities, academics, and NGOs), proper information dissemination (involving local mass media and communities), and through common actions problem-solving cooperation can build strong partnerships with government, with donors, and with NGOs. When work is done in partnership, political and social issues can be raised, confronted, and dealt with up front. In the end, one has tradeoffs between the best assessments of experts and the sociopolitical conditions in the relevant sector. It may be more important to get the process right than to have a perfect solution that cannot be implemented.

Notes

1. It should be noted, however, that about half of Cameroon's forests lie outside the basin.
2. Real growth in Cameroon averaged 7 percent annually between independence in 1960 through 1985. Agriculture was the main source of growth and foreign exchange earnings until 1978, when oil production quickly began to dominate. Such a diversion resulted in higher civil service expenditures, public enterprise subsidies, and low return and capital-intensive investments. In 1985, three major shocks exposed the weaknesses in economic structure and policies. Sharp declines in coffee, cocoa, and oil process led to a 60 percent deterioration in the external terms of trade by end-1988. The long slide in oil output left oil exports in 1994 at about a third of their 1985 level. The real exchange rate appreciated by about 54 percent during 1986-88, greatly reducing Cameroon's competitiveness. By 1993 the country, and its external accounts, had deteriorated significantly.

Cameroon's economy was stabilized by the 1994 devaluation and the subsequent trade, fiscal, and macroeconomic reforms. Yet, while Cameroon's economy has continued to recover slowly but steadily, since the start of the recovery in 1994, per capita GDP has only reached two-thirds of its peak pre-depression levels, most social indicators have not improved, and some have deteriorated further.

3.   The Food and Agriculture Organization's monitoring of the world's forests does not produce accurate measures of change. The monitoring is based on national assessments of often dubious quality for fixed points in time that are then adjusted using a deforestation model, developed to permit the correlation of forest cover change over time with ancillary variables, including population change and density, initial forest cover, and the ecological zone of the forest area under consideration (FAO 1997).

4.   Especially notable here has been the settlement of the Moungo division of the Littoral Province by populations from the West Province and the conversion of forested land for the production of robusta coffee.

5.   Biki, Henriette (WRI/GFW) An Overview of Logging in Cameroon 2000.

6.   Grut and others explain that an export tax is more flexible than an export ban because it can be set to achieve any level of processing incentive. The level of incentive can be adjusted over time in response to tariffs imposed by the industrialized countries on processed products from developing countries. It can also adjusted as the domestic industry develops and matures, and incentives are less needed.

7.   At higher log prices more species, logs, and trees would be used. Furthermore, the use of export taxes as instruments of domestic processing policy become more complex moving from logs to processed products. The domestic processing impacts of an export tax on logs are relatively clear and predictable, but those on an export tax on products are not (Grut et al. 1991).

8.   In principle stumpage values can be estimated from the market price of logs net of transportation and logging costs. In practice, this is difficult because these values vary widely by specie, grade, and distance from market (Grut et al. 1991).

9.   The ECO-OK program certifies products from farms that meet social and environmental criteria for sound farm management and community well-being [24 August 2000, http://www.rainforest-alliance.org/programs/cap/index.html]—and that due to the high rate of forest exploitation, more than 40 species of wild life are threatened with extinction. According to FAO, deforestation rates averaged 0.6 percent a year between 1980 and 1995.

References

Amstrong, Robert P. 1996. *Ghana Country Assistance Review: A Study in Development Effectiveness*. Washington, D.C.: OED.

Angelsen, A., and D. Kaimowitz. 1998. *When Does Technological Change Promote Deforestation? Theoretical Approaches and Some Empirical Evidence*. Bogor: Center for International Forestry Research (CIFOR).

Asheim, Geir B. 1994. "Sustainability: Ethical Foundations and Economic Properties." Policy Research Working Paper No. 1302. Washington D.C.: World Bank.

Ausubel, Lawrence M., and Peter Cramton. 1998. "The Optimality of Being Efficient: Designing Auctions." Policy Research Working Paper 1985. Washington D.C.: The World Bank.

Bayalama, Sylvain. 1995. "Deforestation and Development in the Congo Basin." A Dissertation Presented in Partial Fulfillment of the Requirements for the Degree of Doctor of Philosophy at the University of Denver.

Bawag Besong, Joseph. 1992. "New Directions in National Forestry Policies: Cameroon." In Kevin Cleaver, Mohan Munasighe, Mary Dyson, Nicolas Egli, Axel Peuker, François Wencélius (eds.), *Conservation of West and Central African West Forests.* Washington, D.C.: The World Bank.

Bawag Besong, Joseph, and François L. Wencélius. 1992. "Realistic Strategies for Conservation of Biodiversity in the Tropical Moist Forests of Africa: Regional Overview." In Kevin Cleaver, Mohan Munasighe, Mary Dyson, Nicolas Egli, Axel Peuker, François Wencélius (eds.), *Conservation of West and Central African West Forests.* Washington, D.C.: The World Bank.

Binswanger, Hans, and Klaus Deininger. 1997. "Explaining Agricultural and Agrarian Policies in Developing Countries." Policy Research Working Paper No. 1765. Washington D.C.: The World Bank.

Bromley, Daniel W., and Michael M. Cernea. 1989. "The Management of Common Property Natural Resources: Some Conceptual and Operational Fallacies." World Bank Discussion Paper No. 57. Washington, D.C.: The World Bank.

Bowles, Ian A. et al. 1998. "Logging and Tropical Forest Conservation." *Science* Vol. 280: 1899–1900.

Bulow, Jeremy, and John Roberts. 1989. "The Simple Economics of Optimal Auctions." *Journal of Political Economy.* Vol. 97. No.5: 1060–1090.

Campbell, Donald E. 1995. *Incentives: Motivation and Economics of Information.* Cambridge: Cambridge University Press.

Carret, Jean-Christophe. 1998. *La réforme de la de la fiscalité forestière au Cameroon: Contexte, bilan et questions ouvertes.* Paris: Centre d'économie industrielle, Ecole Nationale Supérieure des Mines de Paris.

CIRAD-Foret. 1997. «Le projet d'Amenagament Pilote Integre de Dimako.» Yaounde: Ministere de l'Environnement et de Forets.

Clayton, Anthony M.H., and N. J. Radcliffe. 1996. *Sustainability: A Systems Approach.* London: Earthscan.

Cleaver, Kevin, and G. Schreiber. 1992. "Population, Agriculture, and the Environment in Africa." *Finance and Development* (June): 34–35.

Coase, Ronald Harry. 1990. *The Firm, The Market and The Law.* Chicago: The University of Chicago Press.

Corden, Max W. 1987. "Protection and Liberalization: A Review of Analytical Issues." IMF Occasional Paper No. 54. Washington DC.: International Monetary Fund (August).

Coté, S. 1993. «Plan zonage du Cameroun du Meridional.» Agence Canadienne de Developmment International et Ministere de l'Environnement et des Forets.

Dixit, Avinash, K. 1996. *The Making of Economic Policy: A Transaction-Cost Politics Perspective.* Cambridge, MA: The MIT Press.

D'Silva Emmanuel H., and D. Kariyawasam (eds.). 1995. *Emerging Issues in Forest Management for Sustainable Development in South Asia: Proceedings of a South Asia Seminar.* Manila: Asian Development Bank.

Dyson, Mary. 1992. "Concern for Africa's Forest Peoples: A Touchstone of a Sustainable Development Policy." In Kevin Cleaver, Mohan Munasighe, Mary Dyson, Nicolas Egli, Axel Peuker, François Wencélius (eds.), *Conservation of West and Central African West Forests.* Washington, D.C.: The World Bank.

Eba'a Atyi, R. 1998. Cameroon's Logging Industry: Structure, Economic Importnace and Effects of Devaluation. Center for International Forestry Research Occasional Paper no. 14. CIFOR; Indonesia.

Ekoko, Francois. 1998. *Environmental Adjustment in Cameroon: Challenges and Opportunities for Policy Reform in the Forest Sector*. Washington D.C.: WRI.

Frischtak, Leila L. 1994. "Governance Capacity and Economic Reform in Developing Countries." World Bank Technical Paper, no. 254. Washington, D.C.: The World Bank.

Garbus, L., A. Pritchard, and Odin Knudsen. 1991. *Agricultural Issues in the 1990s: Proceedings of the Eleventh Agricultural Sector Symposium*. Washington D.C.: The World Bank.

Gartlan, Stephen. 1992. "Practical Constraints on Sustainable Logging in Cameroon." In Kevin Cleaver, Mohan Munasighe, Mary Dyson, Nicolas Egli, Axel Peuker, François Wencélius (eds.). *Conservation of West and Central African West Forests*. Washington, D.C.: The World Bank.

Gaston, G., S. Brown, M. Lorenzini, and K. D. Singh. 1998. «State and Change in Carbon Pools in the Forests of Tropical Africa.» *Global Change Biology* 4(1): 97-114.

Global Environment Facility (GEF). 1996a. Operational Strategy. Washington D.C.

_____. 1996b. The GEF Project Cycle. Washington D.C.

_____. 1996c. Incremental Costs. Washington D.C.

_____. 1996d. A Framework of GEF Activities Concerning Land Degradation. Washington, D.C.

_____. 1997. Project Implementation Review of the Global Environment Facility.

_____.1998a. Summary Report: Study of GEF Projects Lessons. Washington. D.C.

Gockowski J., and M. Ndoumbe. 1999. The Economic Analysis of Horticultural Production and Marketing in the Forest Margins Benchmark of Cameroon. IITA RCMR Monograph No. 27. Ibadan Nigeria.

Grut Mikael, John A. Gray, and Nicolas Egli. "Forest Pricing and Concession Policies: Managing the High Forests of West and Central Africa." World Bank Technical Paper No. 143, Africa Technical Department Series. Washington DC.: The World Bank.

_____. 1998b. GEF Lessons Notes (July). Washington D.C.

Hartwick, John M. 1993. "Forestry Economics, Deforestation, and National Accounting." In Ernst Lutz (ed.), *Toward Improved Accounting for the Environment*. Washington D.C. The World Bank.

Hazell, Peter, and William Magrath. 1992. "Summary of World Bank Forestry Policy." In Kevin Cleaver, Mohan Munasighe, Mary Dyson, Nicolas Egli, Axel Peuker, François Wencélius (eds.). *Conservation of West and Central African West Forests*. Washington, D.C.: The World Bank.

Hodge, Ian. 1995. *Environmental Economics*. New York: St. Martin's Press.

Horta, Korinna. 1997. "La Nuit Coloniale continue a porter son Ombre Immense sur ce Vaste Continent: Cameroon's war against subsistence. A socio-economic and ecological analysis against the background of the Chad–Cameroon oil-pipeline." *The BOS NiEuWSLETTER* Vol. 16 (3), No. 37: 66–75 (November).

IUCN (World Conservation Union). 1994. *Forest Atlas of Africa*. Gland, Switzerland.

Jayaraja, Carl et al. 1996. *Social dimensions of Adjustment: The World Bank Experience, 1980–1993*. Washington D.C.: The World Bank.

Jordan, Lisa. 1997. *Sustainable Rhetoric vs. Sustainable Development: The Retreat from Sustainability in World Bank Development Policy*. Washington D.C.: Bank Information Center.

Kaimowitz, D., and A. Angelsen. 1997. *A Guide to Economic Models of Tropical Deforestation*. Jakarta: (CIFOR).

Karsenty, Alain. 1998. *Environmental Taxation and Economic Instruments for Forestry Management in the Congo Basin.* London: IIED.

Karsenty, Alain, and D. V. Joiris. 1999. *Les Systemes locaux de gestion dans le basin Congolaos.* Libreville, Gabon: Central African Regional Program for the Environment (CARPE), CAROE-IR1.

Kishor, Nalin, and Luis Constantino. 1994. "Sustainable Forestry: Can it Compete?" *Finance and Development* (December).

Klein, Martha, and Mark van der Wal. 1997. "About Tropical Hardwood, Chocolates and Gorillas: Conservation of Forest Fauna in South Cameroon." *The BOS NiEuWSLETTER* Vol. 16 (3), No. 37: 50–58 (November).

Leffler, Keith B., and Randal R. Rucker. 1991. "Transactions Costs and the Efficient Organization of Production: A Study of Timber-Harvesting Contracts." *The Journal of Political Economy,* Vol. 99, Issue 5: 1060–1087 (October).

Lemmens, R. H. M. J., and M. S. M Sosef. 1997. "The Flora of the Congo Basin." *The BOS NiEuWSLETTER* Vol. 16 (3), No. 37: 21–25 (November).

Millington, A. C., R. W. Critchley, T. D. Douglas, P. Ryan. 1994. *Estimating Woody Biomass in Sub-Saharan Africa.* Washington, D. C. World Bank.

Millington, A. C., and K. Pye. 1994. *Environmental Change in Drylands: Biogeographical and Geomorphological Perspectives.* Chichester, U.K., New York: J. Wiley & Sons.

MINEF (Ministere de l'Environnnment et des Forets). 1996. Plan national de gestion de l'environnement au Cameroun (PNGE): Volume II: Analyses sectorielles. Yaounde.

Munasinghe, Mohan (ed.). 1996. *Environmental Impact of Macroeconomic and Sectoral Policies.* Washington, D.C.: The World Bank.

Nashashibi, K., and S. Bazzoni. 1994. "Exchange Rates Strategies and Fiscal Performance in Sub-Saharan Africa." International Monetary Fund Staff Papers Vol. 41 No.1:76–122.

Ndjatsana, M., and Nga T. Ndjodo. 1998. "L'exploitation de l'Azobe au Cameroun: Etude de cas de la Societe Design." Seminaire camerouno-hollandais CIPRE/ICCO sur l'exploitation et la gestion durable de l'Azobe.

Newman, Kate. 1992. "Forest People and People in the Forest: Investing in Local Community Development.' In Kevin Cleaver, Mohan Munasighe, Mary Dyson, Nicolas Egli, Axel Peuker, François Wencélius (eds.), *Conservation of West and Central African West Forests.* Washington, D.C.: The World Bank.

Newman, Kate, and W. Cruz. 1995. "Economy-wide Policies and Environment: Lessons from Experience." World Bank Environment Paper No. 10.

O'Halloran, Eavan, and Vincente Ferrer. 1997. «The Evolution of Cameroon's New Forestry Legal, Regulatory, and Taxation System.» World Bank. Washington D.C.

Peters, Charles M. 1996. *The Ecology and Management of Non-Timber Forest Resources.* Washington, D.C.: The World Bank.

Pezzey, John. 1992. "Sustainable Development Concepts: An Economic Analysis." World Bank Environment Paper No.2. Washington D.C.: The World Bank.

Picciotto R. 1992. "Participatory Development: Myths and Dilemmas." World Bank Working Paper No. 930.

Picciotto R., and Eduardo Wiesner. 1998. *Evaluation and Development: The Institutional Dimension.* Washington D.C.: The World Bank.

Plouvier, Dominiek. 1997. "Short Overview of the Situation of Tropical Moist Forests and Forest Management in Central Africa and Markets for African Timber." *The BOS NiEuWSLETTER* Vol. 16 (3), No. 37: 42–49 (November).

Plouvier, Dominiek, and Jean-Luc Roux. 1997. "Promotion of Sustainable Forest Management and Certification in Timber Producing Countries of West and Central Africa." *The BOS NiEuWSLETTER* Vol. 16 (3), No. 37: 99–108 (November).

Porter, Gareth et al. 1998. *A Study of GEF's Overall Performance.* Washington, D.C.: GEF

Reardon, T. and S. A. Vosti. 1995. "Links Between Rural Poverty and the Environment in Developing Countries: Asset Categories and Investment Poverty." *World Development,* Vol. 23, No.9: 1495–1506.

Redwood III, John, R. Robelus, and T. Vetleseter. 1998. "Natural Resource Management Portfolio Review." Environment Department Paper No. 58. Washington, D.C.: The World Bank.

Ross, Michael. 1996. "Conditionality and Logging in the Tropics." In Robert O. Keohane and Marc A. Levy (eds.), *Institutions for Environmental Aid: Pitfalls and Promise.* Cambridge, MA: MIT Press.

Ruf, F. 1995. *Booms et crises du cacao, les vertiges de l'or brun.* Paris: Editions Kharthala

Salanié, Bernard. 1998. *The Economics of Contracts: A Primer.* Cambridge MA: The MIT Press.

Sandler, Todd. 1997. *Global Challenges: An Approach to Environmental, Political, and Economic Problems.* Cambridge: Cambridge University Press.

Sayer, Jeffrey. 1992. "Development Assistance Strategies to Conserve Africa's Rainforests." In Kevin Cleaver, Mohan Munasighe, Mary Dyson, Nicolas Egli, Axel Peuker, François Wencélius (eds.), *Conservation of West and Central African West Forests.* Washington, D.C.: The World Bank.

Serageldin, I., and A. Mahfouz (eds.). 1995. *The Self and the Other: Sustainability and Self-Empowerment.* Washington, D.C.: The World Bank.

Sharma Narendra P., Simon Rietbergen, Claude R. Heimo, and Jyoti Patel. 1994. "A Strategy for the Forest Sector in Sub-Saharan Africa." World Bank Technical Paper No. 251, Africa Technical Department Series. Washington D.C.: The World Bank.

Shepherd, G., D. Brown, M. Richards, and Kathrin Schreckenberg. 1998. *The EU Tropical Forestry Sourcebook.* London: Overseas Development Institute (ODI).

Shirley, Mary M., and L. Colin Xu. 1997. "Information, Incentives, and Commitment: An Empirical Analysis of Contracts between Governments and State Enterprises." Policy Research Working Paper 1769. Washington D.C.: The World Bank.

Stiglitz, J. E. 1989. "Economic Organization, Information, and Development." In Hollis Chenery and T.N. Srinivasan (eds.), *Handbook of Development Economics,* Vol. I. Amsterdam: Elsevier,

_____. 1996. "The Role of Government in Economic Development." In Michael Bruno and Boris Pleskovic (eds.), *Annual World Bank Conference on Development Economics.* Washington, D.C.: The World Bank.

Struhsaker, T. T. 1998. "A Biologist's Perspective on the Role of Sustainable Harvest in Conservation." *Conservation Biology,* Vol. 12, No.4: 930–932.

Sunderlin, W. D., and J. Pokam. 1998. «Economic Crisis and Forest Cover Change in Cameroon: The Roles of Migration, Crop Diversification and Gender Division of Labor.» CIFOR.

Thenkabail, P. S. 1999. «Characterization of the Alternative to Slash-and-Burn Benchmark Research Area Representing the Congolese Rainforests of Africa Using Near-Real-Time SPOT HRV Data. *International Journal of Remote Sensing* 20 (5): 839-77.

Verdoes, Arie. 1997. "Congo Basin Regional Profile." *The BOS NiEuWSLETTER* Vol. 16 (3), No. 37: 5–12 (November).

von Amsberg, Joachim. 1998. "Economic Parameters of Deforestation." *World Bank Economic Review,* Vol. 12, No. 1: 133–153.

Vooren, A. P. 1992. "Harvest Criteria for Tropical Forest Trees." In Kevin Cleaver, Mohan Munasighe, Mary Dyson, Nicolas Egli, Axel Peuker, François Wencélius (eds.), *Conservation of West and Central African West Forests.* Washington, D.C.: The World Bank.

Warford, J. J., M. Munasinghe, and W. Cruz. 1997. *The Greening of Economic Policy Reform Volume I: Principles.* Washington D.C. The World Bank.

Winterbottom, Robert. 1992. "Tropical Forestry Action Plans and Indigenous People: The Case of Cameroon." In Kevin Cleaver, Mohan Munasighe, Mary Dyson, Nicolas Egli, Axel Peuker, François Wencélius (eds.), *Conservation of West and Central African West Forests.* Washington, D.C.: The World Bank.

World Bank. 1990. World Development Report 1990: Poverty. Washington D.C.

_____. 1991a. The Forest Sector: A World Bank Policy Paper.

_____. 1991b. Forestry: The World Bank's Experience. Operations Evaluation Department (OED).

_____. 1992a. Guidelines for Monitoring & Evaluation of GEF Biodiversity Projects. Environment Department.

_____. 1993. Poverty Reduction Handbook. Washington D.C.

_____. 1994a. Conditional Lending Experience in World Bank–Financed Forestry Projects. Report No. 13820, OED.

_____. 1994b. Global Environmental Facility: Independent Evaluation of the Pilot Phase. Washington D.C.: The World Bank.

_____. 1995a. Mainstreaming Biodiversity in Development: A World Bank Assistance Strategy for Implementing the Convention on Biological Diversity. Paper No. 029. Washington, D.C.: Environment Department Paper.

_____. 1995b. Republic of Cameroon: Biodiversity Conservation and Management: Washington, D.C.: GEF Project Document.

_____. 1995. Working with NGOs: A Practical Guide to Operational Collaboration between the World Bank and Non-governmental Organizations. Washington, D.C.: Operations Policy Department.

_____. 1996a. Resettlement and Development: The Bank-wide Review of Projects Involving Involuntary Resettlement 1986–1993. Washington, D.C.: Environment Department.

_____. 1996b. Maximizing Sustainable Forestry Development Impact in the Countries of the Congo Basin: Strategy for AF3. Washington, D.C: AF3AE, The World Bank.

_____. 1997. Five Years after Rio: Innovations in Environmental Policy. Environmentally Sustainable Development Studies and Monographs Series No.18. Washington, DC.: The World Bank.

_____. 1998a. Cameroon: Country Assistance Strategy¾Progress Report.

_____. 1998b. Assessing Development Effectiveness: Evaluation in the World Bank and the International Finance Corporation.

_____. 1998c. 1997 Annual Review of Development Effectiveness. Washington D.C.: OED.

_____. 1998/99. *World Development Report: Knowledge for Development.* Oxford: Oxford University Press.

_____. 1999. Republic of Cameroon: Country Status Report Prepared for the June 1999 SPA Meeting.

WRI (World Resources Institute). 1994. *World Resource 1994-1995.* New York: Oxford University Press.

_____. 2000. A Global Forest Watch Cameroon Report. "An Overview of Logging in Cameroon." Washington, D. C.

Young, H. Peyton. 1994. *Equity: In Theory and Practice.* Princeton, NJ: Princeton University Press.

6

Forest Management in Indonesia: Moving from Autocratic Regime to Decentralized Democracy

Madhur Gautam, Hariadi Kartodihardjo, and Uma Lele

Indonesia is endowed with the second largest expanse of tropical moist forests in the world—more than three-fourths of its 1.9 million square kilometers are officially classified as forestland.[1] Indonesia's forests are important to both the domestic economy and the global environment. They provide livelihoods and food for an estimated 40 million Indonesians dependent on forest resources, they produce raw materials for a large number of domestic and foreign manufacturers, they contain an extraordinary wealth of biodiversity, and they serve the global environment as a vast sink for the absorption of carbon-based air pollution.

For almost three decades prior to 1997, Indonesia was widely recognized as a model of economic development—it had achieved rapid economic growth with a significant decline in poverty. The economic growth was accompanied by low inflation and was broad-based and labor-intensive. On the social front, too, Indonesia performed well, backed by strong human resource development. Social indicators improved reflecting an improvement in the quality of life of average Indonesians, with reduced infant mortality, higher life expectancy, and higher adult literacy.

Driving this impressive performance was a successful export-led development strategy, diversifying Indonesia's exports out of oil and into, among others, forest products. The initial reliance on exports of logs (in the 1970s) gave way to higher-value added processed products, primarily plywood (in the 1980s).[2] The drive to sustain export earnings has more recently focused on expanding the production of pulp and paper and tree crops, especially oil palm.[3] In addition, Indonesia has pursued policies to promote

167

rapid agricultural growth, to reduce it's dependence on food imports, and transmigration, to reduce regional imbalance in population and alleviate poverty.

Indonesia's economic success, however, has been marred by such fundamental shortcomings as corruption, nepotism, fragile governance, and weak financial and social sectors. Thus, while the forest sector has contributed significantly to Indonesia's growth performance, the gains have been achieved at great environmental and social costs.[4] Not only has the use of forest resources been unsustainable (the rate of deforestation has reached an unprecedented 1.7 million ha per year), the distribution of benefits has been highly inequitable. Large-scale commercial logging interests have dominated the sector, almost completely bypassing the forest-dwelling and forest-adjacent communities, some of whom have inhabited their lands for a long time. Depriving villagers of access to forest resources has been the cause of some of Indonesia's most serious social problems.

Since the inception of Suharto's New Order Regime in 1967, a handful of international conglomerates have dominated forest extraction activities and the wood processing industries. Timber concessions have been granted as a form of political patronage. Industrial interests, particularly the Indonesian Wood Panel Association (a plywood marketing cartel), have had an unusual influence on forest sector policy and governance. These large-scale commercial logging activities have been a leading cause of deforestation and land degradation, although small-scale farmers have become a significant part of the process in recent years.

Indonesia has a highly articulated set of laws, rules and regulations regarding land use and forest management. At the highest political levels, at least externally, Indonesia has projected a strong commitment to the environment. Yet despite these stated intentions, the damage to forests have continued virtually unabated. There is a large gap between the rhetoric and the implementation of existing laws. Serious governance problems have plagued the forest sector, rendering the official forest policy de facto ineffective. The concession system is ironically leading to degradation of forest areas rather than regenerating them: the lack of implementation of rules and regulations governing contracts provides a strong incentive for concession holders not to adopt sustainable practices. Unclear and overlapping forest boundaries have resulted in granting concessions and conversion rights in areas meant to be protected and conserved.

Poor enforcement of laws, often in collusion with officials, is such that almost all domestic demand for logs is now being met by illegal logging, which accounts for more timber removal than legal logging, whereas official concessions account only for processed exports.[5] The governance issues are highlighted by the events following the 1997-98 forest fires which damaged an estimated 9,745,000 hectares. Despite the fact that 176 private companies were found responsible for setting fires to clear land for plantations, including 133 oil palm companies, almost no punitive action was taken.

The recent events in Indonesia have on the one hand brought the forest sector issues to the forefront, but on the other hand they are adding to the pressures on forests. Since the start of the East Asian Financial crisis in 1997, Indonesia has endured severe economic, political and environmental shocks. The substantial devaluation of the Rupiah, the sharp decline in GDP, the collapse of the industrial sector for lack of adequate working capital, and three successive droughts have led to unprecedented increases in food and fuel prices. Economic hardship has forced large numbers of Indonesians to return to their native lands accelerating the rate of deforestation and biodiversity loss. Forest fires, mentioned above, have only made matters worse.[6]

Since 1997, Indonesia has also been through major political changes. The long authoritarian rule of President Suharto came to an end, and Indonesia has since been moving towards a more decentralized democratic form of government. This transition, however, has proved to be challenging—at the time of the writing of this study, Indonesia had its third president. The process of devolving political power to smaller jurisdictions is adding to the administrative problems. This devolution of authority has been more reactionary, responding to regional discontent and external circumstances, rather than a result of deliberative planning. As a result, the central government influence on regional affairs, including natural resource management, has been significantly reduced.

The role of external development partners has also changed substantially. Immediately following the financial crisis in 1997, Indonesia found itself in great need of external economic assistance, providing the international community an opportunity to promote long outstanding reforms in many sectors, including the forest sector. True to experience, however, the adoption of key policy and institutional reforms has been slow except for the relatively easier "stroke of the pen" reforms. For example, a new forest law was put in place in 1999. However, the law is not much different from its predecessor in that it focuses on the state monopoly on forest resources and on the process of awarding concessions. Not surprisingly, there has been little noticeable impact on forest sector management thus far. This experience is in sharp contrast to the actions taken by, for example, China and Costa Rica, who are implementing their forest policies with visible results, as discussed in previous chapters of this book.

The World Bank's involvement in Indonesia's forest sector has a relatively short history. Nevertheless, this brief relationship has been through three distinct phases: a project-lending phase (1988–94), a non-lending phase (1995–97), and an adjustment lending phase—with forest management conditions included in a structural adjustment program (1997 to the present). In general, the Bank's overall assistance strategy prior to the first forest operation in 1988 was very much focused on economic growth, and reducing population pressures and poverty. The Bank did have a forest sector policy at the time, but the impact of macroeconomic policies or the cross-sectoral impacts of other policies, such as for agriculture or population redistribution, were rarely considered. Thus, programs such as the transmigration of people from Java to the outer islands rarely considered their impacts on the indigenous peoples or the forests.[7]

By the early 1990s, the Bank had a reasonably well-developed sectoral strategy for Indonesia. This was laid out in a Bank report in 1993 on Indonesia's forest sector which discussed a wide range of issues. What was then the Indonesian Ministry of Forestry and Estate Crops (MOFEC), however, appears to have been dissatisfied by the report, which explicitly called for far-reaching policy and institutional reforms. As a result, at the sectoral level, the dialogue between the Bank and MOFEC broke down in 1994, and the lending program came to a halt.[8] At the country level, however, till 1995 the Bank ignored forest sector issues in its Country Assistance Strategy (CAS). Until 1997, the Bank remained reluctant to pursue the sensitive issues of policy and institutional reform in the forest sector, with the country department apparently not willing to jeopardize its country relations.

The Bank's adjustment lending following the 1997 financial crisis led to a reengagement with forest sector issues in Indonesia. The Bank sought to resolve long-standing issues by including conditions tied to changes in forest sector policies. Although the government agreed to the reforms and has promulgated new laws and regulations, implementation has been slow despite public acknowledgement by government officials at the highest levels of the weaknesses in Indonesia's management of the sector. The enforcement of forest regulations remains the biggest challenge. This has been further complicated by the unclear functions and authority of forest management organizations at the central, provincial and district levels, following the ongoing decentralization process.

At the same time, it must be acknowledged that some changes in the forest sector are, in fact, occurring in Indonesia, and some reform-minded officials in MOFEC, and others in the government and in civil society, have expressed a keen desire to break with the status quo. In part, slow implementation has been the result of institutional and political instability. The leadership in the Forest Ministry changed when it was merged with the Ministry of Agriculture in 2000. Also in 2000, a presidential decree established an Interdepartmental Committee on Forestry (IDCF) and a working group for coordinating the implementation of forest policy. In 2001, the government announced that, beginning in 2003, all forest concession holders would be required to obtain certificates of sustainability or lose their concessions. While this was a step in the right direction, much remains to be done to improve the management of the forest sector.

There has also been a substantial change in the way the Bank does business with Indonesia. During the preparation of a new CAS in 2001, Bank representatives conducted extensive consultations with NGOs, the academic community, and the private sector in Indonesia. This constituted a break with the past, when such consultations included only the Bank and representatives of the Finance Ministry. During these consultations in 2001, the stakeholders revealed a strong preference for investment in the productive sector and emphasized the need for "people oriented" development approaches as opposed to focusing on environmental concerns. They also urged the use of concessional funds from the IDA rather than loans from the IBRD but rejected the use of grants for projects other than technical assistance.

Looking to the future, it is imperative for Indonesia to develop a clear and comprehensive forest policy and an operational framework that balances environmental sustainability and equitable growth. To be successful, the policy needs buy-in from civil society and hence needs to be developed transparently and with the participation of all stakeholders in a way that reflects the realities of the sector. This would also provide the framework within which external development partners like the Bank can operate and assist.

The policy and the operational framework need to squarely address the sector's governance problems, the long-term sustainability of the economic benefits from forest resources, and the important role of the losers and gainers among rural communities from the past patterns of domestic growth. Insufficient analysis of many forest sector issues has been a particular problem in finding policy solutions—developing a coherent framework and proper sequencing of reforms calls for a detailed understanding of the forest sector and its relationship to other sectors. The overall framework must deal with the legitimate rights to land and access to resources by local traditional communities, develop a far better information system to guide policy implementation by reliably monitoring the use and changes in forest resources, and put in place far more effective enforcement mechanisms.

The experience of other countries can be very helpful in helping Indonesia develop appropriate policy and operational responses. Community participation in forest management is in its nascent stages in Indonesia, but experience in India has been positive. Recent experience in Indonesia is similar also to approaches in Brazil and China that demonstrate that devolution and decentralization by themselves are no guarantee for reducing the rate of deforestation. Some form of resource transfer or compensation may well be needed to induce local communities and regional governments to retain their forests intact. Certification of wood products has started in Indonesia but is still in very early stages; for it to be a fully effective management tool, Indonesia needs to redouble its efforts to build institutional capacity and address related governance issues.

Forest Cover Changes

The Classification of Indonesia's Forests

Some 147 million hectares, about 78 percent of Indonesia's total land area, have been officially designated by the government as forestland and thus under MOFEC control.[9] About 113 million of those hectares are supposed to be administered as "permanent" forest not subject to conversion to other uses (Box 6.1). Another 8 million hectares are designated for conversion to other uses. The official designation of area under different categories of forests has changed over time. The area in protected forests increased from about 30 million hectares in 1984 to about 35 million hectares in 1997 (figure 6.1). Conservation forest area has remained at roughly 19 million hectares. The third category is production forest, which are further sub-classified into normal- and limited-production forests: the area under normal production forests has remained at 34 million hectares but the area under limited-production forests has declined from 30 million hectares to 25 million hectares. The largest decline has been in conversion forests, from about 30 million hectares in 1984 to about 8 million in 1997.

Two categories of land are excluded from official statistics on land with trees: smallholder woodlots and agroforestry lands, and land devoted to perennial estate crops (rubber, coconut, tobacco, oil palm, sugarcane, fruits and nuts, and other plantation crops). While there are no good measures of agroforestry plantings, anecdotal observations suggest that these are significant, particularly on Java. The area in perennial estate crops has grown rapidly, from 5.6 million hectares in 1973 to 12.7 million in 1994 to more than 13.4 million in 1996 (Ministry of Forestry and Estate Crops 1998). The impact of tree crops on the environment is comparable to the impact of the managed forest plantations included in the "official forest" category.

The actual extent of forest cover, however, differs from the officially designated forest lands, including in the "permanent" forests. Recent estimates from MOFEC suggest that well over 20 million hectares of forests have been lost between 1985 and 1997 alone, giving an alarmingly high average rate of deforestation of 1.7 million hectares per year (World Bank 2001). The area under forests is currently estimated at under 100 million hectares.

The extent of damage under different categories of forests is not available but it is clear that the destruction covers all forests. Even the protected and conservation areas have been encroached upon, but the extent to which this is taking place in the aggregate is not known for lack of data. Estimates using limited available official data by Kartodihardjo (2001a) indicate that the highest rate of forest degradation (89 percent) appears to be in production forest managed by concessionaires (table 6.1). Degradation in protection and conservation forests may be as high as 46 percent and 38 percent,

> **Box 6.1**
> **Forest Classification in Indonesia**
>
> **Permanent forestland** is land capable of growing 20 cubic meters of wood per hectare or land with standing trees greater than 50 centimeters in diameter at breast height.
> **State-owned forest area** legally owned by the state. This area is not always covered by forest, which means that a change in the legal forest area may not indicate a corresponding change in the actual forested area. In 1984 the state-owned forest area was determined on the basis of a functional forestland classification system, but in 1997 its determination changed as a result of integration of this classification system with provincial spatial planning. The main forest classifications are:
> **Protection forest**: Forest designated for stabilization of mountain slopes, upland watersheds, fragile lands, reservoirs, and catchment areas. Controlled sustainable extraction of non-wood products could be allowed.
> **Conservation forest**: Forest designated for conservation, including for wildlife, national parks, and tourism.
> **Production forest**: Forest designated for timber harvesting. These are further sub classified into permanent production forests—with sustainable harvest practices allowing for trees down to 50 cm in diameter at breast height (dbh)—and Limited production forests: Where harvests are restricted to trees greater than 60 cm in dbh.
> **Conversion forest**: Forest assigned for conversion of agriculture or other non-forest use.

Figure 6.1
Change in Forest Classifications, 1984-97 (millions of hectares)

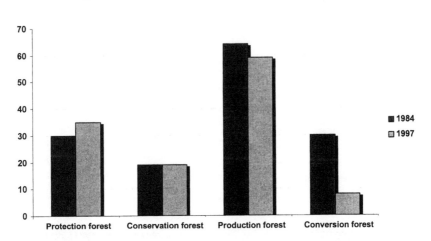

Source: Kartodihardjo and Supriono 1998; World Bank 1993b

respectively. Recent forest mapping work by MOFEC confirms that the indiscriminate nature of the destruction of natural forests: for the three regions of Sumatra, Kalimantan, and Sulawesi, forests cover about 77 percent, 82 percent and 66 percent of the area designated for protection, conservation and production.

Biodiversity

Indonesia is one of the two most biologically diverse countries in the world (Brazil being the other). The main repositories of that biodiversity are forests and coastal regions, and some biota like mangrove swamps are both forest and coastal. To protect its rich biodiversity, Indonesia has designated a network of 35 national parks and 339 other reserves (including coastal reserves). The Indonesian archipelago constitutes only 1.3 percent of the earth's land surface but contains about 25 percent of the world's known species of fish, 17 percent of birds, 16 percent of reptiles and amphibians, 12 percent of

Table 6.1
Recalculation of Areas of Production Forest, Protection Forest, and Conservation Forest

Forest function	Forest condition					
	Primary/virgin forest		Secondary forest, degraded forest, non-forest		Total	
	Million hectares	%	Million hectares	%	Million hectares	%
Production forest (managed by concessions)[a]	18.4	45	22.8	55	41.2	100
Production forest (state-delivered concessions)[a]	0.6	11	5.1	89	5.7	100
Protection forest[b]	6.7	54	5.8	46	12.5	100
Conservation forest[b]	10.8	62	6.6	38	17.4	100
Total	36.5	47	40.2	53	76.7	100

Source: Kartodihardjo (2001a) using MoF data for 2000

a) Based on interpretation of 320 concessions using landsat images dated April 1997 to January 2000.

b) Based on interpretation of air photo and airborne radar (1996-1997). These data present an evaluation of the condition of 42 percent of the total area in protection forest and 58 percent of the area in conservation forest.

mammals, 10 percent of plants, and an unknown number of invertebrates, fungi, and microorganisms (Ministry of National Development Planning 1993).

The current situation with respect to conserving Indonesia's wealth of biodiversity is dire (World Bank 2001). The attention afforded to biodiversity conservation and protected area management, while on the increase in recent years, has been inadequate to curtail significant species extinction or to prevent losses stemming from the destruction of natural habitats. Forest in lowlands are the most biologically rich, but the loss of forest cover has also been mainly in these forests, given their potential for plantations and other large-scale development.

Despite the recognized importance of biodiversity conservation and the availability of resources (domestic and donor), there are important gaps in the protected area system. The protected areas are not secure and their management is weak (World Bank 2001). The management of designated protected areas is well beyond the means of the responsible agency, the Directorate-General of Forest Protection and Nature Conservation in MOFEC. Many areas are subject to overlapping and conflicting claims; the weaknesses in the legal system and governance problem make it difficult to curb illegal activities.

The main approach to conservation in Indonesia has been through the Integrated Conservation Development Programs (ICDPs). While some ICDPs are promising, they have not had any significant impact on biodiversity conservation, and they are not sustainable (Wells et. al. 1999). As discussed in the conclusion of this volume, the problem lies in the seemingly incomplete approach to biodiversity conservation. The ICDPs focus on local communities as the primary threat to protected areas and biodiversity, whereas the major threats are from large-scale operations such as road construction, mining, logging, logging concessions and sponsored migration. At the same time, ICDP efforts to establish incentives for conservation by investing in local development are frustrated by inadequate law enforcement and expropriation of natural resources by powerful non-local interests. Thus, although in principle the past government tried to strike a balance between conservation and the productive use of forests, in practice its actions have shown a preference for the exploitation over conservation.

Causes of Deforestation

The underlying causes of deforestation is a debate related to the extent of deforestation and the relationship of associated costs and distribution of benefits. This debate is significant because of the implications of Indonesia's past experience for the future forest sector policies (Sunderlin and Resosudarmo 1996). In addition to the general lack of data, the debate has been fueled by confusion on individual researchers' definitions of "forests" and "deforestation," as well as the definitions and understanding of traditional "swidden" or shifting cultivation, as opposed to the practices followed by migrant smallholders.

One side of the debate stresses the role of smallholders and, directly or indirectly, shifting cultivation as the primary source of deforestation, a view long espoused by the New Order regime (Barber 1997). The role of smallholders is also stressed in the World Bank's 1991 forest strategy. The other side of the debate, based on empirical research evidence, stresses the power of the international demand forces mentioned earlier, as well as government policies and the commercial interests as the main actors responsible.

Research on the underlying causes has become particularly active in recent years but remains piecemeal. It suggests that multiple factors have in fact contributed (e.g., timber sector, tree crop plantations, transmigration—spontaneous and regular, and shifting agriculture), but the relative importance of government programs and commercial interest is increasingly being accepted (Sunderlin and Resosudarmo 1996).

A major source of deforestation and forest degradation has historically been the large-scale commercial timber interests. From about 1950 to 1985, commercial logging for timber (unprocessed) exports was the main source. Log exports from Indonesia to Japan increased from 6 million m^3 in 1970 to 11.45 million m^3 in 1973 and remained at 8.6 million until 1985, when the log export ban was imposed. Over this period, some estimates suggest that about 33 million ha of forests were logged, roughly at the rate of 1 million ha per year (Barber 1997). From 1985 onwards, with the shift to higher value added products, the pace of forest clearing or degradation has coincided with the rapid growth of the forest product processing industry, particularly for plywood. More recently, the role of the pulp and paper industry and the growth of estate crops, especially oil palm, have accelerated the pace of conversion of natural forest. As discussed later, the current economic incentives favor conversion for all kinds of tree crops have increased considerably since the onset of the financial crisis.

The World Bank has also shifted its views from a predominantly smallholder-led deforestation (World Bank 1990b) to recognizing the significantly greater role of the timber industry in deforestation and degradation of Indonesian forests (World Bank 1993b). However, forests are subject to stress from a number of different sources, often resulting from complex interactions of forestry and non-forestry related policy and regulatory policies (Angelsen and Kaimowitz 1999). The impact of specific policies requires detailed analysis in particular circumstances, but the Bank's economic and sector work (ESW), now called (AAA), has been limited in recent years. As discussed later in this chapter, the analytical work that the Bank has done (World Bank 1995a) recognizes the emerging trends in the forest sector, but has not fully assessed the extent or the pace of development of these trends and their implications for current or future levels of deforestation.

Among the key areas where more detailed analysis is needed include the role of macroeconomic policies, the domestic and international demand for forest based products and their backward linkages to the forest sector, and the forces behind the conversion of forests, primarily the strong incentives provided by the returns to agriculture vis-à-vis those to sustainable management of forests. These pressures are particularly important in the context of Indonesia's political and administrative set up, with an almost complete absence of enforcement of laws, rules, and regulations. This latter greatly reduces the costs and increases the profits from unsustainable forest management and has promoted widespread illegal logging.

The Management of Forests

Indonesian Forest Policy

State ownership, per se, is common in most nations and Indonesia shares this experience. The ownership of most forestland in Indonesia was transferred to the New Order state in 1967 through the Basic Forestry Law (*Undang-Undang Pokok kehutanan No. 5/1967*). However, all traditional or *adat* rights were subordinated to this law and the national forest policy. The rights of the communities who have traditionally lived in and around the forests have been neglected at best, but more generally overruled.

Administrative authority for the state's forest estate was vested in the Ministry of Forestry until 1998. In 1998, estate crops were included in the responsibilities of the new MOFEC. This change has important implications for the future management of forests through the implementation and impact of forest policies. With management responsibility of about three-quarters of the country's land, MOFEC has considerable weight in land use decisions, a major field of public policy.

The Ministry delegates management of "production" and "limited production" forests to private concessions and state-owned enterprises. It designates "conversion" forests for timber harvests followed by conversion to agricultural and other non-forest uses. Conversion forests may be designated for conversion to estate crops or forest plantations, in which case the authority for their oversight remains within the MOFEC; or they may be designed for use by transmigrants, in which case the authority will be transferred to the Ministry of Transmigration and Shifting Cultivation once conversion occurs.

Commercial timber harvests have been the dominant concern in the implementation of Indonesian forest policy. The management of the forest sector has catered to the commercial timber industry based on a system of forest concession rights (*Hak Pengusahaan Hutan* or HPH), industrial forest or timber plantation concessions (*Hutan Tanaman Industri* or HTI), and estate crop plantations. The concessions are licensed to private enterprises or to special state-owned enterprises (*Badan Usaha Milik Negara* or BUMN). State-owned enterprises include *PT. Perhutani* plantations and five PT. *Inhutani*, who are largely responsible for rehabilitating revoked concessions.[10]

The timber and wood processing sectors, and more recently estate crops and forest plantation sectors, are dominated by a few integrated conglomerates. The plywood industry has dominated the processing sector since the mid-1980s, and until recently was tightly controlled by a plywood marketing cartel. As mentioned earlier, the concession system has been the embodiment of the political patronage system of the New Order regime, with significant financial gains accruing to a few politically well connected individuals with an unusual degree of influence on the Indonesian forest and trade policies (Barber 1997). With the changing trends in the processing sector, and emerging market forces, rent-seeking has increasingly turned towards exploiting the HTI system, often in combination with the HPH system, and the conversion of natural forests to estate crop plantations (Kartodihardjo and Supriono 1998).

Indonesian commentators have argued that a significant consequence of the forest policy and the manner in which it has been implemented has been an increase in economically deprived and environmentally poor regions in and around forests. The Bank's own approach to the issues of forest dwelling communities has changed substantially over time, from direct funding of the infamous transmigration schemes in the early 1980s, to the recognition of the local communities as a key "interest group" (World Bank 1993b), to a letter to the government in June 1999 suggesting that it should listen to all stakeholders before rushing to pass the new forestry law.

Industrial Wood: the basic Forestry Law established the basis for commercial exploitation of forests in the Outer Islands by providing MOFEC the authority to grant HPH *timber concession* licenses in areas designated as production and limited production forests. Government regulation number 21 of 1970 provided the HPH holder a non-transferable right for 20 years, and stipulated that the concessionaire follow the principles of sustainable forest management (SFM) as prescribed by the Indonesian selective logging and planting system (*Tebang Pilih Tanam Indonesia* or TPTI). The system prohibits harvesting trees with a diameter less than 50 cm and to follow a 35-year rotation to permit adequate regeneration. The Ministry and the HPH holder sign an agreement that contains rules for long-term planning, harvest levels based on approved annual work plans (*Rencana Karya Tahunan* or RKT), and land rehabilitation after harvests, and community development. The applicant guarantees the establishment of a vertically integrated forest industrial activity (sawmill or plymill) in association with the concession. The

Forestry Agreement is renewable, and in some cases, renewals have been denied on the basis of poor performance. In many cases, however, HPHs have been renewed despite poor management. All *PT. Inhutani* have been assigned management responsibilities for some of the lands from non-renewed or revoked HPH licenses.

Despite the requirement that concessionaires establish mills in association with their concessions, there never has been a requirement that concessions supply only their own mills. Concessions generally do provide raw material for their own mills because the mills and the concession are in the same timber shed. Nevertheless, when other concessions and mills occur within the same timber shed, concessionaires have a history of allowing the local market to allocate their timber harvests.[11]

Since the mid-1980s, the government has promoted, financed out of the Reforestation Fund (proceeds from the reforestation fee discussed below), industrial forest or *timber plantations* through the HTI program. The aim of the program was to encourage the establishment of a large industrial forest estate to meet the country's long-term needs (World Bank 1993b). Prior to 1989, the HTI scheme required the HPH concession holders to undertake plantation activity as part of the agreement. However, poor results and quality of stands established led to a new approach in 1989, which granted a land use right in the form of an HTI concession with an understanding that the developer would have the rights to the wood produced.

According to government regulation (no. 7, 1990), HTI development can take place within production forests, and the permit allows the holder to clear cut a designated area and to replant it with commercial tree species (Barr 1999b). The scheme was designed to rehabilitate unproductive or degraded forests, with a residual standing forest inventory of less than twenty m^3 per hectare of commercial species with a minimum diameter of 30 cm. Private investors, cooperatives and state-owned companies (or joint-ventures among these) can apply for an HTI permit for a period of 35 years. Their management distinguishes them from the concessions on which selective harvest practices are required as a means to obtain natural regeneration and maintain the existing forest.

To establish HTIs, the government has provided financial incentives to private investors. The scheme requires only a 21 percent equity investment for the plantation's total capital requirements. Firms entering joint-ventures with one of the *Inhutani's* can secure 14 percent of the project's total cost as a nonrefundable allocation from the Reforestation Fund, and can also get an interest free non-collateralized loan for a period of 10 years equivalent to 32.5 percent of the investment from the Restoration Fund.

There are three distinct types of HTIs: pulpwood plantations, non-pulp, and HTI-transmigration. In consonance with the governments efforts to promote the pulp and paper industry (also since the mid-1980s), pulp plantations have been regulated with a different set of rules than the other, longer rotation timber plantations. Whereas the concession size of non-pulp timber plantations is limited to 60,000 hectares, the pulp plantation size limit is 300,000 hectares. Further, while all area of non-pulp plantations must be planted, pulp plantations are allowed to plant a portion of the area but can log the rest for use as pulp until the pulpwood production comes on stream. HTI-transmigration scheme, introduced in 1992, allows clear-cutting on an HPH site, provided 10 percent of the area is reserved for transmigration purposes. The rest of the arrangements are similar to other HTI contracts.

MOFEC has also taken other measures to benefit the pulp and paper industry by introducing regulations, in 1992, requiring all Production Forests within a 100 km radius of a pulp mill to be utilized for pulpwood plantations. The Ministerial Decision 442/1992 circumvents the original HTI regulations on converting productive natural forests, permitting clear-cutting of significant stands of commercially valuable timber.

The government attaches three basic fees to the operation of forest concessions:

- The IHPH (*Iuran Hak Pengusahaan Hutan*) is an annual area-based fee paid at the granting of the concession. It typically runs in the range of US$3-10 per ha. The MOFEC collects the IHPH and redistributes 80 percent to local governments (16 percent to provincial government and 64 percent to regency—kabupaten-government) and 20 percent to the central government.
- The reforestation fee (*Dana Reboisasi*) is a fee per cubic meter of wood harvested. It varies by region and species group. The MOFEC recalculates this fee semi-annually. The current (January 2002) average fee is in the neighborhood of US$16.50 per cubic meter. This fee contributes to a fund that was designed to cover reforestation costs. In the past, it had become a source of general support for the MOFEC. It is also widely known that these funds have been an easy source of discretionary funds for special political interests, and especially higher political interests external to the Ministry. Based on Law No. 25/1999, reforestation fees included one of the sources of specific allocation fund (Dana Alokasi Khusus) collected by MOFEC and redistributes 40 percent to local government and 60 percent to central government.
- The IHH (*Iuran Hasil Hutan*) was a royalty on logs charged on the basis of weight or volume, collected by the MOFEC. The IHH varies by region and species group. This royalty was semi-annually based on the check price (the local market price for the lowest quality log) identified by the Ministry of Trade and Industry. Following the conditions in the IMF emergency package, the IHH has been replaced by a forest resource royalty (FRR or Pajak Sumberdaya Hutan-PSDH). Currently, the FRR is to be revised periodically to ensure capture of at least 60 percent rent from timber. (The Bank's adjustment loans required that

the revision be made by the end of 1998, but MOFEC did not think it was necessary. Eventually, the MOFEC announced a compromise increase to ten percent.)

Before 1998, IHH revenues were distributed 45 percent to local governments (30 percent provincial and 15 percent district) and 65 percent to three central government accounts: 15 percent to a MOFEC account to be allocated to forestry activities within provinces, 20 percent to the central government for forest rehabilitation and forestry activities, and 20 percent for PBB (Pajak Bumi dan Banguan), a property tax on land and buildings which is transferred to the Ministry of Finance. A presidential decree in April 1988 combined the latter two in a central government account for forestry activities. Based in Law 25/1999, MOFEC collects the PSDH and redistributes 80 percent to local governments (16 percent to provincial government and 64 percent to Kabupaten) and 20 percent to central government.

The funds collection from DR and IHH are the largest by far, and their calculations and allocations are important topics in discussions of policy reform. Collections from the *DR* range upward from Rp. 800 billion in 1996 (US$340 million at the average annual exchange rate for 1996 of 2348 Rp per dollar), Rp 1.5 trillion in 1998 (US $196 million at the average annual exchange rate of 7619:1), and they are growing at a rapid rate. According to an external audit, for the five years ending March 31, 1998, the reported total amount of the reforestation fund was US$1.73 billion. The audit (conducted by Ernst and Young) also noted that based on realistic estimates of timber yield of 60 cubic meters, the reforestation fund should have been US$4.388 billion, suggesting a receivable loss over the five year period of US$2.658, plus an additional loss of $US1.56 billion in interest.

Log Allocation and the Processing Industries

A 200 percent export duty on log exports replaced a log export ban in 1992. Both regulations effectively restrict international participation in Indonesia's log market and reduce local prices. These regulations provide effective subsidies for the domestic wood processing industries. While these restrictions reduce the draw on forests by decreasing export demand, the lower prices also encourage domestic processing demand and decrease the incentive to reforest.

More recently, the export tax has been revised following IMF-World Bank structural adjustment conditions. The 200 percent duty was decreased to 30 percent in 1998 as a first step in getting rid of it altogether. Nevertheless, there was little increase in log exports in 1999, perhaps because domestic mill demand is high and demand from Indonesia's traditional markets for processed products (Japan and Korea) is low, but also because exports require an export license. The Ministry of Trade and Industry has approved only 21 export licenses for 479,390 m³ of logs. No new licenses were approved in 1999. Actual official exports were only 114,000 m³ as of December 1998, with the majority shipped to China and India. The trade restrictions were, thus, effectively still in place. In 2001, a ban on log exports was reimposed.

While these restrictions tend to decrease log consumption below what international market conditions would predict, the government also subsidizes forest processing industry. In the past, there have been capital investment subsidies for mills and export subsidies on forest products. These further improved the international position of the wood processing sector. Preferential export treatment (export taxes on sawnwood and rattan, but not on plywood or furniture) provided further advantages for finished wood products. The capital subsidies for mills have been discontinued. The export duties on sawnwood and rattan were to be reduced as part of the IMF reform package in 1998, making export duties uniform across all wood processing industries.

The producers' associations for plywood (APKINDO) and molding (ISA) added their own deviations from competitive market behavior. These associations used marketing boards to allocate export quotas before the reforms of 1998. Membership in APKINDO was compulsory for plywood mills. Some argue that compulsory membership was a means of regulating entry to the industry—but it is also true that the plywood industry was characterized by excess capacity. The pulp and paper industry association (APKI) has no history of marketing boards or other domestic or export controls. However, the government has a stated policy of improving its market share of the world pulp and paper industry.

Land Conversion Policy

The conversion of forestland to estate crops has not been constrained by either government or industrial infrastructure to control the market. Licenses for forest conversion are obtained upon request. Both large and small estate operations have obtained licenses but the area allocated to large-scale commercial operations has increased significantly in recent years. The current policies also permit the same company to operate an HPH, an HTI, and an estate crop plantation at the same time.

Government regulations stipulate that estate crop plantations be established on Conversion Forest areas. However, the existing rules of land allocation and forest classification are widely ignored. The process by which forest areas are declared as conversion forest is neither serious nor transparent. The problem is perpetuated by the lack of clarity of existing boundaries between conversion and non-conversion forests, and variable definitions of what constitutes a conversion forest.

Among the uses that converted lands are put to, the government since the late 1960s has vigorously promoted oil palm estates. The strategic importance of oil palm (foreign exchange earnings, domestic cooking oil supply, and rural labor absorption) has made the sector a top priority for the government (Casson 1999). Schemes providing incentives to domestic and international investors have facilitated the growth of the sector.

Since the financial crisis in 1997, there have been a number of changes in policy that are likely to affect the rate of conversion of forests (Casson 1999). These include reduction of export taxes on palm oil, liberalization of foreign investment in the sector, revoking of conversion permits for failure to develop the estates, limitations on plantations sizes, granting permission to state forestry companies to convert 30 percent of their concessions to oil palm (inside production forest boundaries), increased autonomy of local administration through decentralized decision making and increased budgetary allocations, and a new regulation that permits plantation companies to establish tree crops along with timber plantations in non-productive production forests formerly allocated to logging companies.

The second use of converted forestland is for settlement by transmigrants. Fifty-nine percent of Indonesia's 195 million population (in 1995) is concentrated on Java, while the outer islands contain 93 percent of the nation's land area. The outer islands are an attractive source of land to younger Indonesians, especially from Java's denser regions. In fact, Indonesia has experienced a net migration outflow from Java to the outer islands.

The government has three programs for encouraging transmigration. The first provides land, facilities, training, and financing for an initial period to acceptable applicants. The second program is entirely dependent on voluntary action, with no government assistance but they must obtain permission from the Ministry of Transmigration and Shifting Cultivation for the land they do settle. The third program occurs in association with the private sector. In this program, the MOFEC provides land for new settlers while forest plantations (HTI) guarantee employment. This program was designed to assist plantations in less settled regions in attracting labor for their forest operations. The Ministry adds lands to this program upon its approval of requests from the plantations.

While many have taken advantage of these programs, the programs also have their serious critics. The Indonesian criticisms of these programs have been that the lands allocated to transmigrants are generally of low quality for agriculture and that transmigration, by separating extended families, imposes heavy personal costs. These programs have also had significant negative impacts on indigenous forest dwellers and on the forests themselves. Transmigrants have resorted to unsustainable slash and burn practices, either for lack of adequate land, lack of appropriate agricultural skills or poor soil productivity.

Community Participation

The highly centralized "top-down" management of the forest sector reflects the mindset of the New Order Regime since it took over in 1966. This
manner of operation allowed the state to get a firm control over the country
politically and economically, and inevitably had negative consequences on
many peoples, but perhaps most significantly on the poor who live in or near
the forests.[12] In Indonesia, as elsewhere in the developing world, the struggle
for land and access to forest resources is not simply between the large-scale
extraction companies (in forests and mining) and the poor, but has increasingly led to social and ethnic conflicts between the poor and the poor, particularly the transmigrants and the indigenous people.

Indonesia's many cultures operate under norms, rules, resource management strategies, and spiritual belief systems known collectively as *adat*. Under the New Order regime, *adat* laws and institutions are recognized so long
as they do not impede the state's political or economic objectives. But *adat*
has weakened in many regions because of pervasive government intervention. (Barber 1997). The basic philosophy of the New Order state resisted
diversity, and denied the existence of distinct "indigenous peoples" with
autonomous claims over territory or resources, or independent local systems
of spiritual beliefs and political authority. Any attempts to emphasize diversity were perceived as subversive threats to the national unity (Evers 1995).

The New Order considered traditional swidden agricultural practices to be
environmentally destructive and wasteful. Instead, it appropriated land for
redistribution, logging, commercial agriculture, and resettlement. The Indonesian Forestry Action Programme of 1991 considered shifting cultivation a
significant source of deforestation, although other research has since shown
that traditional practices can be sustainable (World Bank 1993b; Tomich et
al. 1998).

In addition to large-scale commercial interests, indigenous dwellers have
had to contend with transmigrants for access to resources. As a result conflicts
between local communities and logging concessions, plantations,
transmigrants, and other state-sponsored activities have become endemic
(Barber 1997). But only in the past few years have these conflicts started to
gain attention. The state was once able to contain conflict and discontent
through an efficient military and domestic security apparatus. Now, following the financial crisis, with increasing resource scarcities, more poverty, and
less law and order, the conflicts and violence have become more serious and
widespread (Kartodihardjo 1999b).

The issues of *adat* rights and tenure are critical not only as basic human
rights issues but also as a potentially useful system for sustainably managing
the remaining forests. Although the benefits of participation and consultations have been recognized for some time, the development of community

participation (community forestry) is still in its infancy (Sève 1999; Potter and Lee 1998). Laws passed in 1992 recognize community territorial rights, the rights to cultural autonomy, and the priority accorded to historically vulnerable communities (World Bank 1993b). The laws also establish the communities' rights to be consulted on new activities affecting their historic areas.

But the laws required local governments to formally recognize the preexistence of traditional rights, a difficult process. Further, the commercial use of forest products by these communities was explicitly restricted. Reflecting New Order biases, shifting cultivators were deemed destroyers of the environment and of local and national development, and were to be resettled outside forest areas.

As problems continued, in 1995 the Bank's sector work again called for increased participation in forest management, consultations with local communities prior to commercial activities, revenue sharing for regenerating activities, and increased stewardship roles for local communities. It also recommended that the government alter the forestry act and other legislation and regulations to facilitate titling of forest dwelling and adjacent communities in forestland (World Bank 1995a). So far, however, little progress has been made on these issues.

Donors, research institutes, and NGOs have also tried to implement community-based forest management, most of them through tree planting. While the projects have yielded important lessons, they have had only isolated impacts. Few programs have been officially established, and innovative ones are generally viewed as marginal to the agendas of central or local governments.

Certification

Forest certification, or eco-labeling, emerged in the 1990s as a way to improve the environmental and ecological quality of the world's forests while maintaining a sustainable level of production. Though the concept is likely to gain importance as environmental consciousness grows, the definition of sustainability and the economic and equity implications of forest certification are still open to debate.

Indonesia is among the few countries to establish a national certifying body, the Indonesian Eco-labeling Institute (*Lambaga Ekolabel Indonesia or* LEI). This followed the government commitment to comply with ITTO guidelines for sustainable forest management by 2000, and the Bank contributed by providing a start-up grant. While both of these are welcome moves, in reality, they have had little influence in moving Indonesia toward sustainable forest management.

LEI has taken important steps toward designing an effective and credible certification system. It has sought the participation of national and international stakeholders to improve the implementation and effectiveness of its domestic program (for example, the Forest Stewardship Council to facilitate a Joint Certification Program, trade and industry associations in importing countries, and the WWF-sponsored Buyers Group of Certified Wood Products). The effectiveness of certification in modifying logging practices in Indonesia is likely to be limited for some time. Several constraints, including limited institutional and human capacity, need to be addressed before local certification can be considered a practical tool for promoting sustainable forest management. The problem of general governance and corruption requires an orderly and open process of local certification. A complicated system reduces the incentives to certification. Beside lack of incentive, to be effective, the certification system should be supported by improved regulations that support sustainable forest management. These challenges will take time to resolve, and while local certification is a potentially long-term solution, in the short and medium term it offers little.

One possibility is to use external or international certifying agencies. But even if proper certification apparatus could be established, questions remain about the effectiveness of certification if there is limited or no demand from export-destined, especially low-income countries. The more expensive certified forest products may not be very appealing to these importers. Equity is another important issue. Certification is costly and likely to hit the smaller producers harder than the large conglomerates. At the same time, certification could have the same effect as non-tariff barriers, reducing demand and depressing forest product prices and thereby helping accelerate the conversion of forests to other uses (see the sections on reduced impact logging and certification in the last chapter of this volume).

Pressures on Forests

Industrial Demand

Indonesia's four major log-consuming industries are the sawmill industry, molding and building components, plywood and particleboard, and pulp and paper.

With the ban on log exports since 1985, replaced by prohibitive taxes in the early 1990s, most of the timber was processed domestically into pulp and paper, plywood, sawnwood, chipwood, and other products. The impact of the policies promoting these industries on forests can be gauged by considering their log consumption. Recent estimates put industrial capacity at 53.4 million m^3. The estimated 1996 log consumption was 44.57 million m^3 and the official estimates of log supply for 1996-97 was 26 million m^3 (Barr 1999a). Based on information available in 1995, the Bank estimated the sustainable level of log harvest at that time to be about 22 million m3 in 1995 (World Bank 1995a). Considering the current, higher rates of deforestation, the sustainable level is likely to be lower than this estimate. This unsustainable volume of extraction highlights two key issues. One is the impact of poor commercial logging practices, which reflect the current policies governing the logging and processing industry. The second is the extent of illegal logging commonly attributed to filling the difference between estimated consumption and official records of log supply. While some of this was probably supplied by smallholder farmers (e.g., from agro-forests and trees from their own land, not on the forest estates), a substantial amount of it represents illegal logging activity.[13] It is widely perceived that a large share of the illegal supply originates from the HPH and HTI concessions, reflecting the poor enforcement of existing regulations and rule of law. More recently, significant illegal logging has been documented in national parks, conservation areas, and protected forests (EIA/Telepak 1999; Merrill and Effendi 1999).

Sawmills, Molding, and Building Components

The great expansion in both the sawmill and plywood industries occurred in the decade preceding the financial crisis. The sawmill industry has the greatest number of establishments of any of the forest products industries. Its numbers range upward of 3,000 in various estimates. Official BPS statistics account for the 670 sawmills in 1996 that employed more than five workers each. The numerous uncounted smaller sawmills are indicative of how little capital is required to get started in this industry. Small sawmills are mobile and easily shifted in and out of operation as local resource supplies and economic conditions change. The fluid nature of sawmill operations is also reflected in the large difference between permitted and installed capacity in the industry. Most of the production of these two industries was consumed locally to support the construction industry. Indonesia is one of the five largest producers of tropical sawnwood. Over 80 percent of its production was consumed in domestic markets in the 1990–97 period.

Plywood

Since the mid-1980s, plywood has been the dominant wood products industry in Indonesia. The log export ban ensured a cheap source of raw material, and an export marketing cartel aggressively pursued overseas markets. The total wood consumption of the industry is three times that of the sawmill and molding industries combined. It employs twice as many workers, and at a higher average wage. Approximately 10 percent of Indonesia's plywood production is consumed in domestic markets, and the rest is exported (figure 6.2)

Figure 6.2
Change in Production, Imports, and Exports

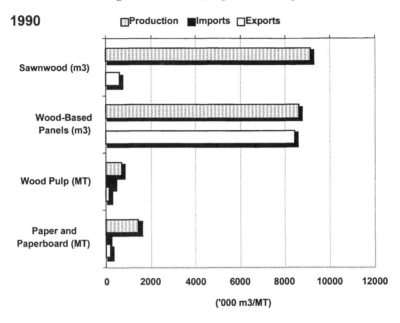

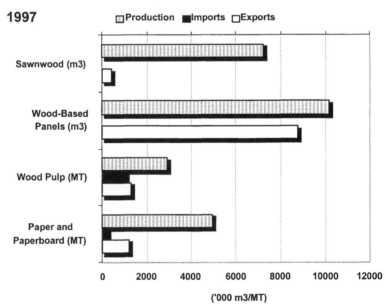

Source: FAO

Figure 6.3
Exports of Selected Wood and Pulp Products

1990
Export value = $3,183,021,000

1997
Export value = $5,095,399,000

□Sawnwood (4.5%)
□Wood-Based Panels (86.9%)
■Wood Pulp (2.2%)
▣Paper and Paperboard (3.6%)
□Industrial Roundwood (0.8%)
□Other (1.9%)

□Sawnwood (4.9%)
□Wood-Based Panels (67.8%)
■Wood Pulp (10.4%)
▣Paper and Paperboard (14.1%)
□Industrial Roundwood (0.5%)
□Other (2.2%)

Source: FAO

Until 1997, the plywood industry's export earnings dominated the sector, with Indonesia producing twice the volume of the world's second-largest producer of tropical plywood (Malaysia or Japan) and exports more than twice as much as its nearest geographical competitor (Malaysia). Unofficial estimates indicate that plywood may no longer be the highest foreign exchange earner among wood products, having been replaced by pulp and paper. Trends in total production indicate that until 1997 plywood production had stagnated since about 1991, although it remained very high (Figure 6.4). This slowdown in growth is attributed largely to increasing scarcity of logs.

Pulp and Paper

Pulp and paper production is concentrated at fewer locations than sawmills or plywood, and it employs fewer workers than sawmills or plywood. It was second to plywood in its value-added contribution to the economy in 1996—and it is growing rapidly. The pulp and paper industry expanded rapidly in the 1990s. Installed capacity doubled from 1990 to 1997 and output of wood pulp and paper and paperboard has almost tripled (Figure 6.5). Although the major share of the output of pulp and paper products is for domestic consumption, the value of exports has increased almost five times (figure 6.3). The demand for exports is expected to continue increasing with the economic recovery in East Asia and elsewhere.

The high-fixed-cost and immobile natures of pulp and paper mills make their managers more concerned with sustainable resource supplies than, say sawmills and plymills. These features, and the rapidly growing demand for their products, make the pulp and paper industry the leading commercial

Figure 6.4
Plywood and Sawnwood Production (1990–97)

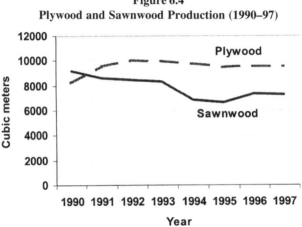

Source: FAO

Figure 6.5
Production Trends in Pulp and Paper Sector, 1990–97

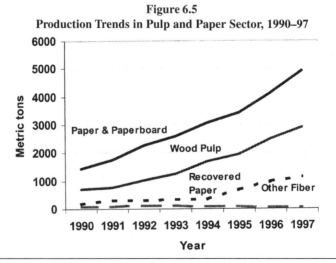

Source: FAO

force for sustainable forest plantations. However, in practice, the rapid expansion in capacity and the need to operate at high levels of capacity to maintain profitability increasingly has forced the mills to rely on natural forests for raw materials. This has put significant pressure on the forests, while the availability of cheap fiber supplies through illegal logging has been a strong disincentive to invest in pulp plantations. The pace of expansion of the pulp and paper mills is rapidly become the most significant threat to natural forest degradation, especially since the demand for fiber creates added incentives to clear-cut logged-over forest lands.

Forest Concessions and Plantations

Forest extraction and the conversion of forest land for other uses have been at the heart of Indonesia's modernization strategy. In addition to the direct pressure from the heavy demand placed on the forest resources by the processing sector, a set of complex intersectoral and macroeconomic issues have had indirect effects. The indirect effects, however, have been largely ignored in most analytical work on Indonesia until recently, including by the Bank in its macroeconomic, agricultural, and forest ESW.

HPH operations, among other factors, have been the dominant cause of forest degradation (Kartodihardjo and Supriono 1998). As of June 1998, out of the total production and conversion forests, 69.4 million had been allocated to HPH, 4.7 million reserved for HTI, and 3 million for large-scale plantation development. Despite a clear policy on where HPH and HTI can be sited, there have been numerous cases of encroachment, including into protected and conservation forests. Those responsible have included large-scale HPH and HTI holders, including some state-owned enterprises, and smallholders. For example, about 22 percent of the total area allocated for HTI, or 1 million ha, is in primary natural forest. Meanwhile, several protection and conservation forest areas, for which no change in function is permitted, have been encroached by plantation activities, by timber plantations, and by shifting cultivation degradation (Kartodihardjo and Supriono 1998).

By June 1998, forest degradation resulting from HPH operations had reached 16.57 million (Kartodihardjo and Supriono 1998). The government has stated that it will rehabilitate, change to different status or function, and reserve this area for other purposes. But there also appears to be a change in the forest ministry's management of the concessions since the economic crisis and the IMF and Bank adjustment packages. Of the 35.5 million ha (nearly half of the area reserved for concessions) managed by 359 HPH, whose first 20-year term had expired, the rights of only 96 HPH, with a total operational area of 14.3 million ha (about a quarter of the total), had been extended to the second term. Of the revoked concessions, 33 for 3.3 million ha have been awarded to other concessionaires, while the rest (9.5 million ha) were so poorly managed as to need rehabilitation.[14] These have been given to the *Inhutanis*.

The reduction in the number of HPHs suggests that the importance of concessions may be declining, evidently a result of resource scarcity in traditional logging areas such as Kalimantan and Sumatra. However, MOFEC appears to be shifting its focus toward opening new areas such as Irian Jaya. Between 1987 and 1997, the MOFEC allocated 40 HPHs covering 9.7 million ha in Irian Jaya alone. More recently, the Indonesian selective logging and planting system, TPTI has been weakened, which is likely to lead to even less prudent management practices by HPHs.

While the HPH system continues to be a major force affecting forests, the plantation sector is significantly adding to the pressures on forests. This added pressure reflects the increasing demand from the pulp and paper industries, ostensibly for timber plantations, and from the palm oil processing industry. In response to a slow down, and perhaps even a decline, in the growth of plywood production, there appears to be a change in MOFEC strategy, a result of the desire to maintain a steady, and cheap, supply of fiber to the pulp and paper processing sector. At the same time, there is increasing allocation of forest areas for conversion, and the *Inhutani*'s or state companies are reportedly looking for private sector partners to allow log extraction on lands intended for "rehabilitation," often with the objective of eventually establishing oil palm plantations.

The growing importance for conversion is evident from the increasing volumes of wood produced through the Wood Utilization Permit (Izin Pemanfaatan Kayu, or IPK), which permits logging companies to clear-cut logged-over or areas designated by the MOFEC for conversion (Barr 1999b). The IPK has become popular because of its various incentives: it allows non-selective harvesting techniques, there are minimal royalties, and no restoration fee. In addition, as part of its policy to promote plantations, the government has also provided subsidy for HTI. This policy has been very popular with the private companies, who have used the HTI subsidies and the IPK advantages, but have generally failed to comply with the key element of the HTI permit: to establish tree plantations. The record of planting has been very poor, with only 23 percent of the planned area being realized for the period 1990–97 (Kartodihardjo and Supriono 1998). This in turn has promoted further illegal logging, as the pulp and paper industry continues to search for raw material from standing natural forests.

The 1998 government reorganization of the Ministries of Forestry and Agriculture to give the mandate for estate crops development to the new MOFEC suggests an apparent change in the government's strategy. One view of this change is that it makes the de facto policy of forestland conversion de jure, with potentially damaging consequences for forests. An alternative view is that the previous arrangement did not prevent land conversion anyway.

Given adequate staffing and appropriate institutional arrangements, the reorganization may provide an opportunity to improve the conditions of forests by ensuring a consistent application of regulations.

Indonesia has been the lowest cost producer of palm oil in the world and this comparative advantage has been reinforced by the devaluation as it has also increased the profitability of all exports from Indonesia. The government's strategy to promote investment in oil palm, both for exports and domestic processing, have led to a strong demand from private foreign investors for land conversion, often from natural forests.[15]

Despite the incentives, however, as in the case of timber plantations, the rate of establishment of oil palm plantations is also very low (Casson 1999). Given that many of the companies that have shown an interest in oil palm plantations are also logging companies, it is evident that at least in the first instance, the investors are more interested in the timber that can be harvested from the plantation sites. Those genuinely interested in oil palm are likely to target Sumatra because of its better soils and infrastructure. However, with the decline in the area of conversion forest, increased demand for land has put pressure on the remaining natural forest for tree crop development.

The pressures for forest conversion have accelerated in other ways since the economic crisis, apart from economic profitability of plantation crops, and the declining quality of forest land which makes conversion to tree crops attractive. The problems brought about by the crisis and other external factors include the rising urban unemployment, reduced access to credit and agricultural inputs promoting extensive agriculture, the increased use of fire— as the least capital intensive way of land clearing in light of economic hardships, inflow of foreign investment for oil palm plantations, and government imperative to increase foreign exchange earnings resulting in increased conversion of land to quicker-payoff tree crops relative to sustainably managing forests and the unrelated, but more frequent, droughts resulting in increased fire outbreaks.

Consumptive Uses of the Forest: Rural Households and Non-Timber Forest Products (NTFPs)

Rural households rely on the forest for a part of their own consumption of non-timber forest products (NTFPs) like fuelwood and bamboo and rattan. Some of the latter are the basis of domestic production activities resulting in market sales and personal income. Some even make their way to international markets.

Estimates of the level of direct and final household use of the forest are difficult to obtain. Approximately 63 percent of Indonesia's population is rural and a large proportion of rural households rely on the forest for some of their consumption of fruits and nuts, meat (from hunting), wood for fuel and construction, and many other uncultivated or minimally managed products. Some of the poorest households worldwide are dependent on forests. Current estimates suggest that at least 40 million Indonesians (World Bank 1998) are highly dependent on forest resources for their basic livelihood (World Bank 2001).

Furthermore, forests act as an insurance policy on which rural households increase their reliance in times of economic hardship. For example, ICRAF's Alternatives to Slash-and-Burn research project anticipates that the financial crisis of 1997 and the collapse of Indonesia's currency may increase local reliance on slash-and-burn forest conversion and cultivation, and that the financial crisis has increased the local profitability of many tree-based agricultural systems—at least in Sumatra (Tomich et al. 1998).

Forest Fires

One of the world's largest environmental disasters in recent history was the forest fires that raged across Sumatra and Kalimantan in 1997 and East Kalimantan in 1998, scorching at least 5 million hectares in Kalimantan alone (Casson 1999). Almost all the fires were man-made, initiated by workers at large-scale plantations (34 percent), shifting cultivators (25 percent), agriculturists (17 percent), and new settlers (8 percent) as an inexpensive way to clear land or as a way of resolving personal disputes, especially disputes over land tenure. El Niño caused unusually dry weather in 1997, thus increasing the effects of the fires on the ground and on air quality. Smoke from the Kalimantan fires affected cities as far away as Singapore. The fires and the resulting air pollution caused more than US$9.3 billion in damages (BAPPENAS 1999).

The fires attracted extensive domestic and international attention, leading many to hope that MOFEC would assert greater authority over the use of Indonesia's forest land by corporations in particular, but large businesses have retained their influence in the forest sector. When the former Minister of Forestry—widely recognized by environmentalists for his forward thinking and tough stance on exploitative business practices—released the names of 176 plantation, timber, and construction companies believed to be responsible for large-scale burning (van Klinken 1997; Wakker 1998), only 66 of the companies had their permits temporarily suspended. No logging company had its land concession revoked, and there were no public investigations (Potter and Lee 1998). Once the political and economic situation improves, oil palm companies will probably attempt to establish more plantations on the degraded lands, particularly since the government has already indicated that the burned areas would eventually be allocated to conversion (Casson 1999).

The Impact of the Financial Crisis of 1997

The East Asian financial crisis hit Indonesia in July 1997. Indonesia's currency depreciated approximately 80 percent in the four months following, and has since not recovered much. The immediate impact of the depreciation, however, did not confer advantage in international markets because Indonesia's major trading partners (especially Japan) also suffered from the financial crisis.

Initially, the decline in plywood exports relieved pressure on forests. Shortly thereafter, around April 1998, the demand from China and other regions kicked in for plywood, and the continued exports of pulp and paper have increased the pressure on forests. Even before the crisis, the plywood industry faced supply difficulties because of excess capacity and declining log supplies, with forest fires adding to the problems. As a result, plywood producers are looking in more remote and inappropriate areas for timber. This is made worse by the breakdown of the already poor law and order situation, which has resulted in increased illegal logging and looting of forest resources with the continuing economic crisis (Kartodihardjo 1999b). Adding to the pressure is the demand for fuelwood, as other cooking fuels become more expensive.

Agriculture was seen as an important way to deal with the crisis (Sunderlin 1998): it is less dependent on the dollar economy and hence was expected to be less affected; it commands attention because of the political imperative to assure basic commodities; it helps absorb surplus unemployed work force from the urban areas; it was seen as an important source for both saving foreign exchange (by substitution of costly rice, wheat and soy imports) and a source of foreign exchange (as with other natural resource sectors).

The impact of the crisis itself was expected to put indirect pressure on forests through improved agricultural incentives. A shortage of capital for inputs and an ineffective system of subsidies (which are reportedly being diverted away from poor smallholders to larger farmers or plantations) are expected to encourage extensive agriculture. The sources of this pressure are surmised as smallholders (including a reverse in the declining trend of shifting agriculture), large-scale plantations for oil palm and spontaneous forest clearing for cocoa, coffee, shrimp, rubber and pepper as economic forces make these crops attractive in the wake of the rupiah devaluation. The biggest threat was perceived to be from large-scale operators and the relatively more wealthy individual farmers with the wherewithal to undertake forest-clearing activities. Expansion of oil palm plantations often puts the "developers" in direct conflict with the forest communities, who are often displaced. The crisis was expected to add to the already rapid pace of expansion of oil palm estates and the conversion of forests (with a high risk of going well beyond the designated conversion forests and into protected and production forests).

The limited evidence that is available, however, suggests that the adverse impact on forests may not be as bad as anticipated (Angelsen and Resosudarmo 1999). Different crops have been impacted in different ways. Expansion of oil palm was checked by a decline in world price (as demand from other Asian countries fell), and government policies affecting crude oil palm exports. The government first banned such exports from November 1997 to April 1998, and subsequently imposed an export tax of 60 percent (reduced to 40 percent in January 1999). Thus, the domestic price has been relatively insulated from the exchange rate fluctuations, translating into less impact on oil palm expansion than anticipated.

In addition to these "incentive" effects, the timber and oil palm companies have reduced their investments because of the limited funds available. Since forest conversion is a capital-intensive operation, preliminary evidence suggests that at least the large-scale operations may not have increased as much as expected as a result of the crisis.

As regards farming, those involved in export-oriented crops had mixed experiences. Cocoa producers benefited from the crisis. The producers of rubber, the largest smallholder cash crop, gained little as the crisis was accompanied by a fall in world prices (as result of decline in demand for rubber and low oil prices, which affect the price of synthetic rubber). The impacts on forests have also been varied by location and by crop (e.g., of coffee on North Sumatra conversion forests, and shrimp on South Sulawesi mangroves).

The impact on forests from smallholders has generally been smaller than expected. Small farmers generally lack the resources (either capital or family labor) to open a new swidden field. The groups that were able to take advantage of the opportunities from the crisis were the relatively better-off farmers, immigrants with capital and urban entrepreneurs who were able to finance forest conversion to export crops.

Need for Reforms

Forest policy reform is essentially a political issue (Ross 1996; World Bank 1993b). Contrary to its publicly declared positions, the government has viewed forests as assets to be liquidated to help economic growth and diversify the economy. Forest resources have been under-valued, ostensibly to promote domestic "value added," generating enormous economic rents. At the same time, rent capture has been kept low, and forest management practices and policies have been governed by political and patron-client interests.

Before the financial crisis and the change in Indonesia's central government, the key domestic actors in the forest sector were doing well under the existing rules and with the benefit of a stable economic and policy environment. The leading member of the forest industry was a close friend of the president. He easily could obtain hearing for any policy change he desired. Several members of the president's family were directly involved with timber conglomerates, making it personally very profitable to ensure that the industry's interests were well served by the official policy. MOFEC was well financed, largely through the reforestation fund created from revenues from Dana Reboisasi. The army received benefits of unidentified magnitude from forest concessions managed by regional commanders and largely off the books with respect to MOFEC or Ministry of Finance accounting. The MOFEC and BAPPENAS (the National Planning Bureau) disagree over the allocation of the revenues from the Dana Reboisasi, whose funds have often been used for non-reforestation purposes, even for non-forestry purposes. The ministry relies on its current control over these funds for its regular operation, and the government has generally used these funds for various political purposes. BAPPENAS prefers to allocate these funds to the central treasury. Otherwise, the domestic incentives for policy reform were limited.

Indonesian smallholders, local communities, and indigenous populations were largely left out of the political and policymaking process. They have received little benefit from the lands they have historically occupied. Many local groups and some environmental NGOs expressed their unhappiness with decisions regarding forests, and some were quite vocal. Nevertheless, despite the increasing level of complaints and demonstrations, civil society has had little effect on forest policy or management decisions.

This means that the arguments for policy reform had to come from external sources. In light of their past experience with implementation in the forest sector, most donors stayed out of the sector since the mid-1980s. Some donors with forestry interests did take up technical advisory roles, but they have generally tended to stay away from policy advice and have not actively pushed for policy reforms. The World Bank, however, remained engaged through the early 1990s, breaking ranks with other donors in the sector. This also left the Bank as a major actor pushing for policy and institutional reforms, with limited interactions with other donors through the consultative group meetings. Many of the donors feel, however, that the Bank has largely been working in isolation, with little or no consultation on key policies or reform areas. There has been a change following the recent events, with the donors showing significantly greater unanimity in calling for reforms. In the most recent meeting, the consultative group has strongly endorsed a focus on forest reforms.

Given the state of Indonesian forests, and the pace at which forests have been depleted, the focus of the Bank's policy advice since early 1990s has been on sustainable forest management. It has specifically targeted production forestry to bring it under control, moving the forest sector toward the proper valuation, albeit in a market sense, of the forest resources. For this, the Bank has made proposals for removing policy distortions that drive a wedge between world prices and domestic prices of logs. The basic argument has been the need for providing appropriate incentives for economic efficiency, sustainable management of standing forests, and for plantations to substitute for natural forests.

Among the needed reforms, several observers (as noted in Sunderlin and Resodudarmo 1996) have noted the need for improving the concession management system by:

- Raising royalty fees and government rent capture (Gray and Hadi 1990; Ascher 1993; D'Silva and Appanah 1993; Ramli and Ahmad 1993; Thiele 1995; Ahmad 1995)
- Lengthening the concession cycles and increasing tenure security for concessionaires (D'Silva and Appanah 1993; Thiele 1995; Kartodihardjo 1995)
- Enhancing competition in the allotment of concessions (Gray and Hadi 1990; Thiele 1995)
- Increasing area-based as compared to volume-based concession fees (Gray and Hadi 1990; Thiele 1995).

The most challenging and perhaps the most difficult to address is the issue of illegal logging, which has the potential to render most policy recommendations ineffective.[16] Illegal logging manifests a deeper problem of governance. To address these issues, both internal and external observers, including the Bank, have called for addressing the complex issues of local participation, property rights, consultative process for decision making for resource use, revenue sharing, and greater decentralization and devolution of authority to regional and local governments (Barber 1997; Kartodihardjo 1999b; World Bank 1993b, 1995a, 1998). Yet, until the legal issues surrounding land titling can be resolved and new approaches in community participation can be developed, the Bank has argued for a more substantive involvement of the local communities and provincial governments, through revenue sharing and direct participation, in the improved management and protection of forest resources.

At the root of many of these issues are the economics of sustainable forest management and the competitiveness of land allocation. Research indicates that under prevailing conditions sustainable forest management is unlikely to be competitive with plantation crops, especially oil palm (Tomich et al. 1998; Scotland 1998; Kartodihardjo and Supriono 1998). Other results indicate that sustainable forest management may be profitable at world prices (World Bank 1995a; Tomich et al. 1998). How sustainable forest management fares against alternative uses of land is not known (Scotland 1998; Kartodihardjo and Supriono 1998; and World Bank 1995a). It is highly likely that the profitability of sustainable forest management will vary depending on the location and type of forests, but the bottom line is that not enough is known about the competitiveness of sustainable forest management, even under ideal policy circumstances.

These results—based on financial timber prices—do not fully value the externalities provided by forests, which are relevant from a social (long-term individual, intergenerational, national, and international) point of view. A full economic valuation of forests should incorporate all benefits, including biodiversity, carbon storage, and NTFPs, properly valued at their "economic" prices (Pearce et al. 1999). If alternatives to natural forests are indeed more profitable, then the tradeoffs among local, national, and international interests will have to be managed. These would include non-market measures to provide incentives to keep forests intact, such as by compensating local governments and owners of forest resources for sacrificing their benefits for the sake of national and global social benefit.

The World Bank and Indonesia: Promoting
Ownership and Sustainable Management

Management and conservation of a country's forests is primarily the country's responsibility. Policy advice and investments funded by external partners such as the World Bank and IMF can make a difference to the forest outcomes, but their effectiveness depends on how the advice and assistance is utilized by the countries. Even the right advice may not lead to desired outcomes because of the lack of domestic political will, institutional and human capacity or the wrong incentive system. The Bank and the IMF have a mixed record in Indonesia. They have not been able to prevail when their advice was right, and often have been shunned by the government for their advice. On the other hand, at times, with the benefit of hindsight their advice and the process by which it was imparted or the policy conditionality imposed was less than optimum.

Given the state of Indonesian forests and the pace of their depletion, the focus of the Bank's policy advice since the early 1990s has been on sustainable forest management. It has tried to bring production forestry under control, encouraging the forest sector to properly value, at least in a market sense, its forest resources. For this the Bank has made proposals for removing policy distortions that drive a wedge between world and domestic log prices. The basic argument has been the need to provide appropriate incentives for economic efficiency, sustainable management of standing forests, and substitution of plantations for natural forests.

The Bank and the Forest Sector: Varying Degrees of Involvement

The Bank's relationship with the government of Indonesia in the forest sector can be divided into three phases. The first was the lending phase from

1988 to 1994, which ended when the government decided to stop borrowing from external sources for forestry. This began the non-lending phase, from 1995 to 1997, during which the Bank maintained a presence in the sector through conservation activities, but lending and policy dialogue came to a halt. With no activity in the sector there was no economic and sector work— MOFEC was not interested in having the Bank involved in the sector in any substantive way. The reform and adjustment phase started with the financial crisis and the inclusion of forest sector conditions in the IMF reform package to Indonesia, agreed to by the government through its letter of intent in January 1998. The IMF loan was followed by the Bank's first policy reform support loan in 1998 and a second one in 1999.

At the finalization of this volume the Bank was involved in a broad consultative process aimed to develop a longer-term strategy for more equitable and sustainable development of the sector.

Lending: Pre-1991 Projects

In the period before the Bank's 1991 forestry strategy paper, the Bank's investment program in Indonesia included 12 agriculture projects, eight power projects, two urban projects, one mining and oil project, and four transportation projects that could have had impacts—mostly harmful—on the forest sector.

The Bank supported Indonesian transmigration through seven loans totaling $560 million, one in the 1970s and the others from 1980 to 1992. The main project components were clearing land, building villages and the related social and physical infrastructure, building settlers' houses, providing agricultural services, planting trees, and building drainage systems. A 1994 World Bank review noted that although settlers had benefited, the program had a major negative, and probably irreversible, impact on the indigenous peoples, particularly the Kubu, who depend on the forest for their economic and spiritual well-being (World Bank 1994b).

Projects that helped the forests included the Forestry Institutions and Conservation Projects (FICP I and FICP II), approved within 18 months of each other in 1988 and 1990. Although the projects were designed before the Bank's 1991 forest strategy became effective, their objectives, design, and intent were consistent with the strategy.

FICP I had two components. The first was institutional strengthening through sectoral and policy studies, information generation, and research. The second was conservation by rehabilitating terraced lands and associated conservation structures, planting trees on private lands, conserving forests on state lands, and managing five existing nature conservation areas. The objectives of FICP II were to reduce the pace of deforestation in Indonesia and to sustain and maximize the flow of benefits from forest resources. The project components included natural forest management, plantation planning, research planning and development, and conservation of forest environments. It was designed to provide investments supplementing the implementation of FICP I.

Despite implementation delays, the implementation completion report for FICP I claimed substantial success in improving sectoral planning, management, and human resources (World Bank 1997b). Other achievements included improving forest research capacity and addressing critical conservation needs through investments in five national parks around the country.

The implementation completion report also identified some challenges that made the sustainability of the project's achievements uncertain. These included a lack of government commitment to the project's initiatives and to carrying out the institutional and policy reforms in the sector, lack of coordination among governmental agencies, and government reluctance to address difficult land-use issues by enforcing a clear and effective policy for demarcating and protecting the forest areas with the greatest biodiversity and environmental value.

FICP II did not fare as well. During the project the government informed the Bank of its decision not to proceed with the concession management component and not to extend the project. The government also seemed unhappy about the amount of technical assistance and the number of studies and plans in the project. The total project cost at completion was $11.44 million (the appraisal estimate was $33.1 million), and more than 50 percent of the Bank's $20 million loan was cancelled. At the same time the government asked the Bank not to proceed with a third project the Bank was preparing. FICP I was still active, however, and continued to its original closing date, as did the remaining components of FICP II and a Global Environment Facility conservation project cofinanced by the Bank.

Post-1991 Projects

The Bank financed no new direct forest projects in Indonesia after 1991. But the Watershed Conservation Project, a natural resource management project, had a significant component directly related to forests. The Bank has also financed five projects in the agricultural sector that had components for tree crop development and two Global Environment Facility (GEF) projects.

The Watershed Conservation Project, approved in 1994, allocated $400 million of its $487 million budget to a forest-related component. The project objectives were to improve watershed environmental quality, protect downstream watershed resources, and improve living standards of poor upland farmers by improving and restoring the production potential of the resource base. The project components included institutional strengthening to improve the regreening and reforestation program guidelines and policies, investment support for regreening and reforestation, and development of the Upper Cimanuk Watershed.

According to recent project status reports, progress on strengthening national institutions and getting investments for regreening and reforestation continue to be rated unsatisfactory. Since a demonstrated methodology for underpinning the watershed intervention strategy has not yet evolved, the government has asked that the regreening and reforestation component be cancelled. The Bank has responded by reducing the loan more than 70 percent.

Two GEF projects are relevant to forests. The Biodiversity Collections Project was approved in 1994 for $11.4 million, of which GEF provided a grant for $7.2 million. The objective is to strengthen the institutional capacity of the Research and Development Center for Biology of the Indonesian Institute of Sciences. The project is consistent with the CAS objectives of improving environmental management and strengthening government capacity.

The second GEF project is the Kerinci-Seblat Integrated Conservation Development Project, approved in 1996 for $45.9 million, with the Bank providing $19.2 million. Forest-related components constitute about 33 percent of the cost. The project objectives include improving park protection and management (including involvement of local communities) and promoting sustainable management and maintenance of permanent cover in the remaining buffer zone concession area. In addition to support for park management, the project includes improving land use planning, land use rights, and community resource management in areas with forest interests.

The project is expected to benefit the environment by protecting the 1.3 million hectares of national park and the surrounding buffer zone. About 13,400 households would directly benefit from the investment funds, and about 300,000 households would indirectly benefit from improved biodiversity conservation. But there are some significant environmental and land use and socioeconomic development implications.

A major challenge facing the project includes the desire by two of the four bordering provinces (West Sumatra and Bengkulu) to expand tree crop and estate development around the park and to build roads through it (Wells et al. 1999). The road moratorium was broken in West Sumatra in 1996 but restored as a result of persistent Bank efforts to get the central government to intervene. In contrast, Jambi Province depends on the park for watershed protection and has demonstrated support for the project by canceling some road building.

Another challenge is the lack of incentives for concessionaires to practice sustainable forestry. Subsidized loans to convert concessions to oil palm or timber plantations further skew the incentives and reduce the prospects for conserving biodiversity in Kerinci-Seblat's lowland forests. The local NGOs

have limited capacity to help communities develop village plans or to negotiate agreements with park authorities and local governments. Finally, the
project depends on effective and coordinated action by three separate agencies and four provinces. Central leadership is limited for lack of field presence and field staff capacity. These challenges considerably reduce the
prospects for the project's sustainability.

These challenges demonstrate the problems with the integrated conservation development program (ICDP) approach to biodiversity conservation
adopted by Indonesia. A recent assessment of ICDPs in Indonesia concludes
that very few "can realistically claim that biodiversity conservation has been
or is likely to be significantly enhanced as a result of current or planned
activities" (Wells et al. 1999: 2–3). The threat is not pressure from local
people, as is implicit in the projects' rationale, but failure to address the real
issues of economic planning or land use decision making (the main threats
are identified as road construction, mining, logging concessions, and sponsored immigration). The project is showing that a piecemeal approach that
does not address broader sectoral and cross-sectoral issues affecting the forest
sector is unlikely to be successful, regardless of its admirable objectives.

Through the WWF/World Bank Forest Alliance for Conservation and Sustainable Use, Bank and the World Wide Fund for Nature are working with
governments, the private sector, and civil society to significantly reduce the
loss and degradation of forest types worldwide. The Forest Alliance activities
in Indonesia are still being formulated, but have faced such problems as
scarce resources, a political climate unconducive to conservation, and a disconnect between global and local objectives or even consultation of the
local offices of the two organizations when the alliance was conceived and
being implemented. For the alliance to be effective, World Wide Fund for
Nature local offices must take more ownership, and Bank staff and Indonesian agencies must make a greater commitment.

Policy Advice: Bridging the Regulatory and Implementation Gaps

Since 1991, the Bank has undertaken a significant amount of high-quality
formal economic and sector work (ESW) covering forestry, the environment,
and agriculture. Most of this work was done in the early 1990s (the forest
sector report was completed in 1993). Since then Bank staff have circulated
informal discussion notes (World Bank 1995a, 1998), but until 1998 no more
resources were made available for undertaking formal economic and sector
work.

The forest sector report and the subsequent environment sector report explicitly recognized the need to balance economic development and environmental concerns (Word Bank 1993b, 1994a). The forest sector report
highlighted the political nature of the line separating permanent forests (con-

servation, protection, and production) and conversion forests. The focus of the report was sustainable forest management because substantial work on conservation and biodiversity had already been undertaken. It argued that regaining control of production forestry was necessary for conservation and preservation, and that the two activities needed to be pursued simultaneously to address the most pressing issue in forest management: unsustainable logging. It also noted that although Indonesia had made decisions at the highest political level to help protect forests—committing to maintaining 84 million hectares of forest cover, implementing the International Tropical Timber Organization guidelines by 2000—there remains a gap between policy and implementation.

In addition to its call for improving forest policy and implementing existing rules and regulations, the report argued for a more equitable distribution of gains from forestry. It recommended that local (forest dwelling and adjacent) communities be given a more proactive role in the sustainable management of forest resources. To improve enforcement of policies, the report recommended mobilizing stakeholder resources—NGOs, private sector, academics and others.

The report marked the beginning of Indonesia's (particularly MOFEC's) dissatisfaction with the Bank. The significant policy and institutional reforms it suggested—involving forest communities in managing forests and ensuring sustainability along the guidelines established by the International Tropical Timber Organization—implied a departure from management practices that served the interests of the military and the politically connected.

After the report had been discussed with the government, the then director of the Bank's Indonesia country department decided not to officially issue it. This decision restricted the report's availability and muted potentially valuable discussion. As it became clear that MOFEC and the government were not serious about implementing the reforms in the report, the Bank and the government agreed to end their lending relationship in the sector, with the exception of some conservation-related activities.

The government did not want the Bank involved in policy and institutional reforms because the government did not like what the Bank was recommending. At the same time, the Bank's top management at the time was not willing to jeopardize its relationship with the country over disagreements in the forest sector, which constituted a minor part of its total portfolio and there was relatively little overt understanding within the Bank at the country assistance level then of the full ramifications of the complex relationship between Indonesia's exploitation of natural resources and its economic growth process. Overall lending to Indonesia throughout the 1990s remained the same until the 1997 crisis but due to governance and other reasons had declined to third of the level in the pre-crisis period by 2001.

Although it never represented the Bank's official position, the 1993 report contained a fairly comprehensive strategy for the development and sustainable management of the forest sector, and its recommendations conformed to the Bank's forest policy. It has provided the foundation of Bank thinking on the forest sector, and some of the main policy recommendations were included in a Bank report on the environment (World Bank 1994a) that was discussed with the Indonesian government and officially issued by the Bank. But the government adopted none of the recommendations on sustainability, equity, and institutional reforms in the forest sector.

Since 1993, the Bank has focused its advice on economic efficiency and the proper valuation of natural resources illustrating that the internal technical knowledge did not always provide input into policy decisions but also illustrating the role of long term policy and institutional reforms in comparison with the stroke of the pen reforms introduced through adjustment type lending. The report argued for policy reforms to correct the distortions that create disincentives for good management of forest resources. The main recommendations by the Bank before the 1997 financial crisis are summarized in a 1995 working paper (World Bank 1995a). The paper concluded that Indonesia would be better off economically if it introduced policy changes to induce more efficient and sustainable use of its natural forests. It identified the disincentives to sustainability as:

- Raw material pricing and allocation policies that discourage investment in timber plantations and efficient extraction and use of wood.
- Industry policy based on inefficient export taxes and official sanction of a cartel controlling processed exports.
- Exclusion of communities living in or near the forests from title or participation in forest management.

Other suggested reforms covered the method of log sale, which placed heavy demand on MOFEC for monitoring and encouraged corruption; concession terms (short leases and non-transferability), which discouraged private interest in sustainability; and land use decisions based on ill-defined boundaries and unclear responsibilities for supervision, which encouraged forest degradation and misuse. These policy areas are related to the direct mandate and practices of MOFEC.

The Bank thought that higher prices could be achieved by introducing auctions of timber concession rights. Where long-term concession rights are in place, or genuinely competitive auction is not feasible, the government could set log prices according to residual appraisal formulas calculated from international price levels. By phasing in such pricing strategies, following firm policy announcements, the government would allow industries time to restructure and would encourage potential investors to locate log supply sources before investing in a new processing capacity. A phased approach to reforms would be a reasonable compromise between introducing log parity prices immediately and doing so little about introducing market signals that rent seeking became institutionalized at the expense of development of competitiveness and efficiency.

An efficient, competitive log market would produce a better concession system. Elimination of excessive rent seeking in the concession licensing system would allow for greater flexibility in allocating ownership and leasing rights over forests, and in the introduction of multiple use of forestry resources, including the full range of biodiversity conservation, ecotourism, and other global considerations. The resulting system would probably blend auctioning (or other forms of sale) of timber extraction rights to interested purchasers and rights or contracts of management to other interested groups (which might include local communities) and provincial governments—all in the context of a firm government policy on the broad parameters of natural forest conservation (Box 6.2).

But the Bank's economic and sector work in the forest sector also had shortcomings. First, it failed to adequately integrate poverty reduction. The Bank consistently expressed concern about communities that depend directly on forests for their livelihoods, many of which are poor. Yet the forest-dependent poor had not been fully integrated into the Bank's poverty reduction strategy. Nor had the Bank linked its CAS or macroeconomic policy dialogue to forest sector issues affecting the poor. The OED country assistance review noted that the quality of the Bank's poverty analysis has slipped in recent years, and the issues of regional distribution and vulnerability of the near poor have not been adequately studied (World Bank 1999), as an assessment that the 2001 country assistance report has taken on board.

Second, the Bank's economic and sector work did not fully acknowledge, and perhaps does not to date, the cross-sectoral impacts of forest sector policies, which may be more important than their direct impact. That includes the effects of agricultural incentives and the need for countervailing measures to conserve forest resources (for global or national public services) (World Bank 1992, 1994a)[17] and the link between economic growth and the unsustainable exploitation of natural capital. In the drive to diversify exports, no effort had been made until about 2000 to link the government's policy of building the capacity of processing industries to the demand pressures industries place on forests. This has implications not only for equity but also for the long-term sustainability of economic growth as the natural capital base is rapidly depleted.

Third, the idea that sustainable forest management is economically viable and competitive with alternative uses of land—the assumption underlying the Bank's advice—is questionable at least for the foreseeable future (Barr 1999a). Some studies note that current financial incentives appear to favor forest conversion, notably for oil palm production (Tomich et al. 1998; Potter

---

Box 6.2
Bank Recommendations for Improving the Forest Sector

The 1995 report, "The Economics of Long-Term Management of Indonesia's Natural Forests," recommended that the government:

- Progressively replace log export taxes with higher royalties to better value the forest resources and increase rent capture.
- Comprehensively review export taxes on sawn timber.
- Remove the link between logging concessions and processing plant capacity.
- Eliminate the plywood marketing cartel and promote competition.
- Offer longer concession leases and permit transferability of concession rights.
- Stop approving conversion of forestland until a more effective classification of the forests is completed.
- Increase the share of revenues going to provincial and local governments—if they improve their performance in managing and regenerating areas and protected forests.
- Change the forestry act and other legislation and develop supporting regulations to facilitate land titling in forest-dwelling and forest-adjacent communities. As a precursor, facilitate award of concessions or share in concessions to communities identified as traditionally linked to forestland to promote cooperation in regeneration, protection, and management of forest resources.
- Improve monitoring and revenue collection by introducing log sales by area, performance bonds for regeneration and proper management, and an independent inspection system.
- Protect regenerating forests by revising the HTI scheme to make it consistent with new restrictions on the use of regenerating forest land, and accelerate the KPHP [Kesatuan Pemangkuan Hutan Produksi/Production Forest Management Unit] process—a new forest land-use management system, and include provisions in leases requiring consultations with local communities in project activities and follow-up.

Source: World Bank 1995a

and Lee 1998). While other evidence (Scotland 1998) suggests that world market prices may improve the returns to concession management, the evidence is limited and the results are questionable, suggesting a need for further detailed study using better models and data.

The Bank had not tried to validate its policy advice because it had not allocated resources to forest related economic and sector work since 1993. While Bank staff have kept in touch with the emerging issues in the sector, they have not had the resources for in-depth analyses. This situation is changing as donors are beginning to work more closely to undertake what the Bank describes as Analytical Advisory Activities (AAA) and annual donor allocations to technical assistance of over $500 million in 2001 were higher than the World Bank's proposed annual commitments of $400 million. In the consultations leading up to the World Bank's CAS, Indonesian stakeholders questioned the use of loans for technical assistance and asked help in building a broad range of Indonesian institutions. This area of drawing on national researchers, supporting them and building their capacity instead of technical assistance still needs improvement.

Structural Adjustment: Recognizing the Significance of the Forest Sector

Once the Bank was effectively excluded from the sector between 1995 and 1998, it had no opportunity to share its viewpoints. And with the termination of the lending program, the Bank undertook no new economic and sector work. But many of the recommendations from economic and sector work in 1993 and the analytical work in the 1995 report formed the basis of IMF conditionality for the forest sector in 1998.

When President Suharto resigned in May 1998 after 30 years in power, details of the deep-seated corruption, cronyism, and nepotism in Indonesia's government hit the press. The deteriorating economic and social conditions created a political crisis for the New Order, which led to an IMF standby agreement with the government in late 1997. With continued deterioration of the rupiah, the government and the IMF agreed on a reform package in January 1998. At the last minute, the IMF asked the Bank to recommend forest-related conditions to be included in its reform package. This was an unusual step, so far taken in only two other countries as part of IMF packages (Cambodia and Papua New Guinea, two relatively small countries with considerably greater leverage for the IMF and the World Bank). These reforms for Indonesia were intended to increase government revenues and increase exports and to address issues of sectoral governance, competitiveness, and environmental impacts.

The IMF reform package provided an opportunity to take up some of the outstanding policy reforms and reinitiate a dialogue on others. For the first time the significance of the sector—its policies and performance in the national economy—were fully recognized in an IMF and later in the Bank programs. Policy conditionality, however, raised issues of ownership, sequencing, and appropriateness of the lending instrument, and whether the reforms would be effective.

These initial conditions were pursued by the Bank through two Policy Reform Support Loans (in April 1998 and April 1999). According to the government, the reforms are intended to address the need for increased transparency and anticorruption measures. Following up on its earlier commitments, the government promised to increase consultations with all stakeholders before it enacts further reforms but this is an area in which its performance has been less than stellar. It also undertook to adopt strong measures to identify community groups living in and around forest areas that have legitimate claims to share in the benefits of forest use and management.

Reforms in the terms and conditions of concession awards were to be incorporated in the new forest law passed in early 1999 that deals with concessions and revenues and the regulations that govern concession operations. The government agreed to increase concession license terms and to make concessions tradable. It will no longer require corporate linkage of concessions to large processing facilities, so that any group can manage concessions. It agreed to develop a system for demarcating forest land into its best uses, based on the need to encourage local communities to participate in forest management and the need to protect the rights of forest-dwelling indigenous people. The government also agreed that no new concessions will be granted until these reforms are in place.

The structural adjustment program had mixed results (see Boxes 6.3 and 6.4 on the conditions and their implementation). The conditionality achieved some reforms, including tax reductions, reform of concession contractual terms, and the abolition of the plywood marketing cartel and the transfer of the restoration fund to the ministry of finance. But some observers question whether it wise to replace the ban on palm oil exports with an export tax or to encourage foreign direct investment in the oil palm sector and large-scale investments in oil palm estates (Barr 1999a; Kartodihardjo 1999b). These policies are seen as inconsistent with the intent of the conditions calling for sustainable forest practices and reduced land conversion targets. Oil palm production is significantly more profitable today than other land uses in Indonesia, and external investors are eager to invest. Considering the threat that oil palm development poses to natural forests, reducing the tax and encouraging large-scale foreign investment is expected to increase the incentives to deforest.

Bank staff maintain that these reforms need not increase deforestation; there is enough degraded forestland that could be used for oil palm expansion. The reduction in tax is intended to promote the optimal use of (degraded) land, not more deforestation. Other conditions, including the breakdown of enforcement capacity, are expected to ensure that all new oil palm development will occur on designated conversion land. In reality, most of the attractive conversion areas are already planted (Casson 1999).

In other places, poorly enforced regulations for plantation management, unclear boundaries of conversion or degraded forest areas, and nontransparent concession operations make it almost certain that the policy change will have some negative impact. Plantations can also have negative social impacts: they mark the final dispossession of local communities' land and provide fewer alternatives for income generation (Potter and Lee 1998). In short, the wisdom of blanket conditions on export taxes needs to be questioned under the current governance structure.

Box 6.3
World Bank Conditionalities for the Policy Reform Support Loan I

The following elements were incorporated as conditionalities in the Policy Reform Support Loan I, in April 1998. GOI agreed to (** indicates second tranche release conditionality):

- Introduce system of resource royalties on forestry products, linked to world market prices and operating costs, independent of end use. [completed]**
- Reduce export taxes on logs, sawn timber and rattan to maximum of 30 percent by 12/31/98 and adopt and announce a program to reduce this to 20 percent by 12/31/98 and 10 percent by 12/31/00. [completed]**
- Allow transferability of concession permits by sale. [completed]*
- Remove requirement to have a processing facility in order to hold a concession permit. [completed]**
- Lengthen concession period. [completed]
- Reduce land conversion targets to environmentally sustainable level. [no progress]
- Authorize a performance bonding system for concessions. [regulation issued authorizing system]

Box 6.4
World Bank Conditionalities for the Policy Reform Support Loan II

GoI agreed to include the following conditionalities in the Policy Reform Support Loan II of April 1999 (* indicates condition for Board presentation):

- Audit the Reforestation Fund. [completed]
- Reduce export tax on logs, sawn timber and rattan to maximum 20 percent by 3/31/99 and 10 percent by 12/31/00. [on schedule]
- Draft design for area-based collection system for timber concession revenues by 6/30/99 [incomplete]
- Prepare draft implementing regulations for performance bonding system and submit for stakeholder consultation by 6/30/99 [draft prepared; consultation not completed]
- Establish system for independent inspection teams in concession areas by 6/30/99 [incomplete]
- Establish outcome-based criteria and performance bond implementing regulations 6/30/99 [incomplete]
- Review and refine the resource rent royalty to ensure that it captures at least 60 percent of economic rent [1998 review completed*; 1999 rev incomplete]
- In cooperation with the Bank, determine financial arrangements to utilize the Reforestation Fund. Use findings of audit. [incomplete]

cont. on next page

- Initiate a multi-stakeholder consultation process by which all proposed regulations and legislation will be publicly reviewed and discussed up to the final drafting stage [process initiated* but performance inadequate]
- Using the consultative process, prepare draft forest legislation that defines a transparent and consultative process for changing the nature of forest land and accommodates rights and responsibilities for traditional use areas. [consultation on the forest bill inadequate]
- Map existing forest cover for all of Indonesia using recent satellite imagery – 5 provinces by 6/30/99, the remainder thereafter. [Kalimantan, Sumatra, Sulawesi and Maluku finished, good progress and quality on Irian Jaya]
- Locate priority conservation areas on the maps [incomplete]
- Provide an acceptable timetable for completing designation and gazettement of these areas. [incomplete]
- Make the maps publicly available as they are completed [maps available on MoFEC website]
- Until maps are in place, implement and maintain a moratorium on new conversion of state forest land and alteration of main land use patterns. Any future conversion or land use status change is to be reviewed through a transparent and consultative process. [Minister asserts he is maintaining moratorium but conversions continue, perhaps with Governors' or other authorization.]
- Implement a mechanism for rationalizing state forest boundaries, taking into account existing forest cover.
- Revise concession boundaries in accordance with new permanent production forest boundaries and regulatory requirements. [not yet due]
- Using the consultative process, draft a community forest participation regulation defining clear and transparent procedures which: establish equitable representative organizations; establish terms and conditions for community participation in benefits from and management of forests; and protect the interests of local communities in forest use programs. [consultative process not yet operating properly]

Others wonder whether increased efficiency will promote forest conservation. Recent evidence suggests that in the face of declining log supplies, some plymills have already invested in more efficient technologies, allowing them to extract more from each log (Barr 1999a). Firms are going back to logged-over areas to log trees before the optimal cutting cycle. Although the Bank has identified illegal logging and enforcement as key issues and recommended including local participation in management of forests, appropriate sequencing can avoid adverse outcomes.

Another concern is whether the government can continue to extract large resource rents. Rents are probably declining as timber supply diminishes, but the magnitude of the rents needs further study. In addition, collecting royalties and rental taxes on resources amid widespread corruption will probably be impossible. This again raises the issue of governance and sequencing; the Bank has long been aware of both.

While stroke of the pen reforms could be carried out, for more fundamental reforms, progress is likely to be limited by a lack of a supporting environment (Kartodihardjo 1999). Key elements of such an environment include accurate information on forest resources and their social environment, results-based performance indicators, community participation in implementation and control of resources, and transparency and accountability in forest management. While the conditions on the adjustment loans have been expanded to address some of these issues, the lack of political will, the political changes at the top and the ensuing changes in the leadership of in MOFEC, first its split and then its merger with the ministry agriculture, the rapid pace of proposed decentralization all pose problems for implementing the spirit of the reforms and effectively dealing with governance issues.

A precondition for reforms is the reform readiness of the country. Within this framework the Indonesian case is particularly complicated. While the reforms proposed by the Bank have support and ownership in the Ministry of Finance, support from MOFEC, the implementing agency, is almost completely absent. MOFEC has demonstrated its lack of commitment to reform in several ways. Reforms that are implemented are often ineffective, and some-times-complementary conditions have not been implemented. And some-times other measures negate the reforms' effects (export licensing, for example).[18]

This lack of government commitment and political will raises the issue of ownership more generally. Before 1998 the Bank did little to build support for its reforms either among non-government stakeholders or by leveraging its policy dialogue by engaging other donors. As a result the Bank criticism it faced from NGOs, academics, and a civil society, and the donor community, unaware of the details of the structural adjustment reforms, the Bank has radically changed its approach opting for a far more transparent and consultative style of operating.

Analysts and Indonesian NGOs generally agree that the Bank's efforts since 1997 are on track—they agree with many of the reforms promoted and the direction taken by the Bank (Kartodihardjo 1999a). Stakeholders nevertheless have deep reservations about adjustment lending and even the Bank's intentions (Dubash and Seymour 1999). Some criticisms of specific conditions reflect differences of opinion on the relative importance of reform priorities. But a more significant problem for the Bank's credibility among some local advocacy groups has been the lack of knowledge of the Bank's strategy. Consistent with its mode of operation until 1998, the Bank did not articulate its phased approach to reforms or the difficulties and rationale involved in the reforms. Nor did it make any attempt to publicize its sector work or engage civil society in formulating a reform agenda. It appears to be doing a better job now by translating its CAS in Bahasa and widely discussing it in the country.

The criticisms of the adjustment lending reflect an incomplete understanding of the conditions under which the Bank was operating in 1997 still continues to operate today. The circumstances surrounding the Bank's approach to structural adjustment in Indonesia and the complex issues in the sector complicate a clear-cut assessment of the program. First, a structural adjustment loan is by nature short term, and while it provides the leverage to initiate certain policy changes, it cannot ensure their sustainability without complete ownership or lack of political will by the borrower. Many critics of the adjustment lending conditionality are rightly concerned about longer-term, institutional development-type reforms, which are not appropriate for a short-term program. Given the situation at the end of 1997 the Bank had to identify realistic changes to pursue. And it had to be selective in choosing reforms that could be included as policy conditionality.

Second, the Bank had a short time to react, with no opportunity for broad stakeholder consultations. The IMF and the Bank could have better analyzed the potential conflicts among conditionalities, considered the realities, and identified the potential impact on forests. The motivation in the standard neoclassical prescription of uniform (and low) export and other taxes is furthering economic efficiency and facilitating smoother trade flows. However, in the presence of market failures, as is the case with forests and their non-valued public goods and services, appropriate consideration of the impact of an unfettered goods market and commerce on forests needs special attention. This was lacking in the design of the conditionalities, especially those on export taxes on agricultural and forest-related goods.

Finally, the conditions in the structural adjustment loan were part of a larger strategy for sectoral reform. Indonesia mainly needed institutional reforms. Some reforms, primarily pricing and tax reforms, can be achieved by decree; some of these have been archived, including the transfer of the restoration fund from MOFEC to the Finance Ministry. The remaining, and arguably more important, reforms can only be achieved over time, after sustained incremental institutional change and the Bank began to pursue them through its long term assistance strategy working jointly with other development partners.

These operational realities aside, there are areas where the Bank could have been more prepared. For example, regular, in-depth economic and sector work (AAA) would have been helpful in high-priority areas. Alternatively, the Bank could have fostered greater collaboration and partnerships with other donor and research agencies to maintain its knowledge base in the absence of resources or opportunities for economic and sector work. Because of its dissociation with MOFEC and limited opportunity for sector work, the Bank did not fully recognize the speed and magnitude of changes in the sector. Thus, although the Bank was aware of the rapid expansion of the pulp and paper and oil palm industries, it did not have the benefit of a rich assessment of the magnitude and pace of their development, nor of their potential impact on forests. The Bank assumed that plantation development would be restricted to degraded land and conversion forests as called for in the existing rules.

In this situation, with other problems of enforcement and governance, the Bank has been criticized for focusing only on the supply side by promoting sustainable production. In the current legal and regulatory environment it is unlikely that any measure to control the destruction of forests would succeed. In the short run, sequencing problems could mean putting more pressure on forests in the light of strong vested interests and economic incentives to deforest. An alternative strategy for the short run could have been to include measures to control the demand for forest products more directly. For example, slowing down the excessive capacity generation in the pulp and paper industry, or a judicious use of taxes and subsidies on finished forest products may be more effective until the broader policy and governance issues are resolved.

Although gaps remain in the Bank's structural adjustment program approach, whether the program succeeds in changing the direction of the sector remains to be seen. However, the Bank has put the forest sector high on the economic reform agenda for Indonesia. It has created a significantly higher level of awareness, raised the level and the quality of debate on forest issues, and helped make decision making on policy more participatory and consultative. This is particularly important in Indonesia, where civil society has been unable to push the government to enact reforms, despite environmental disasters of unprecedented proportions. The Bank has also succeeded in bringing about some key policy changes. The main problem has been sequencing, whereby inappropriate or inadequate institutional reform threaten even nominal reforms.

Community participation is central to the new approach in the forest sector. In the short term the Bank intends to pursue tasks aimed at securing and protecting the forested estate, improving monitoring and enforcement in forest operations, establishing collaborative forest management and sharing the benefits through strong community participation. In the medium term its goal is to manage the transition to a more participatory forest sector, including institutional reform and decentralization. The long-term goal is to develop a new forest sector paradigm in a participatory and consultative manner that is acceptable to all the key stakeholders.

Conclusion: Analyzing Findings and Lessons for Continued Improvement

Although Indonesia has successfully used its forests to promote economic growth, it has not achieved equitable growth or conservation. With better governance and the participation of forest-dependent communities, Indonesia's natural capital could have been used more efficiently, equitably, and sustainably. The lessons from Indonesia's experience are important for the government, for Indonesian society, and for the World Bank as a partner in more just and sustainable economic development.

With Indonesia losing an estimated 1.7 million hectares of forests a year and natural resource benefits almost completely bypassing forest-dwelling and forest-adjacent communities, the outcome of forest sector policies must be judged highly unsatisfactory. Extremely weak governance has been the most debilitating problem. Under the system of corruption, cronyism, and nepotism cultivated under the "New Order Regime," this can be attributed partly to the political influence of strong vested interests from outside the Ministry of Forests (MOF), the official custodian of the nation's forest resources. But the ministry has shied away from its responsibility. Lack of enforcement of rules and regulations, lack of an effective custody system, poor management and implementation capacity, and the key role that officials at various levels have played in the patron-client relationship have resulted in unscrupulous exploitation of Indonesian forests.

Could these poor outcomes have been avoided? The answer to this question debatable. Had the government, particularly MOFEC, followed through with the established rules and regulations, Indonesia could have managed its forests sustainably and equitably. However, counteracting the strong economic incentives for exploiting forests requires a government committed to ensuring social justice and protecting the country's long-term interests over short term economic and political gains. To Indonesia's credit, and unlike in many other countries, Indonesia at least did achieve rapid economic growth and a substantial improvement in the living standards of its people, thereby generating political support for a regime that benefited greatly from Indonesia's natural capital.

Since the International Monetary Fund and the World Bank included forest policy reform in the Letter of Intent in 1998, and since the Consultative Group for Indonesia (CGI) used the issue as a condition for debt relief, international institutions have continued efforts to improve forestry performance. The Inter-Departmental Committee on Forestry (IDCF) was set up following CGI pressure last year in Jakarta. Although the committee has already arrived at a comprehensive framework and action plans to control forest degradation, the agenda has yet to be implemented.

Some activities have been carried out by the Ministry of Forestry; however, the high priority action plans, such as those related to illegal logging, restructuring of the timber industry, and reform of forest management systems in line with decentralization—which need inter-departmental coordination—have not resulted in significant progress.

The degradation of Indonesia's forest is a result of structural problems: the gap in allocation of the rights to utilize forest resources, conflicting claims, and conflicts of interest among bureaucrats, including law enforcers. All these make people pay less attention to sustaining the forest. Private parties are able to afford the extra, high costs entailed because they have the opportunity to gain from illegal logging or over cutting as compensation, and upholding the law becomes difficult.

Small success stories on forest degradation control are due to the presence of people capable of reforming the role of bureaucracy and at the same time win over the support of the local community. Improvements are needed for an open and credible bureaucracy, which enables the making of decisions together with the community. The key is in the commitment of the local government leaders, especially the heads of regencies.

There have also been problems in the way the decentralization process is taking place. The central government's policy instrument, used as a reference to implement regional autonomy, was late in its release. Although the authority of the central and regional governments was defined by January 1, 2001, the function of forest management organizations at central, provincial, and district levels had not been established. Internal disagreement in the implementation of regional autonomy, especially in the field of forestry, has been a problem.

There remains a serious conflict between the central and regional governments over questions of authority. Immediately prior to the implementation of regional autonomy, the central government was still releasing new, long-term concession permits. During the same period, most regional heads had also released hundreds of licenses to use forest products. The implementation of regional autonomy has also been hindered by the activities of Forestry State-Owned Enterprises. As centralistic forest management institutions, these enterprises (e.g., *PT. Perum Perhutani in Java and PT. Inhutani in the Outer Islands*) have not defined their position, even after the era of regional autonomy had begun. In this situation, the MOF came out strongly in favor of state-owned enterprises being designated to conduct forest management together with the local government, but initiative was rejected by local governments. (Kartodihardjo 2001b).[19]

With diverse perceptions and priorities among stakeholders, an approach stressing instructions from the center—such as the issuance of a presidential decree or instruction—would not receive support or produce a positive result. The weak implementation of the presidential instruction and Ministry of Forestry decree on the moratorium of ramin (*Gonystillus bancanus*) cutting and trading is a clear example.

Transaction costs for legal logging businesses are very high compared with the costs and risks of illegal ones. Research conducted in 1998 shows that to secure their various necessary permits for many activities, private companies had to spend around 26 to 48 percent of their variable costs. A preliminary result from this year's study by the Ministry of Industry and Trade together with Sucofindo shows that transaction costs amount to Rp

203,000 per cubic meter. The costs included "supporting costs" for guidance and control of forest concessions by the government which reached Rp 900 million per year for a forest concession with an annual log production of 45,000 cubic meters.

A crucial issue forest management is how the international agenda and national commitment can be linked to the commitment of local government, and how the bureaucracy can be reformed. The failure of last year's multi-sector agenda under the Inter-departmental Committee on Forestry and other previous international programs were due to the absence of intensive communication to link those international commitments with national, as well as local, concerns.

Governance and bureaucracy problems are the most important causes of forest degradation. International initiatives cannot be more than a trigger to further work in this area. Experience in the last two years has shown that the forest reform agendas that could be carried out were only those agreed through intensive communication among the central and local government as well as other stakeholders, followed by bureaucracy reform and strengthening. Any one agenda could be better than any other, but it would be futile without sufficient commitment and institutional capability.

Notes

1. How much of the classified forestland is actually covered by forest is not known for lack of reliable data but is estimated to be about 100 million hectares.
2. This transformation was achieved through a ban on the export of logs (phased in over the period 1982–85) and incentives to establish the processing industry. Under-priced logs, low rent capture, and an officially sanctioned aggressive marketing cartel have made Indonesia a world leader in tropical plywood. By 1988, Indonesia had become the leading exporter of tropical plywood, and since then it has controlled about 70 percent of the world market.
3. The bulk of pulp and paper output has so far been marketed domestically, but exports are growing at a rapid pace. Over time, together with Malaysia, Indonesia has taken over the African export markets for palm oil, rubber, coffee, cocoa and coconuts, with production based mostly in the outer islands.
4. The growth strategy has been criticized by some as the major cause of the loss of the rainforests (Dauvergne 1997). Accounting for the loss of natural capital, some have argued, may reduce Indonesia's growth performance from the impressive to the ordinary (Barber et al. 1994). Similar arguments have led to a plea for explicit accounting of natural resources in the measurement of GNP in order to gain a better picture of the net benefits of economic development.
5. Illegal logging during the 1994-97 period to meet the demands of national sawmills and plywood mills was estimated to be 20 million m3 annually. Because of growing demand from the pulp and paper industries, illegal logging is estimated to have risen as high as 56.6 million m3 in 1998 and probably rose again in 1999. In September 2001, the Bank's country director for Indonesia noted that illegal logging was costing the government about $600 million a year.

6. Most of the forest fires were man-made. The total damage caused by these fires is estimated at $9.3 billion—$7.9 to the domestic economy and rest to the neighboring countries as a result of carbon emissions.

7. Although the rationale of the transmigration program was poverty reduction in Java, the social conflicts between transmigrants and poor Indonesians in the outer islands were not anticipated.

8. Even though there were no direct forest-related operations after 1991, the Bank has remained engaged in conservation related activities through projects in conjunction with the Global Environment Facility, the incorporation of tree-planting components in non-forest sector projects, and analytic and advisory work.

9. This section draws extensively on Kartodihardjo (1999a) and Hyde et.al. (1999). Data used are mostly from MOFEC or Biro Pusat Statistic (BPS), and occasionally from other agencies or industry associations. The data from different sources are not always consistent. For example, 143 million rather than 147 million total forest hectares is a commonly quoted number, even by MOFEC. The data and their interpretations preferred by MOFEC, the World Bank, or other observers can be very different. Nevertheless, the magnitudes and ordered rankings of MOFEC data are consistent with other observations.

10. Three *Perum Inhutani* are on Java, which are largely teak plantations, and one in E. Nusa is a sandalwood plantation.

11. This point must be noted because external observers often assume, incorrectly, that the Forest Agreement ties harvests to the mill officially identified with each concession. In fact, Indonesian concessions act just like North American firms with integrated operations. They often send timber to competing mills if the competing mill will match their reservation price for either stumpage or logs. Mills in vertically integrated operations may purchase more than 10 percent of their logs on the open market. One large group of mills, the Barito Pacific Group, purchases more than 40 percent of its logs on the market (Barr 1999a). It would be useful to inquire more closely of the patterns and sources of log flows.

12. Estimates of direct forest-dependent peoples range from 1.5 million, based on a restricted definition of "isolated people" used by the Ministry of Social Affairs, to 65 million, including all forest dependent peoples (indigenous people and transmigrants) (World Bank 1994a). Recent estimates put the number of people directly and substantially dependent on forest resources for their livelihood at about 40 million (World Bank 2001), and the inhabitants of "forest villages" at 14.5 million (Muljadi, Fraser and Prodjosaputro, 2001). Whatever the exact number, it is clear that a large proportion of the Indonesian population is directly forest dependent for their livelihood. As worldwide some of the poorest households are the most dependent on the forest it is highly likely that most of the Indonesians relying on forests are also likely to be among the poorest in the society.

13. One observer goes so far as to assert that illegal logging is the source of all consumption for domestic use. Illegal logging is common in all the countries studied for this review, including two countries with strong political will to preserve forests, China and India. China also has a strong enforcement system.

14. By June 1998, 69.4 million ha of forest areas had been allocated to 651 HPH. Of these, 34 million ha are still under the first-term management by 291 HPH. Of the concessions whose first term has expired and not been renewed, 14 percent will be rehabilitated, 6 percent will be reserved for other as yet undetermined uses, 4 percent will be managed by HPH in partnership with state owned enterprises (*Bumn Kehutanan*) and the private sector, and the remaining 5 percent will be changed to different functions, such as tree plantations and transmigration. The

largest-ever land conversion took place in the peat forest of Central Kalimantan converting to agriculture an area of 1 million ha that had previously been managed by an HPH.

15. Among tree crops, rubber, coffee, and coconut are primarily smallholder crops. The majority (66 percent) of oil palm production is in the hands of large-scale commercial plantations, which have been growing rapidly in recent years. The total area of oil palm plantations (2.5 million ha) is smaller than that under rubber (about 3.5 million ha). However, the growth rate of the former between 1986 and 1997 has been 14 percent, while the latter has grown at about 2 percent per year.

16. Tempting as it may be, we should resist concluding that the policy changes should be put on hold until after the governance issues are resolved. While appropriate sequencing is necessary, the basic policy distortions should not be ignored, as they are likely to provide a strong incentive to resist institutional change.

17. The 1994 strategy review for the rural sector in the Eastern Islands contains almost no discussion of the impacts of forest-related issues. The 1992 agricultural sector work report identifies deforestation as a major concern in siting and managing tree crop development in the outer islands, but does not discuss the impact of agricultural policies on forests.

18. A case in point if the redrafting of the Basic Forestry Law. Following the mandated consultative process, the government undertook a series of consultations with key stakeholders. But the final draft of the law submitted by MOFEC did not adequately reflect the recommendations from these consultations, specifically those relating to recognizing local community rights on forests.

19. Kartodihardjo 2001b. Structural Problem on Implementing New Forestry Policy. CIFOR.

References

Ahmad, M. 1995. "The Role of Timber Production in Indonesian Economy: Reality or Illusion?" Konphalindo, Jakarta.

Angelsen, Arild. 1995. "Shifting Cultivation and 'Deforestation': A study from Indonesia." *World Development*, 23(10):1713-1729.

Angelsen, Arild, and David Kaimowitz. 1999. "Rethinking the Causes of Deforestation: Lessons from Economic Models." *The World Bank Research Observer*, February, 14(1):73-98.

Angelsen, Arild, and Daju Pradnja Resosudarmo. 1999. "Krismon, Farmers and Forests: The Effects of the Economic Crisis on Farmers' Livelihoods and Forest Use in the Outer Islands of Indonesia." Mimeo, Center for International Forestry Research (CIFOR), Bogor, Indonesia.

Ascher, W. 1993. "Political Economy and Problematic Forestry Policies in Indonesia: Obstacles to Incorporating Sound Economics and Science." The Center for Tropical Conservation, Duke University, July.

Barber, Charles Victor. 1997. *The Case Study of Indonesia, Project on Environmental Scarcities, State Capacity, and Civil Violence.* Published by the Committee on International Security Studies, American Academy of Arts and Sciences.

Barber, C. V., N. Johnson, and E. Hafield. 1994. *Breaking the Logjam: Obstacles to Forest Policy Reform in Indonesia and the United States.* Washington, D.C.: World Resources Institute.

Barr, Christopher M. 1999a. "Banking on Sustainability: A Critical Assessment of the World Bank's Structural Adjustment Reforms in Indonesia's Timber Sector." Working Draft, CIFOR, Bogor, Indonesia.

_____. 1999b. "The Development of Indonesia's Wood Based Industries During the New Order Period, 1966-98." Preliminary Draft, CIFOR, Bogor, Indonesia.

Casson, Anne. 1999. "The Hesitant Boom: Indonesia's Oil Palm Sector in an Era of Economic Crisis and Political Change." Working Draft, CIFOR, Bogor, Indonesia.

Dauvergne, Peter. 1997. *Shadows in the Forest: Japan and the Politics of Timber in Southeast Asia.* Cambridge: The MIT Press.

Dubash, Navroz K., and Frances Seymour. 1999. "The Political Economy of 'Environmental Adjustment': The World Bank as Midwife of Forest Policy Reform." Paper presented at a conference on International Institutions: Global Processes—Domestic Consequences, Duke University, April 9-11.

D'Silva, E., and S. Appanah. 1993. "Forestry Management for Sustainable Development." EDI Policy Seminar Report No. 32, The World Bank, Washington, D.C.

EIA/Telepak. 1999. "The Final Cut: Illegal Logging in Indonesia's Orangutan Parks." Environmental Investigation Agency and Telepak. London, U.K. and Bogor, Indonesia.

Evers, P. 1995. "A Preliminary Analysis of Land Rights and Indigenous Peoples in Indonesia." World Bank, Draft Working Paper.

Garrity, Dennis. 1999. Personal Communication.

Gelb, Alan, and Associates. 1988. *Oil Windfalls: Blessing or Curse?* New York: Oxford University Press for the World Bank.

Gillis, M. 1988. "Indonesia: Public Policies, Resource Management, and the Tropical Forest." In R. Repetto and M. Gillis (eds.). *Public Policies and the Misuse of Forest Resources.* Cambridge: Cambridge University Press.

Gray, J., and Hadi Soetrisno. 1990. "Fiscal Policies in Indonesia Forestry." Directorate General of Forest Utilization, Ministry of Forestry, Government of Indonesia and Food and Agriculture Organization of the United Nations, Jakarta. April.

Hafild, Emmy. 1999. Personal Communication.

Hanson, Arthur J. 1999a. "Indonesia's Transition: Environmental Governance and Sustainability." Paper presented to Lokakarya Lingkungan Hidup Reofrmasi Lingkungan; Tantangan Bagi Indonesia Baru; Environmental Governance Project, BAPPENAS/UNDP.

_____. 1999b. "Environment and Resource Management: Environment and Governance In Indonesia." Paper presented at the OED Indonesia Workshop for the Country Assistance Review, Operations Evaluation Department, The World Bank, Washington, D.C.

Hyde, William F., H. Kartdodihardjo, A. Khan, and Erwinsyah. 1999. "OED Forest Policy Review: Indonesia Case Study." World Bank, Jakarta.

Kaimowitz, David, and Arild Angelsen. 1999. "The World Bank and Non-Forest Sector Policies that Affect Forests." Mimeo, Center for International Forestry Research (CIFOR), Bogor, Indonesia.

Kartodihardjo, H. 1995. "Kegagalan teori rente ekonomi hutan." *Prisma* (2): 43-60.

_____. 1999b. "Toward an Environmental Adjustment: Structural Barrier of Forestry Development in Indonesia." World Resources Institute, Washington, D.C.

_____. 1999b. "Forest Management Policy Reform in Indonesia: The Need of Accountable Direction." Mimeo.

_____. 2001a. "Which Way Forward? Forests, Policy, and People in Indonesia.» CIFOR. Jakarta, Indonesia.

Kartodihardjo, Hariadi, and Agus Supriono. 1998. "The Impact of Sectoral Development on Natural Forest Conversion and Degradation: The Case of Timber and Tree Crop Plantations in Indonesia." January. 2000 Occasional Paper No. 26(E). Center for International Forestry Research (CIFOR), Bogor, Indonesia.

Larson, D. F. 1996. "A Review of the Palm Oil Subsector in Indonesia." International Economics Department, Commodity Policy and Analysis Unit, The World Bank, Washington, D.C.

Merrill, Reed, and Elfian Effendi. 1999. "Impact of Indonesia's Crisis: IV. Protected Areas Management." *NRM News* 1 (1): 15. Natural Resource Management Project. Jakarta, Indonesia.

Ministry of National Development Planning. 1993. Workshop on Indonesian Biodiversity Conservation and Management. Bogor, Indonesia.

Ministry of Forestry and Estate Crops. 1998. Direction, Strategy and Policy of Forestry and Estate Crops Development. Government's Response to Working Report of Komisi III DPR (House of Representatives), 1997/1998. Jakarta.

Muljadi, A. I. Fraser, and Siswanto Prodjosaputro. 1998. "Sustainable Forest Management Through Local Community Participation." Mimeo, ITFMP, Jakarta.

Pearce, David, Francis Putz, and Jerome K. Vanclay. 1999. "A Sustainable Forest Future?" Natural Resources International. UK and UK Department for International Development.

People's Consultative Assembly of the Republic of Indonesia. 1999. "Draft Law of the Republic of Indonesia Concerning the Fiscal Balance Between the Central Government and the Regions." Jakarta.

Potter, Lesley, and Justin Lee. 1998. "Tree Planting in Indonesia: Trends, Impacts and Directions." Center for International Forestry Research, Jakarta.

Ramli, R., and M. Ahmad. 1993. "Rente Ekonomi Pengusahaan Hutan Indonesia." Wahana Lingkunan Hidup Indonesia, Jakarta.

Ross, M. 1996. "Conditionality and Logging Reform in the Tropics." In R.O. Keohane and M.A. Levy (eds.), *Institutions for Environmental Aid: Problems and Prospects.* Cambridge, MA: The MIT Press.

Scotland, Neil. 1998. "The Impact of the Southeast Asian Monetary Crisis on Indonesian Forest Concessions and Implications for the Future." Report No. PFM/EC/98/3. Indonesia-UK Tropical Forest Management Programme, Jakarta.

Sève, Juan. 1999. "A Review of Forestry Sector Policy Issues in Indonesia." Natural Resources Management Program, Jakarta.

Sunderlin, William D. 1998. "Between Danger and Opportunity: Indonesia's Forests in an Era of Economic Crisis and Political Change." CIFOR.

Sunderlin, William D., and Ida Aju Pradnja Resosudarmo. 1996. "Rates and Causes of Deforestation in Indonesia: Towards a Resolution of the Ambiguities." Center for International Forestry Research, Jakarta.

Thiele, R. 1995. "Conserving Tropical Rain Forests in Indonesia: A Quantitative Assessment of Alternative Policies." *Journal of Agricultural Economics* 46(2): 187–200.

Tomich, T.P., M. Van Noordwijk, S. Budidarseno, A. Gillison, T. Kusumanto, D. Murdiyarso, F. Stolle, and A.M. Fagi. 1998. "Alternatives to Slash-and-Burn in Indonesia." Summary Report and Synthesis of Phase II. International Centre for Research in Agroforestry S.E. Asia, Bogor, Indonesia.

Wakker, Eziz. 1998. "Lipsticks from the Rainforest: Palm oil, Crises & Forest Loss in Indonesia: The Role of Germany." A forest campaign project of WWF Germany in collaboration with WWF Indonesia. World Wide Fund for Nature.

Wells, Michael, Scott Guggenheim, Asmeen Khan, Wahjudi Wardojo, and Paul Jepson. 1999. "Investing in Biodiversity: A Review of Indonesia's Integrated Conservation and Development Projects." East Asia Region, World Bank, Washington, D.C.

Whiteman, A., and A. Fraser. 1997. "The Value of Forestry in Indonesia." Report No. SMAT/EC/97/1. Indonesia-UK Tropical Forest Management Programme, Jakarta.

World Bank. 1988. "Forestry Institutions and Conservation Project." Staff Appraisal Report, Report No. 7002-IND, Country Department V, Asia Regional Office. The World Bank, Washington, D.C.

_____.1989. "Indonesia Forest, Land and Water: Issues in Sustainable Development." Report No. 7822-IND. Country Department V, Asia Regional Office. Washington, D.C.

_____. 1990a. *World Development Report 1990: Poverty.* The World Bank, Washington, D.C.

_____. 1990b. "Indonesia: Sustainable Development for Forests, Land and Water: Country Study." Report No. 9212. Washington, D.C.

_____. 1990c. "Second Forestry Institutions and Conservation Project." Staff Appraisal Report, Report No. 8603-IND, Country Department V, Asia Regional Office. The World Bank, Washington, D.C.

_____. 1992. "Indonesia: Agricultural Transformation Challenges and Opportunities Vol. II." Report No. 10504-IND. Agricultural Operations Division, Country Department III, East Asia and Pacific Regional Office. Washington, D.C.

_____. 1993a. "The East Asian Miracle: Economic Growth and Public Policy." Oxford University Press.

_____. 1993b. "Indonesia Production Forestry: Achieving Sustainability and Competitiveness: Draft Working Paper." Report No. 11758-IND. Washington, D.C.

_____. 1994a. "Indonesia Environment and Development: Challenges for the Future." Report No. 12083-IND. Environment Unit, Country Department III, East Asia and Pacific Region. Washington, D.C.

_____. 1994b. "Indonesia Transmigration Program: A Review of Five Bank-Supported Projects." Report No. 12988. Operations Evaluation Department. Washington, D.C.

_____. 1995a. "The Economics of Long-term Management of Indonesia's Natural Forests: Draft Forestry Report." Washington, D.C.

_____. 1995b. "Indonesia: Country Assistance Strategy: Memorandum of the President." Report No. 13988-IND. Country Department III, East Asia and Pacific Region. Washington, D.C.

_____. 1996. "Second Forestry Institutions and Conservation Project—Implementation Completion Report." Report No. 1529. The World Bank, Washington D.C.

_____. 1997a. "Indonesia: Country Assistance Strategy: Memorandum of the President." Report No. 16691-IND. Washington, D.C.

_____. 1997b. "Forestry Institutions and Conservation Project—Implementation Completion Report." Report No. 16725. The World Bank, Washington D.C.

_____. 1998. "World Bank Involvement in Sector Adjustment for Forests in Indonesia: The Issues." Washington, D.C.

_____. 1999. "Indonesia: Country Assistance Note." Report No. 19100. Operations Evaluation Department. Washington, D. C.

_____. 2001. *Indonesia: Environment and Natural Resource Management in a Time of Transition.*

7

Brazil's Forests: Managing Tradeoffs among Local, National, and International Interests

Uma Lele, Virgilio Viana, and Adalberto Verissimo*

World Bank lending was held at least partly responsible when there were reports of accelerated rates of deforestation in the Brazilian Amazon in the 1980s, and those reports significantly influenced the design of the Bank's new forest strategy in 1991. However, the possibility of "guilt by association" with any deforestation in Brazil's Amazon basin since that time continues to hobble the Bank's involvement in the Brazilian forest sector. On the other hand, the Bank's limited experience in the 1990s in Brazil demonstrates that the institution can play a small but catalytic role in improving our understanding of the processes and causes of deforestation, thus ensuring that the future deforestation that is inevitable in Brazil will be more efficient, equitable, and less damaging to the environment.

Brazil's vast size, per capita middle-income status of $3,467 (IBGE 2000) and highly skewed distribution of income and wealth (Gini coefficient of 0.6 in 1999) are all intertwined with the processes of deforestation. In recent years, Brazil has gone through several major transitions: from military dictatorship to thriving democracy, from a centrist government to one that is increasingly highly decentralized, and from an import-substituting industrialization strategy to a liberal trade regime. These changes provide immense opportunities for a more informed, planned, efficient, and equitable process of deforestation, but they also pose many challenges.

Under Brazil's decentralized system of government, the rich and the powerful have greater impact on local and state level politics than does the central government. And given Brazil's abundant forest resources, there continues to be considerable divergence in the costs and benefits as perceived by the local, national, and global interests. Our knowledge of the processes and

*The authors have benefited from extensive comments on earlier drafts by Robert Schneider, Sector Leader, the Latin American and Caribbean Region, World Bank.

underlying causes of deforestation in Brazil is still inadequate to devise an effective policy and an implementation strategy. Hence, a policy of completely protecting all of the Amazon while neglecting Brazil's other forests— a stance that the international environmental community persuaded the Bank to adopt in 1991—was not the right policy. The challenge is to ensure that all of Brazil's forests (including those in the Amazon) serve a variety of interests, including timber production for broad-based and sustainable development, and that those forests that are most endangered receive attention in conservation.

Brazil's Forest Resources

Brazil's forests cover more than 65 percent of its 8.5 million square kilometers. This vast resource accounts for 60 percent of the forests of tropical South America and a little over a quarter of the world's tropical forests.[1] In 1998, Brazil had 3.32 hectares of forest per capita, more than twice that of Indonesia and Cameroon, the other forest-rich countries covered in this volume. Brazil's forests are extraordinarily rich in species and globally significant in biological distinctiveness. About 90 percent of the country's forest cover is in the Amazon (World Bank 1994a) and in the broad savanna in central Brazil where much of the agricultural development of the past decade has taken place.

The Amazon Region

The so-called legal Amazon covers 5 million square kilometers (or 500 million hectares) in the northern states of Acre, Amapá, Amazonas, Pará, Rondônia, Roraima, and Tocantins), as well as in Mato Grosso and in parts of Maranhão. About 65 percent of the legal Amazon (about 350 million hectares) is under forest and contains a commercial stock of 60 billion cubic meters of timber, large stocks of carbon (140–350 tons per hectare), and possibly more than half the world's biodiversity (Verissimo et al. 1997; Fearnside 1999). Savannas and natural grasslands occupy about 20 percent of the Amazon territory, while about 15 percent has been deforested (Veríssimo et al. 1997).

Estimates of the rates of deforestation in the Amazon's original forest cover vary. It has been estimated that during the period 1978-81, an average of 21,000 square kilometers of forest were cleared each year. Estimated annual rates of deforestation also varied during the 1990s, but by 1999 total deforestation is believed to have exceeded 550,000 square kilometers. Most of the deforestation has occurred in the southern Amazon basin (a region commonly referred to as the deforestation arc), reflecting the shift of the agricultural frontier from Brazil's central west region into the Amazon basin (Schneider et al. 1999).

Cattle ranching accounts for 77 percent of land use in Brazil's forested areas. An estimated 7 percent is under annual crops, and a meager 2 percent under perennial crops. The remaining 14 percent are degraded lands (IBGE 1996). Unequal land distribution in the Amazon region has resulted in debate as to whether large ranchers have replaced small settlers as the major source of deforestation, an issue we return to later.

Only 1 percent of the establishments in the Amazon are larger than 2,000 hectares, but they account for 52.7 percent of the total cultivated area. At the other extreme, the 54 percent of landowners with less than 20 hectares hold only 1.1 percent of agricultural land (Schneider et al. 1999). Those who hold between 20 and 2,000 hectares account for the other 45 percent of landholders.

The Atlantic Forest

Brazil's long Atlantic coast is the site of the remaining fragments of the Atlantic Forest. Only 7.3 percent of the original 1.3 million square kilometers of coastal forest remain in existence. Despite the shrinkage, Brazil's Atlantic forest still has one of the highest levels of biodiversity on the globe. It houses many endemic mammals, birds, amphibians, reptiles, and butterflies, and at least 146 bird species and 68 subspecies. A large number of these are in danger of extinction. The small remaining parts of the Atlantic forest are far more threatened than the Amazon forest and should be a top priority for conservation. Over the years, attention to deforestation in the Amazon eclipsed concern for this highly fragmented and degraded forest, and the World Bank's 1991 forest strategy was no exception. Its focus was on the conservation of tropical moist forests. But the consensus is rapidly shifting, and a recent study of global hotspots has rated Brazil's Atlantic forest as one of the hottest (Mittermeier et al. 2000). The Operations Evaluation Department (OED) *Review of the 1991 Forest Strategy and Its Implementation* questioned the focus on tropical moist forests and recommended that Bank strategy be broadened to address conservation of more endangered forest ecosystems, such as the Atlantic forest and the Western Ghats forest in India.[2]

Deforestation in the Atlantic forest began many centuries ago, but most of it has occurred in the last several decades. Until the 1970s, most of the domestic demand for wood in southern Brazil was met by logging in the Atlantic forest. Timber production in the area declined sharply as a result, since there was little reforestation and no management for sustainability. The decline in timber production in the Atlantic forest then prompted increased demand for Amazonian timber. Today, many of the processes that have whittled away the Atlantic forest are affecting the Amazon. Hence, an understanding of the interplay of logging, roads, industrialization, and agricultural expansion in the Atlantic forest can provide lessons for preserving far more of the Amazon region.

Where economic returns to agriculture in the Atlantic forest were higher, deforestation was more rapid, particularly in areas suitable for coffee plantations in the states of Sao Paulo, Minas Gerais, and Parana. Where economic returns to agriculture were lower, as in Espirito Santo and Bahia, logging helped finance agricultural expansion. The area continued to lose tree cover in the 1990s, with more than 5,000 square kilometers disappearing in the first half of the decade (SOS Mata Atlantica; INPE, ISA 1998). A study in Parana (Sonda 1999)[3] found that deforestation continued in most of the western plateaus of the Atlantic forest (Parana, Sao Paulo, and western Minas Gerais) because farms there enjoy low transportation costs, productive soils, favorable topographic conditions, and good agricultural technology. High returns to agriculture also give new migrants an incentive to clear the land. Forest cover is more dense in areas close to the coast; the topography there tends to be unfavorable for mechanized agriculture, soils are poor, and transportation costs are high.

The Atlantic forest retains a high capacity for carbon dioxide storage in more than 20 million hectares of degraded areas, and provides other environmental services (particularly watershed protection) to more than 100 million Brazilians. It is thus a potential candidate for reforestation under the newly emerging carbon credit schemes.

Other Natural Forests in Brazil

Other associated ecosystems include the coastal restinga (sandy soil vegetation) and mangrove vegetation. Deciduous seasonal forests are found behind portions of the Atlantic forest, and the semi-arid caatinga is found in northeastern Brazil.

Plantation Forests

Brazil has 55,000 square kilometers of some of the most productive plantation forests in the developing world. They reflect Brazil's favorable growing conditions and an advanced research system supported by the private sector. The plantation forests have become an important source of charcoal for manufacturing, thereby reducing pressures to cut trees in natural forests. Until the early 1980s, annual revenues from natural forest extraction were greater than those from plantation forests, but this relationship has since reversed (IBGE 1997). The Bank's investments have contributed to this reversal. The synergistic relationship between plantations and natural forests must be better understood and actively developed to meet the growing international and domestic demand for Brazil's forest products.

Overall, the forest sector—including native forest, plantations, and non-timber forest products—accounts for 4 percent of Brazil's gross national product (GNP). While declining in importance (down from 13 percent in 1970), forest-dependent industry represented almost 11 percent of the total revenue in what Brazilians term the "transformation industry" in 1994.

A Proposed Forest Strategy for Brazil

A recent study jointly carried out by the Bank and Imazon, an environmental NGO and research institution (Schneider et al. 1999), offers several conclusions and recommendations for a future strategy for managing the Amazon forest. It provides a useful context in which to review knowledge about the underlying causes of deforestation. The report concludes that agriculture (including ranching) has the greatest chance of success in the drier zone (with less than 1,800 mm rainfall) that occupies about 17 percent of the Amazon basin (or 85 million hectares). For the remaining 83 percent, from a social and environmental point of view, the most promising alternative form of land use is a mosaic of protected areas, extractive reserves, indigenous reserves, and areas of sustainable forest management (SFM). Based on an analysis of forest species and economic accessibility, the report concludes that about 115 million hectares of economically accessible forests in the Amazon have commercial potential and could be designated for SFM. Within those 115 million hectares, however, there are about 44 million hectares of forests of high biodiversity that should be placed under strict protection.

Sustainable management and harvesting of the remaining 70 million hectares (about 20 percent of the Amazon rain forest) could meet the foreseeable demand for Brazilian Amazon timber. To restrict the expansion of unsustainable logging and the agricultural frontier, a combination of command and control and other instruments (zoning for parks, extractive reserves, public forests) would be needed. It would also call for rigorous application of independent third-party certification and auditing procedures. If market forces continue to operate freely without such a strategy, land use will be dominated by the predatory logging associated with extensive ranching and Amazonian communities will continue to experience a boom-to-bust economic cycle. Sustainable forest management would provide a more stable economy (income, employment, and tax revenues) than that produced by agricultural expansion, which will result in the impoverishment of soils and social misery for local communities.

Proactive intervention by the federal and state governments is needed to slow and eventually halt the current pattern of development. With obvious tradeoffs between short-term benefits to a variety of stakeholders and the long-term global and national benefits, whether the government would effectively be able to protect these areas of the Amazon without substantial transfer of resources to compensate the losers, is questionable.

The Role of International Trade in Brazil's Forest Products

Up until now, international trade has accounted for only a small share of the market for products from Brazil's native forests. Although forest-related exports grew from $100 million in 1985 to about $430 million in 1999, Brazil supplies only 4 percent of the global market for tropical wood (Barretto et al. 1998). Since 1980, the relative importance of the forest sector to Brazil's international trade has increased only slightly, rising from 5.4 percent to 7.1 percent of total exports and from 1.2 percent to 2 percent of imports.[4] About 50 percent of exports are in the form of cut wood, 25 percent plywood, and 12 percent laminates (Verissimo and Lima 1998). Considering the entire forest sector (including plantations), the forest sector was responsible for 7.14 percent of exports and 1.98 percent of Brazilian imports in 1998 (Bacha and Silva 1999).

However, trade liberalization, along with a boost from the joint customs union known as Mercosur[5] and from currency devaluations, is virtually certain to produce an increase in the global market for forest product exports from Brazil as other traditional suppliers of tropical timber, such as Indonesia and Malaysia, deplete their resources. Market pressure as an incentive to deforest was overlooked in the formation of the Bank's 1991 forest strategy.

The Role of the Domestic Market in Brazil's Forest Products

Understanding the nature of the domestic market is the key to the formulation of future forest strategies. Brazil's domestic consumption of tropical timber, estimated at 34 million cubic meters of logs in 1997, exceeded timber consumption in all of the Western European countries combined. An overwhelming 84 percent of Amazon timber is sold on the domestic market.

Timber consumption in Brazil takes various forms. Use as firewood is particularly important in the northeast region, where natural caatinga forests provide 35 percent of the energy supply in the region and generate 700,000 jobs in forest related industries (MMA 2000). In the country as a whole, demand from the manufacturing sector accounts for a large share of domestic consumption. Iron and steel production relies heavily on wood energy and is the highest revenue earner, followed by the pulp and paper, timber, and furniture industries.[6] In 1997, 85 percent of all charcoal produced in Brazil was used by the iron and steel sector (Bacha and Silva 1999). Historically, demand for charcoal has exerted major pressure on Brazil's natural forests. But that dependence declined from 82.6 percent in 1985 to 25 percent in 1997 as other energy sources were substituted for charcoal.

In 1999, Brazil's forest sector employed 2 million people. Most were involved in the extraction and processing of forest products. During the 1970–85 period, the forest sector accounted for roughly 14 percent of total employment in the transformation industry, but by 1994 that share had dropped to 11 percent (Bacha and Silva 1999). Timber milling creates the most forestry-related jobs (29 percent in 1994), followed by furniture (26 percent), iron and steel (24 percent), and pulp and paper (21 percent). The changes between 1985 and 1994 were minimal. In 1985, these segments accounted for 30.5 percent, 29.3 percent, 21.6 percent, and 18.6 percent of employment, respectively.

The Effect of Macroeconomic Policies on Deforestation

There are no studies and no convincing time series evidence to suggest that rates of deforestation have changed significantly over the last four decades as a result of the country's major changes in macroeconomic policies and strategies. With respect to deforestation, the complex role of structural factors at the economy-wide level (income and asset distribution) and sectoral level (in the industrial, agricultural, and forest sectors), in combination with such aspects of development as increased domestic demand, urbanization, and migration, would in any case make it difficult to capture reality in a model.

In the post-World War II period, Brazil pursued an aggressive policy of import-substituting industrialization. In the protected industrial sector, this policy created a considerable increase in demand for wood-based charcoal. The state of Minas Gerais, which produces 85 percent of Brazil's steel and pig iron, then became the world's largest producer and consumer of charcoal. In 1985, annual consumption of fuelwood in Minas Gerais was about 115 million cubic meters, of which 77 percent was converted into charcoal. Some 85 percent of this fuelwood came from native forests. In 1991, the state government enacted legislation requiring all wood-using industries to use only wood from plantation sources by 1998, and by the end of the century, almost all the fuelwood used in the state came from the plantation sector.

Brazil's import-substituting industrialization strategy led to impressive economic growth through the 1970s but left the country vulnerable to the oil shocks that occurred late in the decade which led to stagnating economic growth and rampant inflation in the 1980s. The effects of the oil shocks and the industrial slowdown, later investments in energy (such as the Brazil-Bolivia gas pipeline), the electric power shortages of early 2000, and the rapid growth of solar energy on the use of charcoal in Brazilian industry are not known.

Rapid trade liberalization in the 1990s resulted in the removal of almost all nontariff barriers to trade and a reduction in import tariffs that lowered the cost of agricultural machinery and other agricultural inputs. One result of these changes was rapid forest conversion. Trade liberalization has supported Brazil's comparative advantages in agricultural and livestock production, and it has also stimulated expansion of the services and durable goods sectors (EIU 1999b). What it also did, however, was to spur the growth of agricultural and livestock production along the forest margin, leading to further encroachment on the forest.[7]

One of the few macroeconomic studies on the subject explores how changes in the policy regime and in technology may have affected deforestation in the Brazilian Amazon. Using a computable general equilibrium model, Cattaneo (1999) shows that a currency devaluation shifts agricultural production in favor of exportable products. How devaluation affects agricultural production incentives in different regions, however, depends on migration flows. If migration occurs only between rural areas, a 30 percent devaluation increases the rate of deforestation by 5 percent, but if urban labor migrates to the Amazon to work in agriculture, the deforestation rate increases by 35 percent.[8] Vosti et al. have done similar modeling at the agricultural sectoral level.

Some recent studies have argued that agro-ecological factors, including heavy rainfall, provide natural protection to a large part of the Amazon region and hence put limits on land conversion. Technological change, however, has injected considerable dynamism into Brazil's agriculture, and government investment in roads to open up additional parts of the Amazon region for agricultural development is an important part of Brazil's development strategy.

Questions about the Role of Agriculture in Deforestation

Despite many studies on land use in the Amazon region, several agricultural issues of critical importance for rural land use policy remain debated and unanswered. They include:

1. The roles of small and large farmers in deforestation
2. The returns to livestock ranching in comparison to returns from better forest management
3. The roles of ecological and technological factors in deforestation
4. The role of agricultural finance in deforestation.

Without clear answers to these questions, it will be difficult to reach political consensus among competing stakeholders about land use planning and its implications for policy, laws, regulations, and enforcement.

The Roles of Small and Large Farmers in Deforestation

Large-scale migration into the Amazon region began in the 1960s as a consequence of the government's plans for regional development and resulted, among other things, in the establishment of large livestock ranches financed by generous subsidized credit schemes (Dean 1993). From the beginning, regional development plans included major land tenure and resettlement programs whose goal was to remedy regional disparities in wealth and land distribution.

The subsidies for migration into the Amazon in the 1970s and 1980s were sizable. They have now declined in size, but the migration has continued. The resettlement of small farmers through the government's resettlement agency (INCRA) also continued in the 1990s. The government claims to have met its target of resettling 280,000 families in the Amazon region between 1994 and 1998 at a cost of $7 billion—nearly double its total spending on agricultural reforms in the previous three decades (*The Economist* 1999).

To reduce the impact of new settlements on the Amazon forest, INCRA has prohibited such settlements in forested areas, but data on deforestation obtained by Brazil's National Institute of Space Research (INPE) in the 1999-2000 period suggest an apparent increase in the participation of small settlers in deforestation.

Others have questioned this conclusion and have argued that the role of large ranchers in logging and farming is increasing (Margulis 2001). They argue that 77 percent of all cleared land in the Amazon basin is used to pasture livestock (Chomitz and Thomas 2001). A large share of the cleared land belongs to a few large landowners. Hence, large farmers must be an important source of deforestation. An alternate hypothesis, as argued by Mahar et al., is that after a large number of smallholders had taken possession and cleared the land, the large landholders bought them out.

The Returns to Livestock Ranching in Comparison to Returns to Better Forest Management

On the basis of a review of the literature on livestock ranching and some modeling, Schneider et al. (1999) offer evidence of low returns to ranching compared to those for forest management to support their argument that market forces are leading to a boom-bust cycle in agriculture. They report average internal rates of return to ranching of 4.3 percent in isolated cases and 13 percent with reformed practices.[9] These rates are very low compared to the estimates of others.

For managed forests, on the other hand, Verissimo et al. (1997) (using a forest management system developed and described by Imazon, Embrapa, and the Tropical Forest Foundation),[10] report an internal rate of return of 71 percent. That rate of return (and some others reported later under our discussion of certification) is very high compared to the 8 to10 percent reported by Pearce et al. on the basis of an extensive review of the literature on improved forest management (Pearce 1999). The argument for low returns raises an important question: if indeed the returns are low, why is large-scale ranching and continued deforestation so prevalent?

A low return also raises the question of whether improved forest management, albeit from a close to zero base, is likely to be quick enough to significantly reduce the rate of deforestation in the Amazon in the foreseeable future.

There are several possible explanations for the continuing deforestation in the Amazon basin. One is that the rate of return to livestock ranching is far higher than the rates suggested by Schneider, Pearce, and their colleagues. In a recent work on agents of deforestation, Margulis (2001) suggests that "even if logging opens up access roads and helps finance future deforestation, deforestation will take place anyway because cattle ranching is potentially very profitable, and clearing the jungle is a classic way of claiming land rights."

In other words, even though logging reduces the costs of land clearing, the ultimate causes of deforestation are the profitability of cattle ranching and the fact that deforestation is the cheapest way of claiming land rights. Margulis goes on to argue that the persistent emphasis on loggers deflects attention away from the agents who really benefit from deforestation, namely, cattle ranchers.[11] His hypothesis is consistent with the Cattaneo study, which reported that livestock has the highest rates of return among all agricultural activities. It is also consistent with the Carpentier results (reported by Lele et al. 2000) that dairying by small-scale farmers has the highest return of all agricultural activities in the western Amazon and is greater than the returns generated by forest extractive activities.

Carpentier et al. (1999) concluded that it is the demand for cleared land for pastures that drives deforestation and offered four reasons: (1) livestock production systems are more flexible than cropping or forestry and require less labor, although they may not always offer the highest possible return to land; (2) seasonal labor requirements preclude broad expansion of labor-intensive but environmentally less destructive activities; (3) market risks are higher for many other potential activities; and (4) it is costly to switch out of ranching to other agricultural activities. Carpentier and colleagues say that cattle operations are attractive to small farmers because they improve profitability, productivity, liquidity, food security, and risk avoidance simultaneously.

Therefore, smallholders would suffer dire environmental and income consequences if replaced by large farm enterprises. Large farms might contribute more significantly to regional agricultural GDP, but well-capitalized smallholders who were displaced closer to the forest margins might cut down trees more quickly than poor migrants from urban areas, due in part to the demonstrated profitability of smallholder cattle production systems (dual-purpose dairy systems). The Carpentier findings refer to cattle operations in the drier areas of Acre and Rondonia, where transportation links and market access are well established. Carpentier et al. (1999) also reported that local municipalities in those states provide access to infrastructure, tax rebates, and tax holidays to entrepreneurs desiring to establish meat and dairy processing plants. These researchers also contend that while the broad social benefits of forest management may be greater than the private benefits of agriculture, there are no mechanisms for monetary transfers to compensate farmers or potential farmers for the loss of income that would result if they could not farm.[12] That is what would happen unless the farmers were compensated for not being able to benefit from such potential landholder assets as carbon storage or biodiversity or ecotourism, or unless the cost of land clearing was made prohibitive by imposing a tax on land cleared unsustainably so as to reduce the benefits from farming, a solution proposed by Schneider et al. (1999).[13]

The Role of Ecological and Technological Factors in Deforestation

On the basis of a study of weather patterns, Schneider et al. (1999) argue that agricultural success in the Amazon region is strongly influenced by the amount of annual rainfall in any given year and by the length of the dry season. Statistical analysis shows that (maintaining other factors constant) a higher level of rainfall reduces the rate of land conversion to agriculture and also reduces pasture productivity.[14] In the wettest areas there is an increase in the rates of land abandonment and soil degradation. In addition, agricultural productivity decreases as rainfall increases, with a consequent decline in economic return.

The Schneider et al. (1999) study, however, defined agriculture in terms of soil crops and livestock and did not take into account the possibilities of tree crop production. Such production is a better possibility under high rainfall conditions, particularly the domestication of wild strains of tree crops that already prosper in such conditions.

Moreover, technological change is greatly increasing the possibilities for sustainable agriculture through new combinations of crop rotation, soil and farming systems management, and chemical inputs. Thanks to agricultural research by EMBRAPA (Brazilian Agricultural Research Corporation) on zero tillage technology, soybean production in Brazil and other parts of the world has expanded to areas that were previously considered unsuitable for growing soybeans. Changes in rainfall could also have an effect. Since 1998, annual rainfall in the Amazon has declined, making the region more fire-prone. If that trend continues, additional areas may become suitable for farming.

Clearly, fine-scale mapping of rainfall patterns and soil patterns in the western Amazon region should be an essential part of long-term planning of agricultural enterprises as well as timber plantations. Exploration of location-specific land use options could significantly contribute to land use sustainability. Such information would be crucial to the government in making politically difficult decisions about land use.

Because of labor shortages and the high costs of mechanical clearing, fires that have been set deliberately by owners have been the most cost-effective way to clear land for agricultural purposes in the Amazon region. Escaped fires, however, burn a large amount of land unintentionally and release stores of carbon into the air. Moreover, annual rainfall in the Amazon has declined since 1998, making both escaped fires and natural fires more likely. A series of large wildfires in 1998 burned some 40,000 square kilometers (20 percent) of the state of Roraima, including 9,254 square kilometers of closed-canopy forests and extensive savanna, agricultural, and Indian reserve areas (Nepstad et al. 1999). Since 1998, Brazilian states have put satellite monitoring systems into place, and this technology has helped to greatly reduce the destructiveness of forest fires.

The Role of Agricultural Finance in Deforestation

Some studies assert that cheap agricultural loans have encouraged the conversion of forest land to agriculture in Brazil in past years, but others argue that the phase-out of cheap credit during the 1980s also had the same effect. Additionally, real interest rates moved to positive or near-positive levels in the mid-1980s, and the subsidy element was eliminated altogether in 1987 (World Bank 1990). The decline in credit volume is thought to have promoted expansion of agricultural land use by small-scale producers in the Amazon region, and probably to further migration in search of additional land for farming.

Under the Northwest Region Integration Program in Rondonia in the 1980s, some farmers began operating government-promoted high-input production systems for tree crops, which are more environment-friendly than other crops. Given the long-term nature of tree crop investments, the systems were predicated on the availability of cheap credit. When that credit was no longer available, farmers could not afford the required inputs and reverted to less sustainable practices, such as swidden farming and extensive ranching (Mahar 1989). Mahar argues that the rapid pace of pasture formation in Rondonia in the 1990s might have resulted, in part, from the tightening of the credit supply. Further, with little credit available, the farmers also resorted to cutting the fruit trees to finance their agricultural pursuits.

Vosti (1999, personal communication) argues that if credit is made available to small farmers, it will in all likelihood also increase their conversion of forest land to agricultural pursuits. That may not be the case, however. Small farmers seem to decide to make this conversion based on the perceived potential of returns to agriculture vis-à-vis forestry. Whether it is financed by credit or by cutting down trees seems to be a secondary issue. Nevertheless, the role of the financial sector (whether formal through institutional loans or informally through private savings) and its relationship to logging is one about which little seems to be known with certainty. Still, Schneider observes it should be noted that managed forestry requires control of many thousands of hectares, meaning that no smallholder could ever earn a living through managed forestry (Schneider 2000).

Policy Impacts

Schneider (1994) and Schneider et al. (1999) argue that the result of national development policy and the glut of cheap land in the Amazon basin has been "nutrient mining," the exhaustion of the natural resource base through a progression of economic activities. "The process of nutrient mining varies from region to region along the frontier, depending on the quality of soils, ease of forest access, availability of labor, credit, and land tenure relationships."

Policies directed toward forest ownership are also an issue. As long as forest ownership is not limited by an active land policy and combined with restrictions on road access, and land prices do not reflect the true value of forest resources (biodiversity, carbon sequestration, and the like), intensification of land use and more sustainable management practices will not be economically attractive. This calls for an active policy of land-use planning.

Public policies and legislation have historically been biased against maintaining standing forests and in favor of other land uses. The seemingly endless supply of cheap land in the Amazon has made land-extensive activities economically more attractive than land-intensive investments.

A related policy question in the Schneider et al. (1999) paper is whether the demand for improved forest management can be stimulated through active policies. Although there is some evidence of increased interest among large entrepreneurs, the reason for the still quite limited interest could be that substantial rewards are still available from logging. Verissimo et al. (1997) report that returns to predatory logging may reach as high as 121 percent. That is twice the rate they report for improved forest management.

The Increase in Predatory Logging

Logging in the Amazon is becoming much less selective than it was 20 years ago. The Brazilian government acknowledges that more than 80 percent of the logging in the Amazon is illegal and that it has contributed to rapid growth of the region's timber industry (Verissimo and Amaral 1998). Between 1976 and 1998, forest production (in logs) in the Amazon increased from 4.5 million cubic meters to 28 million cubic meters. Growth in timber production in the region is expected to continue at a rate of 5 to 7 percent annually to keep pace with domestic and international demand (Stone 1997; Arima et al. 1999).

Protection of Brazil's Amazon forest beyond the short term requires an increase in the valuation of standing forest, an increase in the costs associated with unsustainable logging practices, and an increase in the incentives for, and profitability of, sustainable (or improved) forest management. It must pay owners to retain trees and other forest products in the forest and to improve management practices. At the same time, predatory exploitation of timber must become unprofitable.

In evaluating measures that might address these challenges, it is useful to distinguish between the processes taking place at the forest-agriculture frontier and those taking place beyond it, deep in the forest. At the frontier, agriculture, logging, and road-building create a mutually reinforcing system of forest conversion. Beyond the frontier, illegal logging of higher value tree species threatens protected areas and the livelihoods of indigenous communities and extractivists.

Illegal logging is intertwined with governance and political economy. The rapidly increasing economic importance of timber production in the Amazon has increased the political influence of the timber sector at all (municipal, state, and federal) government levels. Timber interests play a strong role in state politics and influence the design and implementation of state policies that are favorable to the current unsustainable logging practices (Mahar 1998). The politics of logging has also limited the effectiveness of Bank projects (discussed below).

Extensive predatory logging in the Amazon is stimulated in part by the construction of roads and other infrastructure. While the direct contribution of logging to deforestation is significantly less than agriculture's contribution (particularly including cattle ranching), its indirect contribution is large. Roads built for logging purposes stimulate colonization, which in turn brings more farming. Meanwhile, landowners who sell extraction rights to the logging industry use the money to invest in agriculture, using newly cleared land to produce sufficient returns to extend the agricultural frontier or to intensify farming on cleared lands (Arima et al. 1999).

Uncontrolled timber extraction in the Amazon is a result of poor enforcement of regulations. Even when management plans are submitted to the Brazilian Institute of the Environment and Renewable Natural Resources (IBAMA), they are rarely implemented as written. Independent verification of planned implementation is present in very few operations, and few qualify as "well-managed." Insufficient efforts by rural extension agents from EMATER (Empresa de Assistencia Tecnica e Extensao Rural) to promote proper forest management are another reason, as is the low level of timber-processing technology[15] (see Box 7.1).

The intervals between extraction cycles in the Amazon are getting shorter, leaving an estimated 41 tree species at risk of extinction (Verissimo et al. 1997; Martini et al. 1994) out of a commercial stock of some 350 tree species

Box 7.1
Brazil's Timber Industry

About 2,500 mills in 75 production centers in Brazil produce approximately 11.2 million cubic meters of processed wood annually, 63 percent of it being sawn wood. The remaining 37 percent goes to the manufacture of higher value-added products: veneer (18 percent), plywood (10 percent), and flooring, doors, room dividers, and other improved wood products (9 percent). Capital investment costs can be as low as $3,000 for a micro sawmill, $300,000 for a mill with a band saw, and as much as $2 million for plywood and laminate operations (Verissimo et al. 1992; Barros and Uhl 1995).

(Martini et al. 1994). The number of species exported from the Amazon increased from just a few (principally mahogany and virola) in the 1970s to more than 40 in 2000 (Veríssimo Comunicação Pessoal), and there has been severe depletion of mahogany and virola. About 90 percent of the commercial species fetch prices of less than $60 per cubic meter, compared to more than $200 per cubic meter for natural mahogany (Verissimo et al. 1997). As extraction cycles get shorter, the agricultural frontier lags farther behind the logging frontier, which allows time for the logging of lower value trees prior to conversion of the land to agriculture.

Only 32 to 40 percent of every cubic meter of timber is transformed into sawn wood, plywood, or veneer. The remaining 60 to 68 percent is wasted. Obsolete equipment, poor storage of cut logs, and a thin market for small pieces of wood all contribute to this low productivity. As wood becomes scarcer, however, productivity may be improving through investments in better processing technology (Arima et al. 1999).

The Lack of Incentives for Better Forest Management

Evidence on the financial returns to managed forests in the Amazon is limited. As reported earlier, some of it suggests that returns are barely adequate relative to interest rates. When returns on managed forests are compared with the returns to predatory logging or the opportunity cost of capital—in clearing land for agriculture, for example—they seem unattractive. But Schneider (1992) argues that there is only one study by Southgate on financial returns that shows they are "barely adequate relative to interest rates." The only other study was done by Howard in Bolivia which calculated an NPV of 200-260 hectares at a 10 percent discount rate. Schneider et al. (1999) obtained $100 per hectare at 10 percent, which only falls to zero at a discount rate of 71 percent. Schneider et al.'s recent economic analysis comparing the costs of timber production under good forest management practices to those normally used in predatory logging has produced unexpected results. Barreto et al. (1998) analyzed the costs and benefits of improved forest management on an experimental plot of 100 hectares and found that management is more profitable than predatory logging because of greater efficiency of machine use and better utilization of logs. The authors observed an NPV per hectare of $430 with a discount rate of 20 percent. A study sponsored by the Forest Service of the U.S. Department of Agriculture and conducted by Holmes et al. (2000) produced results similar to those of Barreto. The Holmes study compared an industrial-scale managed forest of 500 hectares with a predatory logging system and also found management to be more lucrative (a return of $11.60 per cubic meter versus a return of $9.84, or a return of $294 per hectare versus $250 per hectare).

Most of the research on managed forests, including that of the Brazilian Agricultural Research Corporation, has assessed financial and economic costs and returns under varied geophysical conditions and size of logging operations. In any case, small-scale loggers have limited capacity to introduce new technology unless policies on credit and extension improve.

Based on the notion that SFM is not possible in primary tropical forests, the Bank's 1991 forest strategy declared that the Bank "will not under any circumstance finance commercial logging in primary tropical moist forests as a precautionary policy towards utilization." The OED review has documented the chilling effect of that declaration on the Bank's involvement in forest management. By the late 1990s, even without Bank involvement, there was extensive evidence of illegal logging, and some of the Bank's borrowing countries in the tropics were attempting some form of improved natural forest management on an experimental basis on both the industrial and community scales. The beneficial impact of this improved forest management on soils and biodiversity is small, difficult to measure and its beneficiaries are difficult to identify compared to the impacts of illegal logging or other economic uses of the land (agriculture, pasture, mining).

In the course of the OED review, the Brazilian analysts working on this case study and progressive elements of the Brazilian private sector argued that the World Bank and the International Finance Corporation (IFC) should actively support research, policy and institutional reforms, and investments in improved forest management practices in the Amazon to minimize the adverse effects of predatory logging. In other words, the Bank and IFC should get involved in efforts to improve conditions in Brazil's forest sector rather than assume that continuing the 1991 policy—that is, not providing financing for commercial logging operations, will somehow correct the problem of poor forest management and discourage deforestation. Hence, they urged that the Bank's 1991 forest strategy be revised to address the extensive, new, on the ground evidence of illegal logging (Viana et al. 1996).

The OED review also noted that the 1991 policy was inconsistent with the agreement between the Bank and the World Wide Fund for Nature (WWF) on bringing 200 million hectares of land globally under some form of SFM and has recommended such a change in Bank policy that will enable the Bank to be more proactive in its operations in helping countries to improve management of their forests. The Bank's new forest policy was still being reformulated at the time of publication of this volume.[13]

Migration to the Amazon Region

The geographic isolation of the Amazon ended in 1964 with the completion of the Belem-Brasilia highway. This new access road to the forest, combined with tax and credit incentives, caused population in the highway's zone of influence to balloon from 100,000 in 1960 to an estimated 2 million 10 years later. In 1968, completion of the Cuiabá-Porto Velho highway opened the previously isolated territory of Rondonia to a wave of migrants.[16] In contrast to the state's original settlers, the new migrants were primarily small-scale farmers from the southern state of Parana. Many also arrived from Mato Grosso, Minas Gerais, Espirito Santo, and Sao Paulo.

Farmers in southern Brazil leave their land for the Amazon, where land has been cheaply available, for a number of reasons, including a desire to take advantage of the scale economies in agriculture, a result of technical changes in the production of soybeans and other crops, and thus overcome the competitive disadvantage of small producers relative to their larger counterparts. Migration from the Northeast and parts of the Amazon itself (e.g., in the Southern arc) seems to have been prompted by a combination of drought episodes and land degradation.

Word of the discovery of fertile land in Rondonia prompted massive migration to the state. By the late 1970s, Rondonia's population had quadrupled, and the state government faced a growing demand for construction of infrastructure and other governmental services. In the 1980-83 period, before the Cuiaba-Porto-Velho highway was paved, an average of 65,000 migrants entered Rondonia each year. Afterwards, in the 1984–86 period, the average number of migrants rose to 160,000. A study of 624 municipalities throughout the Amazon found that from 1991 to 1994, 81 percent of deforestation occurred within 50 kilometers of major roads in the southern part of the Amazon region in what is now known as the deforestation arc (Alves and Strada 1999).

Transportation costs play a key role in decision making at the frontier, where land tenure is unclear and government institutions are weak. Lower transportation costs in the deforestation arc, coupled with available credit technology, and abundant and cheap land, have favored such major export crops as soybeans. Lower transportation costs also fuel the expansion of uncontrolled logging, which in turn finances secondary and smaller roads that are often constructed by private land owners and that facilitate encroachment on forested lands by both small-scale farmers and large ranchers (Arima et al. 1999). While the Brazilian government has become increasingly sensitive to ecological issues raised by the development of the Amazon's resources and has taken steps to increase forest protection, it continues to view the Amazon as an opportunity for economic growth that can help alleviate poverty and accelerate the overall development of the country. As a result, such government efforts as the "Brazil in Action" plan,[17] which includes significant road building in the Amazon, continue to threaten the region's forests (see Box 7.2). Many investments in transportation are undertaken with little or no consultation with the Ministry of Environment, in much the same way that agricultural expansion generally involves little attention to the zoning attempted in the Bank's rural development projects in the Amazon, and discussed below. Trade liberalization and currency devaluations have already increased exports of primary products, intensifying already existing economic pressures on the forests.

Improving environmental assessment and mitigation procedures where road building is essential to intensify agricultural production in areas already cleared for agriculture can clearly help achieve the goal of sustainable development of the Amazon by taking long-term environmental as well as short-term economic costs and benefits explicitly into account.

The Role of Indigenous People in the Amazon

There are dozens of small indigenous populations in the Amazon. It is generally believed that indigenous societies have a comparative advantage in forest management because of their rich knowledge base and skilled methods. Viana et al. (1996) argue that forest management (both timber and non-timber production) may become an economic alternative for these communities. A significant body of literature documenting successful long-term management of forests by local people is available, but little of it demonstrates increased incomes and improved well-being. Herein lies the tension between the objectives of forest management and maintenance of cultural life-styles, on the one hand, and improved living standards, on the other. An important policy challenge is to demonstrate that indigenous people can achieve both successful forest management and improved incomes and living conditions while continuing their traditional way of life.

Only a few well-documented experiences with natural forest management and improved living standards in indigenous reserves exist. A noteworthy case is the forest management project in the Xikrin Indian Reserve. A private partner, Compania Vale do Rio Doce, cofinances the project with Global Environment Facility funding. It is the first forest management project for timber production in an Indian Reserve. The project has generated interest in a number of other indigenous groups and support from key NGOs.

Box 7.2
Brazil in Action

In 1996 the government launched "Brazil in Action," a development initiative that includes ambitious infrastructure and transport components, several of which are particularly relevant to the Amazon:

- Paving highway BR-174, linking Manaus to Venezuela and crossing the state of Roraima.
- Extracting natural gas from the Urucu fields in the Jurua River basin of Amazonas state. The projected output of 4 million cubic meters a day would benefit both the Manaus industrial region and the states of Acre and Rondonia.
- Improving the navigability of the Madeira river to permit grain shipments from Rondonia and Mato Grosso to Amazonas, and from there to the Atlantic Ocean.
- Recovering the road link from Cuiabá to Rio Branco, then providing an overland link to Peru.
- Installing an energy transmission line from Tucurui to benefit the west and south of the state of Para.
- Creating the Tocantins-Araguaia Waterway to transport grain from the Center-West to the Maranhao port of Itaqui.
- Paving around 1,147 km of the Santarem-Cuiaba highway (from the Guarantâ do Norte, Mato Grosso, to Santarem, Pará) .
- Paving 981 km of Transamazônia (BR 230) from Marabá (Para) to Ruropólis (Pará).

Brazil in Action has been an important step in opening the Amazon and integrating it into the Brazilian economy. Many of these undertakings will facilitate exports and regional integration with neighboring countries.

But along with these infrastructure developments are environmental risks.

For example, "The paving of federal roads in Acre completely modifies the conditions for access and exploitation of natural resources of the state and of many border areas, opens up possibilities for population movements, accelerates the sale of land, and places previously rather isolated indigenous populations in contact with non-Indians" (GTA 1998). By opening a link with Peru, the paving of these roads may also lead to international labor flows into Brazil, thus relieving labor constraints on forest clearing for small-scale agriculture in the Amazon.

Additionally, the Brazil in Action initiative is intended in part to facilitate an increase in soybean exports. Expansion of soybean cultivation (Kueneman and Camacho 1987) will replace important natural habitats in the country's Center-West region.

Box 7.3
Indigenous Peoples

Brazil's indigenous population of about 320,000 is scattered among all five geographic regions and comprises 206 ethnic groups who speak some 170 languages. The government has taken significant steps in securing land tenure rights for these people.

According to the National Indian Foundation, there are 559 areas classified or claimed as Indigenous Lands, covering 84 million hectares, or about 9.85 percent of the country. A significant portion of the indigenous lands is of great importance for the conservation of biodiversity. In the Brazilian Amazon alone there are 160 ethnic groups living on 358 tracts of indigenous lands. Because of their large size, many of these areas still preserve the reproductive cycles necessary for conservation of their diverse flora and fauna.

Although Carpentier et al. (1999) suggest that providing formal land titles for small-scale agriculturalists may increase forest conversion, demarcating and giving clear title to indigenous people has generally been found to benefit forest conservation.

The indigenous lands component of the Pilot Program to Conserve the Brazilian Rain Forest (PPG7), which started in 1995, aims to enhance the well-being of indigenous people and promote conservation of the natural resources by completing the legalization of the indigenous areas in the Amazon and assisting in their protection. This $22 million project is funded by grants from the Brazil Rain Forest Trust Fund and the German government. With technical assistance from NGOs under the supervision of Brazil's National Indian Foundation (FUNAI), the program has supported a number of alternative approaches to demarcation that are carried out by indigenous people themselves. It also supports work to improve the other steps in the land legalization process, such as funding studies on adding environmental diagnosis to the process. This will help identify the full range of natural resources and microenvironments used by indigenous people and ensure that mapping does not eliminate or disrupt important activities. As of August 2001, some 17 million hectares in 28 indigenous areas had been demarcated and titled, and an additional 28 million hectares (132 indigenous areas) were in process of regularization.

The program also assists in procedures designed to support a more efficient and participatory process of indigenous land identification, demarcation, and legislation. In addition, support is being provided for ethno-ecological studies on resource patterns, training, monitoring, and evaluation of demarcation procedures, and the preparation of surveillance and protection strategies.

Land held by indigenous groups is often invaded by large landowners, timber companies, mineral prospectors, or sharecroppers, as well as by the public sector for such activities as creating new municipalities and building new roads and hydroelectric plants. High-value mahogany stocks are a principal impetus for many of the invasions (Verissimo et al. 1997). Thus, giving title to indigenous groups will have to confront many challenges, including the following:

- Federal and state agencies lack a strong political mandate or the necessary enforcement capacity to punish invaders of indigenous lands, and indigenous communities have little power to defend themselves.
- Corruption in government institutions often permits a vicious cycle of land invasions and extraction of natural resources that compromises natural ecosystems and weakens social organizations (Viana 1998).
- Public resources from Brazil's government for demarcating indigenous lands are scarce. To date, the government has mostly used external resources from bilateral and multilateral sources, including the Bank. This creates problems for indigenous communities that exist outside the Amazon and rely exclusively on ever tighter federal funds. Regional economic and political interests oppose federal demarcation of indigenous lands, which leads to land disputes, and sometimes, even physical violence.
- Finding economic alternatives to meet the social requirements of indigenous people, particularly to cover health costs, poses a challenge.

Extraction of Non-Timber Forest Products

Non-timber forest products—medicinal plants, nuts, berries, and the like—are important to the livelihoods of tens of thousands of Brazilians living in extractive reserves (Carpentier et al. 1999).

Medicinal plant extraction in the southern state of Parana is an example of how non-timber products can benefit the community. Klabin, a private pulp and paper company, maintains a public health program for the municipality of Telemaco Borba that is supervised by a team of doctors and pharmacists and relies heavily on phytotherapy, based on traditional medicinal plants. The initiative receives funding from the Brazilian Biodiversity Fund Project, supported through a GEF grant, to establish a partnership with the Brazilian Foundation for Sustainable Development, and to prepare a business plan for a company that will market medicinal plant products (FBDS 1999). EMBRAPA has recently funded a similar program in Parana that is attempting to develop a commercial market for traditional medicinal plants through contracts with supermarkets and state health services. The results of these initiatives will shed light on the financial viability of such enterprises and the possibilities of scaling them up to make a difference to the lives of people. Their transferability to the Amazon is a challenge because infrastructure, institutions, and markets are far less developed in the Amazon than in southern Brazil.

Another example of forest product use is the creation of fashionable hand-bags made of rubber tapped from forest trees. The handbags are sold in Rio or exported. Whether and to what extent this has increased financial returns to the rubber tappers is not yet known.

Given current trends in the policy environment, the question is whether the extraction of non-timber forest products will be profitable on a scale large enough to significantly improve forest conservation and improve the liveli-hoods of indigenous people. Extraction is not competitive with agriculture and has been declining over the past few decades. In the Amazon this decline is predictable and is explained by a combination of factors: low productivity per unit of land, competition with more economically attractive plantation-based products, competition with chemical substitutes, and government policies, in-cluding import tariffs. This same general pattern of decline has been documented in the Atlantic forest (Homma 1993; Reserva da Biosfera 1999). Homma argues that domestication of extractive products is the best way to assure a market and thus long-term sustainability for them, a view that has been controversial among proponents of support for extractivist activities. Extractivists, according to Vosti (1999) are among the poorest residents of the Amazon, with some in extreme poverty. Further international assistance, such as that noted below, would seem to be merited for both poverty alleviation and environmental reasons.

In 1989, the Brazilian government recognized extractive reserves as a new type of conservation unit. In these reserves, traditional communities receive long-term concessions to reside in them and use their natural resources in exchange for sound stewardship.

In 1992 the Brazilian Institute of the Environment and Renewable Natural Resources (IBAMA) created the National Center for the Sustainable Devel-opment of Traditional Populations (CNPT) with a mandate to establish and help in maintaining extractive reserves. Then, in 1995, and with the assis-tance of $9.4 million provided by the Rain Forest Trust Fund, an Extractive Reserves Project was started to provide support to the first and largest of the extractive reserves, which encompasses 21,600 square kilometers. The project provides support to complete the establishment and legalization of four re-serves while strengthening community organizations, improving subsistence and commercial crop production, and improving management of natural re-sources. In 1999 the European Commission provided an additional $74 mil-lion for a second four-year phase of the project.

Considerable progress has been made toward completing legalization of the reserves, strengthening local community organizations, and installing infrastructure. The project is helping to introduce the cultivation and use of natural vines and medicinal plants, handicraft production, ecotourism, and the use of fallen timber for small-scale processing. All four reserves have natural resource utilization plans in place and are completing long-term de-velopment plans.

Project documents say that local participants show strong ownership of the four reserves and that they constitute one of the best examples of shared management of conservation areas. But while much is known about project inputs, little concrete information on project benefits to participants—such as increased security of land tenure and increased incomes—is available.

As a rule, public policies have not supported extractive production systems. Brazil nut productivity in native forests, for example, can be improved by simple management practices (Viana et al 1998). But only in the past few years has the Amazon Development Bank (PRODEX) created a credit line for extractivist activities. Successful cases of community projects supported by the Extractive Reserves Project could serve as a basis for Bank or GEF support. Mid-level institutions that either provide funding for sustainable practices or act as negotiator between smallholders and markets may offer a new way of organizing for long-term sustainability.[18]

Shortcomings in the Protected Areas System

Along with extractive reserves and indigenous lands, Brazil has five other types of protected areas: national parks, ecological stations, biological reserves, national forests, and environmental protection areas. Additionally, states and private landowners may set aside areas for protection. Although the federal government has 86 conservation areas under strict preservation— covering almost 160,000 square kilometers—these protected areas do not necessarily represent Brazil's biological diversity.

A 1994 Bank study discussed two critical shortcomings of Brazil's protected area system. These shortcomings still exist. First, severe understaffing of management agencies limits effective policing and protection of these areas. Amazonian parks, for example, have only one field agent for every 6,000 square kilometers, compared to one agent for every 82 square kilometers in the United States (Terborgh and Peres 1995).

Second, the government has to deal with the complexities of having people reside within the boundaries of protected areas. By 1994, about 20 percent of the land within national parks, biological reserves, and national forests was in private hands. Few alternative strategies have been pursued for managing protected areas without removing the people who live there (World Bank 1994b), although Mamiraua State Park and Jau National Park (both in the state of Amazonas) show that achieving forest protection despite the existence of resident communities is possible (Verissimo 1999).

According to a recent study by Conservation International, the parks are an effective means of protecting tropical biodiversity. The study concentrated on well-established parks in regions subject to heavy land-use pressure and concludes that a majority of the parks were successful in halting land clearing and, to a lesser extent, in reducing logging, hunting, animal grazing, and the use of campfires. Effectiveness was found to be correlated with effort devoted to basic management activities, such as enforcement, boundary demarcation, and compensation to local communities. This would suggest that even modest increases in funding would go a long way in increasing the protectiveness of the parks. It should be noted that this view has been contested (see chapter 8).

The critical issue for Brazil's protected area system is insufficient funding and implementing capacity to protect and manage conservation units. Although Brazil is the largest recipient of international support for protected areas,[19] the support is quite small on a per hectare basis. IBAMA has given greater administrative autonomy to conservation units, thereby allowing managers to use part of the revenues generated locally through ecotourism, for example. The government, through the Ministry of Environment and IBAMA, is also developing a strategy to improve protected area management through partnerships with the private sector. Some NGOs have expressed concern about private participation in conservation units, in the belief that such participation could result in disputes with people living in the protected areas. NGOs are likewise increasingly involved in preparing management plans for protected areas.[20]

Brazil has several parks with high potential for tourism (Iguaçu, Orgãos, Itatiaia, Bocaína, Chapada dos Veadeiros, et al.). Domestic and international expertise would be helpful in making the parks financially viable and determining the roles of the private sector and NGOs. The Bank and the GEF need to do more to develop and disseminate quantitative information about the environmental, socioeconomic, and financial success of protected areas both inside and outside Brazil, including successful participation by the private sector (Viana et al. 1996).

Toward a More Sustainable Forest Sector Strategy

Solutions to the problems of forest management have included several specific elements, including a growing interest in the usefulness of forest certification.

The Growing Interest in Certification

Because domestic consumption of wood accounts for 85 percent of the wood produced in Brazil, the promotion of certification of timber in large urban centers like Sao Paulo is the key to success in improving the forest management practices of loggers. Demand for certified timber in this market is growing rapidly, together with a campaign to promote certification and efforts to set standards (Smeraldi and Verissimo 1999).

The amount of land where timber is managed rose from almost nothing in 1993 to nearly a million hectares in 2000. These figures include 277,000 hectares of fully certified forest (by FSC standards), 467,000 hectares of forest under processing of certification (see chapter 8), and more than 200,000 hectares being managed but not under the FSC scheme (for example, Flonas Tapajós, Flona Antimari in Acre). Although a million hectares is relatively small, given that the Amazon forest extends over more than 350 million hectares, this is an important beginning.

International donors have been working with local NGOs to support pilot initiatives on forest management of both commercial and community-based operations (Box 7.4). Uncertainties surrounding the certification program, however, raise questions: How effective will it be? How credible? Will it be well monitored? The importance of independent certification to sustainable timber production in the Amazon will depend not only on the growth of the international and domestic markets and prices for certified products relative to the cost of establishing certification, but also on the implementation of public policies to encourage forest management and prohibit illegal logging. It will also depend on private investments in improved forest management on operations of all sizes.

Certification can be expected to provide producers with three benefits: improved attractiveness to environmentally conscious international purchasers as well as a small segment of the domestic market; better (perhaps premium) prices; and improved access to credit and investment funds (Viana 1996). Provided there is credible independent capacity to monitor forest management, certification can help improve the government's limited capacity to monitor the industry by serving as independent verification of sustainable management of private operations. Further, certification should stimulate change in employment practices.[21] How long, and to what extent international and particularly domestic consumers will pay premium prices for certified products is unknown. Hence, the costs and benefits of certification are still unknown, particularly for small-scale forest managers. Nor is there agreement on whose standards on forest management should be used.

The best-known commercial initiative in forest management is Mil Madereiras, an 80,000-hectare Swiss operation in Itacoatiara, near Manaus, that has substantial access to international capital. It is the first commercial-scale forest sector operation in Brazil to invest significantly (more than $20 million) in natural forest management. Timber producers skeptical of the economic viability of natural forest management have become frequent visitors to Mil Madereiras. Some have shown interest in the potential economic gains of adopting similar methods (particularly in reducing legal problems, improving product marketing, and reducing harvesting and transportation costs), and are assessing the feasibility of improving their management systems to qualify for certification. An improved business image and greater receptivity among environmentally conscious consumers, government, and NGO circles is an important motivation for certification. To what extent this

---

Box 7.4
Home-Grown Certification

Brazil is actively developing national standards for good forest management. The Forest Stewardship Council's framework, while not universally accepted, is making headway. A working group of the council, currently chaired by the Worldwide Fund for Nature, includes participants from the private sector and environmental and social groups, along with observers from the government and academia. This broadly consultative process initially focused on developing national standards for natural forest management in the Amazon and for plantation forestry. NGOs participated in the structuring of Forest Stewardship Council International in 1993, and, more recently, in the Brazilian Forest Stewardship Council (FSC) working group. A Brazilian NGO representative is the vice-president of the Council's board of directors. Many NGOs view independent certification as a positive step in encouraging good forest management and discouraging predatory logging. The Brazilian Buyers Group, chaired by Friends of the Earth's Amazon Program, has more than 60 participants, including some large manufacturers. The forest plantation industry has also sponsored a certification program, known by the acronym CERFLOR, through the Brazilian Silviculture Society (SBS). This program had credibility problems at first—few NGOs supported the initiative because it was perceived by many as industry-oriented. SBS recently handed the program over to the Brazilian Association of Technical Standards, which is attempting to revitalize it. The program's future depends largely on the perceptions of key stakeholders—particularly NGOs—of the program's independence and on the economic viability of the program vis-à-vis alternatives.

---

will translate into economically viable operations remains to be seen. Gethal (the largest producer of plywood in the Amazon), Cikel (a large timber company in the Amazon), and Juruá Madeiras (also in the top 15) all received the Forest Stewardship Council (FSC) label in 2000 and 2001. Five more big timber companies, including Guavirá (Mato Grosso) and Rosa Madeireira (Pará), are now undergoing formal auditing prior to certification.[22]

Forest Plantations: An Important Source of Timber

Brazil's large-scale plantations are highly productive and have become a growing source of woodfuel. Yet such plantations tend to be controversial in Brazil, as elsewhere, both on environmental and social grounds. Whether large or small, plantations cannot match the biodiversity of natural forests, and large ones are often thought to succeed at the expense of small-scale plantations, which are believed to be more sustainable both environmentally and socially. Large-scale plantations have brought about significant concentrations of landholdings, and some research shows that the unit cost of reforesting tends to be higher on large-scale plantations than on small-scale plantations (Bacha and Silva 1999). However, the unit cost of marketing from small-scale plantations tends to be higher than that of large plantations, leading to outgrower schemes, several of which have had problems in working out marketing arrangements that are beneficial both to the growers and the purchasers of forest products. Experience elsewhere in small-scale agriculture is highly relevant here. The production of tea in Kenya by smallholders used to be one of the few examples where markets were efficiently organized to increase the incomes of small farmers.[23]

Brazil's strong plantation industry is an important alternative source of raw materials for the pulp and paper and iron and steel industries. Some 5.5 million hectares are under plantation reforestation, primarily eucalyptus and pine. Productivity in Brazilian plantations is among the world's highest, and time will tell whether plantations can become a cheaper source of timber than natural forests. If so, logging may be subtracted from the logging-agriculture-roads combination at the frontier, thereby reducing pressure on Amazonian forests.

Some plantation forestry companies, particularly in pulp and paper, are making significant investments in increasing their environmental performance and reaching out to small farmers. The National Association of Pulp and Paper Producers created a working group to address environmental issues and is actively involved in discussions on public policy matters. Likewise, the Association of Charcoal Producers is engaged in many public policy forums. Several companies have set aside more than 25 percent of their lands for environmental protection. Such environmental policies have a direct impact on carbon sequestration and biodiversity conservation.

The Role of Carbon Sequestration in Forest Preservation

Land use and forestry changes have been receiving substantial attention in the industrialized countries as a cost-effective way of meeting carbon emission quotas under the Kyoto Protocol. The Brazilian government's position on forests and climate change is also evolving. In negotiations on the Clean Development Mechanism,[24] Brazil has moved toward accepting payment for carbon sequestration, but only for forest plantations and only if the scheme is limited to developing countries (Schneider 1999). This excludes the possibility of carbon payments for the Amazon. However, carbon trading could have profound indirect effects on the demand for natural forest products, given that Brazil has large tracts of degraded land (unused and abandoned pasture and crop lands) outside the Amazon that are prime candidates for reforestation and management.

Schneider (1992) concluded that "on a global scale, prevention of deforestation in the Amazon may be one of the lowest-cost ways to reduce greenhouse emissions," with both donors and Brazil benefiting from transfers. He later (1994) estimated that the carbon sequestration value of Amazon forest land would be between $600 and $7,000 a hectare (compared to a land market value of $250-300 per hectare) and added that the inability of people in

Sweden—who pay a carbon tax of $45 per ton of carbon released—to transact with farmers preparing to clear land in Brazil was a pity because it resulted in a global welfare loss of perhaps more than $4,500 a hectare. Kishor and Constantino (1993) estimated that only transfers of $717 per hectare for small farmers and $1,573 per hectare for large farmers would offset the opportunity cost of income forgone. In part, the payment for carbon will depend on the number of countries that ratify the Kyoto agreement, whether it becomes a binding agreement, and the willingness of developing countries to supply land for conversion to forests. The price could decline considerably if large countries such as Brazil, China, Indonesia, and India get into the carbon market, making it attractive for international businesses to pay for land conversion to meet their quotas under the agreement, but a lower price might make it less attractive for individual landholders to set land aside for carbon sequestration.

Inadequate Spending on Forest Research and Technology

Research in agriculture has been expanding production possibilities to previously unsuitable areas in Brazil. Agricultural research in developing countries tends to receive far better funding than forestry research as a share of agricultural GDP, in part because the food security of urban populations depends on it, and in part because the share of rural populations dependent on agriculture tends to be larger than those dependent on forestry. International agencies, including international and regional banks, have also spent less on research and experimentation on improved forest management relative to the value of the sector compared to their investments in agricultural research, using the same criteria.

Brazil is no exception to these funding realities. EMBRAPA spends less than 10 percent of its annual funding for forestry research, and only a small share of it goes to research on the management of national forests.

But this picture may be changing. Over the past decade or so, EMBRAPA research stations in the north of Brazil, in partnership with many other research institutions, NGOs, and universities, have dedicated increasing amounts of financial and human resources to understanding the "forest side" of the forest margins. EMBRAPA has placed special emphasis on assessing forest ecosystem responses to timber off-take at different rates and through different extraction technologies, in order to identify methods for improving the management of forested areas, especially those held by small-scale agriculturalists. For some types of tropical moist forests, improved management strategies have been identified, tested, and are being replicated in several parts of the Amazon in a joint effort between the Amazon Institute of People and Environment and the Tropical Forest Foundation. But gaps remain in the knowledge base. These gaps will need to be filled, since timber off-take is profitable and the pressure to open new land for agriculture remains strong.

The Role of the International Community

The government of Brazil has repeatedly reminded the rest of the world of Brazil's sovereignty and has resisted anything that might suggest "internationalization" of the Amazon region, even informally. Promoting Brazilian ownership of any environmental program is thus the key to its success. The interactions of external actors with Brazil on the problems of the Amazon clearly show that aggressive positioning by the Bank, international NGOs, or the grant-giving donor community is likely to be counterproductive.

Furthermore, the vested interests of powerful stakeholders in the Amazon, combined with Brazil's fragile but rapidly growing environmental constituency, require a low-key, consensus-building approach in which the interests of all key stakeholders are taken into account and joint ownership of policy is guaranteed. External actors have made progress in working with the federal and state governments, the research and extension community, Brazilian NGOs, and the private sector. If the objective is to help Brazil construct a realistic and workable strategy on the ground in terms of improved forest management and more efficient, more equitable, and more sustainable solutions, then much progress will have been made.[25]

Active collaboration between the World Bank, often seen by donors as the convener of the interests of the international development community towards the Amazon, and the Government of Brazil increased considerably in the 1990s, particularly through economic and sector work. The Bank has remained ambivalent about direct engagement in the forest sector, based on past experience and concern about the reputational risk in doing so. Its limited leverage comes from the power of its ideas, mainly in the forms of analysis, use of its convening power, and persuasion. Cautiously, it is preparing a forest sector loan for the Amazon that has been requested by the Brazilian Government and reflects an increase in mutual trust between the two since the disastrous episodes of the late 1980s. If approved, the loan would be the first such loan in the forest sector after the series of less than fully successful projects in the region initiated in the 1980s. In contrast to this deliberate and modest approach by the Bank, other external organizations (particularly the international NGO community and the development- assistance- granting institutions of the northern industrial countries) have tended to have high expectations in pursuing their agenda and less patience for the subtleties of dealing with Brazil.

The World Bank and the Forests of Brazil

Brazil has been one of the Bank's top five borrowers, receiving loans totaling $9.3 billion between 1992 and 1999. But the Bank's annual commitments of $1 billion to $1.5 billion to Brazil are small in comparison with the total external private capital flows to Brazil of nearly $35 billion annually.[26]

Through its lending experience of the 1980s and the analytical and sector work in the 1990s, the Bank has become sensitive and risk averse so as not to be criticized by Brazilians for overstepping its bounds—for example, by insisting on reforms that are out of step with the domestic political consensus, institutional capacity, or national "ownership." The Bank, on the other hand, sees considerable reputational risk from being involved in situations where it cannot produce outcomes on forest conservation or indigenous people that are sought by its NGO critics. Besides, taking credit for such outcomes would irritate Brazilians and endanger further Bank involvement, a phenomenon that external actors pushing for reforms have not fully appreciated.

The Bank's enthusiasm for forest-related investments has been tempered by project experience in Rondonia and Polonoreste. Funded by six Bank loans totaling almost US$500 million, the Polonoreste project aimed, among other things, to improve rural settlements in areas with good potential for agricultural development, encourage environmentally friendly agricultural production in existing production areas, and establish and maintain national parks, forest reserves, ecological stations, and research programs. A mid-term review mission was "stunned by weak program coordination, institutional inefficiencies, and undisguised lack of political support for environmental and Amerindian protection" (Mahar and Ducrot 1998). Attempts to introduce forest management techniques were largely unsuccessful. Commercial loggers progressively removed valuable tree species, and in the process disturbed the surrounding forest and opened up additional areas for occupation by squatters and land speculators (Redwood 1992). Improvements in transportation allowed access to the region's natural resources by a variety of economic agents, including miners, loggers, and ranchers, who operated with virtually no attention to environmental goals. The Bank clearly overestimated Brazil's and its own effective capacity to attain the program's social and environmental objectives, and Polonoroeste became one of the Bank's biggest environmental headaches.

Deforestation in the wake of the Bank-financed paving of BR-364 under the project prompted unprecedented negative reactions from NGOs. The Bank conducted evaluations of the environmental consequences of the project, including a 1992 OED environmental review of four Bank-funded projects in Brazil (Redwood 1992). The problems uncovered by the review illustrated the difficulty of letting local and regional institutions take control while introducing legal covenants to ensure that the federal government (i.e., the borrower) met the environmental standards expected by the Bank. The two evaluation processes contributed greatly to the development of the 1991 World Bank forest strategy and other social and environmental safeguard policies. The Bank sought to learn from its mistakes in its later lending for the Rondonia (known as Planafloro) and Mato Grosso projects. Both projects were intended to provide a coherent incentive framework for sustainable development, conserve the states' biodiversity, and protect and preserve conservation areas.

Planafloro had a lengthy list of components,[27] but a central one was land-use zoning of the state of Rondonia, the outcome of which is relevant to understanding the Bank's adoption of its 1991 forest strategy. While prescriptive land-use zoning was first proposed in the late 1980s to impose rationality on land use in the Amazon, Planafloro was the first effort to implement it on a large scale. The zoning was intended to intensify agriculture in settled areas in the hope of increasing the incomes of farmers and thus diminishing their incentive to clear more land. Mahar and Ducrot (1998) point out that one of the biggest challenges was to assure effective coordination between federal and state governments, and between the state government and local communities. Between 1992 and mid-1995 the National Institute of Resettlement and Agrarian Reform attempted to establish seven settlements that conflicted with Rondonia's zoning law. Many of Planafloro's difficulties resulted from the prescriptive nature of the zoning, which imposed land-use rules that "often differed greatly from those that would have prevailed had economic agents been left to make their own decisions." The lesson learned the hard way from Planafloro was that zoning is inherently political and will not succeed in the absence of broad public support.

There were also difficulties in managing the consultative process with stakeholders. Bank representatives had little direct contact with the stakeholders who were most likely to oppose the zoning (i.e., ranchers and loggers). Bank staff sensed that such discussions were likely to be perceived by international NGOs and their national counterparts as "pandering to vested interests." But the lack of consultation ensured the opposition of loggers and ranchers to project zoning plans. Meanwhile, the intended beneficiaries, (small farmers and settlers) represented by local NGOs, requested an investigation of the project by the Bank's Inspection Panel. The potential beneficiaries claimed that they had been harmed by the Bank's failure to enforce its loan agreements and policies, particularly regarding land tenure. The Inspection Panel determined that material harm had in fact occurred and could be linked to policy violations, and recommended that the Bank's board authorize a full investigation. The board refused (Udall 1997), but the Inspection Panel made several recommendations for project improvement that were implemented when the project was restructured.

The Legislative Assembly of Rondonia, siding with powerful local interests, declined to approve the zoning. It introduced unilateral modifications of the zoning law that were ultimately agreed to by the federal government and the Bank. The assembly's actions, however, considerably weakened the legal framework for zoning. A late project status report stated that interruption of the project would prevent completion of the socioeconomic zoning and the consolidation of environmental and socioeconomic activities, therefore jeopardizing the returns to all investments made to that point.

The Bank has since adopted a much more active but low-key sectoral approach that is believed to have contributed to the revision of the Brazilian Forest Code and Provisional Act, enacted in June 2000. The Act, intended to harmonize ecological, economic, and social goals, draws on all stakeholders to develop a consensus on the strategy and its implementation. It provides a basis for strengthening command and control mechanisms to prevent illegal logging, adoption of economic incentives for the conservation of private forests, and development of knowledge and regulations on biodiversity, reforestation, and forest management. The government also has established a National Protected Areas System to better protect forested areas. Definition of what constitutes areas of "sustainable use" is being established.

The government has also created a National Forest Program (PNF) to coordinate the forest sector and develop a forest strategy to ensure that at least two-thirds of the 350 million forested hectares of the Amazon will be permanently protected, and to improve management of natural forests, establish a network of protected areas, and support the development of sound legislative, institutional, and fiscal policies. The PNF and its 10 thematic lines to develop a strategy provide the Bank with an opportunity to contribute to forestry sector development. This was the context for the OED report, which recommended that the Bank should be willing to be more proactive and take risks. Active debate in the Bank on the Bank's role with regard to Brazil's forests was ongoing at the time of this volume's publication.

The Bank's Role as Facilitator of International Forest Efforts

The thrust of the Bank's forest-related activity in Brazil centers on the World Bank-WWF Alliance, the GEF, and the multi-donor Rain Forest Trust Pilot Program to Conserve the Brazilian Rain Forest (the so-called PPG 7, an effort funded by seven donors). PPG-7 is an outgrowth of the 1990 summit of the G-7 industrialized countries in Houston, Texas, where German Chancellor Helmut Kohl proposed establishing a pilot program to reduce deforestation in Brazil's tropical forests.[28]

Formally launched in 1992, PPG-7 is funded by the European Union, Canada, France, Germany, Italy, Japan, the United Kingdom, and the United States and administered by the Bank; its 12 projects had an estimated total cost of $340 million. Although the program did not deliver the expected impact on Brazil's strategy towards the management of the Amazon, PPG-7's many small programs address a variety of specific issues that have increased donor understanding of the realities of the Amazon. Additionally, the increased emphasis on participation embodied in the projects enabled the much-needed involvement of civil society. The innovative program raised expectations among the rainforest constituency both in Brazil and internationally and invited criticism from an external review panel for failing to address strategic objectives.[29] While it has been understandably slow in achieving its strategic objectives, which were far too ambitious given the importance of constituency building needed, it has facilitated economic and sector work by the Bank collaboratively with Brazilian institutions such as Imazon and is helping to develop a constituency composed of Brazilian NGOs and environmentalists. Responsibility for implementation of the program now rests with the Brazilian government.

In December 1997 the government of Brazil pledged to join the WWF/World Bank Alliance, and in early 1998 the president of Brazil signed a decree creating new protected areas in the Amazon region and the Atlantic forest and pledged to work with the Alliance to bring 10 percent of the area in the Amazon under protection. The total area to be converted into preservation units under this new initiative is 25 million hectares—the size of Sao Paulo state—which would constitute half of the Alliance's total global target. Efforts were underway at the time of this book's publication to establish an endowment fund, the proceeds of which would finance day-to-day management of the protected areas.

Brazil's pledge will allow the Alliance to meet its global targets. Nationally, the benefits are more complex. Those who favor bringing additional areas under protection argue that even poorly managed areas help set aside lands that would otherwise be devoted to development, increase the scarcity value of land, and provide incentives for its improved management. But given the poor management of existing protected areas and competing demands on the limited fiscal resources at the disposal of the government, there is no consensus on whether Brazil should bring additional areas under protection. Brazilian institutions also feel strongly that a strategy should be defined through a participatory process that is domestically oriented. Fundraising for establishing an endowment fund, on the other hand, entails consultations with interests outside Brazil, who would naturally prefer to see their own agenda pursued. The challenge is to establish enough of a balance so that a national sense of ownership of the concept is established. The government's pledge to the Alliance was externally driven and was announced without internal consultations either in Brazil, or with the Bank's country department resident in Brazil. It subsequently became controversial in Brazil, stirring an intense debate. Efforts were then made to develop broad-based internal ownership of the effort in Brazil's NGO community and within the Bank. A first-phase Amazon Protected Areas Project funded by the GEF as part of the larger policy strategy oriented program of land use was underway in the fall of 2001.

Global Environment Facility (GEF) Projects in Brazil

The two GEF forest projects in Brazil are small relative to Brazil's biological resources and needs. They provide one-time support to pay the incremental costs of protection for biodiversity of recognized global value and thus must be catalytic to be sustainable. The National Biodiversity Program (PROBIO) is intended to help pay the incremental costs incurred by Brazil's government in initiating a program for the conservation and sustainable use of biodiversity by identifying priority actions, disseminating biodiversity information, and stimulating the development of subprojects by facilitating partnerships between the public and private sectors. The project is supported by a $10 million GEF grant and an additional $10 million in host country matching funds. Implementation has suffered from a shortage of counterpart funds, and the government had to ask the Bank for an extension and amendment to reallocate grant proceeds. The GEF project also raises issues of internal ownership.

A Brazilian Biodiversity Fund (FUNBIO) began in 1996 with a $20 million grant from GEF and $10 million from other domestic and international partners. It later became a private non-profit organization to pay the incremental costs of establishing long-term support for conservation and sustainable use of biological diversity by promoting and supporting partnerships among the government, nonprofit organizations, academic institutions, and the private business sector.

The Bank's low key and slow approach has helped to gain the confidence of the Brazilian policymakers and institutions, and built some capacity of the Brazilian professionals to take up the cause, but the results have been slow in coming, and unpredictable. The Bank's and the donor community's impact on demonstrating a few approaches has been significant (e.g., simplified administrative procedures of the Demonstrative Projects through Banco do Brasil), a number of successful forest management (timber and non-timber) and agroforestry pilots and in stimulating interest in the private sector in improving forest management by getting it involved in consultations on forest management, but its impact on the goal of slowing down the rate of deforestation in the Amazon has been minimal so far.

Conclusion: Learning to Balance the Needs of Multiple Stakeholders

Controlling deforestation in Brazil, as this chapter shows, will be tremendously difficult, given the large number of local, national, and global forces and actors whose actions affect it in one way or another. The forests are threatened by fundamental economic forces in the context of a lack of effective policy instruments and institutional capacity to influence, control, or monitor vast areas, and lack of sufficient knowledge about the natural resource base to articulate its economic value and possible uses. In the face of these circumstances, there is intense struggle for control of forest resources. Perhaps more importantly, global and national economic forces beyond the reach of policymakers seem to dwarf even the mightiest of national policy instruments. Evidence of the force of some of these macroeconomic events, such as liberalization of trade, the strength of the domestic market, and decentralization and the power of the local elite, is present in Brazil as elsewhere. In the short and medium term they offer powerful incentives to deforest, even when perverse policies, such as the subsidies identified in the Bank's 1991 forest strategy, are removed.

Brazil has clearly moved a substantial distance in the right direction since the Bank formulated its forest strategy in 1991. The Bank, too, has learned a great deal from the mistakes it has made and perhaps understands better the policies, institutions, and multi-stakeholder approaches needed to address the issues of deforestation.

But the most important underlying factors that are causing deforestation, such as the relative returns to land use, the domestic demand and substitutes that influence it, the weaknesses of planning, implementation, enforcement, and the power of the stakeholders are much less understood, as this chapter illustrates.

Understanding the sources and causes of deforestation, which are far more complex now than in 1991, is insufficient to achieve the strategy's objective of slowing deforestation. On the contrary, the evidence suggests that local actors may tolerate a far higher rate of deforestation in the Amazon than the international community or even the federal government deems appropriate.

Notes

1. These figures represent all forest types, not just tropical moist forest. Although Brazil is richly endowed with forests, not all of its forests are richly endowed—in fact, Brazil's forests are quite heterogeneous.
2. Lele et al., *The World Bank Forest Strategy: Striking the Right Balance*, Operations Evaluation Department, The World Bank, 2000.
3. This study was commissioned by OED and financed by EMBRAPA (the Brazilian Corporation for Agricultural Research).
4. Even though Brazil has maintained a positive trade balance in forest products since 1980, between 1995 and 1998 Brazil's overall wood trade balance was negative (Bacha and Marquesini 1999).
5. In 1991, Brazil, Argentina, Uruguay, and Paraguay signed the Treaty of Asuncion to create a customs union with common tariffs. Known as Mercosul, this common market formally came into existence in 1995. Chile became a member of Mercosul in 1996, Bolivia in 1997. Mercosul's goal is to incorporate all other South American countries by 2005 and then to join hands with the North American Free Trade Agreement (NAFTA). The devaluation of the Brazilian real and the dollarization of the Argentinian peso have placed great strains on Mercosul.

6. The iron and steel sectors are major consumer of forest charcoal. In Brazil iron and steel have traditionally been included in the forest sector because of their heavy dependence and influence on native *cerrados* and plantations to meet its demand for forest products. It is the most important part of the forest sector in such states as Minas Gerais. Forest charcoal is a major source of income for many smallholders worldwide, and a major cause of deforestation as subsistence farming is replaced by reliance on cash for food, etc.

7. Using a computable general equilibrium (CGE) model to determine how the magnitude and impact of deforestation in the Brazilian Amazon are affected by changes in policy regimes and technology, Cattaneo (1999) shows that devaluation shifts agricultural production in favor of exportable products. How devaluation affects agricultural incentives in different regions depends on migration flows. If migration occurs only between rural areas, a 30 percent devaluation increases deforestation rates 5 percent. If urban labor is willing to migrate to the Amazon and farm, the deforestation rate increases 35 percent. Environmental sector work on Brazil argues that rainfall determines agricultural production's potential and may mute some of the effects of improved incentives from globalization. Technical change, on the other hand, may expand agricultural options even in high rainfall areas. These examples merely demonstrate the complexity and location-specificity of outcomes.

8. San et al. (1998) analyzed the short- and medium-term impacts of structural adjustment through devaluation on regional production, deforestation, factor markets, income distribution, and trade for the Sumatra region of Indonesia. The study found that devaluation encourages deforestation; exports of forest products as both the final products and intermediate inputs for the wood processing industries increase.

9. Schneider et al. (1999), Sustainable Amazon, Limitations and Opportunities for Sustainable Rural Development, World Bank/Imazon report, Appendix 1.

10. Using selective harvest, based on an inventory of commercial trees, planning of roads, patios and skid trails, vine cutting, directional felling and planning of skidding, stimulation of growth of commercial trees and an annual harvesting schedule.

11. Margulis Sergio, comments on summary comments, "who are the agents of deforestation?" August 29, 2001, unpublished.

12. Lele et al., *Forests in the Balance*, Operations Evaluation Department World Bank, 2000, p. 28.

13. Schneider notes that only two of the cases reviewed by Pearce included log processing as well as extraction and thus would be comparable to his calculations. One of Pearce's calculations was of NPVs , while the other used annual returns to capital. At 10 percent for NPV, Mendoza and Aymou get $160 per hectare. Schneider's calculations at 10 percent yield $100.

14. Schneider et al. (1999), p. 12.

15. The internal market is strongest in the Southeast (38 percent of total) followed by the South (18 percent), Northeast (14 percent), and the Center-West (5 percent). The Amazon consumes 10 percent of forest production. The United States and Europe have traditionally been the largest importers of Amazonian wood products, followed by Japan. Amazonian exports to other Asian countries (Indonesia; the Philippines; the Republic of Korea; Taiwan, China; and Thailand) began in the 1990s (Smeraldi and Verissimo 1999).

16. This road was not paved until the late 1980s.

17. A new government program known as Move Forward Brazil has been proposed by the federal government and is now being analyzed by the Brazilian Congress. The program is similar to Brazil in Action.

18. See www.ecotrust.org and the many examples from International Association for the Study of Common Property. Also see, *Linking Social and Ecological Systems*, by Berkes and Folke (1998).
19. Brazil and Mexico received 45 percent of the $3.26 billion committed through 3489 conservation projects mostly for national parks during 1990 and 1997. Ganzalo Castro et al., *Mapping Conservation Investment: An Assessment of Biodiversity Funding in Latin America and the Caribbean*, USAID and the World Bank, Biodiversity Support Program, Washington, D. C., n. d., p. 7.
20. In Jau National Park, for example, the NGO Fundacao Vitoria Amazonica is successfully assisting IBAMA.
21. In the case of Mil Madereiras, all workers are officially registered and, as a result, have access to social security benefits.
22. A Bank-sponsored workshop on Opportunities for Sustainable Forest Management, held in Manaus in October 1999, brought together producers, buyers of certified timber, private ecological investment funds, leading Brazilian and international NGOs, certifiers, and government representatives. The meeting was seen as a historical event for the future of forest management in the Amazon. For the first time, market advantages (premium prices, access to investment funds, access to markets, corporate image, and the like) of certifiable forest management appeared to be greater than perceived costs.
23. "Growth and Structural Change in East Africa: Domestic Policies, Agricultural Performance, and World Bank Assistance, 1963-86," with L. Richard Meyers. MADIA Discussion Paper No. 3 (Washington, D.C.: World Bank, 1989).
24. The Clean Development Mechanism was created as part of the Kyoto Protocol in 1997 to lower the overall cost of reducing greenhouse gas emissions released into the atmosphere and to support sustainable development initiatives within developing countries. It allows developed countries to invest in low-cost abatement opportunities in developing countries and receive credit for the resulting emissions reductions. Developed countries can then apply this credit to their 2008–12 targets, reducing the cutbacks that would have to be made within their borders (Clean Development Mechanism, www.wri.org/cdm, June 1, 2000).
25. The World Bank/Imazon Report 2001 has a foreword from the Secretary of the Environment ministry.
26. This is a small amount relative to Brazil's annual GNP of $760 billion.
27. Indigenous reserves, public forests, and extractive reserves prevent illegal deforestation, wood transport, and forest fires, promote integrated farming systems with permanent agriculture, agroforestry, and nonwood forest products, promote agroecological zoning by supporting priority investments in socioeconomic infrastructure and services and consolidate the technical and operational capacity of state institutions, particularly those responsible for agricultural and forestry support services.
28. Through 12 projects, the Pilot Program to Conserve the Amazon Rain Forest (PPG-7) has aimed to: demonstrate that sustainable economic development and environmental conservation can be pursued simultaneously in tropical rain forests.
29. A blue-ribbon panel review of the institutional arrangements was critical of the Bank and other donors. It concluded that: The (disappointing) state of affairs [within PPG-7] reflects lack of an agreed pilot program strategy, weak program management, inability of the participants to address and resolve fundamental program issues, as well as complex project designs and financing plans which have led to costly and time-consuming project processing. Slow coalition-building with Brazilian civil society and with the private sector has deprived PPG-7 of needed support . . . The existing institutional arrangements (of vesting responsibility for the program with the World Bank) have not succeeded in

catalyzing the needed Brazilian ownership and leadership of the pilot program, and have allowed weak structure, poorly defined accountabilities and unclear and over-lapping role assignments to compound the performance problems of most, if not all of the participants.

References

Alston, Lee J., Libecap, Gary D., and Robert Schneider. 1996. "The Determinants and Impact of Property Rights: Land Titles on the Brazilian Frontier." *JLEO* 12(1):25-61.

Alves, D., and I. Strada. 1999. "Roads and Deforestation in Amazon." Brazil Country Study Background Paper. Operations Evaluation Department (OED). World Bank.

Amaral, P. Manejo florestal comunitário na Amazônia. Porto Dias: WWF/SUNY.

Amaral, P., A. Versissimo, P. Barreto, and E. Vidal. 1998. Floresta Papa Senore: um manuel para a producao de madeira na Amazon. IMAZON. Belem.

Anderson, A. B. 1999. "From local Communities to Biomes: The Pilot Program's Effort to Influence Land Uses in the Brazilian Amazon." In *Patterns and Processes of Land Use and Forest Change in the Amazon.* Center for Latin American Studies, University of Florida.

Arima, Eugenio Y., Adalberto Verissimo, and Carlos Souza, Jr. 1999. "A Atividade Madeireira e o Desmatamento na Amazonia," IMAZON.

Bacha, Carlos, and M. Marquesini. 1999. "Plantation Forestry." Brazil Country Study Background Paper. Operations Evaluation Department (OED). Washington DC.: The World Bank.

Bacha, O. L., and J. C. Silva. 1999. Evolução do reflorestamento no Brasil—impactos de políticas públicas e tendências. Reflorestamento no Brasil. IICA—Instituto Interamericano de Cooperação para a Agricultura Agência de Cooperação para a Agricultura. Piracicaba, SP.

Bacha, Carlos, and M. Marquesini. 1999. "Plantation Forestry." Brazil Country Study Background Paper. Operations Evaluation Department. The World Bank, Washington, D.C., unpublished.

Barreto, P., and A. Verissimo. 1998. Sugestoes para a criacao e implementacao de florestas nacionas na Amazonia. Relatorio Técnico. Projecto FAO/UTFRA/047. MMA e FAO. Brasilia.

Barreto, P., E. Vidal, P. Amara,l and C. Uhl. 1998. "Costs and Benefits of Forest Management for Timber Production in Eastern Amazon." *Forest Ecology and Management* 108: 9-26.

Banco da Amazonia S/A (BASA). 1998. Programa de Aplicação dos Recursos para o Exercício de 1999, BASA-Belém, PA.

Barros, A., and C. Uhl. 1995. "Logging along the Amazon river and Estuary: Patterns, Problems and Potential." *Forest Ecology and Management* 77:87-105.

Berkes, F., and C. Folke (eds.). 1998. *Linking Social and Ecological Systems: Management Practices and Social Mechanisms for Building Resilience.* New York: Cambridge University Press.

Bernardes, M. 1999. Lucro difícil de extrair. pág. 436 a 447. Agrianual. São Paulo, Editora FNP.

Biller, Cassells, Becerra Meyer. 1996. *Pursuit of Sustainable Forestry Policy in the Americas: Current Initiatives and Opportunities for Regional Cooperation.* Latin American and the Caribbean Technical Department. Washington, DC: The World Bank.

Binswanger, Hans P. 1989. Brazilian Policies That Encourage Deforestation in the Amazon. Environment Department Working Paper No. 16, Washington, DC: The World Bank.

BRACELPA. 1997. Annual Report 1997. Associacao Brasileira de Celulose e Papel, Sao Paulo.

Brazil: National Biodiversity Project. 1996. Washington, Global Environment Division.

Brown, P., s/d. Climate, Biodiversity, and Forests. Issues and Opportunities Are Emerging from the Kyoto Protocol. World Resources Institute.

Byron, Neil, and Michael Arnold. 1999. "What Futures for the People of the Tropical Forests?" *World Development* 27(5):789-805.

Camino, V., and Müller. 1993. Sostenibilidad de La Agricultura y los Recursos Naturales Bases para Establecer Indicadores. Instituto Americano de Cooperacíon para la Agricultura/Proyecto IICA/GTZ, San José, C.R.

Carpentier, Chantal Line, Gomes, Steve Vosti, and Julie Witcover. 1999. Impacts of Soil Quality Differences on Deforestation, Use of Cleared Land, and Farm Income (c). Unpublished manuscript, IICA/EMBRAPA/OED, Brasília.

Carpentier, Chantal Line, Gomes, Steve Vosti, and Julie Witcover. 1999a. Smallholder Deforestation and Land use: A Baseline. Unpublished manuscript, IICA/EMBRAPA/ OED, Brasília.

_____. 1999c. "Policy-Deforestation Links: The Case of Small-Scale Agriculturalists in the Western Brazilian Amazon" (draft).

_____. 1999d. Impacts of Distance to Market and the Absence of Markets on Deforestation, Use of Cleared Land, and Farm Income. Unpublished manuscript, IICA/ EMBRAPA/OED, Brasília.

_____. 1999e. Impacts of Changes in Input and Output Prices on Deforestation, Use of Cleared Land, and Farm Income. Unpublished manuscript, IICA/EMBRAPA/OED, Brasília.

_____. 1999g. Impacts of Forest Payments on Deforestation, Use of Cleared Land, and Farm Income. Unpublished manuscript, IICA/EMBRAPA/OED, Brasília.

_____. 1999h. Impacts of Subsidized Brazil Nut Prices on Deforestation, Use of Cleared Land, and Farm Income. Unpublished manuscript, IICA/EMBRAPA/OED, Brasília.

_____. 1999b. Technical Note—Small-Scale Managed Forestry, Unpublished manuscript, IICA/EMBRAPA/OED, Brasilia.

_____. 1999f. Impacts of Changes in Wage Rates and Farm-Level Labor Flows on Deafforestation, Use of Cleared Land, and Farm Income. Unpublished manuscript, IICA/EMBRAPA/OED, Brasília.

Cattaneo, Andrea. 1999. "Technology, Migration, and the Last Frontier: Options for Slowing Deforestation in the Brazilian Amazon." Environmental Research Service, USDA.

Chomitz, Kenneth M. 1999. Transferable Development Rights and Forest Protection: An Exploratory Analysis, Development Research Group. Washington, DC: The World Bank.

Chomitz, Kenneth M., and Kanta Kumari. 1996. The Domestic Benefits of Tropical Forests: A Critical Review Emphasizing Hydrological Functions. Policy Research Paper 1601, Policy Research Department, Environment, Infrastructure and Agriculture Division. Washington, DC: The World Bank.

Chomitz, Kenneth M., and Timothy S. Thomas. 2001 "Geographic Patterns of Land Use and Land Intensity in the Brazilian Amazon" Policy Research Working Paper. World Bank.

CIFOR. 1998. "EMBRAPA and CIFOR—A Partnership Generating Technologies for Amazonia." *CIFOR News*, Number 18, March.

Coorporación Financeira Internacional. 1998. Cartera de Inversiones. Corporación Financeira Internacional, Washington, DC.

Costa, J. P. O. 1997. Avaliação da Reserva da Biosfera da Mata Atlantica. Reserva da Biosfera, São Paulo, SP.

Davis, Shelton, and Alaka Wali. s/d. *Indigenous Territories and Tropical Forest Management in Latin America*. Washington, DC: The World Bank.

Dean, W. 1989. A Luta pela Borracha no Brasil, Um estudo de história ecológica. São Paulo, Nobel.

Dean, W. 1989. *A Luta pela Borracha no Brasil, Um estudo de historia ecológica*. Sao Paulo: Nobel.

The Economist. 1999. "Brazil Survey" (special insert section). March 27.

Economist Intelligence Unit. 1999a. Country Report, Brazil, First Quarter 1999.

_____. 1999b. Country Profile, Brazil, 1998-99.

Edwards, S. s/d. *The Evolving Role of World Bank. The Latin American Debt Crisis*. Washington, DC: The World Bank.

Economist Intelligence Unit. 1999. Country Report, Brazil, First Quarter 1999.

EMBRAPA. 1999a. Program 08: Forestry and Agroforestry Production Systems (pamphlet).

_____. 1999b. Manejo Florestal na Amazonia Brasileira (Situacao Atual e Perspectivas).

ESMAP. 1994. Energy Efficiency and Conservation: Strategic Pathways for Energy Efficiency in Brazil. Based on a workshop conducted by Instituto nacional de Eficiencia Energetica, March 21-22, 1994, Rio de Janeiro.

Faminow, M. D. 1998. *Cattle, Deforestation and Development in the Amazon: An Economic, Agronomic and Environmental Perspective*. UK: CAB International.

Faminow, Merle D., and Steve Vosti. 1998. "Livestock-Deforestation Links: Policy Issues in the Western Brazilian Amazon." In A.J. Nell (ed.), *Livestock and the Environment International Conference*. Wageningen, The Netherlands: World Bank, Food and Agriculture Organization of the United Nations, and the International Agricultural Centre.

Farraz, Patricia. 1998. "Quem Desmata a Amazonia e Voce." *Jornal da Tarde*, June 21.

Fearnside, P. M. 1999. "Does Pasture Intensification Discourage Deforestation. Patterns and Processes of Land Use and Forest Change in the Amazon." Center for Latin American Studies, University of Florida.

_____. 1998. Forests and Global Warming Mitigation in Brazil: Opportunities in the Brazilian Forest Sector for Responses to Global Warming under the "Clean Development Mechanism." Biomass & Bioenergy. Instituto Nacional de Pesquisa da Amazônia (INPA), Amazonas.

_____. 1997a. "Monitoring Needs to Transform Amazonian Forest Maintenance into a Global Warming-Mitigation Option." In J. Sathave, et al., *Mitigation and Adaptation Strategies for Global Changes*.

_____. 1997b. Environmental Service as a Strategy for Sustainable Development in Rural Amazonia. *Ecological Economics*, vol. 20:53-70.

Ferreira, L. V. et al. 1999. *Áreas protegidas ou espaços ameaçados?* Brasília: WWF-World Wildlife Fund.

FUNBIO-Financiando o uso sustentável da biodiversidade. 1998. FUNBIO-Fundo Brasileiro para a Biodiversidade. Rio de Janeiro.

Government of Brazil. 1997. Agenda 21 for Amazonia: Basis for Discussion. Ministry of the Environment, Water Resources and the Legal Amazonia, Secretariat for the Coordination of Amazonian Affairs, Brasilia.

GTA and Friends of the Earth International (FOEI). 1998. Coherent Public Policies for a Sustainable Amazon: The Challenge of Innovation and the Pilot Program.

Guatura, Corrêa, Costa, and Azevedo, 2ª ed., 1997. A Questão Fundiária, Roteiro para a solução dos problemas fundiários na Áreas Protegidas da Mata Atlântica. Reserva da Biosfera, São Paulo.

Holmes, T., G. Blate, J. Zweede, R. Pereira, P. Barreto, F. Boltz, and R. Bauch. 2000. *Financial Costs and Benefits of Reduced-Impact Logging in the Eastern Amazon*. Tropical Forest Foundation, Alexandria, Virginia.

Homma, A. K. O. 1993. Extrativismo vegetal na Amazônia:limites e oportunidades. Empresa Brasileira de Pesquisa Agropecuária. Centro de Pesquisa Agroflorestal da Amazônia Oriental. Brasília.

IBGE (Instituto Brasileiro de Geografia e Estatistica). 1996, 1997, 2000. Recursos naturais e meio ambiente: uma visao do Brasil.

IMAFLORA/IMAZON. 1999. Consumo de madeira no mercado interno brasileiro e estratégia para a promoção da certificação. São Paulo.

INPE (Instituto Nacional de Pesquisas Espacias). 1999. Monitoring of the Brazilian Amazon Forest by Satellite, 1998-1999. Brazil.

IPCC Working Group III, for the Subsidiary Body for Scientific and Technological Advice (SBSTA) to the UNFCC, United Nations. New York, NY.

Instituto De Manejo E Certificaçào Florestal E Agrícola (IMAFLORA). 1997. Protocolo Verde: Uma análise Preliminar dos Bancos Signatários. Instituto de Manejo e Certificação Florestal e Agrícola-IMAFLORA, Piracicaba, SP.

International Advisory Group (IAG). 1998. Relatório do Grupo Consultivo Internacional, Programa Piloto para a Proteção das Florestas Tropicais do Brasil-PPG-7, Brasil.

IUCN. 1988. Brazil: Atlantic Coastal Forests (draft). Cambridge: Conservation Monitoring Center.

_____. 1998. Arborvitae, August 1998.

Kaimowitz, David. 1996. *Livestock and Deforestation, Central America in the 1980s and 1990s: A Policy Perspective.* Jakarta: Center for International Forestry Research.

_____. 1999. Notes from presentation, Inter-American Development Bank, Forest Policy Roundtable. Washington D.C., June 28.

Kaimowitz, Vanclay, A. Puntodewo, and P. Mendez. 1999. "Spatial Econometric Analysis of Deforestation in Santa Cruz, Bolivia." Patterns and Processes of Land Use and Forest Change in the Amazon. Center for Latin American Studies, University of Florida.

Kaimowitz, David, and Arid Angelsen. 1998. Economic Models of Tropical Deforestation: A Review. Center for International Forestry Research, Indonesia.

Kirmse, Robert D., Luis F. Constantino, and George M. Guess. 1993. Prospects for Improved Management of Natural Forests in Latin America, LATEN Dissemination Note #9. Latin America Technical Department, Environment Division. Washington, DC: The World Bank.

Kishor, Nalin M., and Luis F. Constantino. 1993. Forest Management and Competing Land Uses: An Economic Analysis of Costa Rica. Latin America and Caribbean Regional Office, Technical Department, Environment Division. Washington DC. The World Bank.

Kolk, Ans. 1998. "From Conflict to Cooperation: International Policies to Protect the Brazilian Amazon," *World Development* 26(8):1481-1493.

Kueneman, Eric A., and Luis Camacho. 1987. "Production and Goals for Expansion of Soybeans in Latin America." In S. R. Singh, K. O. Rachie, and K. E. Dashiell (eds.), *Soybeans for the Tropics.* John Wiley & Sons Ltd.

Kumar, Nalini, Naresh Chandra Saxena, Yoginder K. Alagh, and Kinsuk Mitra. 1999. Alleviating Poverty Through Participatory Forestry Development: An Evaluation of India's Forest Development and World Bank Assistance. Unpublished manuscript. Operations Evaluation Department, The World Bank.

Lele, Uma. 1998. "Forests and the World Bank: OED Study of Forest Policy and Implementation, Proposed (tentative) Framework for Country Case Studies: The Case of Brazil, Scope of the Study, Terms of Reference, Organization and Management, and Staffing." October 1 (work in progress).

Lele, Uma, Virgilio M. Viana, Adalberto Verissimo, Stephen Vosti, Karin Perkins, and Syed Arif Husain. 2000. *Forests in the Balance: Challenges of Conservation with Development. An Evaluation of Brazil's Forest Development and World*

Bank Assistance. Operations Evaluation Department. Washington D.C.: The World Bank.

Lozez, Ramon, and Claudia Ocana. 1999. "Why Latin America Should Participate in Global Trade in Carbon Emissions: Carbon Trade as a Source of Funding for Sustainable Development." Inter-American Development Bank, Forest Policy Roundtable, Washington D.C., June 28.

Mahar, Dennis J. 1988, 1989. Government Policies and Deforestation in Brazil's Amazon Region. Environment Department Working Paper No. 7. Washington DC: The World Bank.

Mahar, Dennis J., and Cecile E. H. Ducrot. 1998. Land-Use Zoning on Tropical Frontiers: Emerging Lessons from the Brazilian Amazon. Washington, The World Bank, Development Institute of the World Bank. EDI Case Studies. Washington. DC: The World Bank.

Manfrinato, W., and V. M. Viana. 1999. Sequestro de Carbono como parte de uma estratégia de desenvolvimento sustentável de Bacias Hidrogáficas. Projeto Carbono. Documento apresentado no Workshop Mudanças Climáticas Globais e Agropecuária Brasileira. Embrapa e Meio Ambiente Ministério da Ciência e Tecnologia-MCT-Campinas-SP.

Margulis, Sergio. 2001. Comments on summary comments, "Who are the Agents of Deforestation?" August 29, unpublished.

Martín, A., N. Rosa, and C. Uhl. 1994. "An Attempt to Predict Which Amazonian Tree Species May Be Threatened by Logging Activities." *Environmental Conservation* 21 (2): 152-162.

Martini, A., N. Rosa, and C. Uhl. 1994. "An Attempt to Predict Which Amazonian Tree Species May be threatened by Logging Activities." Environmental Conservation 21(2): 152-162.

Ministério do Meio Ambiente dos Recursos Hidricos e da Amazônia Legal, Secretaria Executiva. 1997. A Caminho da Agenda 21 Brasileira, Princípios e Ações 1992/97.,Brasília, DF.

Mittermeier, R. A., Normal Myers, Cristina goettschr Mittermeier, and Norman Myers. 2000. *Hotspots: Earth's Biologically Richest and Most Endangered Terrestrial Ecoregions.* Chicago: University of Chicago Press.

Murphy, L., F. Pichon, C. Marquette, and Bilsborrow. 1999. "Land Use< Household Composition and Economic Status of Settlers in Ecuador's Amazon: A review and Synthesis of Research Findings, 1990-1999." *Patterns and Processes of Land Use and Forest Change in the Amazon.* Center for Latin American Studies, University of Florida.

Nepstad, D. C. et al. 1999. "Large Scale Improvements of Amazonian Forests by Logging and Fire." *Nature* 398 (6727):505-508.

Operations Evaluation Department (OED). 1998. Forests and the World Bank: An OED Review of the 1991 Forest Policy and its Implementation: A Design Paper. Unpublished manuscript. The World Bank.

Pearce, D., F. Putz, and J. Vanclay. 1999. "A Sustainable Forest Future?" Natural Resources International, UK and UK Department for International Development.

Pesquisa gestão ambiental na indústria brasileira. 1998. Brasília: BNDES.

Pfaff, Alexander S. P. 1997. What Drives Deforestation in the Brazilian Amazon? Evidence from Satellite and Socioeconomic Data. Policy Research Working Paper No. 1772, Environment, Infrastructure, and Agriculture Division. Washington DC: The World Bank.

Pilot Program to Conserve the Brazilian Rainforest. 1999. Review of Institutional Arrangements, July.

Prada, and Costa. l997. Protocólo verde: uma análise preliminar dos bancos signatários. Piracicaba: BMDES/BASA/BNB/CEF/BB, IMAFLORA-Instituto de Manejo e Certificação Florestal e Agrícola.

Presidência da República, Governo Fernando Henrique Cardoso. 1998. Real: Quatro anos que mudaram o Brasil, Brasília, DF.

Psacharopoulos, George, and Harry Anthony Patrinos. l994. *Indigenous People and Poverty in Latin American: an Empirical Analysis.* Washington, DC: The World Bank.

Razetto, Fernando T. 1999. "Perspectivas de las Empresas Privadas." Inter-American Development Bank, Forest Policy Roundtable, Washington DC., June 28.

Redford, Kent H., and Christine Padoch (eds.). c. 1992. *Conservation of Neotropical Forests: Working from Traditional Resource Use.* New York: Columbia University Press.

Redwood, J. 1992. World Bank Approaches to the Environment in Brazil: A Review of Selected Projects. Report No. 10039, Operations and Evaluation Department. Washington D.C.: The World Bank.

Rozelle, Scott, Jikun Huang, Syed Arif Husain, and Aaron Zazueta. 1999. From Afforestation to Poverty Alleviation and Natural Forest Management: An Evaluation of China's Forest Development and World Bank Assistance. Unpublished manuscript. Operations Evaluation Department, The World Bank.

San, Nu Nu, H. Lofgren, S. Robinson, and S. A. Vosti. 1998. *Macroeconomic Policy, Labor Migration, and Deforestation in Sumatra: Progress Report.* Washington, D. C.: International Food Policy Institute.

Schneider, R. 1992. Brazil: An Analysis of Environmental Problems in the Amazon. Report No. 9104-BR. Washington D.C.: The World Bank.

_____. 1994. Government and the Economy on the Amazon Frontier, LAC Technical Department, Regional Studies Program. Report No. 34. Washington D.C : The World Bank.

Schneider, R., A. Verissimo, and V. Viana. 1999. "Logging and Tropical Conservation." *Science* magazine. Submitted.

Schomberg, William. 1999. "Brazil Relaxes Amazon Deforestation Ban." Reuters, March 25.

Sedjo, Roger A. 1999. "Carbon Projects in Latin America." Inter-American Development Bank, Forest Policy Roundtable, Washington D.C., June 28.

Serrao, Emmanuel, S. Adilson, Daniel Nepstad, and Robert Walker. 1996. "Upland agricultural and Forestry Development in the Amazon: Sustainability, Criticality and Resilience." *Ecological Economics* 18(1996):3-13.

Simula, Markku, and Oy Indufor. 1999. "Do Global Conventions Bring Benefits to Forest Owners and Managers?" Inter-American Development Bank, Forest Policy Roundtable, Washington D.C., June 28.

Smeraldi, R., and B. Milikan. 1997. PLANAFLORO Um ano Depois. Análise Critica da Implementação do Plano Agropecuário e Florestal de Rondônia um Ano Após o Acordo para sua Reformulação. Amigos da Terra e OXFAM-Associação Recife-Oxford para a Cooperação ao Desenvolvimento, São Paulo.

Smeraldi, R. org. l997/l998. Políticas Públicas para a Amazônia: Rumos, Tendências e Propostas. Amigos da Terra-São Paulo.

_____. Políticas Públicas Coerentes. Para uma Amazônia Sustentável. O desafio da Inovação e o Programa Piloto. Amigos da Terra, Brasília, DF.

Smeraldi, Roberto, and Adalberto Verissimo. 1999. "Acertando o Alvo: Caracterizacao do Consumo Interno de Madeira da Amazonia." IMAFLORA and IMAZON.

Smith, Nigel, Jean Dubois, Dean Current, Ernst Lutz, and Charles Clement. 1998. Agroforestry Experiences in the Brazilian Amazon: Constraints and Opportunities. Pilot Program to Conserve the Brazilian Rain Forest.

Smith, Warrick, and Ben Shin. 1995. Regulating Brazil's Infrastructure: Perspectives on Decentralization. Economic Notes Number 6, Latin America and the Caribbean Region. Washington D.C.: The World Bank.

Sonda, C. 1999. "Dynamics of Land Use in the Atlantic Rainforest." Brazil Country Study Background Paper. Operations Evaluation Department (OED). The World Bank.

Southgate, Douglas. 1999. "Markets, Institutions, and Forestry: The Consequences of Timber Trade Liberalization in Ecuador." Inter-American Development Bank, Forest Policy Roundtable, Washington D.C., June 28.

Stuart, D., and Pedro-Moura Costa. 1998. Climate Change Mitigation by Forestry: A Review of International Initiatives. Policy That Works for Forests and People: Discussion Paper. Publications, International Institute for Environment and Development, London.

Terborgh, J. W., and C.A. Peres. 1995 "Amazonian Nature Reserves: An Analysis of the Defensibility Status of Existing Conservation Units and Design Criteria for the Future." Conservation Biology 9: 343-46.

Tosta Faillace, Sandra. 1999. Impactos Sociais das Atividades Florestais no Brasil: Exploracao madeireira em Terras Indigenas.

Udall, Lori. 1997. The World Bank Inspection Panel: A Three Year Review. Washington D.C.: The Bank Information Center.

University of Florida. 1999. Amazon: A Review and Synthesis of Research Findings, 1990-1999. Patterns and Processes of Land Use and Forest Change in the Amazon. Center for Latin American Studies.

Verissimo, Adalberto, Carlos Souza Jr., Steve Stone, and Christopher Uhl. 1997. "Zoning of Timber Extraction in the Brazilian Amazon." Conservation Biology 12 (1):128-36.

Verissimo, Adalberto, and E. Lima. 1998. Caracterizacao dos polos madeireiros da Amazonia Legal. IMAZON.

Viana, Ervin, Donovan, Elliott, and Gholz. 1996. Certification of Forest Products Issues and Perspectives. Washington D.C.: Island Press

Viana, J. R. A. org. 1998. A Estratégia dos Bancos Multilaterais para o Brasil, Análise Crítica e Documentos Inéditos. Instituto de Estudos Sócio-Econômicos, Brasilia.

Viana, Virgilio M., and A. Verissimo. 1999. "Forests and the World Bank in Brazil." Brazil Country Study Background Paper. Operations Evaluation Department (OED). Washington D.C., The World Bank.

Vosti, Steve, C. Carpentier, and J. Witcover. 1999. "Land Use Dynamics in Western Amazon." Brazil Country Study Background Paper. Operations Evaluation Department (OED). Washington D.C.: The World Bank.

World Bank. s/d. Learning from the Past, Embracing the Future. Washington D.C.: The World Bank.

_____. 1998a. "Feeder Roads in Brazil." Precis. Operations and Evaluation Division, Number 160, Summer 1998.

_____. 1998b. Land Management I Project—Parana. Implemantation Completion Report. Washington DC: The World Bank.

_____. 1998c. The World Bank Annual Report. Washington D.C.: The World Bank.

_____. 1998d. "Environment Matters." Annual Review. Washington D.C.: The World Bank.

_____. 1998e. "Sustaining Tropical Forests: Can We Do It, Is It Worth Doing?" Tropical Forests Expert Discussion Meeting. Meeting Report. Part I & II." Forests Team. Natural Resources Program. Environment Department. Washington D.C.: The World Bank.

_____. 1997a. Brazil: Multimodal Freight Transport: Selected Regulatory Issues. Report No. 16361-BR. Washington D.C.: The World Bank.

_____. 1997b. Country Assistance Strategy of the World Bank Group for the Federative Republic of Brazil. Report No. 16582-BR, Country Operations Unit 1, Country Department I, Latin America and the Caribbean Regional Office. Washington D.C.: The World Bank.

_____. 1996a. "Brazil: Financial Sector Policies in a Stabilized Economy." Report No. 15743-BR, Country Unit I, Country Department I, Latin America and the Caribbean Region. Facimile (confidential).

_____. 1996b. "Effectiveness of Environmental Assessments and National Environmental Action Plans: A Process Study." Report No. 15835. Operation Evaluation Department. Washington D.C.: The World Bank.

_____. 1996c. Environmentally Sustainable Development. "The World Bank Participation Source Book." Washington D.C.: The World Bank.

_____. 1996d. The Inspection Panel, International Bank for Reconstruction and Development/International Development Association, Report August 1, 1994 to July 31, 1996, Washington D.C.

_____. 1995a. Country Assistance Strategy of the World Bank Group for the Federative Republic of Brazil. Report No. 14569-BR, Country Operations Unit 1, Country Department I, Latin America and the Caribbean Regional Office. Washington D.C.: The World Bank.

_____. 1995b. Brazil: A Poverty Assessment. Report No., 14323-BR, Human Resources Operations Division, Country Department I, Latin and the Caribbean Region. Washington D.C.: The World Bank.

_____. 1994a. Brazil: The Management of Agriculture, Rural Development and Natural Resources. Report No. 11783-BR, Natural Resources Management and Rural Poverty Division, Latin America and the Caribbean Region. Washington D.C.: The World Bank.

_____. 1994b. Brazil–Environmental Conservation and Rehabilitation Project, EA Category B: Summary of Environmental Analysis. Report E0053. Washington D.C.: The World Bank.

_____. 1994c. _Making Development Sustainable. The World Group and the Environment_. Washington D.C.: The World Bank.

_____. 1993. _World Development Report—Environment_. Washington D.C.: The World Bank.

_____. 1991a. A World Bank Policy Paper: The Forest Sector. Washington, D.C.

_____. 1991b. Brazil: Medium-Term Strategy Paper for the Infrastructure Sectors. Report No. 9473-BR, Washington D.C.: The World Bank.

_____. 1990. Brazil Agricultural Sector Review: Policies and Prospects. Report No. 7798-BR, Country Operations Division, Brazil Department, Latin America and the Caribbean Region, Washington D.C.: The World Bank.

_____. 1987. Staff Appraisal Report, Brazil, Minas Gerais Forestry Development Project. Washington D.C.: The World Bank.

_____. Undated. "Assessing Development Effectiveness: Evaluation in the World Bank and the International Finance Corporation." Operations Evaluation Department. Washington, D.C.: The World Bank.

World Wildlife Fund. 1999. WWF-Forests for Life: Forest Protected Area Triples in Brazil's Amazon, http://www.wwf.org/forests/ff.htm.

8

The Way Ahead

Uma Lele

Managing a Global Resource: Challenges of Forest Conservation and Development, and the World Bank's OED review on which it is based, grew out of a conviction that World Bank strategy (and by implication the strategies of the international development community) toward the forests of developing countries must be based on the economic development aspirations of developing countries and on realistic assessments of multiple, sometimes conflicting needs. Bank strategy and lending policies must be responsive to the needs of all stakeholders, especially the poor in borrowing countries. Where there are tradeoffs, they should be recognized and their implications for policies and incentives should be explicitly explored, such as between the global objectives of saving forests and the national or local objectives of creating livelihoods for forest-dependent people.

Six implications of these case studies were highlighted in the OED review:

1. Concessional *incremental* financial resources—over and above those currently provided through traditional development assistance—need to be mobilized internationally. This needs to be done on a sustainable basis, recognizing that developing countries will be unable to protect forests of global significance using borrowed funds or short-term grant funds given other high-priority demands on their own fiscal and financial resources, and competing demands on their forests.
2. The livelihood and employment needs of the forest-dependent poor need to be addressed, especially where the incidence of poverty is large.

The section in this chapter on the Prototype Carbon Fund has benefited from the work of Kenneth Newcombe, but the views expressed here are those of the authors. Syed Arif Husain contributed substantially to all of the sections concerning Carbon. The treatment of the section on Biodiversity relied heavily on analysis conducted by J. Gabriel Campbell and A. Martin, 2000 (see references).

3. The Bank's strategy and policy need to be inclusive, going beyond conservation of tropical moist forests, given that the largest number of the poor in the developing world makes a living from other forests, where biodiversity is the most endangered.
4. The alternative sources of demand for forest products and their supply need to be explored and forest concerns need to be incorporated in the macro cross-sectoral country considerations.
5. Illegal logging, governance and enforcement through improved property rights, forest certification and similar measures need to be addressed.
6. Partnerships with a variety of stakeholders are needed. Given the competing and often-irreconcilable claims on forests, forest conservation and development is often a conflict-resolution issue.

Mobilize Additional Incremental Concessional or Grant Resources

The cases of the six countries illustrated in this book help to identify some of the global trends in forest production and consumption and clarify the role forests play in poverty reduction, carbon sequestration and biodiversity conservation. These case studies demonstrate that convergence between global and national objectives has been greater in forest-poor countries like China, India and Costa Rica than in forest-rich countries. The forest-poor countries have already reached the limits of exploiting their extensive land margin for agricultural production, already experienced considerable forest cover loss, and adopted policies to reverse it. In contrast, forest-rich countries like Brazil, Indonesia and Cameroon are continuing to lose forest cover at a considerable rate. Although some of this forest cover loss is environmentally unsustainable and socioeconomically inequitable, the loss itself is also inevitable. The challenge for the international community is to increase forest and agricultural productivity, help ensure that the loss is minimum in extent and least damaging socially and environmentally, rather than operate under an assumption that it can be averted all together.

Land needed for agricultural use, production forestry and that which is likely to be left protected due to natural protection from the lack of economic access to the land is of considerable interest. The FAO has estimated that globally another 150 million hectares of land might be needed by 2015 (Alexandratos 1996) to meet world food production needs, assuming 80 percent of those needs are met by agricultural intensification made possible by the use of *ex-situ* biodiversity conservation to improve crop productivity. Some forestland in parts of Latin America or Eastern Europe may be naturally protected by its remoteness, its unsuitability for agricultural production, or a lack of current or anticipated investments in infrastructure. Land that is naturally protected may not need international transfers to keep it under protection. Hence, the estimates of the amount of land available in Latin America for potential forest protection reported in chapter 1 would need careful scrutiny, together with the amount of financial transfers needed to protect the forests on that land.

Forest-poor countries need international transfers for compensating the forest-dependent people for the opportunity cost of their forest resources, due in part to the extremely low per capita incomes of these households and the inability of their governments to compensate poor populations. Although India, China and Costa Rica are politically and socially committed to conservation and have domestic policies, institutions, and investments geared up or gearing up to support sustainable forest conservation, they use only a small share of their borrowed funds for these efforts. India has too many competing demands on the uses of concessional IDA funds to deploy those resources in the forest sector. And China and Costa Rica are loathe to use costly IBRD loans to invest in the benefits of conservation, which are long-term, risky, and more global than local. Alternative uses of these funds (for example, in such activities as girls' education) have considerably higher and quicker returns. For these countries, the period over which international grant transfers are needed is likely to be limited to the time when currently nascent international, regional and domestic markets for environmental services in carbon, biodiversity and water conservation would be developed.

The bottoming out of deforestation in these countries is a result of additional factors to increasing agricultural productivity, reaching the end of the extensive land margin for agriculture, and bringing more land under forest protection. They include:

- Banning logging in natural forests
- Curtailing domestic demand for forest and forest-dependent products
- Increasing the supply of wood from planted forests
- Finding substitutes and other products for forest products
- Increasing imports.

The case studies have shown that some of these actions, such as the bans on logging in natural forests, have serious socioeconomic consequences at the local level, substantial fiscal implications for the state at the national level, and in any case inadvertently result in "exporting" deforestation—that is, giving other countries an incentive to supply the timber not produced in the original country. Moreover, bans and similar actions may be difficult to enforce without creating alternative sources of income and employment for those dependent on forests or agriculture and without addressing the issue of increased demand for and supply of forest products.

Global Production and Consumption Patterns

Global production and consumption of wood are likely to increase about 26 percent between 1996 and 2010 (see table 8.1). Production and consumption are in close balance within regions, but there is substantial intra-regional trade. Demand from China, India, and Japan, for example, has been met largely by Southeast Asian countries, including Indonesia (Dauvergne 1997). More than a fifth of global consumption of industrial wood in 2010 is expected to be concentrated in Brazil, China, Indonesia, and the Russian Federation.

To contain deforestation and the degradation of forest resources, countries need substitutes for products originating in natural forests. Investments in alternative sources of wood—ranging from small-scale tree planting to the creation of forest plantations on degraded lands—are becoming important. Plantation forests now offer great promise for wood production. Improved genotypes and recent advances in silvicultural technologies have led to spectacular yields. Growth rates of 20 to 30 cubic meters per hectare a year, common on research stations in tropical areas, are being realized on many private lands.

The amount of industrial wood available from one hectare of a plantation can easily equal the amount available from 5 to 20 hectares of natural forest (Binkley 1999). Plantations not only relieve pressures on natural forests— they also offer reliable supply, uniform product, and competitive cost, and could potentially satisfy most of the global demand for forest products (LEEC

Table 8.1
Expected Increases in Industrial Wood Production and Consumption, 1996–2010 (million m³ a year)

Region	1996 Production (consumption)	2010 Production (consumption)
Africa	66 (59)	81 (72)
East Asia and the Pacific	304 (339)	421 (466)
Europe and Central Asia	380 (380)	547 (556)
Latin America and the Caribbean	141 (131)	164 (143)
Middle East and North Africa	7 (8)	10 (11)
South Asia	31 (31)	57 (58)
Other	560 (546)	593 (574)
World	1,490 (1,493)	1,872 (1,881)

Source: *Whiteman 1999*

1993). They also provide environmental benefits by reducing soil erosion, protecting watersheds, conserving biodiversity that would otherwise be lost through land clearing in natural forests, and sequestering carbon. Large or small tree-planting operations, if economically, environmentally, and socially responsible, provide the poor with substantial employment and income opportunities, either as tree owners or as plantation workers and in post-harvest operations.

A decade ago, intensively managed forests supplied 7 percent of industrial wood. Today they supply about 26 percent, and by 2040, possibly 40 percent. More than half of wood production in industrial countries now comes from managed forests and plantations. Productivity is already high in plantation forestry in Brazil, which has a progressive private sector and a strong research system partly funded by the private sector. But this is not typical of other developing countries, and small-scale planters in all developing countries need investment help. Real interest rates tend to be high, making it next to impossible for small farmers to obtain credit.

In Brazil and China, representatives of private companies made surprisingly similar suggestions during OED's fact-finding missions to China and Brazil. Give Bank/IFC loans to wood processing enterprises that join small farmers in operating tree plantations, while the government provides research and extension services. Countries as diverse as Argentina, Brazil, Chile, Indonesia, New Zealand, South Africa, and Uruguay are investing in industrial plantations. Discussions at the World Bank's CEO Forum suggest that prospects for forestry investments in developing countries are strong if a favorable investment climate can be assured.

The Bank's experience in Brazil and China offers some important lessons about socially and environmentally sustainable plantation forestry. The government of the state of Minas Gerais, in Brazil, is so convinced of the future of plantation forestry that a credit extended under a previous Bank loan has been converted into a commercially operated revolving fund to help small farmers establish plantations. In several developing countries, particularly in the tropics, millions of hectares of degraded lands are suitable for tree planting. Investments in plantation forestry in these countries—combined with greater commitment to bringing natural forestland under protection, while ensuring productive livelihoods for forest-dependent communities—can meet urban and export demand, create livelihoods, and substantially reduce continued pressures on the world's natural forests. China's small farmer plantations and India's social forestry experience demonstrate the importance of investment in tree planting.

Tree-planting operations will succeed in replacing wood from poorly managed and unsustainable operations in natural forests only if tree planting is economically competitive with products originating from natural forests. It is crucial to improve governance and to eliminate the perverse incentives, market distortions, and constraints on valuation currently associated with natural forest operations. To develop economically and environmentally competitive tree-planting operations, it is also necessary to provide clear and secure property rights, access to finance, and payments for environmental services. In countries where legislation has supported such related initiatives, such as Costa Rica, tree planting has increased the forest cover; in countries without such incentives, tree planting and investment in plantations have plummeted. An important question is whether new instruments such as carbon trading can mobilize finance from non-conventional sources.

Forests' Role in the New Instruments to Address Climate Change

A consensus has emerged that global warming in the past 50 years is largely attributable to human activity, a belief reinforced by the work of the Intergovernmental Panel on Climate Change (IPLC). Global warming has affected hydrological systems as well as terrestrial and marine ecosystems in many parts of the world, contributing to the rising socioeconomic costs of climate change. Almost 80 percent of all anthropogenic emissions of greenhouse gases (GHG) come from industrial countries, and their per capita emissions exceed those from developing countries. But it is the developing countries that have been penalized the most by climate change, while the industrialized countries are largely the beneficiaries. So, greater variability in climate suggests greater effects on the poorest of the world.[1]

Under the Kyoto Protocol, developing countries have an opportunity to earn revenue from carbon trading. Except for the United States (the largest emitter of carbon dioxide), the industrialized countries have collectively committed themselves to reducing their GHG emissions by 5.2 percent below the 1990 levels between 2008 and 2012. These commitments amount to a 30 percent reduction from their anticipated growth in GHG emission levels over the next decade. But for an international agreement to make a difference in the global climate, the parties to the agreement must pledge to supply an agreed amount of carbon. And the agreement must be supported in a way that makes it in the interest of all the parties to deliver on their pledges.

Carbon Emissions and Biological Mitigation

Humans release 7 to 8 billion tons (GtC) of carbon into the atmosphere each year, about 6 GtC are released from combustion of fossil fuels and 1 to 2 GtC from forest fires, land clearing, and soil erosion. The oceans absorb about 2 GtC of these emissions and plants between 1.5 and 2.5 GtC, while the remaining 3.5 GtC are released into the atmosphere. These emissions could be reduced or offset by reducing the use of fossil fuels, employing environmentally friendly technologies, and reversing deforestation. The options to reduce global warming include investments in energy efficiency, renewable resources, forest preservation, reforestation, and sustainable management—options that vary in their availability, costs, risks, and timing.

Forests, agricultural lands, and other terrestrial ecosystems offer significant potential for carbon mitigation—by conserving carbon pools, increasing the size of carbon pools, and substituting sustainably produced biological products. These strategies can help in reducing emissions if leakages can be prevented and the socioeconomic drivers of deforestation and other losses of carbon pools can be addressed.

Forests store nearly two-thirds of terrestrial carbon—nearly one trillion tons—and provide the longest-lived storage sink in the carbon cycle. But forests have historically been a net source of atmospheric carbon dioxide that has been released into the atmosphere through the decimation of 80 percent of the world's original forest cover. Moreover, under "business as usual," according to IPCC, the world could lose an additional 650 million hectares of tropical forests over the next 60 years, which would release as much as 77 GtC of carbon. Globally, six hectares of woodland are deforested for every hectare of trees planted. The situation in Africa is worse, with only one hectare planted for every 32 hectares deforested (Totten 1999). In total, the world is losing tropical forests at an alarming rate of 15 million hectares a year, equivalent of more than one Bangladesh or one Nicaragua a year.

The cumulative global potential for biological mitigation is estimated to be about 100 GtC by 2050—about 10 to 20 percent of potential fossil fuel emissions over the same period. This estimate is based on the assumption that some 700 million hectares of land might be economically attractive for forest carbon programs and that an additional 29 GtC of carbon emissions could be avoided by substituting woody biomass for fossil fuels.[2] This means that some of the drier open forests, which are generally eclipsed by attention to closed forests, would be included in the sequestration effort. Many of the world's poorest forest-dependent people rely on these open forests, and carbon trading would benefit the efforts to conserve those forests.

In short, the largest biological potential for atmospheric carbon mitigation is in subtropical and tropical regions of the world. Cost estimates for biological mitigation vary significantly—from $0.1/tC to about $20/tC in several tropical countries, and from $20/tC to $100/tC in non-tropical countries suggesting opportunities for trade.[3] These biological mitigation options, if properly implemented, could also provide such benefits as biodiversity conservation, watershed protection, sustainable land management, and rural employment. But if implementation is inappropriate—through excessive reliance on and replacement of natural forests with plantation forestry—it poses such risks as loss of biodiversity, community disruption, and groundwater pollution, among others.

International Carbon Trading

OECD countries can reduce their stated emissions of carbon through international trade in carbon-trading certificates under the flexible mechanisms of the Kyoto Protocol. But if the OECD countries confine actions to reduce emissions only to their own economies, they will miss their agreed obligations by 20 to 30 percent. Therefore, they will have to trade under the protocol's flexible mechanisms of Joint Implementation (JI) (Article 6), Clean Development (Article 12), and Emissions Rights Trading (Article 17) to make up the difference.

The impetus for investment and trade in emissions reductions with developing and the transition countries of Eastern Europe and Central Asia comes from this opportunity provided for by the Kyoto Protocol. Even without the cooperation of the United States, momentum is building to reach concrete agreements. But without ratification of those agreements by industrial countries' parliaments, the OECD countries' actions will be of little value in protecting the global climate. In the meantime, many private companies in the industrialized countries are preparing to trade in carbon.

Mitigation of climate change will involve complex interactions among economic, political, institutional, social, and technological processes and will have significant international and intergenerational implications for global equity and sustainable economic development. The potential mitigation options and their costs and benefits will vary by sector, nation, and region, owing to differences in their mitigation capacities.

Industries and services related to renewable energy, including forests and solar energy, are expected to benefit in the long term from price changes and the availability of financial and other resources. But fossil fuel industries (coal, oil, and natural gas) and certain energy-intensive sectors, such as steel production, may incur economic costs in the short run.

Policies such as the removal of subsidies for the use of fossil fuels and investments in energy-efficient technologies can potentially increase total environmental benefits to society through gains in economic efficiency if the new technologies are both economically efficient and environmentally desirable.

Other policies, such as exempting carbon-intensive industries from taxes, tend to redistribute benefits but increase total environmental costs to society. Studies show that the distributional effects of a carbon tax on polluting industries tend to have negative effects on the income of low-income groups unless the tax revenues are used directly or indirectly to compensate those groups.[4]

Successful implementation of GHG mitigation strategies will need to overcome these and other technical, economic, political, social, and institutional barriers. The poor in any country face limited opportunities to adopt technologies or change their social behavior, particularly if they are not part of a cash economy and if there are no markets to involve them and their physical environment in the process of carbon trading. Encouraging small-farmer forest production or forest management is a win-win-win from environmental, social, and economic viewpoints. What does this require in developing countries? A great deal: broader access to data and market information, greater availability of advanced technologies, more financial resources, training and capacity building, and assistance for poor forest-dependent households interested in environmentally friendly initiatives in land use changes.

The effectiveness of mitigation policies can thus be enhanced when climate policies are integrated with the non-climate objectives of national and sectoral policies, turning them into broad strategies to achieve long-term sustainable development and climate change objectives.

Coordinated action among countries and sectors will help to reduce mitigation costs. If the governments of the world decide to stabilize the atmospheric concentration of carbon dioxide at 550 ppm, about twice the pre-industrial level, global emissions would peak by about 2025 and fall below current levels by 2040 to 2070. This would mean that all regions would have to deviate from most "business-as-usual" scenarios within a few decades.

Given that long-term stabilization of the atmospheric concentration of greenhouse gases cannot be achieved without global reductions, the issue is who should do what in the short term while not losing sight of the challenge in the long term.

Carbon Trading: International Initiatives and Conventions

If the Kyoto Protocol is ratified and the current commitment period of 2008–12 is retained, perhaps 500 million to 700 million tons of carbon emissions a year will have to be offset through trade each year during that period. Analysts speculate that the market-clearing price globally, in a perfect world, would be $20–50 per ton of carbon. Compare that with the value of carbon saved per hectare ($198–809) and the price (rent) per hectare ($7–12) at which developing countries can supply this carbon (Lopez 1999). Developing countries can meet this volume of demand with estimated benefits to industrial countries (in terms of cost savings) of between 2 and 10 times the payments to developing countries.[5]

Some estimate that a trade volume on the order of $10 billion a year in emissions rights and project-based emissions reductions is feasible if the Kyoto Protocol provides an enabling regulatory environment for private investment. Because financing of trade in carbon will make up only 10–20 percent of total project financing, this volume implies a substantial boost in investment in cleaner technologies—and in climate-friendly and environment-friendly infrastructure for the Bank's client countries.

Experience in Costa Rica shows that the governments and private sectors of the developing countries have only a limited capacity to facilitate the trade in carbon rights, particularly to deliver services in this time frame. They will need assistance to help establish the institutional capacity to enable public and private agents (including small farmers) to participate in carbon trading. Opportunities for developing countries will also depend on the trade policies of the industrial countries. Unfortunately, the European Union is inclined to cap the proportion of an OECD country's emissions reductions obligations that can be met through trade, with the intention of forcing the United States and other countries to make hard decisions about their current energy policies.

Developing countries have the market capacity to deliver a significant volume of low-cost project-based emissions reductions to the OECD countries in this time frame. But in reality, very few countries may benefit from this trade, which could easily come to resemble the highly skewed distribution of foreign direct investment. China, India, and Brazil could be the main beneficiaries, with Russia and Ukraine potentially large beneficiaries if they can gain the confidence of the market. Other developing countries have not defined or articulated their self-interest in the convention process and are ill-equipped to defend their interests.

Most of the poorer agrarian economies will have only one significant way of benefiting from the Clean Development Mechanism—that is, the potential to become carbon sinks as a means of reducing emissions. But most of them are silent on the issue because they have limited capacity to analyze the potential benefits of carbon trade to their agroecosystems, degraded landscapes, and livelihoods of the rural poor.

Driven by the Clean Development Mechanism, project-based investment in the industrialized countries to reduce greenhouse gas emissions could be the single most powerful incentive for the development of clean technology transfer. But without the benefits of trade in carbon, especially through flexible mechanisms, the cost of compliance for companies in the OECD countries will be so high that it is unlikely they will be willing or able to reduce emissions on a large scale.

The key concern of most stakeholders is the environmental credibility of traded emissions reductions. The market can only exist if the supposed climate benefit is real. If it is not, the trade will collapse. What reasonable, affordable transactions and processes could achieve environmental credibility while creating this new market commodity? Is there a suitable convergence between the transactions costs that will assure the environmental usefulness of the product while being manageable transactions costs in the carbon trade?

Recent Kyoto Protocol Developments of
Relevance to Developing Countries

The parties to the United Nations Framework Convention on Climate Change (UNFCCC) agreed on the core elements for the Buenos Plan of Action

(1998) to implement the Kyoto Protocol during the Sixth Conference of the Parties (CoP6) in Bonn. Several countries were waiting for such an agreement on the rules of implementation before they would consider ratifying the Kyoto Protocol.

The parties to the Kyoto Protocol agreed to create three new funds to be managed by the Global Environment Facility (GEF):

- *The Special Climate Change Fund*: To support activities, programs, and measures for adaptation, technology transfer, and sectoral programs to help developing countries achieve economic diversification while limiting its adverse impacts.
- *The Least Developed Countries (LDCs) Fund*: To support the development of National Adaptation Programs and ensure that they are eligible for assistance under the Special Climate Change Fund.
- *The Kyoto Protocol Adaptation Fund*: To support adaptation projects in the developing countries that will be financed with a 2 percent share of the proceeds from investments under the CDM.[6]

Flexibility Mechanisms of the Kyoto Protocol

The parties agreed that the use of mechanisms "should be supplemental to domestic action, and domestic action shall thus constitute a significant element of the effort made by each party included in Annex 1 to meet its quantified limitation and reduction commitments..." Annex 1 parties are requested to provide relevant information on their supplemental activities that can be reviewed by the Compliance Committee's facilitative branch, but this provision does not include financial or other penalties that can be enforced by the Compliance Committee in case of noncompliance.

- To participate in the Kyoto Mechanisms, parties will have to comply with methodological and reporting requirements under article 5, paragraphs 1 and 2, and article 7, paragraphs 1 and 4 of the Protocol.
- Annex I parties agreed not to use reduction of emissions from nuclear facilities under the CDM or the Joint Implementation Mechanism.
- Afforestation and reforestation activities eligible under the CDM, with rules and modalities to be developed by CoP9.

Land Use, Land-Use Change, and Forestry (LULUCF)

The Kyoto Protocol recognizes that the enhancement and improved management of "carbon sinks," including afforestation and reforestation measured as verifiable changes in carbon stocks, could be used by parties to meet their emission reduction commitments through domestic policies and measures and through the Joint Implementation Provision (article 6) of the Protocol.

- The Protocol requires the CoP/MoP to define additional LULUCF activities that will contribute to a party's effort to meet its emission reduction target.
- It was agreed that the industrial countries can adopt all LULUCF activities—forest, grassland, and agricultural-land management—as part of their domestic actions to meet their commitments. Caps were negotiated for the amount of credit a country can claim from forest management activities.
- The ability of parties to account for significant quantities of "domestic sink" credits to meet their emission reduction commitments has implications on the demand for emission reductions through the flexibility mechanisms, particularly since the largest potential buyer of emission reductions will likely not be a party to the Protocol.

Compliance

The parties to the Protocol agreed to adopt procedures and mechanisms to address noncompliance. This would include a Compliance Committee with an Enforcement Branch to determine the consequences of noncompliance and a Facilitative Branch to assist parties that have difficulty meeting their obligations.

- The parties agreed that a significant consequence of noncompliance with the emission reduction target will be inclusion of excess emissions in the subsequent commitment period multiplied by a penalty factor of 1.3 and the development of a compliance action plan for review and assessment by the Enforcement Branch.

Implications

The ratification of the Protocol will create a demand for emission credits among the industrialized countries to fulfill their commitments. This will be especially true if the compliance regime is legally binding, or caps adopted at the domestic level have binding consequences, and if the agreement on the commitment period reserve is respected.

But some of the 2001 decisions could have serious consequences for the demand for CDM and JI projects. It is possible that the OECD's gross annual demand for reductions will be met through domestic policies and measures—and hot air.[7] This would also mean that the cost of emission reductions in CDM and JI projects would be lower than originally anticipated. But there is also a possibility that the market for emissions reductions from CDM and JI projects could be larger than anticipated, given their desirability from a policy perspective. For instance, investment in sustainable development in developing countries may be more attractive than investments in hot air. Moreover, greater market demand may be created by domestic, subnational, and regional initiatives, such as regulations passed by individual states in the United States and voluntary corporate targets.[8]

Prototype Carbon Fund (PCF)

The Prototype Carbon Fund (PCF) was established in 1999 to provide practical experience in implementing the Clean Development and Joint Implementation mechanisms. It demonstrates the usefulness of a financial instrument in paying for reducing emissions while simultaneously providing an effective vehicle to help developing countries meet their sustainable development objectives. It has three strategic objectives:

- Demonstrate how project-based emission reductions transactions can promote and contribute to the sustainable development of developing countries and countries with economies in transition and lower the cost of compliance with the Kyoto Protocol.
- Provide the parties to the UNFCCC, the private sector, and other interested parties with an opportunity to "learn by doing" in the development of policies, rules, and business processes for the achievement of emissions reductions.
- Demonstrate the potential for public-private partnerships in mobilizing new resources to address global environmental problem through market-based mechanisms.

The second objective is particularly sensitive because the regulatory framework for the Kyoto Protocol is still being developed. The Bank has been testing the application of the Protocol through rules still being negotiated. Often in developing a product, the GEF and, by association, the Bank are accused of "getting ahead of the Convention." After substantial debate, the Bank's board, most stakeholders, and OED's forest strategy evaluation agreed that "learning-by-doing" has a potentially enormous value.

The Fund has a funding cap of $180 million. The contributors (governments and the private sector) are its participants, and the Bank serves only as the trustee. Each public sector participant has contributed $10 million, and each private sector participant $5 million. The Fund is now $145 million, obtained from 6 governments and 17 private sector companies.[9]

The Fund places shareholder funds almost equally between JI and CDM projects. It distributes carbon purchases as widely as possible across climate-friendly renewable energy and energy-efficient technologies and regions of the world. The Prototype Carbon Fund will deliver certified emissions reductions with an average target price of about $20 per Ct at Fund liquidation in 2012. Yet, the more interesting product is knowledge gleaned through the process of "learning by doing." All stakeholders, including NGOs, the private sector, and host countries stand to learn much through carbon purchases and the maintenance of carbon-based assets in line with the Kyoto Protocol's requirements.

An important challenge is creating a high-value asset up front by establishing a credible baseline of what would have happened without the project, and defending this baseline through independent validation and verification. What would have happened under "business as usual?" The subject of this book, therefore, is of considerable interest to those involved in the carbon market. Procedures that allow independent arbiters of high professional standing to certify a baseline are being put in place. The environmental credibility of countries is of crucial importance in this process: there has to be confidence that certification of emissions reductions means that mitigation of climate change actually materializes.

Biodiversity and Protected Areas

Although laboratory conservation of diverse species has been highly beneficial to people, most notably through increased agricultural productivity, *in situ* conservation has received considerably more attention in recent years as a way of maintaining ecosystems.[10] Biodiversity conservation also includes ensuring habitats for migratory species, maintaining biosphere functions, and providing opportunities for the bio-prospecting of medicinal and other useful plants.

Understanding the distribution of the global, national, and local benefits and costs of conservation is crucial because of the implications for preserving biodiversity. Clearly, benefits that are global should be financed globally. Such financing must be available as long as needed to establish sustainability and to ensure that biodiversity conservation of global importance does not come at the cost of and divert attention from traditional developmental assistance.

The GEF has adopted an approach of incremental costs to finance biodiversity conservation of global significance. But this section demonstrates the conceptual and practical issues in defining biodiversity of global significance. Short-term external financing will not ensure biodiversity conservation over the long term.

Without resolving a variety of these issues at the global level, the World Bank has preferred to justify financing (loans and IDA credits) for biodiversity conservation as a way of removing barriers until a conducive domestic environment is ensured for conservation at the national level. The size of benefits within the national borders, especially those that can result in mobilizing financial and, where necessary, fiscal resources, are crucial for generating commitment to conservation in developing countries, given the competition for resources.

From a development perspective, over 90 percent of the biodiversity of value to developing countries tends to be outside the protected areas. Though such traditional approaches as protected areas have had relative success in bolstering national commitments toward conservation, such methods alone cannot address the underlying cause biodiversity loss or reduce its associated threats. "Protected areas inevitably lose species when surrounded by land-scapes that bring alien invasive species, pollution and development pressure" (IUCN 2000). Research attests that if only the current protected areas remain as wildlife habitat, between 30 and 50 percent of the species will be lost, because the reserves do not contain populations large enough to maintain the species.

Furthermore, agriculture has been identified as presenting the greatest threat to species diversity, and almost half the areas currently protected for biodiversity are in regions where agriculture is a major land use, where food supply, employment, and incomes of the poor are at stake. Populations, especially in tropical wilderness areas, are increasing at rates twice the world's average growth. Therefore, agro-biology through agriculture and livestock production is of increasing importance in ensuring biodiversity, whereas much of the emphasis today on biodiversity conservation has been through a conventional protected-areas approach. While external funding is necessary it is not sufficient. Generating and demonstrating economic benefits from biodiversity conservation net of costs incurred by various agents including users is the only way to ensure sustainability.

Predictions that more than half the world's remaining species will be lost in the next 50 years through forest clearing have led to a global movement for biodiversity conservation. But the goal poses a number of challenges. There is only a limited consensus on global conservation priorities at the international level. There is no concerted effort to pool together goals and data on such issues as diversity, endemism, threat, viability and ecological function (Mace 2000). Despite efforts to reduce duplication of effort across organizations, more still needs to be done to eliminate redundancies of effort across environmentally oriented organizations. Conservation International, WWF-US, Bird Life International, IUCN, World Resource Institute and Nature Conservancy are all involved in assessing biodiversity of high priority, each using different criteria and standards, at huge costs involving independent data and analysis (Mace 2000). Considerable resources are devoted to these efforts. Those by international NGOs are additional to the resources provided through traditional development assistance. But many are not of a long-term sustainable nature. Some, such as WWF, have a combination of regional programs, policy programs and campaigns in 70 countries. In the case of the resources mobilized by GEF there is no way of establishing that these are additional to the traditional development assistance. Evidence after 10 years of the GEF existence is limited on the extent to which it is leading to sustainable conservation practices or sustainable financing of conservation beyond the efforts of national governments. Bank staff working on GEF projects recognize the conceptual and practical issues in defining biodiversity of global significance, with incremental cost financing and with the insufficiency of short-term external financing to ensure biodiversity conservation in developing countries over the long term.

Some of them have preferred to justify financing for biodiversity conservation in Bank borrowing countries as a way of removing financial obstacles until a domestic environment conducive to conservation efforts is assured. For this to work, benefits within national borders are crucial for generating social and financial commitment to conservation in developing countries. Clearly, in this case, priorities of developing countries matter in conservation, as they should. The extent to which they address conservation of global biodiversity is not clear, although GEF's current portfolio covers quite a wide range of areas.

How to Define and Tackle Biodiversity

Only 1 to 4 percent of the earth's biodiversity has been documented. Particular attention in identifying biodiversity has been given to 25 so-called hotspots—areas that contain at least 0.5 percent, or 1,500 of the world's estimated 300,000 plant species. Of the 25 hotspots, 10 contain at least 5,000 plant species. This approach applies such criteria as species endemism and degree of threat of extinction for biodiversity documentation. Few scientists from developing countries are involved in this process, however, because their knowledge tends to be confined to species in their own countries.[11] The analysis omits invertebrates, which are largely undocumented and constitute perhaps 95 percent of all animal species; most are insects.

A threatened area of biodiversity is defined as an area that has lost at least 70 percent of its vegetation. Eleven of the 25 hotspots have lost 90 percent, and three 95 percent. Since endemic species of all kinds are estimated to be found on only 2.1 million square kilometers, or 1.4 percent of the earth's land surface, this relatively small area should make it easier to establish priorities in biodiversity conservation. An estimated 15 of the 25 hotspots are in tropical countries. Five are estimated to contain 45 percent of all the hotspots' endemism. This makes it potentially a very attractive approach to global priority setting, in a Noah's Ark style, given the limited resources.

Proponents of the hotspot approach argue that their analysis can be complemented by the endemism among higher taxa, such as families and genera. For example, Madagascar possesses 11 endemic families and 310 endemic genera of plants, 5 endemics and 14 genera of primates, and similarly for birds. Others have suggested that there is strong congruence between the presence of indigenous cultures and biodiversity endemism.[12] But others argue that the hotspot approach does not use advanced techniques for mapping species to balance the representation and conservation efficiency with socioeconomic costs (Mace 2000).

WWF advocates "eco-regionally based conservation" on grounds that "it is no longer appropriate to focus on protecting a single species without due consideration for what might be happening to its habitat. Neither is it appropriate to consider conservation apart from the needs of communities. Also, trans-boundary cooperation in protecting species and their habitats is essential."[13] WWF has identified 900 eco-regions, which are defined as relatively large units of land or water containing a geographically distinct assemblage of species, natural communities, and environmental conditions. Decisions about biodiversity conservation in such large areas would have to take socioeconomic costs into account, but such costs typically are not included in current analysis.

A pilot *Millennium Ecosystems Assessment*, funded jointly by the Bank, GEF, and other partners has embarked on assessing the impacts of human activity on the developing world's two ecosystems by involving governments and institutions of developing countries with a view to addressing intergovernmental bodies. The project leadership involves some of the scientists who play a key role in the Intergovernmental Panel on Climate Change, giving considerable credibility to the effort. Strong social scientific input would be critical for this to succeed.

Lack of knowledge of the core processes limits conservation. A recent study by IUCN and Future Harvest stresses that more than 1.1 billion people live within the 25 hotspots, and that hunger runs rampant in at least 16 of them. Half of the world's 17,000 major nature reserves intended to protect wildlife, and 45 percent of the protected land reserves, are being heavily used for agriculture. As a consequence, many of the protected areas are highly degraded. A recent review of biodiversity in China by a prestigious group of international and Chinese scientists came to a similar conclusion.[14] So, unless ecosystems are managed for multiple uses and factor in the need of feeding people, biodiversity will remain threatened.

Considering that representation of several taxa, including invertebrates, is also needed, and that biological priorities must be combined with socioeconomic realities, the hotspot approach fails to address conservation of the key ecological and evolutionary processes critical to maintaining the patterns of biodiversity.

Cost of Saving Biodiversity

Pimm et al. (2001) have argued that the global community can afford the costs of saving biodiversity by estimating a one-time cost of $25 billion because reserves in tropical wilderness areas and hotspots need only cost a fraction of the $30 billion needed annually to reach 15 percent of the global reserve network in each continent.[15]

This amount assumes a one-time payment for the land, presumably to be made by the global community to the countries in question. It also assumes that the payment would cover the recurrent costs of protecting biodiversity, including regulation, enforcement, and maintenance. This may or may not be a valid assumption unless developing countries see an economic benefit in such a potential offer.[16] Nor is it clear that incremental official development assistance will be forthcoming on a long-term sustainable basis to meet global biodiversity objectives.

Funding for biodiversity conservation comes from a variety of sources, but there are no known estimates of the global total, particularly those from non-traditional development assistance, an issue of considerable interest. In a rare study of funding for Latin America, Castro et al. (2000) estimated that in 1990 and 1997, 3,489 conservation projects were funded by 65 sources, with $3.26 billion, or 70 percent, for protected areas.

Protected Areas

Developing countries have greatly expanded their protected areas in recent years, as shown by the six country cases. Environmentalists have encouraged the expansion of protected areas as the single most important way of saving biodiversity before population pressures cause increases in land values that make enlargement of protected areas financially infeasible.

But saving global biodiversity and protecting areas requires a holistic view of land, fiscal and other sector policies (toward agriculture and fisheries as well as forestry and wildlife and infrastructure), transfers from polluting to green industries, the introduction of cost-recovery principles including fees for parks, revenue-sharing with local communities to increase their stake in protection, mobilization of private capital, stronger links with local NGOs and research institutions, and the exchange of information about successful experiences within and across countries and regions. These are the types of multi-sectoral approaches and actions Costa Rica has developed over the past 20 years. Brazil is doing the same on a smaller scale in some of its southern states by promoting local and national ecotourism, charging fees for access to parks, involving national research institutions in biodiversity inventories, and imposing local ecological taxes.

The Bank and GEF portfolios show how the global community has addressed the challenges of biodiversity conservation. GEF's implementing agencies have been responsible for developing projects with their client countries and implementing them through executing agencies, including government bodies, NGOs, and regional project authorities. These international agencies are also charged with integrating ("mainstreaming") GEF objectives and activities in their own operations and in their client countries' activities. Unlike the work of the international NGOs, the *raison d'être* of the GEF is its ability to fulfill convention commitments, which are fundamentally intergovernmental in character. The GEF is the only intergovernmental international financing mechanism for raising and transferring funds to recipient countries for global environmental purposes. It involves commitments made by donor countries to recipient countries in accordance with international environmental conventions and priorities.

Ensuring that funds raised for global environmental purposes supplement and do not displace funds for development is fundamental to the ability of the international community to raise funds through the replenishment process. Related issues are the extent to which GEF programs are catalytic, sustainable, replicable, cost-effective, and able to leverage additional finances through cofinancing.

GEF's implementing agencies' commitment to mainstreaming and country-drivenness, including particularly the interface and congruence between global and national priorities, is also crucial. In 1992 in Rio, governments agreed on broad requirements for a politically responsive governance structure as part of an agreement on the conventions for the interim GEF to become universal, democratic, balanced, and transparent. The first GEF evaluation[17] of its pilot phase in December 1993 stressed the lack of strategic direction for these perspectives and set the pace for restructuring the GEF. Consequentially, interested governments negotiated the *Instrument for the Restructured Global Environment Facility*—including the GEF Assembly (with political representation), the GEF Council (with a critical role in the formulation and adoption of policy and funding commitments), and a CEO and Chairman with responsibilities to determine the content of the work program and recommend projects to the Council for approval on the basis of Council-approved strategy, programs, and criteria. The Secretariat was proposed to advise the CEO on the quality and composition of the work program and prepare strategic and policy documents for the Council.

As the trustee of GEF, and the largest lending agency, the Bank was expected to provide GEF with a unique opportunity to "mainstream" biodiversity conservation. That is why the GEF Secretariat was housed in the World Bank, with UNDP and UNEP as the two other implementing agencies.[18]

Each agency has established its own GEF coordinating unit through which all project proposals flow to the GEF for approval (see Council paper on Executing Agencies for Expanded Opportunities; these agencies will eventually be able to channel funds directly from the GEF Trust Fund to the countries without the GEF IAs). While the involvement of the Bank, UNDP, and UNEP has helped GEF to develop projects of all sizes, the independent approaches of the three entities have not yet fostered integrated strategies to national biodiversity in all cases, although there are some interesting examples of cooperation in Honduras and Madagascar. Expansion to include other agencies will certainly expand GEF activities more rapidly and increase competition among agencies, which will be its strength, but based on the historical experience of the implementation by three agencies it could further fragment, possibly undermining a coherent approach to biodiversity conservation by developing countries at the national level.

GEF's impact, the roles of the various partners and the comparative advantage of a publicly funded facility in catalyzing appropriate action for global environmental improvement were the issues addressed by the OED review in relationship to the forest sector only and most recently by GEF's second evaluation which focused on GEF impacts, known as OPS 2.

World Bank-financed GEF project proposals are prepared in accordance with the Bank's regular preparation and appraisal procedures, often in association with regular projects, while ensuring that they also meet GEF criteria. From 1991 until June 1999, the World Bank has managed two-thirds of the total GEF portfolio and took on implementation of 162 projects with GEF grant funding, approximately 44 of which were forest projects with commitments of $370 million. The total value of these projects with co-financing from a variety of sources, including co-financing of $181 million from the World Bank, was over $1 billion. As is the case with World Bank lending, GEF projects in other sectors also affect the forest sector.

Some of the achievements of the GEF include institutional regional approaches that span several countries (something the Bank's country-focused lending cannot do), promotion of participatory approaches that involve substantial involvement of local communities and domestic and international NGOs, and establishment of the precedent that international funding can be provided for conservation activities. But the global community's efforts to protect biodiversity have faced conceptual and practical challenges while the sums committed by GEF are small, relative to the various estimates of requirements presented earlier. GEF projects, however, can provide lessons through monitoring and evaluation so that the large sums needed in the future could be spent more effectively.

What is needed to design the right strategy for saving global biodiversity? First, there seems to be a need for an agreed set of criteria on how to measure biological diversity or determine biological diversity of global significance. Biological diversity, however defined, is not equally distributed. This has led to continuing debate on GEF's selection of ecosystems and its choice of projects, which is based on guidance from the Convention on Biological Diversity (CBD) on balancing global biodiversity criteria with country priorities by favoring "ecosystem representation."

But favoring ecosystem representation raises another strategic question: will developing countries feel an obligation to save biological diversity of global significance if most of the benefits do not accrue to them, and if the economic value of diversity is not seen by the stakeholders who make the most demands on these resources? Some regard this issue as more political than technical,[19] a debate that continues even in the NGO community. It rarely involves either debate on what constitutes biological diversity of global value or on the economic considerations that drive land and resource use in developing countries.

Another critical issue is financing incremental costs and measuring global benefits. Incremental cost financing for a period of five years—as is currently practiced by the World Bank, assumes that the country will finance these activities after donor financing ends.

But unlike Bank-funded projects, GEF project benefits do not all accrue only to the grant-receiving country. Can developing countries be expected to fund biodiversity conservation of global significance if it is not a priority of theirs with substantial national benefits?

There are even more significant issues for GEF's regional projects. Can these investments be sustainable if the financing is small in relation to the opportunity cost of resources? If it is provided only over a period of five years? And if it does not address issues of making the protected areas financially sustainable without addressing such policy measures as introduction of user fees, cross-sectoral taxes and subsidies, and sharing revenues with locals?

To work toward sustainability, some Bank staff are suggesting that GEF should increase the length of its support for some projects to up to 15 years. And in other cases GEF is setting up endowments, the interest from which can be used as the working capital for the management of protected areas. But the resources needed to establish trust funds are conservatively 20 times the operating costs, since only about 5 percent of the endowment can be used to operate biodiversity projects (there are many other types of trust funds in which the GEF has participated. See the report "Experience with Conservation Trust Funds" [GEF Evaluation Report 1-99]). And in several cases, the working capital ends up being used for social activities at the community level rather than for the protection of biodiversity. Because baselines were not established in early projects and the conceptual and empirical issues of how to establish baselines remains thorny, monitoring and evaluation have been weak and it is difficult to assess how much the GEF is ensuring sustainable financing.

The 44 forestry-related GEF projects managed by the Bank through 1999 faced some of these challenges. A large number of them focused on protected area management, but relatively few resources went into addressing the fundamental threats to biodiversity or to investigating the value of conserving rather than exploiting those resources. The OED review of the GEF forest operations[20] found that the World Bank task managers designing these projects used a variety of biodiversity criteria in justifying financing of the projects. From the perspective of some biologists and conservationists, this appeal to different criteria for different countries, and the failure to develop a prioritized list of ecosystems and criteria, lessens the GEF impact on global biodiversity conservation (IUCN 1997). At least implicitly, this argument is based simply on the existence value of biodiversity and the future risks that might emanate from its loss for uses that are currently unknown. Perhaps the weakest part of the biodiversity conservation effort globally has been the attempt to sort out the different global, national, and local benefits, their actual and potential consumers, and hence the implications for sustainability.

From a pragmatic, country stakeholder perspective, however, this willingness to accept a variety of criteria is an honest reflection of the lack of consensus on global biodiversity prioritization and indeed even the prospect for consensus and an essential recognition of the importance of enlarging both global support and national ownership of the overall objectives of biodiversity conservation. As other evaluations have also concluded, there is room for improving the biological criteria and their application to project selection while continuing to recognize the need for global buy-in and equity in fund distribution (Porter et al. 1998). While the debate on this issue continues, NGOs have accepted both points of view as valid and coexistent, even if not completely reconcilable. That may help them forge more meaningful approaches to biodiversity conservation in place of their past adversarial purist conservation approaches, and hopefully bringing additional resources to conservation instead of diverting existing resources away from development assistance. Credible monitoring and evaluation of biodiversity projects, whether funded by GEF or by the World Bank in partnership with others, remains a challenge.

The treatment of people in the protected areas, many of whom tend to be poor and of minority communities, also raises issues. The advocates of minority peoples' rights argue for increased delegation of resource control and use rights to the minorities—usually on the assumption that this will result in increased conservation. Other conservation advocates argue for decreasing the use of the forest by both indigenous peoples. Thus, this too is an issue which needs greater monitoring to assess impact on the ground in place of the current idealistic, and sometimes, ideological solutions.

Meanwhile, the private sector is also arguing for increased investment in sustainable forest management, and address the development aspirations of developing countries on grounds that demonstrating the realization of private profit is the best means for maintaining biological diversity.

The Bank's current strategy, like the GEF's,[21] attempts to achieve an acceptable compromise by avoiding these more controversial issues. Yet the GEF guideline not to finance sustainable forest management, while appealing to those who argue that primary tropical forests "cannot be managed sustainably" and require complete protection, defies the growing recognition of the importance of promoting economic uses of land as the most hopeful way, in many cases, of saving biodiversity.

Notwithstanding these issues, the Bank's partnership with the GEF has allowed it to pursue conservation aspects of the 1991 forest strategy that might not otherwise have been possible, since few countries are able or willing to borrow IBRD or even IDA funds for biodiversity conservation. But it would be difficult to conclude that these relatively modest GEF interventions in the forest sector have significantly helped the mainstreaming of biodiversity issues into country strategies or addressed the real biodiversity conservation challenges on the ground.

Mainstreaming long-term global concerns about biodiversity into country plans and the Bank's forest sector lending is ambitious, considering the many pressing economic and social concerns the Bank's borrowing countries face. Grants that focus on demand-driven biodiversity and improvements in countries' own strategies to address major threats to biodiversity of national significance have a better chance of succeeding, but GEF's mandate is to support activities of global importance.

Greater effort is needed not just to mobilize international grant funds for saving biodiversity of global importance but also to address the relationship between global and national priorities, incidence of costs and benefits, including how they can coincide to ensure greater attention to economic, livelihood, and sustainability issues.

The second independent evaluation of GEF (OPS 2) has addressed some of these issues and, like the OED review, it has concluded that the GEF has been successful in transferring international resources for biodiversity conservation and promoting participatory approaches in protected areas but to a lesser extent in production landscapes. However, OPS 2 concludes that the extent to which GEF is strategically saving global biodiversity—an expectation of the convention for which it is a financing mechanism—is not clear for various reasons. There is little information available on GEF's impact on saving biodiversity of global importance, and little reporting of it to the convention because monitoring and evaluation of projects has been weak. The situation is reportedly now being rectified by initiatives being taken by the GEF Secretariat and by biodiversity assessment projects supported by the GEF, such as the Millennium Ecosystems Assessment. According to OPS 2, a review of a group of newer forest-related projects reveals that almost all of them have been carried out, or propose to carry out, biological and socioeconomic baseline studies.

Further issues addressed include the concern that operational focal points in the countries are not clear as to the GEF mission. Country ownership of programs is weak and awareness of GEF and global environmental issues is low in the civil society. OPS 2 recommended clearer lines of accountability and common reporting systems across all IAs/EAs for ensuring that broad-based, inclusive participation is a feature of GEF projects. Relatedly, stakeholders must be clearly defined and the term stakeholder must be understood to include more than institutional stakeholders alone.

OPS 2 argues that IAs, including the Bank, have not put in place incentives to persuade borrowing countries to mainstream GEF activities. Private sector financing outside of the transitional economies is still limited and the financial sustainability of the GEF programs is unclear.

There is much confusion among GEF stakeholders in the identification of global environmental benefits and incremental costs that should be attributed to the global benefits. OPS2 found that "many country partners, some IA staff and other GEF stakeholders, were unfamiliar with both the economic concepts and GEF Operational Strategy relating to the incremental costs of delivering global environmental benefits" (p.65).

It goes on to observe that GEF Secretariat's existing staff capacity is too weak to address issues of operational strategy or to demonstrate that the funds mobilized by it are additional, particularly as GEF-funded projects have not mobilized much private finance and there is lack of clarity on whether the implementing agencies or the GEF have the responsibility for private resource mobilization. Cooperation with IFC to undertake the kinds of collaboration Costa Rica has forged in its investments has been weak. But some of the recent successes include establishments of trust funds and endowments to manage protected areas on a long-term sustainable basis. Projects in the pipeline take these lessons into account.

Integrated Conservation and Development Projects (ICDPs)

Integrated conservation and development projects (ICDPs) are becoming attractive to local governments and donors because they not only address the threats posed by local people to forest biodiversity but also because they provide a potential mechanism to compensate local communities for the loss of livelihood typically associated with restrictions on resource use and investment in protected areas. A recent review of ICDPs in Indonesia comments:

> Why are ICDPs so popular? First, because they offer a simple and intuitively appealing alternative to earlier, unsuccessful approaches to PA management which have come to be regarded as politically infeasible. Second, because ICDPs offer the attractive prospect of contributing to three of the most sought-after goals on the sustainable development agenda: more effective biodiversity conservation, increased local community participation in conservation and development, and economic development for the rural poor. These features seem virtually irresistible to many NGOs, government departments, and development agencies. (Wells et al. 1999)

The government's inability to protect the protected areas and concern that those in charge of maintaining law and order have been sharing in the benefits of exploiting valuable biodiversity in the protected areas, has been widespread.

OPS 2's observations in this regard are also of interest. It states that the integrated area conservation projects lack innovation. There continues to be too much focus on community conservation initiatives and not enough on such major threats as pressures on buffer zones, poor logging practices by concessionaires, road construction, and weak in-country ownership.[22] Governments have failed to enforce adequately the existing laws, rules, and regulations designed to protect against global biodiversity loss, and projects have not adequately helped improve enforcement.

The policy against Bank financing for commercial logging in tropical moist forests may have hindered even GEF support for promising experiments in forest management by local communities and the private sector. GEF's Interim Guiding Principles for Projects Associated with Logging go much beyond the Bank's 1991 forest strategy. They indicate that GEF will not support logging in *any* primary forests, not just tropical moist forests, and that GEF financing will not be used to meet baselines for pursuing sustainable forest management, the cost of forest certification, of improving timber harvesting methods to meet Forest Stewardship Council/International Tropical Timber Agreement criteria or to finance reduced-impact logging, among other things. Weaknesses in the monitoring of environmental and forest safeguard applications in infrastructure projects with often large but indirect impacts on biodiversity also remain unaddressed. NGOs believe the Bank should remain active to maintain influence on maintenance of law and order. But cancellation of grants/credits/loans provides the problems of corruption and mismanagement the necessary publicity and creates awareness of the problem so that national constituencies can address the longer-term law-and-order issues with greater information. Financing of workshops on illegal logging and training of nationals to undertake forest watch are some useful steps GEF and WWF are taking to help strengthen priority to law and order.

To summarize, the development community must use its influence to persuade governments to live up to their international commitments on the environment. But it is unclear if biodiversity of global significance can be saved without:

- Establishing clear global priorities for its protection
- Adequately analyzing the real threats to biodiversity
- Providing assured long-term financial support for its protection, through such arrangements as trust funds
- Creating national capacity for policy, planning, monitoring, and evaluation so that countries are able to address these issues better.

The GEF and the Bank/WFF Alliance must address such fundamental issues as incentives and financial resources in their quest to increase protected and sustainably managed forest areas. The World Bank Institute's link with operations must be strengthened to realize this potential.

Reduced-Impact Logging and Sustainable Forest Management

The many definitions of sustainable forest management (see glossary) are testament to the controversy surrounding the concept. But there is a widening consensus on the need to improve forest management from its often-predatory nature. Indeed, the Bank–WWF Alliance's global target of 200 million hectares to be brought under sustainable management by 2005, though unrealistic in its ambition, reflects the well-intentioned goal of increasing the area under improved forest management. Partly translating the conceptual controversies, economic assessment of forest management makes three potential assessments to a financial analysis using opportunity costs, environmental and social costs, and global values (see glossary).

Conservation International believes that trying to make commercial logging operations more sustainable will not help to conserve forests.[23] Rice et al. (1998) have argued for some time that donors have little to show for the hundreds of millions of dollars they have invested to promote sustainable forest management. Why? Because companies find it more profitable to practice non-sustainable logging, and because governments find it difficult and costly to manage forests sustainably.

As noted earlier, natural forests grow slowly. Timber prices have risen only slightly faster than inflation. And in most tropical countries, high interest rates are a powerful disincentive to long-term investment. So it makes little economic sense for companies to invest in long-term forest activities. Rice et al. (1998) admit that reduced-impact logging practices may improve companies' profits, since careful planning of skid trails and directional felling may make their operations more efficient. Still, they argue that such practices alone are unlikely to make commercial logging sustainable.

Even so, reduced-impact logging has begun to resonate with environmentalists and foresters worldwide because of its purpose of reducing the environmental and social impacts associated with timber harvesting.[24] Some describe it as transfer of well-established technology from temperate forests to the tropics.

Holmes et al. (2000) have estimated that it would be possible to save as many as 150 million hectares of tropical forest lands between 2001 and 2050—depending on the assumptions about demand growth in forest product use, alternative sources of forest products, and the extent of annual improvement in utilization—if reduced-impact logging were to spread. They argue that properly planned and supervised harvesting operations not only meet conditions for sustainability but also reduce harvesting costs. Pilot projects in Indonesia have shown cost savings of $0.3/m^3 but without including the costs of training and planning.[25] These cost savings are due to better planning, supervisory control, and more efficient use of felled timber.

But others question if reducing damage to the stand alone is really the objective of reduced-impact logging (Sist et al. 2001). They argue that harvesting guidelines should not only tell us how to plan skid trails but how many trees should be felled, which species can be harvested, which should be protected, and implications for future timber yield. So the integration of silvicultural principles and treatment is crucial. Implicit in the argument is a call for location-specific adaptability of principles to suit diverse conditions. This means not only technically competent planners, loggers, and supervisors—it also means location-specific ecosystem research and extension. Without skilled planners and loggers, even the promoters believe that there is little hope for reduced-impact logging to work on a large scale. Sarre and Efransjah (2001) argue that it is too early to predict its impact because the costs associated with training and planning and investment in new equipment and infrastructure are not known.[26] Studies on the same subject cited in the chapter on Brazil suggest high rates of return to managed forests, though still only half as much as those from predatory logging. By contrast, authors of the Indonesia chapter express doubts about the financial viability of better forest management.

There is also a debate about what constitutes reduced impact. How much reduction in impact is enough environmentally, and is it sustainable financially? There clearly appear to be tradeoffs between the two. Furthermore, the returns to reduced-impact logging of timber grown in natural forests at a level acceptable to all concerned must compare well with alternative uses of the land. That raises issues ranging from trade, tax, and subsidy policies to institutions for regulation and enforcement in both the forest sector and in sectors competing with forestry. So partnerships of various stakeholders—foresters, scientists, private businesses, NGOs, and civil society—together with an optimum combination of command and control with incentives, are crucial in determining the prospects for reduced-impact logging. It goes to show why forest conservation and development pose multi-sectoral, multilevel, and multi-temporal challenges.

Notes

1. IPCC, Synthesis Report to the TAR, September 30, 2001.
2. Recall that the introduction to this volume quoted Lopez, who contends that 650 million hectares are potentially available for protection in Latin America alone. About 150 million hectares are estimated to be needed to meet world food needs by 2010, on the assumption that 80 percent of the growth in food production would come from land intensification. (Alexandratos 1996).

3. These may be upper bounds, given that other studies suggest the land base estimates for expanding carbon sinks are grossly overestimated when tenure, institutional capacity, ecological, and other constraints are taken into account.
4. Based on reports prepared by working groups of the Intergovernmental Panel on Climate Change.
5. The short-run marginal cost of supply in the already energy efficient and hydropower or nuclear- dominated economies of Japan, Norway, and Sweden, for example, is already above $40/t/Carbon.
6. After the adoption of the text, a group of countries (EU, Canada, Norway, New Zealand, Switzerland, and Iceland) declared that they would provide a minimum of $410 million per year in predictable and reliable funding for climate-change activities (including their climate-change contributions to the GEF), beginning in 2005. Canada announced an immediate grant of US$6 million to seed the Adaptation Fund. All of these countries also called for a "streamlining of GEF processes." The United States announced that it would intensify its bilateral and regional programs as well as preexisting multilateral ones (and made a distinction between Convention Funds and Protocol Funds).
7. Hot air is the headroom available from the difference between emissions in 1990 and current emissions in various East and Central European countries.
8. Oregon State: Carbon dioxide emissions standard for new energy utilities. Price cap: $0.57/tCo2. Utilities can offset emissions using project-based mechanisms. Washington State: New plants must demonstrate the use of best available techniques for carbon dioxide emissions control. Massachusetts State: Carbon dioxide emissions cap for energy utilities effective in 2005. Utilities can offset excess emissions using project-based mechanisms.
9. Governments: Canada, Finland, Japan (through Japan Bank for International Cooperation, Netherlands, Norway, Sweden. Private Sector: BP-Amoco, Chubu Electric, Chugoku Electric, Deutsche Bank, Electrabel, Fortum, Gaz de France, Kyushu Electric, Mitsui, Mitsubishi, NorskHydro (Norway), RaboBank, RWE–Germany, Shikoku Electric, Statoil (Norway), Tohoku Electric, Tokyo Electric Power.
10. This pertains to soil quality characteristics, including texture, porosity, chemical balance, moisture retention, and fertility that the presence of various materials, including micro-organisms, provide.
11. Five key factors include number of endemics and endemic species/area ratios for both plants and vertebrates and habitat loss.
12. WWF's Global Conservation Programme, 1999/2000, A WWF International Publication, Dr. Chris Hails, Programme Director.
13. Ibid.
14. China Council for International Cooperation on Environment and Development (CICED) Report: Biodiversity Working (Phase Two) on China. Fifth Report (2001), June 2001 Xining, Qinghai.
15. "Tropical wilderness forests, predominantly the relatively intact blocks of the Amazon, Congo, and New Guinea, are remote and sparsely populated. Land values are low and sometimes equivalent to buying out logging leases. Recent conservation concessions suggest ~$10/ha for acquisition and management. Securing an additional approximate 2 million km2 and adequately managing 2 million km2 already protected for biodiversity and indigenous peoples requires a one-time investment of about $4 billion. Land prices for the densely populated hotspots are much higher. Of the 1.2 million km2 of unprotected land, some will remain intact without immediate intervention, some is already too fragmented, and perhaps one-third

constitutes the highest priority. A study of the South Africa fynbos hotspot suggests a one-time cost of about $1 billion, and so by extrapolation, about $25 billion for the protection and adequate management of all hotspots. Additional marine reserves would likely require about $2.5 billion. Pimm et al., *Science* 2001, September 21; 293: 2207-2208

16. Cameroon recently rejected such an offer. Personal conversations with Giuseppe Topa, lead forest economist, The World Bank's Africa Region.
17. GEF: Independent Evaluation of the Pilot Phase by UNDP, UNEP and World Bank.
18. By June 2000, of the 753 GEF projects, 53 percent were implemented by UNDP and 30 percent were implemented by the World Bank. However, of the total GEF allocation of 2,947 million by that date, World Bank-implemented projects received 60 percent and UNDP projects received 31 percent.
19. Response by GEF Secretariat to December draft report, January 21, 2000.
20. See Campbell and Martin 2000.
21. See annex B of 'Financing the Global Benefits of Forests: The Bank's GEF Portfolio and the 1991 Forest Strategy," *GEF's Interim Guiding Principles for Projects Associated with Logging,* Campbell and Martin The World Bank, Washington, D.C., 2000.
22. Biodiversity loss is a major issue in several countries, but it is not clear whether it is high on the agenda of governments that face many other developmental challenges (see Africa portfolio review, Kumar et al. 2000).
23. Rice et al. 1998.
24. RIL requires pre-harvest inventory and mapping of individual trees, planning of roads and skid trails, pre-harvest vine cutting, construction of roads, landings, and skid trails, the use of appropriate felling and bucking techniques, the winching of logs to planned skid trails, systems to protect soils and residual vegetation, and post-harvest survey assessment to provide feedback to the concession holder and logging crews to evaluate the degree to which RIL guidelines were successfully applied. T. Holmes, G. Blate, J. Zweede, R. Periera, P. Barreto, F. Bolts, and R. Bauch, *Financial Costs and Benefits of Reduced Impact Logging in the Eastern Amazon,* Tropical Forest Foundation, Alexandria, Va., 2000.
25. Machfudh, Pinto Sist, Kuswata Kartawinata and Efransjah, Changing Attitude in the Forest: A pilot Project to Implement RIL in Indonesia has created enthusiasm for the practice among concessionaires. *ITTO Newsletter* v11n2/5.html.
26. Alastair Sarre and Efransjah, ITTO, Secretariat, Yokohama, based on above cited reference presented to the RIL conference in Kuching, March 2001.

References

Alexandratos, Nikos. 1996. *World Food and Agriculture: Outlook to 2010.* Rome: United Nations Food and Agricultural Organization.

Brinkley, C. S. 1999 "Forests in the Next Millenium, Challenges and Opportunities for the USDA Forest Service." Discussion Paper 99-15. Resources for the Future, Washington D.C.

Bruner, Aaron G., Raymond E. Gullison, Richard E. Rice, Gustavo A.B. da Fonseca. 2001. "Effectiveness of Parks in Protecting Tropical Biodiversity." *Science* 291 (January 5):125-128.

Campbell J. Gabriel and Alejandra Martin. 2000. *Financing the Global benefits of Forests; the Bank's GEF Portfolio and the 1991 Forest Strategy.* Operations Evaluation Department. Washington, D.C.:The World Bank.

Castro, G. et al. 2000 *Supporting the Web of Life: the World Bank and Biodiversity – a portfolio update (1988–1999)*. Evironment Department Working Paper. The World Bank

Chomitz, Kenneth M. and Kanta Kumari. 1998. "The Domestic Benefits of Tropical Forests: A Critical Review." *The World Bank Research Observer* 13(1):13-35.

Chomitz, Kenneth M. 1999. "Transferable Development Rights and Forest Protection: An Exploratory Analysis." Washington, D.C.:The World Bank.

Chomitz, Kenneth M. 2001. "Fueling carbon offsets from forestry and energy projects: How do they compare?" Washington, D.C.:The World Bank.

Dauvergne, Peter. 1997. *Shadows in the Forest: Japan and the Politics of Timber in Southeast Asia* Cambridge, MA: The MIT Press.

Duraiappah, Anantha K. 1998. "Poverty and Environmental Degradation: A Review an Analysis of the Nexus." *World Development* 26(12):2169–2179.

Easterbrook, Gregg. 2001. "How W. can save himself on global warming." *The New Republic*. July 32, 2001, pp. 22–25.

Ellsworth, Lynn. 2001. "Tenure Security and Community Livelihoods: A Literature Review." *Forest Trends*. September 2001.

IUCN. 2000. "Protected Areas: Benefits Beyond Borders." World Commission on Protected Areas (WCPA).

Kaimowitz, David, and Arid Angelsen. 1998. "Economic Models of Tropical Deforestation: A Review." CIFOR. Bogor, Indonesia.

Holmes, T., G. Blate, J. Zweede, R. Pereira, P. Barreto, F. Boltz, and R. Bauch. 2000. *Financial Costs and Benefits of Reduced-Impact Logging in the Eastern Amazon.* Tropical Forest Foundation, Alexandria, Virginia.

IUCN. 1997. *The Global Environment Facility from Rio to New Delhi: A Guide for NGOs*. Washington, D.C.: Bionet, Climate Network Europe.

Jepson, Paul and Susan Canney. 2001. "Biodiversity Hotspots: hot for what?" *Global Ecology and Biography*. Blackwell Science Limited.

Lecocq, Franck and Kenneth M. Chomitz. 2001. *Optimal Use of Carbon Sequestration in a Global Climate Change Strategy: Is there a Wooden Bridge to a Clean Energy Future?* Development Research Group. Washington, D.C.:The World Bank.

Lopez, Ramon. 1999. "Policy and Financing Instruments for Sustainable Use of Forests" in *Forest Resource Policy in Latin America,* Kari Keipi (ed.). Inter-American Development Bank. Washington, D.C.: The Johns Hopkins University Press.

Mace, G. M. "It is time to World Together and Stop Duplicating Conservation Efforts." *Nature* 405 (May 25,2000):393.

Machfudh, Pinto Sist, Kuswata Kartawinata and Efransjah. 2001. Changing Attitude in the Forest: A Pilot Project to Implement RIL in Indonesia. *ITTO Newsletter* v11n2/5.html.

Newcombe, Ken. 2000. "The Protoype Carbon Fund: Mobilizing Private and Public Resources to Combat Climate Change." Presented at the Workshop on Global Public Policies and Programs. The World Bank.

Ostrom, Elinor, Joanna Burger, Christopher Field, Richard B. Norgaard, and David Policansky. "Revisiting the Commons: Local Lessons, Global Challenges." *Science* 284(9 April 1999).

Pearce, David and Dominic Moran. 1994. *The Economic Value of Biodiversity.* IUCN. London: Earthscan Publications Limited.

Pimm et al. 2001. *Science* September 21; 293: 2207-2208.

Porter, Gareth, Raymond Clemencon, Waafas Ofusu-Amaah, and Michael Phillips. 1998. Study of GEF's overall Performance. Washington, D.C. GEF, World Bank.

Rice, R., C. Sugal, and I. Bowles. 1998. *Sustainable Forest Management: a Review of the Current Conventional Wisdom*. Washington D.C.: Conservation International.

Salafsky, Nick and Eva Wollenberg. 2000. "Linking Livelihoods and Conservation: A Conceptual Framework and Scale for Assessing the Integration of Human Needs and Biodiversity." *World Development* 28(8):1421–1438.

Sarre, Alastair, and Efransjah. 2001. ITTO, Secretariat, Yokohama, presented to the RIL conference in Kuching. March.

Scherr, Sara J., Andy White, and David Kaimowitz. 2001. "Strategies to Improve Rural Livelihoods Through Markets for Forest Products and Services." *Forest Trends.*

Sist P. 2001. "Why RIL Won't Work by Minimum-Diameter Cutting Alone." *ITTO Newsletter*, v11n2/2.html. February.

Sist, P. 2000. Reduced Impact Logging in the Tropics: Objectives, Principles and Impacts. *International Forestry Review* 2 (1): 3-10.

Sist, P., Dykstra, D. and Fimbel, R. 1998. Reduced Impact Logging Guidelines for Lowland and Hill Dipterocarp Forests in Indonesia. CIFOR Occasional Paper No. 15. Centre for International Forestry Research, Jakarta.

Totten, Michael. 1999. *Getting it Right: Emerging Markets for Storing Carbon in Forests.* Washington D.C.: World Resource Institute.

Wainwright, Carla and Walter Wehrmeyer. 1998. "Success in Integrating Conservation and Development? A Study from Zambia" *World Development* 26(6):933–944.

Wallenberg, Eva and Andrew Ingles. 1998. *Incomes from the Forest: Methods for the development and conservation of forest products for local communities.* Bogor, Indonesia: CIFOR.

Wells, Michael, Scott Guggenheim, Asmeed Khan, Wahjudi Wardojo, and Paul Jepson. 1999. *Investing in Biodiversity: A Review of Indonesia's Integrated Conservation and Development Projects.* Washington, D.C.: The World Bank.

Index

Adat, defined, 184
Agriculture Research Corporation, 238
Agro-Environmental Protection System (AEPS), 84
Amazon Cooperative Treaty, 30
Amazon forest management
 financial data lacking, 237-238
 incentives lacking for, 237
 OED review recommendations, 238-239
 World Bank and, 238
Amazon indigenous peoples
 "Brazil in Action" development incentive, 241
 challenges of, 243
 forest management from, 240
 land held by, 242-243
 living standards of, 240
 non-timber products, 243-245
 quantity of, 242
Amazon logging
 governance intertwined with, 236
 predatory logging causes, 236
 protection challenges, 236
 timber industry growth, 235
 tree extinction threats, 236-237
 waste in, 237
Amazon non-timber products
 extractive reserves recognized, 244-245
 fashionable handbags, 244
 medicinal plants, 243
 profitability of, 244
 types of, 243
Amazon policies
 forest management from, 235
 forest ownership, 235
 land use biases, 235
 national development policy, 235
Amazon region
 cattle ranching and, 225
 deforestation rates in, 224
 size of, 224

Amazon region migration
 environment assessment of, 240
 farmer's relocation reasons, 239
 highway access to, 239
 transportation importance, 239-240
Atlantic forest
 carbon dioxide storage in, 226
 characteristics of, 225
 deforestation in, 225-226

Biodiversity
 cost of, 7
 global resources and, 282-292
 India and, 129-130
 Indonesia and, 174-175
 non-protected areas and, 13-14
 See also Brazil's biodiversity; China's biodiversity; Costa Rica's biodiversity; Indonesian biodiversity
Biodiversity Collections Project, 202
Biodiversity Law, 67
Biodiversity prospecting
 Costa Rice markets and, 59
 economy and, 59-60
 parataxonomists purpose, 59
Biodiversity Resource Development Plans, 59-60
Brazilian Biodiversity Fund (FUNBIO), 256
Brazilian Institute of the Environment and Renewable natural Resources (IBAMA), 244
Brazil's biodiversity
 agriculture threats to, 283
 bank borrowing for, 284
 conservation cost understanding, 282
 developing countries and, 283
 financing approaches for, 282
 habitats conservation as, 282
 protected areas and, 286-292
 saving cost of, 286

biodiversity conservation, 59-60
carbon fund, 57
conservation threats, 46
deforestation rates, 45
democracy levels in, 45
economarket project, 58-59
environmental services financing,
    63-64
forest administration changes, 60-61
forest protection steps, 46
forestry sector evolution, 48-52
IFC and, 58
international community and, 46
land use changes, 52
landowners environmental pay-
    ments, 55-57
livestock exports, 55
middle-class characteristics, 45-46
protected area system, 52-55
twentieth-century economic devel-
    opment, 46-48
World Bank future in, 68-69
World Bank influence, 64-68
World Bank relationship with, 61-63
Costa Rica's agriculture
export expansion of, 35
forestland principles, 35
incentives for, 35
Costa Rica's biodiversity
biodiversity prospecting, 59-60
INBIO approach to, 59
protection of, 65
resource development project, 60
Costa Rica's conservation policy
biodiversity protecting, 65
forest sector studies, 64-65
forest service recommendations, 65
natural forest management, 66-67
plantation subsidies, 66
recommendation misconceptions,
    65-66
World Bank projects and, 64
Costa Rica's economic development
agriculture domination, 46
import-substituting policy, 47
meat product support, 46-47
1990's transformation, 48
structural adjustment loans, 47-48
Costa Rica's forestry sector
environmental fiscal incentives, 49-50
Forest Institute establishing, 51
forest to pasture transitioning, 48

government's environmental steps,
    48
land use changes, 52-53
National Parks Service establishing,
    50-51
small farmer incentives, 52
Costa Rica's landowner services
basis for, 56
benefits from, 56
Forestry Law, 1996, 56-57
fossil fuel taxes, 57
funding sources for, 56-57
land registered in, 56
PSAs and, 55
vs subsidies, 55
Costa Rica's protected areas
government steps for, 54-55
growth of, 53-54
Costa Rico's environmental financing
global service negotiating, 63
JI regime establishing, 63
joint implementation approaches, 63
Norway treaty, 63
Costa Rico's forestry administration
customer service focus, 61
decentralization in, 60-61
democratization of, 61
institutional reform, 60-61

Decentralization
national environmental objectives,
    38
negative effects of, 37-38
Deforestation
explaining what it is, 17
grant resources, 271
inevitability of, 3-4
See also Brazil's deforestation;
    Cameroon's deforestation; Indo-
    nesian deforestation
Deforestation causes
decentralization, 37-38
demand varies, 34-35
explosive demand, 33-34
Indonesia and, 175-177
institutional issues, 35-36
land conversion and agriculture, 35
land tenure, 36-37
Deforestation agriculture finance factors
high-input production systems, 234
loan costs and, 234
small farmers and, 234-235